Gold-Bernstein/Ruh Endorsement C

This book's use of real-world case study vignettes really does go to the heart of the subject matter. This stuff is real, it has real applicability to real problems, and, as with most things in life, it shows how it all comes down to real money in the final analysis. This book shows you what your peers are doing to drive costs out of integration projects and to build new applications without re-inventing the entire wheel—just a few new spokes and off you go.

Legacy used to be a word that meant something positive. Careful application of the fundamentals described in this book can again make the word shine in its true light—as something of immense value that you never really knew you had.

This is a good book. Read it.

—Peter Rhys Jenkins, complex systems architect, Candle Corporation

When you get two long-term, acknowledged experts on integration and interoperability together to lay out the current state of the IT universe you expect an immediate return on investment—and this book delivers. It's common knowledge that 90% of total software lifecycle cost is in maintenance and integration, and that needs to drive IT decision-making. With comprehensive coverage of the integration technology landscape, and clear case studies presented at every turn, this book belongs on every IT manager's, every system architect's, and every software developer's bookshelf.

—Richard Mark Soley, chairman and CEO, Object Management Group

Today's myriad of integration technologies and alternatives can be daunting. This book presents a framework and process for the evaluation, design, and selection of the appropriate integration technologies to meet your strategic business needs. You will find the templates a particularly useful mechanism to jump-start documentation and drive your decision-making process.

—Ron Zahavi, CIO, Global Business Transformation, Unisys Global Transformation Team; author of *Enterprise Application Integration with CORBA*

It is refreshing to read a book that presents a good business approach to the integration challenge facing most business leaders today, while at the same time educating them about the major components of the required technologies and management practices changes required. The narrative, examples, and templates establish a common reference point between the business and the technology organizations. A must-read for senior business leaders challenged with the complexities of business integration, as well as Senior IT Leaders challenged with shrinking budgets and lower tolerances for failures.

—Chuck Papageorgiou, managing partner, Ideasphere

Integration has, and will continue to be, one of the success indicators of any enterprise project. Failing to understand the nuances of integration is a critical mistake managers cannot afford to make.

—Marcia Robinson, author of *Services Blueprint: Roadmap for Execution*

A much-needed book; it ties together the business and technology aspects of information system implementation, emphasizing best practices for really getting things done. I believe that both the technical and business communities will benefit from the in-depth material provided in this book.

—Dr. Barry Horowitz, professor of systems and information engineering,
University of Virginia (former CEO, Mitre Corporation)

Enterprise Integration

Addison-Wesley Information Technology Series

Capers Jones and David S. Linthicum, Consulting Editors

The information technology (IT) industry is in the public eye now more than ever before because of a number of major issues in which software technology and national policies are closely related. As the use of software expands, there is a continuing need for business and software professionals to stay current with the state of the art in software methodologies and technologies. The goal of the **Addison-Wesley Information Technology Series** is to cover any and all topics that affect the IT community. These books illustrate and explore how information technology can be aligned with business practices to achieve business goals and support business imperatives. Addison-Wesley has created this innovative series to empower you with the benefits of the industry experts' experience.

For more information point your browser to www.awprofessional.com/itseries

Sid Adelman, Larissa Terpeluk Moss, *Data Warehouse Project Management.* ISBN: 0-201-61635-1

Sid Adelman et al., *Impossible Data Warehouse Situations: Solutions from the Experts.* ISBN: 0-201-76033-9

Wayne Applehans, Alden Globe, and Greg Laugero, *Managing Knowledge: A Practical Web-Based Approach.* ISBN: 0-201-43315-X

David Leon Clark, *Enterprise Security: The Manager's Defense Guide.* ISBN: 0-201-71972-X

Frank P. Coyle, *XML, Web Services, and the Data Revolution.* ISBN: 0-201-77641-3

Kevin Dick, *XML, Second Edition: A Manager's Guide.* ISBN: 0-201-77006-7

Jill Dyché, *e-Data: Turning Data into Information with Data Warehousing.* ISBN: 0-201-65780-5

Jill Dyché, *The CRM Handbook: A Business Guide to Customer Relationship Management.* ISBN: 0-201-73062-6

Patricia L. Ferdinandi, *A Requirements Pattern: Succeeding in the Internet Economy.* ISBN: 0-201-73826-0

David Garmus and David Herron, *Function Point Analysis: Measurement Practices for Successful Software Projects.* ISBN: 0-201-69944-3

John Harney, *Application Service Providers (ASPs): A Manager's Guide.* ISBN: 0-201-72659-9

International Function Point Users Group, *IT Measurement: Practical Advice from the Experts.* ISBN: 0-201-74158-X

Capers Jones, *Software Assessments, Benchmarks, and Best Practices.* ISBN: 0-201-48542-7

Ravi Kalakota and Marcia Robinson, *e-Business 2.0: Roadmap for Success.* ISBN: 0-201-72165-1

Ravi Kalakota and Marcia Robinson, *Services Blueprint: Roadmap for Execution.* ISBN: 0-321-15039-2

Greg Laugero and Alden Globe, *Enterprise Content Services: Connecting Information and Profitability.* ISBN: 0-201-73016-2

David S. Linthicum, *B2B Application Integration: e-Business-Enable Your Enterprise.* ISBN: 0-201-70936-8

David S. Linthicum, *Enterprise Application Integration.* ISBN: 0-201-61583-5

David S. Linthicum, *Next Generation Application Integration: From Simple Information to Web Services.* ISBN: 0-201-84456-7

Sergio Lozinsky, *Enterprise-Wide Software Solutions: Integration Strategies and Practices.* ISBN: 0-201-30971-8

Anne Thomas Manes, *Web Services: A Manager's Guide.* ISBN: 0-321-18577-3

Larissa T. Moss and Shaku Atre, *Business Intelligence Roadmap: The Complete Project Lifecycle for Decision-Support Applications.* ISBN: 0-201-78420-3

Bud Porter-Roth, *Request for Proposal: A Guide to Effective RFP Development.* ISBN: 0-201-77575-1

Ronald G. Ross, *Principles of the Business Rule Approach.* ISBN: 0-201-78893-4

Dan Sullivan, *Proven Portals: Best Practices for Planning, Designing, and Developing Enterprise Portals.* ISBN: 0-321-12520-7

Karl E. Wiegers, *Peer Reviews in Software: A Practical Guide.* ISBN: 0-201-73485-0

Ralph R. Young, *Effective Requirements Practices.* ISBN: 0-201-70912-0

Bill Zoellick, *CyberRegs: A Business Guide to Web Property, Privacy, and Patents.* ISBN: 0-201-72230-5

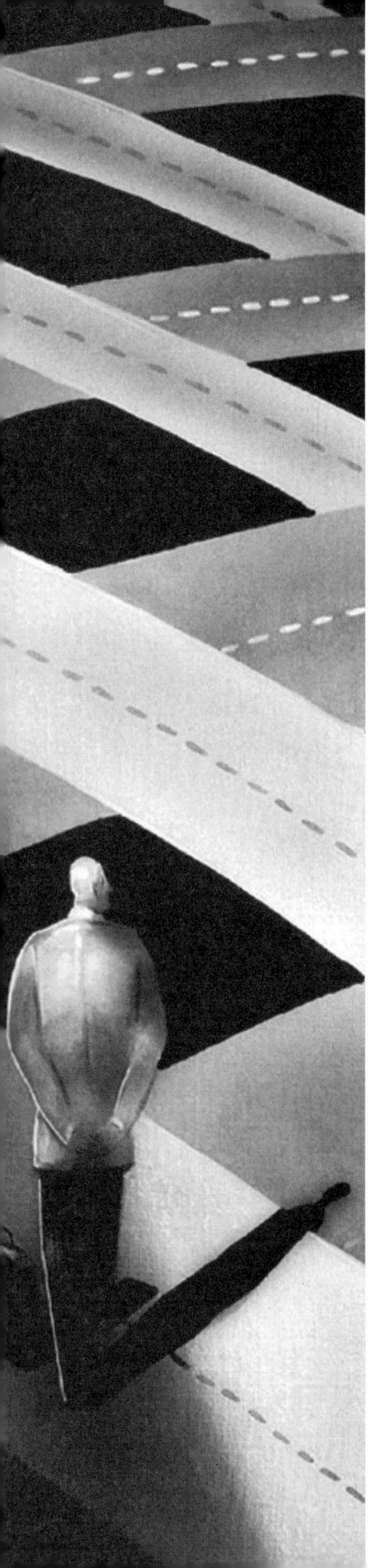

Enterprise Integration

The Essential Guide to Integration Solutions

Beth Gold-Bernstein
William Ruh

Addison-Wesley

Boston • San Francisco • New York • Toronto • Montreal
London • Munich • Paris • Madrid
Capetown • Sydney • Tokyo • Singapore • Mexico City

The publisher offers discounts on this book when ordered in quantity for bulk purchases and special sales. For more information, please contact:

U.S. Corporate and Government Sales
(800) 382-3419
corpsales@pearsontechgroup.com

For sales outside of the U.S., please contact:

International Sales
(317) 581-3793
international@pearsontechgroup.com

Visit Addison-Wesley on the Web: www.awprofessional.com

Library of Congress Cataloging-in-Publication Data

Gold-Bernstein, Beth.
Enterprise integration : the essential guide to integration solutions / Beth Gold-Bernstein, William Ruh.
p. cm.
Includes bibliographical references and index.
ISBN 0-321-22390-X (pbk. : alk. paper)
1. Management information systems. 2. Information resources management 3. Systems engineering. I. Ruh, William A. II. Title.
T58.6.G58 2004
658.4'038'011—dc22 2004010527

ISBN 0-321-22390-X
Text printed on recycled paper
1 2 3 4 5 6 7 8 9 10—CRS—0807060504
First printing, July 2004

Dedicated to Ira, Leah, Jacob, and Kaliji,
who continually inspire me to reach for my highest potential.
—Beth Gold-Bernstein

To my father, who set me on my path
and my wife Karen who keeps me on the path.
—William Ruh

Contents

Foreword

Business in real-time? That seems to be the battle cry for those industry leaders who are looking to automate their business processes both inside and outside of the corporate firewall. Indeed, since 1997 we've seen a growing interest in the science, methodology, and technology for joining applications together so they can truly automate a business, or perhaps an entire vertical, or maybe an entire economy.

Think about it. If we reach such a level of automation, car buyers will be able to determine exactly when their custom-configured car will show up at their dealer, manufacturers will never run out of that one part that holds up production, and terrorists won't have a chance, because law enforcement agencies will have truly coordinated efforts. It's an ideal world, and today we are beginning not only to understand the possibilities, but the mechanisms and approaches, as well.

Corporations today implement several cross-enterprise applications supporting a range of distinct business processes. Moreover, these business processes continue to evolve, and new processes require new services and data. This has lead to a demand to integrate all enterprise applications into a unified set of business processes, composite applications, or a unified data model.

The interest in Enterprise Integration is driven by a few key factors. First, the pressure of a competitive business environment is moving IT management to shorter application life cycles. Rather than creating the same business processes, application services, and data repositories over and over again, IT managers are learning to reuse existing application services and information. Second, this integration of applications to save development dollars is providing a competitive advantage to corporations that need to share application information either within the corporation or among trading partners. A good Enterprise Integration strategy is a requirement for supply-chain integration, not only simple exchange of information but the aggregation and use of application services as well, such as when we use enabling standards such as Web services.

As a rule, we may define Enterprise Integration as the unrestricted sharing of information, services, and business processes among any connected applications or data sources in the enterprise. We need to share this information, services, and processes without making sweeping changes to the applications or data structures. In other words, we must leave it where it lies in order for Enterprise Integration to become cost-effective.

The business value of Enterprise Integration is obvious. Enterprise Integration is the answer to the problem created by the development of the islands of automation over the past twenty or so years. For generations we've been building systems that serve a single purpose and a single set of users. There are, perhaps, instances of these stovepipe systems in your enterprise. Some are inventory-control systems, sales-automation systems, general-ledger systems, and human-resource systems. Typically, these systems were custom built using the technologies of the day, many of which were proprietary and may have used nonstandard data storage and application-development technology.

Despite the fact that the technology is old, the applications still have a great deal of value, and may be critical to the workings of the enterprise. Many of these business-critical systems are difficult to adapt to sharing information or services, and the cost of changing these systems to allow for integration may be prohibitive. A fair share of these applications run on mainframes whose use, contrary to recent reports, is actually growing.

Moreover, with the advent and acceptance of Web services, we have seen Enterprise Integration move to more of a service-oriented model. Of course, we've done service-oriented integration in the past around transaction processors and distributed objects, but we now have a widely accepted and robust standard for sharing services between many remote systems, and leveraging those services to form new applications known as composite applications. The power here is the ability to mix and match services as needed, no matter where those services reside.

In this book Bill and Beth do a great job in not only providing the basic and advanced concepts behind Enterprise Integration and how it's applied, but also provide you with a flexible methodology (guidelines, really), as to how to implement a sound Enterprise Integration project that maximizes your chances of success. Indeed, the included roadmap guiding you through the book serves as a roadmap that may guide you through the process of moving your business to real-time.

What you need to keep in mind as you read this book is the fundamental reality that Enterprise Integration is strategic to many organizations, and should be treated as such. To this end, many organizations have large dedicated teams focused on integrating internal systems as well as systems existing within partner organizations. I have found that these are typically the companies leading their industries, making the strategic investment in time and money to save a lot of money later as well as better serve their ultimate customer.

What's unique about this book is the number of case studies that the book reveals, not only providing you with the conceptual information, but demonstrating how right-thinking organizations implement Enterprise Integration in the real world. This information is invaluable because it allows you to learn from both the successes and failures of others, allowing you to embrace opportunity as well as avoid disaster.

Remember, the ultimate goal of Enterprise Integration is to bind all enterprise systems together in such a way that any application can access any service or any piece of information without delay. It will take some time before this goal is achieved, but reading this book is a first step in the journey.

—David S. Linthicum

Preface

About This Book

The task of developing and managing information systems is no longer dominated by new code development; it is dominated by the integration of new and old, custom and off-the-shelf, and internal and external systems. Organizations need to become expert in the art of integration in order to meet their business needs and compete effectively. At one time, some thought that a "silver bullet" technology would solve our integration problems without much effort. Unfortunately, integration is a much more complex subject, with as much need for processes as for technologies that can be applied to solve a problem. This book is our attempt to guide you through the world of integration—from understanding your problem, to designing your system, to selecting the most appropriate technology. Our hope is to simplify this inherent complexity and provide examples of best practices to enable your success.

The Integration Dilemma

Integration is not a new problem. As soon as computing moved off the mainframe, there was a need to synchronize information across systems. The advent of the network and PC further exacerbated the problem, complicating access to information. The rise of packaged application software increased the need for integration, as these packages needed to interact with other systems. In fact, integration loomed as such a large problem it began consuming up to 70% of project budgets.

Although integration technology was originally created to ease the burden of hand coding point-to-point interfaces between systems, the nature of integration problems has changed, and so has the technology. Today, integration is not merely a technical issue, and integration technology is not merely a more efficient way to solve the hand-coding problem. Integration is fast becoming a core enabler of business agility. The focus of integration solutions is starting to shift from the IT technician to the business manager. In short, integration technology provides the enabling infrastructure for the real-time enterprise. It is fast becoming essential infrastructure for many new types of business solutions: providing self-service applications for employees and customers, supply chain integration, and mobile applications; enabling a unified view of the customer for customer relationship management and call center operations; optimizing business processes and managing them in real time; and implementing packaged industry and compliance solutions.

Indeed, the reach of integration solutions is wide, but integration technology is not a one-size-fits-all proposition. Just as the business solutions are far-reaching and have different requirements, there is a myriad of integration technologies now available on the market, from hundreds of vendors.

The problem is, if companies merely view integration as a tactical solution, there is a likelihood of creating a great deal of redundancy in the infrastructure, which translates into increased operational costs. Moreover, companies will not gain the business agility they seek unless they reuse infrastructure services on new projects to implement a solution quickly and efficiently.

Bringing Simplicity from Complexity

A significant amount of thought, discussion, and consternation went into choosing the title for this book. The topic and the terminology of integration are overloaded to the point where words no longer have clear meaning. Integration, enterprise integration, business integration, process integration, and application integration—the list of terms and marketing jargon is endless. Taken in its entirety, this book is about how good integration can have a profound effect on the business of your enterprise. This book is about how your enterprise can solve its strategic and tactical integration needs by applying the most appropriate process, architecture, and technology.

With this context in mind, we wrote this book as a guide that begins by helping to tie your integration architecture to your specific business strategies and tactical needs. This book will help companies create their enterprise integration architecture while implementing tactical solutions. Using templates, reference architectures, best practices, and case studies, this book will guide organizations through the many decisions that need to be made when implementing business solutions that use integration technology. It will help you reduce risk and increase your return on technology investments.

In Part I of this book we look at enterprise integration from the business user's perspective. The business user is interested in business strategies and tactical business needs. This book looks at the role that enterprise integration can play in supporting the business planning process.

In Part II we focus on defining the integration architecture. The role of the integration architecture is twofold: It is to balance out implementing specific near-term needs while providing a set of reusable infrastructure services to support future implementations and reduce the cost of new business solutions.

In Part III we describe the implementation of a solution, focusing on both the pattern and technology that would be used for implementation. There are four basic implementation patterns to choose from: application, information, composite, and process integration. The architecture is used to implement a specific integration pattern.

Every chapter has a template that provides a process and a context for decisions. In addition, short case studies give some idea of how others are succeeding in these areas. Finally, we discuss best practices that can help an organization build on the shoulders of giants.

Enterprise Integration Applied

We wrote this book to help business and IT managers, architects, and technical staff navigate the complexities of enterprise integration. Our belief is that the biggest benefit of enterprise integration is realized when an organization drives integration strategy and architecture directly from business strategy. When this is done effectively, it bridges a gap within the organization where the IT organization is valued as a critical component of the strategy as much as any other business process, product line, or acquisition. The case studies describe organizations that have excelled in creating this type of environment.

Readers can step into any part of the process, depending on what part of the enterprise integration life cycle they support or what specific problem they might have. The executive overviews, case studies, and best practices will help managers understand the issues and criteria for making integration decisions. The templates will help architects and technical staff design and implement integration solutions.

Finally, the book is excellent as a training guide for the organization or in any college or university setting. It is intended for use in advanced courses in systems analysis and integration. The structure of the book lends itself to a group project, starting with a business problem and leading to a design. The templates help the students structure their projects. This is especially effective as a small group project. The CD gives the instructor a leg up on course materials, as well.

Like any good guidebook, we hope this book remains a desktop reference either physically or, using the CD, digitally. Given the complexities that exist in integrating systems, we hope this will bring simplicity to your enterprise.

The End of a Journey

A book of this breadth and depth is a labor of love for the authors, who have been living with the complexity of integration for a very long time. We were fortunate to have support from a wide variety of friends, associates, and other assorted characters. We wish to thank all of them for being there at our moments of need. First and foremost are our families, who gave us the time and energy we needed over a very long year. Thanks to Ira as well as Karen, Kayla, Kristen, Katie, and Colin.

The process of writing a book requires a significant amount of support from many people. This support comes in the form of reviews, discussion, encouragement, organization, vision, and coordination. We especially want to thank Gary Voight, Deb Zelensky, Gerda Yearwood, Jim Fowler, Ruth Ann Rich, Linda Moulder, Heidi Johnson, Debra Mendes, Martin Steinhobel, Haskell Mayo, Jim Malley, Jonathan Airey, Jonathan Gamlen, Enrique Bertrand, and Markus Roser. Thanks to Les Yeamans and Rick Frey for granting time to write the book. Then there are the great people at Addison-Wesley, including Mary O'Brien, Robin O'Brien, Lynda D'Arcangelo, Elizabeth Ryan, Tyrrell Albaugh, and Brenda Mulligan. Steve Lasko and his team did a great job on the graphics and were a pleasure to work with. Finally, the folks who helped review the book, who shaped this book in ways they may not realize. Thanks to Dave Linthicum, Colin White, JP Morganthal, Marcia Robinson, Ron Zahavi, and Scott Collison.

PART I

Business Drivers for Enterprise Integration

Part I focuses on linking business strategy and drivers with requirements for enterprise integration. Integration is becoming a crucial factor in many new business initiatives, including supply-chain integration, customer-relationship management, compliance solutions, and real-time monitoring of business processes. All of these initiatives require integration. Because integration is becoming critical to business success, it is essential that integration initiatives be closely tied to business goals and objectives.

Chapter 1—The Business Imperative for Enterprise Integration

Chapter 1 describes the fundamental changes occurring in business, from how the business interacts with customers, manufactures goods, to business organization and management. All of these changes are driving a need to manage the business in real-time, rather than through period reports based on historical trends. These changes make enterprise integration crucial to the success and future agility of the business. Business and IT managers seeking to justify integration projects will be especially interested in this chapter as it defines the areas where enterprise integration can deliver a high return on investment.

Chapter 2—Business Drivers and Requirements

Chapter 2 defines the major business initiatives that require enterprise integration. It also includes the Business Drivers and Requirements Specification (full template in Appendix A), which guides companies through the process of creating a requirements specification to be used both on integration projects and when creating the Enterprise Integration Architecture. The template includes a Statement of Purpose, which is a succinct document defining the scope, goals, and organizational impact of the business initiative. It also defines metrics for measuring the business success of the initiative. The chapter includes a section on best practices.

Chapter 3–Enterprise Integration Strategy

Enterprise integration is an inherently complex undertaking. It doesn't come in a box, or in a single product, and can't be accomplished with a single project. The Enterprise Integration Strategy focuses on creating an agile enterprise infrastructure that will deliver value on current and future projects. The chapter focuses on how to succeed in creating an enterprise strategy and key integration architecture concepts. Chapter 3 includes the Enterprise Integration Strategy Specification (full template in Appendix B). The template provides guidelines for creating a team responsible for the integration strategy, templates for mapping business strategies to integration strategies, defining enterprise standards, and business-based metrics.

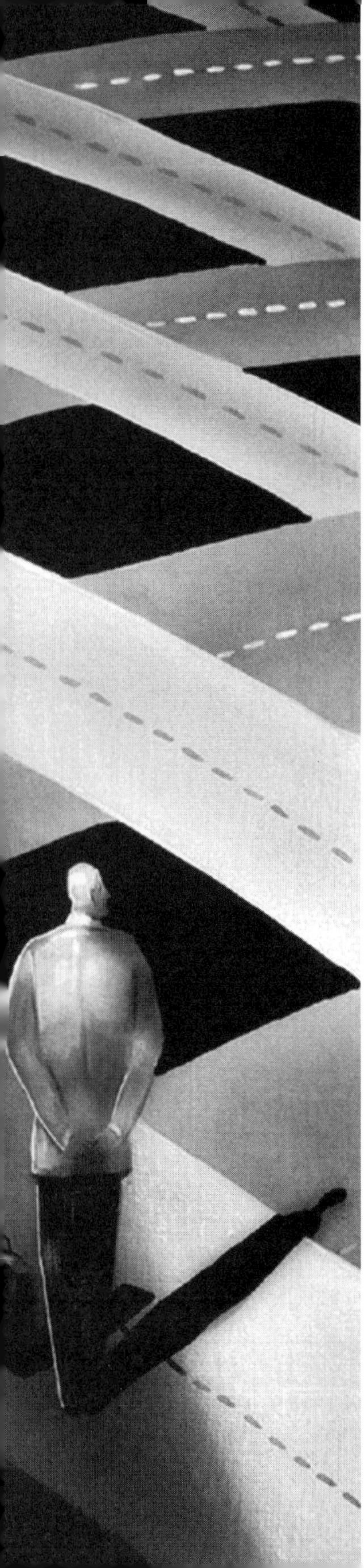

CHAPTER ONE

The Business Imperative for Enterprise Integration

1.1 Executive Overview

Information technology has fundamentally altered the business landscape. In the 1960s and 1970s businesses automated accounting, billing, and other back-end functions. This was the era of the mainframe and the database. In the 1980s information technology provided tools that enhanced the capabilities of workers to be more productive, whether through spreadsheets, word processors, or graphics applications. This was the era of the personal computer and desktop applications. The 1990s opened up communications inside an organization as well as with customers and suppliers. This was the era of the network and the Internet. We are moving into an era driven by the need to improve business processes and to provide increasingly sophisticated capabilities to customers and suppliers to improve how we conduct business. Processing transactions without human intervention, gathering data from multiple sources, and integrating it together or re-engineering business processes are the basic requirements for success in today's environment.

The implementation of these applications and systems will be enabled through enterprise integration. In the same way that organizations have mastered mainframes, databases, back-office applications, personal computers, desktop applications, networks, and the Internet, it will be necessary for them to master enterprise integration. However, integration has always been addressed as a technology and infrastructure topic. In today's business environment the enterprise integration process begins with business problems. Business groups within organizations are rethinking how they interact with customers, partners, and suppliers; manufacture goods; and operate, organize, and manage the business. Business and IT success are dependent upon integration solutions to enable this business change.

As business problems have different requirements, there are literally hundreds of integration solutions available today. The problem is not whether the technology exists; it's which technology to use to solve the business problem. We designed this book to help companies solve pressing business needs while creating an infrastructure that will enable future business solutions as well.

1.2 How Business Is Changing

The need for enterprise integration is being driven by the changing needs of business. Sometime around 500 B.C. Heraclitus said, "Nothing endures but change." Although change may have been a constant from time immemorial, the rate of change is accelerating far faster than ever before, and this is having a profound effect on business. Business cycles are rapidly shrinking. The way business was conducted even a decade ago is no longer acceptable if a business intends to remain competitive. The changes include how the business interacts with customers, how it manufactures goods, and how it is organized and managed. The changes in business are fundamental and pervasive.

1.2.1 Customer Interaction

In the past, customers interacted with companies from defined access points such as stores, over the telephone, or through sales reps, during defined business hours. Now customers may place an order over the Web, ask questions about the order over a telephone, and then exchange merchandise at a physical store. The goal and challenge is to have all customer access and interactions managed consistently across the enterprise, even if the customer uses multiple channels for a single transaction. This requires comprehensive integration of customer information across all possible channels. Barnes & Noble effectively dealt with the threat of Amazon.com by providing seamless integration of an online presence with vast brick-and-mortar operations, turning what had been considered a weakness at one time into a real competitive advantage.

It costs many times more to acquire a new customer than to retain an existing customer. Providing an integrated view of the customer brings together knowledge of the customer that is spread across multiple systems in the organization.

Improving customer knowledge enables the company to maximize the value of each customer.

1.2.2 Manufacturing

The manufacturing process is also changing. Whereas companies used to produce goods to stock with low levels of customization, the trend and competitive advantage is to manufacture products to order with mass customization. Dell Inc. provides a good example of how this capability propelled it to become the number one computer manufacturer and changed the way people buy computers. Whereas retail customers used to purchase personal computers in stores and then customize configurations after the fact, Dell introduced the capability to purchase computers over the Web or by telephone, customized with the amount of memory, disk storage, and other features they may require such as specialized graphics cards or a math coprocessor. It also delivered the customized system to the customers' door faster and cheaper. To compete effectively, the other computer manufacturers needed to do the same to retain customers.

Integration of the design, planning, and manufacturing processes is critical to managing margins, ensuring that the right amount of materials are on hand, and improving inventory turns. Over the last several years this has been the focus of General Motors Corporation's information systems organization. As a result of reducing redundant systems and integrating across the diverse set of systems that support design and engineering, it was able to reduce the design time of a new car from 48 months down to 18 months.

1.2.3 Business in Real Time

Competitive advantage requires making the end-to-end process across the value chain—from requisition to payment—as fast and efficient as possible. The concepts of "zero latency" and the "real-time enterprise" are gaining traction as companies seek to accelerate business processes and reduce business cycle times. The term "real time" refers to being able to view, manage, and control business processes in business time, rather than responding to end-of-month or quarter reports after the fact. This includes integrating, monitoring, managing, and optimizing the end-to-end process across applications, business units, and the entire value chain. Optimization may be based on different metrics, such as time or cost (which in some cases may be conflicting goals). Automating business processes can also go a long way towards reducing business cycle times. Cisco Systems has applied this concept to its finance operations to achieve dramatic increases in performance (Powell 2003). Its story is described in Case Study 1.1.

Case Study 1.1
Cisco Systems: The Importance of Enterprise Integration to World-Class Finance

Many important business strategies and initiatives will be based upon a strong technology-integration foundation. Without the foundation, the building cannot stand. Cisco Systems is an example of an organization where the creation of a world-class finance organization required a solid platform for enterprise integration.

Cisco is a great business success story. In the 1990s, Cisco's finance organization recognized that truly world-class finance required the movement from a gatekeeper role to that of a business catalyst, the difference being one of collection of information versus continuously monitoring and analyzing critical information for more rapid decision making and course correction. The goal was to improve financial reporting and the underlying processes to better support a changing business. For example, strategies changed after 2000, when growth, acquisition, and capturing the growing network volume as business drivers were replaced by the slowing economy, shareholder concerns around disclosure and ethics, and a focus on profitability and productivity.

The finance organization began focusing on real-time metrics to understand the nuances in one of the world's largest businesses. Furthermore, being able to have a virtual close of the books at any time gave management the ability to adjust in real time. If we examine the metrics that were being evaluated constantly, we see that they are a diverse set, including order and revenue status, discounts, product margins, and expenses. In addition, market share, head count, revenue per employee, after-tax profit, business-unit contributions, and balance-sheet information were all collected and analyzed. The finance organization also began looking at nontraditional performance in such areas as sales channels, emerging technology, new opportunities, deal analysis, bookings forecast, and contribution margin. In examining these metrics, we can see that for a global organization such as Cisco, this required the integration of data from diverse systems in diverse locations. Without this integration, the virtual close and ability to perform real-time analysis would not be possible.

The results of this effort are nothing short of tremendous: Productivity doubled, a 30% reduction in cost performance was achieved, and daily reporting became the norm, allowing for improved decision-making. Cisco had a competitive information advantage that was unparalleled in the industry.

Six building blocks were critical to the execution of this strategy:

- Management commitment
- Network and system architecture
- Process reengineering
- Linkage between the IT and business functions
- Focus and review process
- Web-based application

Business strategies that require enterprise integration are the most difficult of all projects to execute. As a result, they require more substantial processes, analysis, technology, and review. However, none of this is as important as the business management commitment and understanding of the complexities of achieving dramatic success.

What can we learn from this example? If we look at these building blocks we see that success is determined by having a business-driven strategy and a good understanding of the problem from a process orientation. With this in hand, it is important to ensure a common understanding between the business and IT functions of the strategy and requirements. Finally, the organization needs to have the right technology to make it all work.

1.2.4 Business Operations

One of the reasons companies are facing the challenges of integration today is the way they were organized in the past. Business operations were organized in functional stovepipes such as sales, order processing, manufacturing, finance, and so on. The back-office computer systems used to manage these organizational stovepipes reflected the specific views and needs of the department, and were not designed to interact with other departmental systems. Each system defined business entities, such as customers and products, without regard to how the other systems represented the same entities. However, the end-to-end business process of the entire interaction with a customer or a business transaction was likely to be supported by multiple business systems.

Lack of integration between systems requires additional manual steps such as rekeying information, increasing the possibility of introducing errors. The cost of fixing errors is not trivial. For example, one high-tech manufacturer integrated the order entry and fulfillment systems, eliminating the need to manually rekey orders, and reduced errors by 40%. Several companies have reported 100% return on investment (ROI) from an integration project within the first year, merely through reducing errors. Automating the flow of information as it crosses stovepipe systems greatly reduces the latency in business processes, reducing business cycle times and enabling the real-time enterprise. FedEx has been a leader in this area. It continues to be on the cutting edge of operational improvement with a focus on field force automation. The details on its latest endeavor can be found in Case Study 1.2 (Brewin 2002).

1.2.5 Business Organization

The globalization of business has fueled the move from centralized to decentralized organizations. Decentralized organizations require access to shared information from multiple locations and systems. This has driven the rise of enterprise portals, which provide front-end, role-based integration. From a browser-based interface, employees, partners, suppliers, or even customers can access the information they require through a single easy-to-use interface that includes information and functionality from multiple back-end source systems.

1.2.6 Management

Moving towards real-time business, or business on-demand, requires real-time management. Previously, defined planning cycles based on historical analysis might have sufficed. However, the company that can recognize and exploit competitive opportunities and react to changes in the market faster than the competition gains competitive advantage. For example, General Electric Company monitors its mission-critical operations across the company's 13 different businesses around the world from "digital cockpits." The cockpits enable GE to respond faster to change, reduce cycle times, and improve risk management. Rather than waiting for end-of-month or quarter reports, the cockpits provide real-time data to GE.

Management practices based on monitoring key performance indicators and real-time metrics tied to the fundamental business objectives, such as reducing business cycle times, will provide competitive advantage to the real-time enterprise. Methods such as balanced scorecard and Six Sigma have shown that management by metrics improves the overall efficiency, quality, and profitability of the company.

Case Study 1.2
FedEx: Improving a Field Force Through Enterprise Integration

FedEx was founded on the principle that through better operational processes it could build a business that would compete with a protected industry. FedEx has become a giant because it has one of the most efficient operations in the world. It has managed the delivery of packages in a way that is still the gold standard in the industry. Next day delivery, electronic package management, and Web-based customer-status checking are all business strategies that require different levels of integration of processes and systems.

FedEx continues to be at the leading edge even today through the provisioning of its field force with custom-built handheld devices based upon Microsoft's Pocket PC operating system. These devices will provide applications to automate courier dispatch, pickup, and delivery. The handheld devices will eliminate paperwork, provide real-time update of information into the core processing systems, and improve the efficiency of managing its field force. It is expected that each transaction can be reduced by ten seconds, which may not seem like a lot, but when aggregated provides a significant increase in productivity. This will result in an estimated yearly savings of $20 million. Furthermore, the real-time update will give enhanced capabilities to manage a package. None of this would be possible without integration with its back-office core systems, such as package tracking. Without enterprise integration, this application would not be able to achieve the dramatic business results that FedEx is expecting.

1.3 Business Agility Is Becoming a Competitive Requirement

The ultimate goal of the real-time enterprise is business agility—the ability to rapidly adapt to change. Business is changing and the rate of change is accelerating. It is becoming clear that maintaining the status quo is no longer adequate. Companies must adapt to change or perish. The real-time enterprise is becoming a strategic initiative because it enables companies to respond rapidly to rapidly changing business conditions. In an audience poll of an ebizQ Web cast (Gold-Bernstein and White 2003), "Critical Success Factors for the Real-Time Enterprise,"

76% responded that becoming a real-time enterprise was a current strategic business initiative, showing that real time is becoming an essential goal for organizations.

One company that has been successful as a real-time enterprise is Wal-Mart. As the world's largest business, Wal-Mart has done extremely well in operational efficiency, managing growth, and scaling its business. The Chief Information Officer (CIO) established three philosophies in the development of its systems that embody its approach to the real-time enterprise. Details are given in Case Study 1.3 (Lundberg, 2002).

Case Study 1.3
Wal-Mart: Philosophies of a World-Class, Real-Time Enterprise

What do you think of when you hear the word Wal-Mart? The largest business in the world, an amazing success story, operational efficiency, or a global retail chain that is the best in the business? All of this has been said of Wal-Mart in the past. Managing the information systems for one of the largest distributed enterprises in the world requires discipline and flexibility. The IT organization in Wal-Mart has three basic philosophies that have made it into the world-class organization that it is today:

- Distributed environment, centralized information systems
- Common systems, common platforms
- Merchants first, technologists second

Wal-Mart's IT organization has been able to manage through phenomenal growth by integrating its distributed empire back into centralized systems in Arkansas. This allows it to have control over its core applications and data while providing the necessary applications to a diversity of locations. Furthermore, Wal-Mart has created in-house teams that focus on integration. These teams do not focus on one product or process, but on the needs of the business. This allows them to have a core competency in their integration needs. These teams form a hub for dispersed networks of people and allow for better interaction between internal and external resources.

Having common systems and platforms allows them to control the infrastructure and train people allowing for more rapid deployment of new capabilities. By having the architecture in place and migrating it over time, the organization is able to build core competencies in its infrastructure enabling better integration.

Lastly, an emphasis on the business means that functionality is driven by the business and the related strategy. This theme is consistent in all world-class organizations that have achieved substantial business results from integration. Since the Internet age began, not one external venture in retail was successful. Almost 70% of these external activities were re-integrated with the parent organization. The rest were shut down.

Wal-Mart represents the kind of company that has been able to develop its own philosophies and core competencies in enterprise integration that make it a world class IT organization. Without this competency organizations will either flounder from a lack of focus and experience or rely entirely on external organizations that cannot understand the business or respond to its needs in the way that Wal-Mart is able to.

1.4 Business Agility Requires Enterprise Integration

Real-time response to business change requires an integrated infrastructure that enables rapid deployment of new solutions while leveraging existing IT investments. An agile business can't afford to rip and replace business systems. It requires real-time connectivity between people, systems, and business entities. Accelerating business processes requires process automation. Although some processes will require human intervention at certain points, especially authorizations and exception handling, increasing the velocity of business requires automating as much as possible; even after automating processes, companies need to monitor and manage them in real time to continually improve and optimize the processes.

Fortunately, advances in technology are enabling business agility. Integration technology, including messaging, application integration, workflow, business process modeling, automation and management, mobile integration, enterprise portals, business-to-business (B2B) integration, Web services, and eXtensible Markup Language (XML) are all helping organizations tie their systems together and manage the processes across them.

Enterprise integration is the underlying enabler of business agility. It provides the infrastructure that supports rapid change. Without enterprise integration, companies will continue to be constrained by the inability to communicate and manage the flow of information and business processes across the enterprise. The real-time enterprise is not possible without enterprise integration.

1.5 The ROI of Enterprise Integration

Companies that have invested in an integrated IT environment have seen dramatic results in business performance. Case Study 1.4 is a compilation of the impact that can result when an organization is able to harness the power of an integrated information system. However, many decision makers require even more data before they agree to pursue a project.

Even if we grant the fact that real-time business requires comprehensive integration, often managers allocating budgets need more tangible paybacks before they will fund an integration project. In fact, there are clearly definable areas where integration projects have been shown to deliver an ROI. Enterprise integration reduces personnel, IT, and business costs and increases revenues. Two other important benefits that companies gain from integration are increasing customer satisfaction and improving overall quality and efficiency through optimizing business processes. An ROI can be calculated in any of these areas to justify a project.

1.5.1 Reducing Costs

Personnel costs can be reduced through automating business processes and reducing head count; providing self-service interfaces for customers, thereby reducing customer support costs; and making information easily and readily available, thereby reducing training costs. For example, through enterprise integration a logistics service company was able to triple its size in five years, going from $80 million to $250 million in revenue, without adding additional head count. It standardized on its product offering, which enabled it to implement new solutions faster, with fewer and less-skilled employees. While saving money, it also increased customer satisfaction and reduced risk.

Through process automation, a Canadian transportation company eliminated 70,000 to 80,000 hand-processed transactions, reducing cost per order from $25 to $5, saving $1.6 million per year. A high-tech parts supplier saved over $166,000 annually by replacing transactions that have gone through Value-Added Networks (VANs) with RosettaNet transactions. It reduced the cost of setting up new partners by 50%. Less-specialized personnel can now perform setups

Case Study 1.4
Achieving Dramatic Business Result

Does mastering business integration have a meaningful effect on an organization? Will an investment in an organizational approach to business integration pay off? A survey of 162 North American information technology executives conducted by NerveWire found that the most highly integrated companies had generated the following results through their integration initiatives (Surmacz 2002):

- 40% increase in revenue
- 30% decrease in cost
- 35% increase in customer retention

We continually see three attributes in successful organizations that benefit from business integration.

1. **Organizational.** Integration is not an administrative or technology task, but one where business interactions are more effectively managed.
2. **Architecture.** Significant emphasis is placed on the architectural aspects of the technology and its application and not on the selection of a specific vendor, product, or approach. In addition, technology coupling is as loose as possible. Tight coupling or proprietary approaches provide only short-term benefits.
3. **Expertise.** Organizations that commit to developing business integration as a core competency achieve more dramatic results than those that outsource their integration. One claim is that 3:1 productivity measures are seen between those that are able to master business integration and those that cannot.

Improving the ability to integrate can no longer be pushed aside as a technology issue; it must be addressed as core to the business strategy.

previously done by senior-level system engineers. Employees no longer have to learn some of their partners' proprietary applications to conduct business. Lastly, it reduced the time and costs related to checking inventory from five minutes over the phone to six seconds electronically.

IT costs can be reduced by reducing error rates and the cost of fixing errors, eliminating rekeying of information, and reducing system support costs through integration. For example, a high-tech manufacturer using RosettaNet reported an 85% reduction in error rates and achieved a 100% ROI in the first year. Reducing errors cropped up frequently in ROI studies, for good reason: The cost of processing disputed transactions is orders of magnitude higher than non-disputed transactions.

Enterprise integration can reduce business costs by reducing the cost of implementing change and optimizing business processes. Integration provides the infrastructure that enables companies to rapidly implement new business solutions or change existing ones to meet new requirements. Rather than having to hand code connectivity to applications and information for each new business solution, the underlying integration architecture provides the necessary connectivity, translation and transformation, intelligent routing, and process management. With a fully integrated infrastructure and process, management business analysts can implement many business process changes without IT intervention, enabling them to implement change at the speed of business.

1.5.2 Increasing Revenue

Enterprise integration can increase revenue by increasing market share and creating new market opportunities. Increased market share is the result of retaining and increasing revenue from existing customers by increasing customer satisfaction and attracting new customers by bringing new products and services to market rapidly in response to emerging opportunities.

New opportunities are created by integrating with partners and suppliers, bringing products and services to market more quickly, and creating new sales or distribution channels through on-line capabilities. For example, a high-tech electronics supplier achieved a 40% increase in sales through implementing real-time order capabilities. In 1999, 81% of Cisco's orders were placed online, representing $11.7 billion annually, with 98% to 99% accuracy. Because of an integrated supply chain, Dell was able to deliver customized PCs in days rather than weeks, propelling the company to market leadership.

1.5.3 Customer Satisfaction

Customer satisfaction is increasingly becoming an important area of focus and spending for many organizations, so we will address it separately here. A major insurance company reported that 1% of retention can equate to nearly $25 million to the bottom line. According to a study by the Insight Technology Group (Dickie 1999), improving knowledge of the customer and customer relationship management has the following benefits:

- 20% increase in customer satisfaction ratings
- 42% increase in revenue
- 35% decrease in sales costs
- 25% decrease in sales cycles

The potential ROI for increasing customer satisfaction is tremendous. Enterprise integration can increase customer satisfaction by making information easily available and responding to customer requests and complaints more quickly. For example, online customer self-service systems enable customers to view their account balances on demand, track orders, and change information. The customer is more satisfied because needs are met immediately, and the company saves money on personnel costs. Integrating customer information from disparate back-end systems enables improving customer interactions at every stage of a transaction, through every channel used for a customer interaction. Companies investing in Customer Relationship Management (CRM) systems are finding that integration is a large part of the implementation process.

1.5.4 Business Process Improvement

Business process optimization holds the greatest potential for ROI. Through process optimization companies can do things better, faster, and cheaper. For example, a large apparel manufacturer reduced inventory costs by 10%, saving millions of dollars through the ability to plan plant capacity better and optimize the manufacturing process. A logistics service company reported that its customers have been able to shrink inventory floor space by 50%, yielding significant savings in inventory carrying costs through enhanced visibility into its logistics supply chain. A high-tech manufacturer projects a 230% ROI over five years through improved business processes provided by implementing RosettaNet Process Interchange Protocols (specifications for automated B2B transactions in the high-tech industry). Business process optimization reduces the latency in business and improves efficiency, quality, and bottom-line profitability.

1.6 The Challenges of Integration

Business drivers and potential benefits are compelling. Integration is essential for moving towards real-time business. Surveys show that companies are focusing IT investment on integration. Morgan Stanley's survey of 225 CIOs consistently ranks integration as either the number one priority in IT spending, or in the top three (Phillips and Rathman 2002). Gartner puts application development and middleware in the top three for annual growth rates (Correia 2002). Companies are increasingly recognizing the need for enterprise integration.

Unfortunately, integration is inherently a complex problem. Providing integration, visibility, and management across hardware platforms, operating systems, programming languages, database structures, applications, and business entities is probably one of the most complex tasks in IT. Integration doesn't come in a box. You can't just install and configure it. There are multiple technologies involved, and different technologies are most appropriate for different types of business requirements. What companies need to avoid is the necessity of integrating the integration solutions.

Enterprise integration is really more of a journey than a solution. Companies will need to continually evolve and optimize their infrastructures to provide better response time to their customers and changes in business conditions. This process involves many decisions along the way.

- Defining the business drivers, requirements, and metrics driving integration. What is the business initiative launching the integration project? What are the business requirements? What are the business metrics that will measure the success of the solution?
- Determining the purpose and scope of the integration. Is it enterprise-wide or linked to a strategic business initiative, or both? Or is it tactical, such as implementing a new application or Web service?
- Deciding whether to make an enterprise commitment to a service-oriented architecture.
- Choosing the type of integration. Integration scenarios include application integration, data integration, process integration, legacy integration or extension, B2B integration, and portals.
- Identifying the technologies necessary for the type of integration. This could include one, some, or all of the following: messaging, data mapping, translation and transformation, intelligent routing, business process management, Web services, XML, B2B integration, and portals.

1.7 How This Book Will Help

This book will guide business managers and IT professionals through the complex decisions surrounding enterprise integration. The ultimate goal is to select the right solution to solve the business problem at hand while increasing business agility. This book is not a rigid methodology. Instead, it is intended to provide guidelines based on best practices for implementing successful integration solutions. We have included templates that we have found to be useful for designing and documenting the integration solution.

The book is designed to be flexible, so it can be adapted based on your project needs. Although the authors truly believe that an enterprise integration strategy and architecture ultimately produces the most agile infrastructure (see Chapter 3), we recognize that tight IT budgets require focus on tactical solutions. Therefore, we offer you guidelines for making tactical decisions while maximizing long-term agility.

Figure 1-1 is a road map to this book. It is our sincere intent and hope that it is a helpful guide on your next integration project.

As the map shows, the first step in the process is to define business drivers and requirements (Chapter 2). This needs to be done regardless of the integration project at hand. This step will determine the scope of your integration initiative, after which you will have some choices of what to do next. However, even if you are implementing a tactical solution, it is important to have an enterprise road map to avoid costly mistakes down the line. Therefore, we strongly recommend that everyone read Chapter 3 on creating an integration strategy, and Chapter 4 through Chapter 9 on defining an integration architecture.

For project work, readers can use the chapters and templates that are most relevant to the solution being implemented.

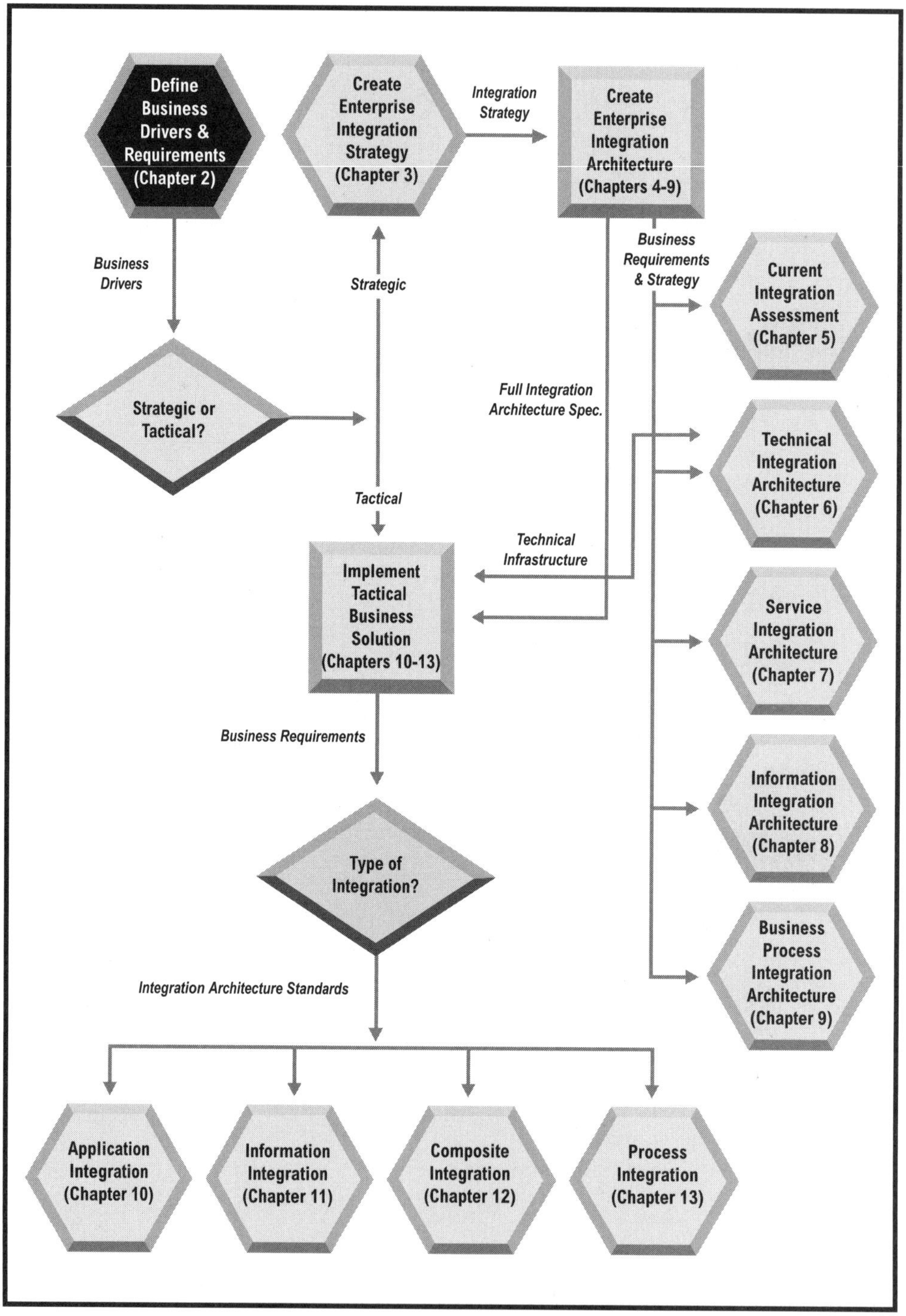

Figure 1-1 Integration Road Map

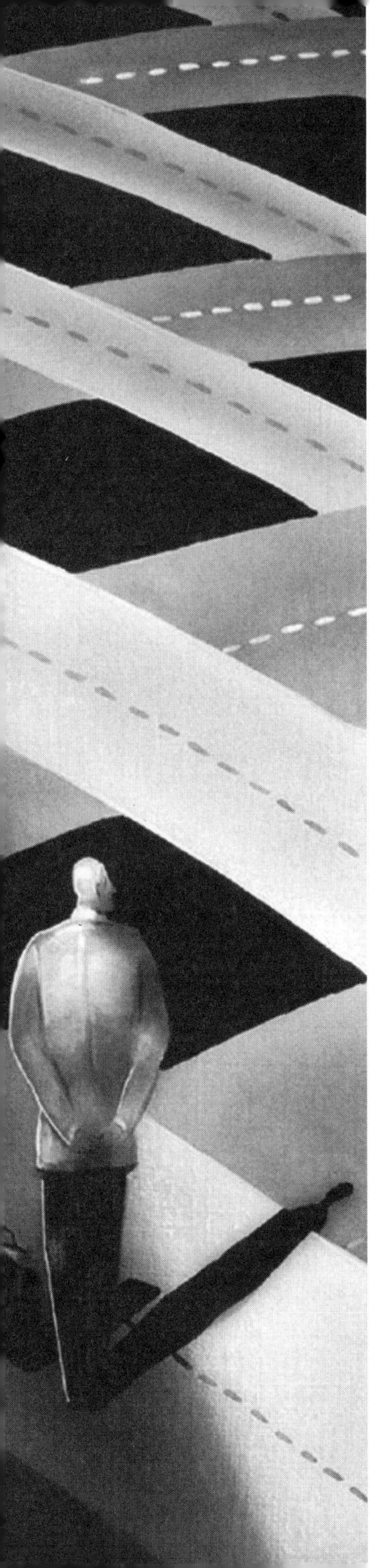

CHAPTER TWO

Business Drivers and Requirements

2.1 Executive Overview

Enterprise business integration is a means to an end. Although an agile infrastructure enabled by integration can have substantial impact on the overall success of the business, technology alone has no value. Two companies can use the same technology and have very different results. For example, when General Motors focused on significantly reducing the time needed to design and engineer cars, it was able to achieve dramatic results that have given it a significant edge over the competition during the downturn in the economy. General Motors' focus on business objectives and improving processes in the context of available technology and an architecture were key to success. The technologies that enabled General Motors to do this were available to all of its competition, but were not applied to the same business initiative. It is therefore critical to tie integration initiatives to business needs as early in the process as possible to ensure success.

There are many approaches, methods, and tools that organizations apply to improve their processes. Six Sigma is one that has achieved a significant following. General Electric has turned Six Sigma into a corporate mantra. Other approaches include the use of balanced scorecards that focus staff on individual and group goals that relate to improving operations. ROI-based approaches calculate the ROI obtained from investing in a given improvement. The application of industry benchmarks is often used to set the goals for improving a process, and can be used in conjunction with balanced scorecards and ROI-based approaches. Many other approaches exist, including a variety of proprietary approaches applied by different consulting firms.

The success of strategic business initiatives depends upon the alignment of IT and business goals. However, without the underlying ability to execute these business strategies and initiatives, they will not yield the same competitive advantage. For example, in the late 1980s business process reengineering (BPR) was the consulting world's latest silver bullet. Many of the great ideas that resulted from a company's BPR efforts did not yield the anticipated results because they required systems to be reorganized and integrated in ways never envisioned when they were created. Radically reengineering core business systems was too disruptive and expensive to achieve an ROI, and many of the plans remained on paper. At the time, the technology was not mature enough to enable companies to leverage their existing systems and integrate them to support new business processes. Without the right technology, the ability to execute on a business strategy and related process improvement is not feasible. What makes Six Sigma and other approaches work is the availability of technology that allows for the integration and implementation of solutions that were not feasible in the past.

The most successful implementations are those that meet the business requirements and contribute to the overall success of the business. IT organizations that use business metrics reflecting key performance indicators (KPIs) have greater success than those that use IT metrics, such as system performance. Meeting business expectations requires correctly defining the drivers, intent, scope, and metrics that measure success. The Business Drivers and Requirements Specification is the document that defines all three. As such, it is used when creating the integration strategy (see Chapter 3) and making technology decisions that ensure alignment with business goals.

2.2 Business Drivers for Enterprise Integration

The most typical types of business initiatives driving integration requirements today include reducing business cycle times to increase efficiency and competitiveness, improving customer satisfaction, mergers and acquisitions, and regulatory compliance. Some of these initiatives are strategic and some tactical. Different business requirements call for different types of integration technologies.

2.2.1 Increasing Business Efficiency and Competitiveness

Companies embarking on initiatives to improve business efficiency can have either a strategic or tactical focus. Strategic initiatives include moving to real-time business processes or integrating transactions across the value chain to reduce time and costs. A strategic approach to improving business efficiency requires integration to automate and manage business processes. Improving business efficiency is an ongoing process, not a finite implementation project. Process simulation provides the ability to analyze process flows as optimized for cost or time. Although still a premium feature among vendors, it will surely become a necessity because those companies that use the technology will gain clear competitive advantage.

Tactical initiatives to improve business efficiency include eliminating reconciliation issues, data inconsistency, and reporting discrepancies across the enterprise. Tactical initiatives typically take less time, consume fewer resources, and cost less than an enterprise solution. The technology necessary to implement tactical solutions is typically only a portion of the full integration platform. However, to avoid having to integrate the integration technologies, even tactical solutions should be considered in light of strategic initiatives so a flexible architecture can be developed and maintained. General Motors has turned this strategy into a science in its organization, creating remarkable business results (Alice Dragoon 1998; Moozakis 2001). This is described in Case Study 2.1.

Case Study 2.1
General Motors: Creating Remarkable Business Results

General Motors has gone through enormous changes in the past two decades. Since 1995, it was able to remake itself into one of the most profitable and efficient carmakers in the world. Technology has played a key role in improving the business of designing and delivering cars under the leadership of the CIO, Ralph Szygenda. When he joined GM, he brought the responsibility and process for IT strategy back into GM. Prior to his arrival as the first CIO at GM, the strategy was conducted in an outsourced manner. Furthermore, he instituted the need for the IT organization to present metrics on how investments in IT provide an ROI to the business.

(continued)

Case Study 2.1 *(cont.)*

An example of a business initiative that would have a profound impact on GM was the need to reduce the time it takes to design and deliver a car. The focus on this initiative and a relentless push on activities to meet this goal had dramatic results. The time to design and deliver a car has been reduced from 48 to 18 months. Additionally, costs for bringing a car to market have been cut by $1 billion. This is only one of many business initiatives that focus the IT group's energies and resources. Large and small initiatives are acted upon if the ROI is compelling to the group. Systems to manage auctions have been put in place to give dealers the ability to bid on cars that have been leased or rented. The ability to squeeze such tremendous value out of an IT organization in itself deserves significant praise. To do this at one of the world's largest and most complex companies demonstrates the power of focusing the process on business drivers and ROI at the beginning of the IT process.

2.2.2 Improving Customer Satisfaction

Companies embarking upon projects to improve customer satisfaction may be considering a number of different technical solutions, including Customer Relationship Management (CRM) systems, portals, mobile integration, sales force automation, or a combination of all or some of these. Again, some of these projects may be enterprise-wide and strategic to the organization, and some may be more tactical in nature.

Customer satisfaction can be measured by

- Customer retention statistics
- Response time to customers
- Number of complaints
- Issue resolution rate (% and time)
- Error rates
- Customer value (computed as sales per customer or lifetime value of customer)

Because of the need to track and analyze customer satisfaction, process management simulation and analytics are key technologies for strategic initiatives.

Tactical solutions typically focus on a particular technology, such as portals or mobile technology, and may also require a combination of technologies. The key is to enable individual technologies to be deployed at the lowest cost and least amount of time possible, and integrate easily with other integration solutions whenever necessary. Companies need to at least have an enterprise road map to enable the infrastructure to be deployed tactically and work on an enterprise strategic level as well. Government organizations are often driven to improve the service to the citizen. There is enormous pent-up demand for these types of initiatives. Oftentimes a modest investment can have extraordinary results as seen in Case Study 2.2 on the work done by Sacramento County (http://www.softwareagusa.com/media/case_studies/pdfs/Sacremento_CR.pdf).

Case Study 2.2
Sacramento County Government:
A Well-Planned, Modest Investment Can Have Extraordinary Results

The government of Sacramento County, California focused its energies to streamline the way it provides a wide range of public records, such as property deeds and real estate tax data, to its citizens. After only six months in service, a Web-based system has logged more than one million online page "hits," making it one of the most popular Web sites in the county. The system reduces phone call volume, decreases the need to travel to the clerk recorder's office, and eliminates the requirement for costly dedicated terminals.

"This solution really has enabled us to provide the citizens of Sacramento County with a higher level of service in accessing records," said Craig Kramer, assistant clerk recorder. "It has also saved the county considerable time and expense."

Every month, as many as 50 thousand new property records are added to the system, which now includes more than a million records dating back as far as 1965. Sacramento County uses Software AG's EntireX to integrate and Web-enable its existing mainframe applications, rather than discarding its legacy system that had been developed over the past 20 years. The county has built a Web-based Recorders Online System Index (e-ROSI) used by homeowners, real estate firms, and title companies to access information from their homes or offices.

(continued)

Case Study 2.2 *(cont.)*

In addition to e-ROSI, the county created a District Attorney and Courts Interface (DICI), which enables the electronic filing of criminal complaints into the county's criminal justice information system. This system comprises data from the state courts, district attorney, public defender, probation department, sheriff's office, and police department. DICI replaces a time-consuming manual-entry process. Hundreds of complaints are filed each day, some as long as 25 pages.

2.2.3 Mergers and Acquisitions

Mergers and acquisitions inevitably result in redundant and incompatible systems, leaving companies with just a few choices:

- Choosing one system over the other and a large data conversion project
- Leaving the systems in place and integrating them
- Implementing an entirely new system, then converting or integrating both

A combination of approaches may also be used. Integration projects resulting from a merger or acquisition are usually treated as tactical projects or one-time conversions. However, companies seeking to improve business efficiency through the merger and acquisition should also consider business processes integration and management across all business units, regardless of where they are located or the technology the systems use. This undoubtedly will require a higher initial investment, but it also offers the highest potential ROI.

2.2.4 Regulatory Compliance

A number of regulatory requirements, including the Sarbanes-Oxley Act, Health Insurance Portability and Accountability Act (HIPAA) in the healthcare industry, and T+1 trade settlements in financial services, can be best be accomplished through enterprise integration. In some cases, regulatory or industry compliance is being defined in such a way that they are at the heart of technology integration. Case Study 2.3 discusses the trend toward the definition of XML-based standards for achieving this compliance.

Sarbanes-Oxley requires auditors to not only certify the numbers, but also the process used to derive the numbers. For example, revenue recognition across

Case Study 2.3
Industry Compliance: The Emergence of XML-Based Integration Standards

Since networks began to proliferate in the 1980s, many industries defined standards for performing business-to-business exchange of information. Hundreds of standards have arisen across every industry to manage the interactions and coordination of business. However, all of these have been in proprietary formats requiring complex custom software or expensive vendor solutions. The Electronic Data Interchange (EDI) standard is one of the better-known business-interchange standards.

A recent phenomenon is the emergence of XML as the preferred approach to defining the next generation of all of these business interchange standards. Independently diverse industries such as health care, financial services, and government have begun to remake the standards under which business and government transactions are conducted. For example, the American Petroleum Institute, the primary trade association representing all phases of the oil and gas industry, has established the Petroleum Industry Data Exchange (PIDX) using XML. In the healthcare industry, the Health Level 7 (HL7) standard has reached its third version in a natural maturation of the standard. The latest version has been defined using XML. The financial-services industry has been one of the leading industries to adopt XML as the preferred manner to define business standards. Diverse standards, such as VISA's XML Invoice Specification for automating purchasing functions and monitoring travel and entertainment expenses, to the Research Information Exchange Markup Language (RIXML), a standard to improve the process of categorizing, aggregating, comparing, sorting, and distributing global financial research, are being defined. The eXtensible Business Reporting Language (XBRL) is a standard that should influence every business because it is a standard format for exchanging business financial information. Within the government, a large number of initiatives are underway, including the Environmental Protection Agency's Central Data Exchange, which supports reporting for critical information on air, water, waste, and toxic substances, using XML-based submissions.

(continued)

Case Study 2.3 *(cont.)*

Business drivers will always exist to exchange information within and across industries to enhance business processes. Initiatives will need to be undertaken to comply with these standards in order to participate in the business community in which an organization participates. These standards will need to be considered by an organization at both the strategy and initiative level, as well as taken into account at the integration architecture level.

a company is an important process that must be certified. Companies can document the process, then manage it after the fact, using end-of-month or quarter reports to fix problems long after they have occurred, or they can implement business-process integration to automate, monitor, and manage critical business processes in real-time.

In addition to all those brochures about patient confidentiality and privacy that you have received from your doctor, pharmacist, and other healthcare providers, HIPAA requires and specifies electronic transactions between payers and providers. Companies needing to be HIPAA compliant are implementing integration technology to accept XML transactions and integrate them with their back-end systems.

The finance industry has been moving towards reducing the amount of time it takes to settle a trade to one day. Although regulatory compliance has been extended until 2005, many financial institutions are moving forward on the initiative now. Long settlement cycles make risk management much more difficult for portfolio managers, and causes reporting discrepancies requiring extensive reconciliation procedures. Therefore, straight-through processing has become a watchword in the financial services industry. The goal is to automate the settlement of the trade across multiple systems, platforms, languages, and technologies. Financial services companies were early adopters of integration technology. As the financial services industry slowly moves towards requiring compliance with the T+1 standard, integration is becoming a requirement. When companies implement solutions to meet these requirements, they will also want to ensure the infrastructure is adaptable to also meet future requirements.

2.3 Defining Requirements

Taking the time to understand and document the business requirements is essential to ensuring the alignment of IT with the business strategy and it makes the project plan easier to sell internally. Failure to accurately define business requirements can lead to wrong decisions and failed implementations. When defining enterprise integration requirements, you need to answer the question, "What is the business problem we are trying to solve?" so that the technical implementation can best meet the business needs. The most critical element of this stage is the identification of the business champion for any strategy or initiative. Empirical evidence suggests that without this champion, the chance of a successful implementation with meaningful impact is substantially reduced.

The requirements process involves the business champion, management and staff involved with the process being addressed, and IT project managers. Projects with enterprise scope may include multiple lines of business in the company. However, even when defining projects with more limited scope, it is helpful to identify related initiatives that could impact architecture or technology decisions.

When defining requirements, it is also important to take the time to understand how the business operates and the impact new business processes will have. Identifying the business benefits of the initiative is an important part of the process; down the road it will help justify technology investments as well as explain the necessity and benefits of change. Therefore, take the time to define the impact and benefits to all parts of the business and all employees who will be affected by the new implementation.

The business requirements will determine whether the initiative is strategic or tactical in nature. As described above, the process, technology, and approach can differ for strategic and tactical projects.

2.4 Business Drivers and Requirements Specification

Achieving the right balance of documentation is often the most difficult part of any project. Too much documentation often wastes time, is not read by the stakeholders, or is poorly maintained as the project naturally evolves. Poor documentation leads to confusion in later stages. Our philosophy is to provide a minimalist approach to documentation. We will focus on the required elements and the process that leads to the creation of the document. These can be tailored to the needs of the organization.

The Business Drivers and Requirements Specification is the document that describes what the business is attempting to achieve. This specification becomes the guiding light of the project and will be used until the system is operational to assess the business impact. When the development team is provided this level of information, it helps them stay focused on the goals leading to a higher probability of success in the development phase. To see the full Business Drivers and Requirements Specification, please see Appendix A. Note that the brackets in the tables refer to specific information to be added to the table.

2.4.1 Introduction

The introduction should be a short executive overview of the specification. In addition, any special aspects of the project should be addressed, including the sponsoring organizations and business champion. A history of the initiative would be helpful as well. At the end of this section the reader should have an understanding of who, what, why, and how the business initiative and strategy evolved.

2.4.2 Scope

This section defines the scope of the Business Drivers and Requirements Specification, specifically whether it is enterprise wide, or for a specific business unit or business initiative.

2.4.3 Key Participants

All stakeholders in the requirements process should be identified, including business managers, the sponsoring organizations and business champions, and owner of the proposed initiative. The artifacts created in this process will be used by enterprise architects and developers to ensure technology solutions are aligned with business requirements.

2.4.4 Statement of Purpose

The statement of purpose is a succinct section used to communicate the business goals and functions of the initiative. It makes the business case for the initiative. It does not include implementation of the technology. One of the more important aspects to address is the impact to the organization once the initiative is complete. Large initiatives will have a major impact that will transcend the technology and affect how people work. Many projects have failed because the corporate culture was not ready for the change.

The business drivers should be a simple and clean statement of the problem. For example, bring cars to market quicker and more cost effectively than before. This section should only have one or two items. Each item should be classified according to the categories we discussed at the beginning of this chapter. If there are too many drivers then the initiative should be reconsidered. Is more than one initiative being addressed?

The business strategy should align with key strategic business initiatives, such as improving business efficiency through process improvement. The functional scope should define the business processes included in the initiative.

The business goals are used to measure and assess the achievement of the business initiative. Examples are reducing design and engineering time from 48 months to 18 months or reducing costs by 20%. These goals need to be realistic to be believed by the business stakeholders as well as the IT organization. This section should outline the benefits to the organization in both subjective and objective terms of achieving the goals. Each of the goals and benefits can then have a value attached to them, whether they are financial, a competitive differentiator, or focused on customer satisfaction. This section makes the business case for the initiative. An extremely useful element of this section is a description or use case of how things will be different as a result of the initiative.

A statement of purpose should be completed for each proposed business initiative. Figure 2-1 (page 30) is an example Statement of Purpose.

2.4.5 Cost Estimates

With the approach in hand, this section of the specification should list high-level costs and an estimated time frame. Costs at this point should be a rough order of magnitude and used for budgeting purposes and estimating ROI. It must be understood that these will be refined in the follow-on phase with the next level of detail. Figure 2-2 (page 31) is an example cost estimate.

Business Initiative

- Online ordering

Business Drivers

- Reduce the order delivery time
- Increase accuracy and decrease delays in providing information to other systems and decision makers

Business Strategy

- Automate business processes to improve efficiency

Functional Scope

- Automate the online order process by integrating transactions with back-end systems
- Automate flow of orders to third-party suppliers
- Provide real-time visibility and management of the end-to-end order process
- Provide online order tracking

Business Goals

- Decrease time between order and delivery
- Decrease error rates of transactions

Organization Impact

- Will decrease headcount for order entry department
- Will change phone order process

Figure 2-1 Statement of Purpose

2.4.6 ROI

This section documents the potential or expected ROI for the business initiative under consideration. Although cost estimates are still at the ballpark stage, it is critical to do an ROI analysis based upon the benefits, cost, and organizational impact.

You can use the template shown in Figure 2-3 (page 32) to guide your assessment of an ROI for any initiative. If the ROI is low, it may be necessary to get a better handle on the costs and the organization might only give a provisional approval to proceed until costs and impacts can be refined.

Costs	Total	Description
Project management	$75000	This is the cost of a project manager for the project for nine months
Hardware	<value>	<description>
Software	<value>	<description>
Development	<value>	<description>
Consulting	<value>	<description>
<Category #1>	<value>	<description>
<Category #n>	<value>	<description>

Figure 2-2 High-Level Cost Estimates

2.4.7 Metrics

The metrics for success refine the business goals into measurable key performance indicators (KPIs). In some cases, the business goals may be of sufficient detail to translate directly into KPIs. Metrics should be defined by business goals. For each goal there can be more than one metric. In addition to the value of the metric, it should include details on how to collect, frequency of collection, and owner, as shown in Figure 2-4 (page 33).

2.4.8 Risks

A risk analysis should be conducted that defines the known areas where there are significant lack of detailed information; difficult issues such as organizational, cultural, technical, or management challenges; and ability to achieve the desired business result.

The risks are a collection of everything that can or may go wrong. The risk analysis may also include a list of assumptions that may be wrong or need further information to be validated. Each risk should be associated with a plan to mitigate the risk and the owner of the risk. Figure 2-5 (page 33) is an example of a risk analysis table.

Reduce Personnel Costs	Reduce head count	<calculation of estimated savings>
	Reduce training costs	<calculation of estimated savings>
	Reduce customer support costs	<calculation of estimated savings>
	Other	<calculation of estimated savings>
Reduce IT Costs	Reduce error rates	<calculation of estimated savings>
	Reduce cost of fixing errors	<calculation of estimated savings>
	Eliminate rekeying of information	<calculation of estimated savings>
	Reduce system support costs through integration	<calculation of estimated savings>
	Other	<calculation of estimated savings>
Reduce Business Costs	Reduce the cost of implementing change	<calculation of estimated savings>
	Reduce costs through optimized business processes	<calculation of estimated savings>
	Other	<calculation of estimated savings>
Increase Revenue	Increase revenue from existing customers	<calculation of estimated savings>
	Attract new customers by rapid response to emerging opportunities	<calculation of estimated savings>
	Create new opportunities through integration with partners and suppliers	<calculation of estimated savings>
	Create new opportunities by bringing products and services to market	<calculation of estimated savings>
	Create new sales or distribution channels	<calculation of estimated savings>
Other	Other	<calculation of estimated savings>

Figure 2-3 ROI Analysis Template

Business Goal	Metric Name	Metric Value	How to Collect	Frequency	Owner
Decrease time between order and shipment	Delivery time	Days	Business activity monitoring solution	On shipment of each order	Line of business manager
Decrease transaction errors	Transaction errors	Number of errors	Exception handling log	Weekly	Operational manager
<goal>	<metric>	<value>	<collection>	<frequency>	<owner>

Figure 2-4 Metrics

Significant unknown			
<issue>	<description>	<mitigation>	<owner>
Organizational issues			
<issue>	<description>	<mitigation>	<owner>
Cultural issues			
<issue>	<description>	<mitigation>	<owner>
Technical issues			
<issue>	<description>	<mitigation>	<owner>
Management issues			
<issue>	<description>	<mitigation>	<owner>
Ability to achieve results			
<issue>	<description>	<mitigation>	<owner>

Figure 2-5 Risks

2.4.9 Conclusions and Commentary

This section should provide any final comments on requirements. It should include any known constraints or other business factors that could affect architecture, design, and implementation.

The Business Drivers and Requirements Specification becomes the guiding light of the project. When the development team is provided this level of information, it helps them to stay focused on the goals, leading to a higher probability of success in the development phase.

2.5 Best Practices

- Ensure that all enterprise integration efforts are closely aligned with business goals and objectives
- Involve IT in strategic business planning
- Appoint business project managers for all IT projects
- Create business metrics to measure success of IT projects
- Revisit business goals and objectives throughout the integration life cycle

2.6 Next Steps

At this juncture the process can differ for strategic and tactical projects, as shown in Figure 2-6. You must define the integration strategy and technology to use on the tactical projects, but it is far better if the recommendation comes from the Enterprise Integration Strategy and Architecture Plan. This ensures that the solution fits into the overall infrastructure and enables agility and reuse on follow-on projects. Having an Enterprise Strategy and Architecture Plan in place is critical to having a long-term supportable environment.

It is especially important to understand how a tactical solution fits into the overall enterprise architecture. For example, enterprises looking to maximize agility and implement real-time processes may view each tactical implementation as a building block in the overall architecture. Rather than take the fastest and most economical path to integration, they may decide to invest in creating reusable business services. Even if the implementation has little bearing on the overall enterprise architecture, it is still important to ensure that enterprise standards are met.

The next step is to create or review the Enterprise Integration Strategy (see Chapter 3).

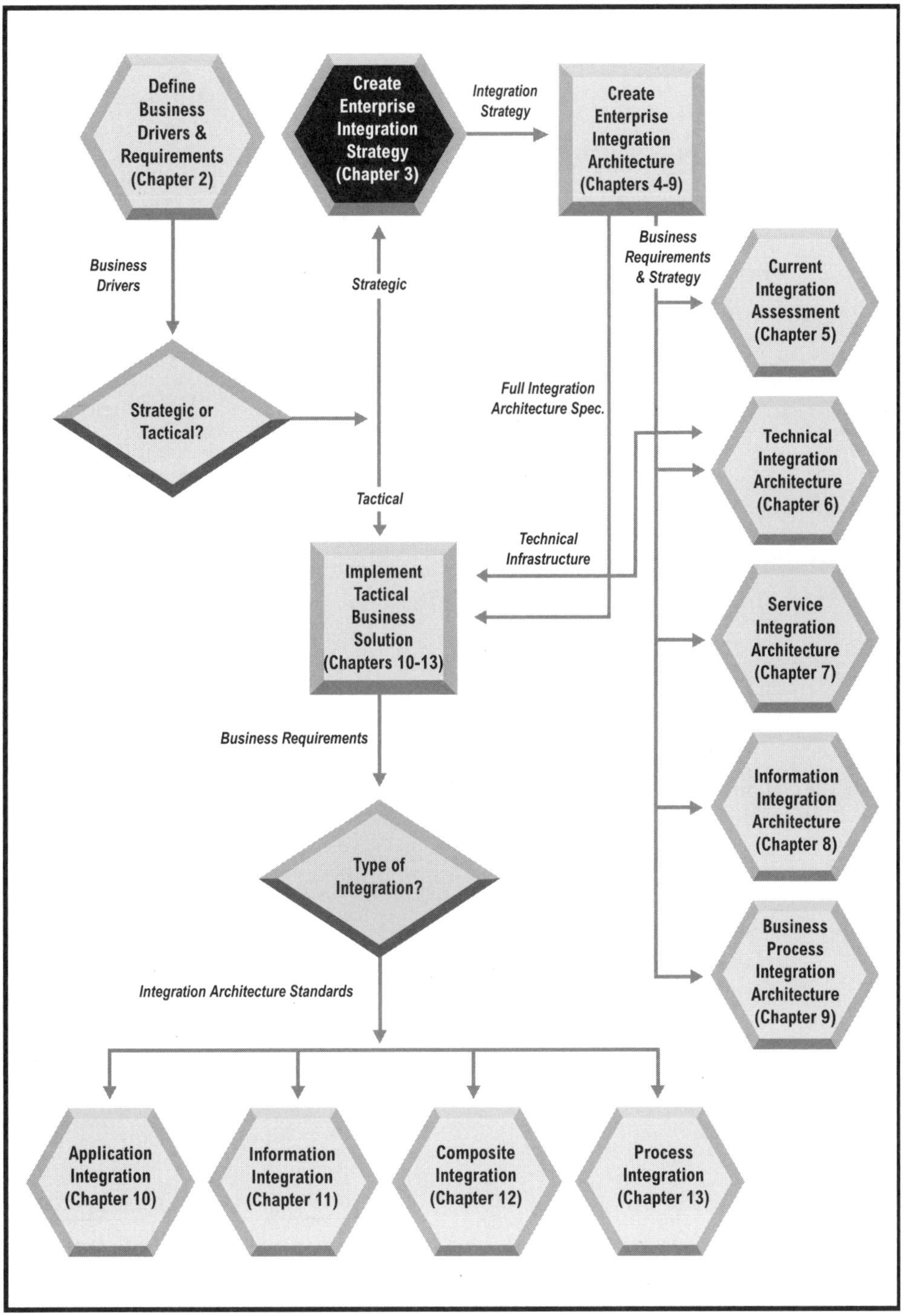

Figure 2-6 Integration Road Map

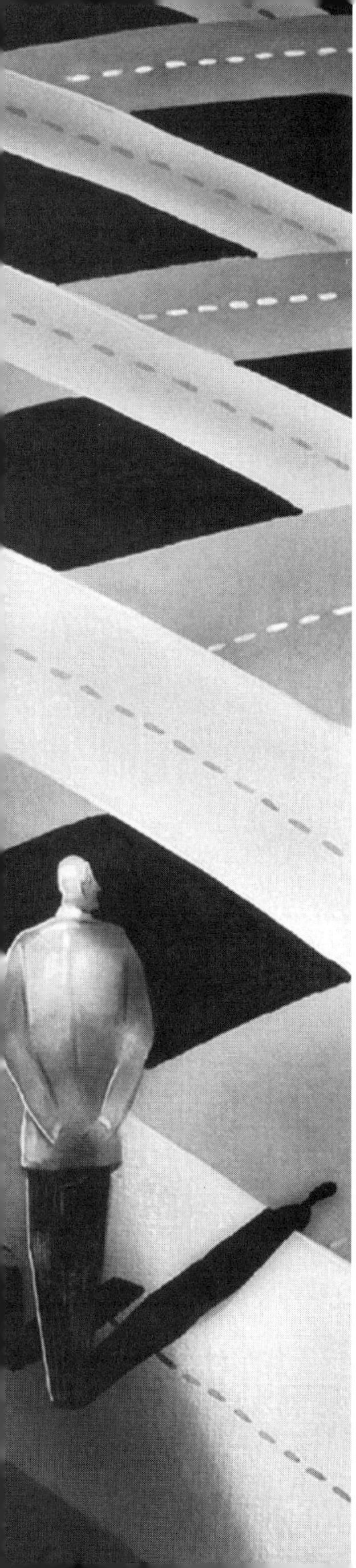

CHAPTER THREE

Enterprise Integration Strategy

3.1 Executive Overview

Enterprise integration does not come in a shrink-wrapped box. Despite the promises and predications of the late 1990s, it is not a single product or technology, nor is it a final end point accomplished with a single project. Enterprise integration focuses on improving the efficiency and effectiveness of the processes that run the business. It includes improving the quality and timeliness of information and providing information on demand where it is needed, regardless of the source system. This level of business agility cannot be achieved simply by implementing integration technology on a project-by-project basis without an overall strategy of how it all fits together. Rapid implementation of the business strategy requires an enterprise-level integration strategy. The enterprise integration strategy ultimately reduces the time and cost of managing information and IT resources.

Enterprise integration is really the natural evolution of computing. It began with networking in the 1980s, which enabled communication between computers as well as with humans, expanding the reach and capabilities of business applications. Improved database access and the ubiquitous browser followed networking, unlocking information and making access easier. The battles over architectural models and standards in these areas are now over and the focus has shifted to improving how information is shared among people and how applications and business processes are supported and improved. Enterprise integration is about laying the foundation for business agility. Like networking in the past, it is at the core of how information systems support an enterprise, and requires standards in order to be truly effective. At some point in the future every enterprise will have embraced enterprise integration in the same way that networking has become an accepted and routine part of an IT environment.

Companies that made good choices for networking and planned out how to design, organize, and use this infrastructure were rewarded with lower costs and a head start over their competition. The same is true for enterprise integration. Long-term success requires laying the groundwork to support both today's business initiatives and evolving needs. However, many companies are taking a tactical approach to integration. A study by the Yankee Group (Derome 2003) stated that enterprise application integration (EAI) demand is declining, resulting in more limited project-based integration spending. EAI implies a corporate-wide information infrastructure capable of managing complex interaction among disparate applications. This lofty IT goal, although technically attainable, has proven unrealistic for most organizations. Instead, companies are buying integration software to meet specific project requirements such as CRM or customer portal integration.

Although tactical initiatives may be the primary drivers of integration, companies that formulate an integration strategy will achieve a much higher level of business agility. Tactical solutions may reduce integration implementation costs on a per-project basis, but the long-term cost reduction will be less significant than an enterprise-wide integration strategy. Remember back to the early days of distributed computing when a project-level approach led to a lack of communication between departments, a multitude of technologies to maintain and understand, a multitude of skill sets required to maintain the systems, skyrocketing of IT support costs, an increase in IT failures, and a corresponding increase in outsourcing and packaged applications. In short, business lost confidence in their IT departments, which makes convincing business managers to invest in infrastructure more difficult, as these investments have not historically paid off. However, the bottom line is that designing for change and agility requires a higher initial investment.

Another problem is that enterprise integration is inherently complex. Different types of projects will require different integration technologies. For example, creating an enterprise portal that allows employees to view, change, and manage their health care and 401(k) plans will require a different technology than integrating electronic transactions from customers and suppliers. It is not possible to solve all integration needs with a single product or technology, nor is it possible to solve all present and future integration requirements with a single project. However, using a purely tactical approach will result in the need to integrate the integration technologies at some point. We have already seen this, and integration technology of the past is quickly becoming the legacy system of the future.

The focus on tactical solutions is the result of the combination of an economic downturn and the failure of large enterprise integration efforts to achieve

Case Study 3.1
CompuCredit: Creating Value Through an Effective Business Integration Strategy

CompuCredit is a leading financial services firm that excels in analysis of financial information, leading to better business decisions with regard to its credit card portfolio. Analysis in any organization is dependent upon the data that is available. Making this information available in a more timely fashion leads to more rapid decision-making. There is significant business value in the form of revenue and profits when the time to act is reduced in the credit business. Guido Sacchi, the CIO of CompuCredit, realized the value of providing a business integration strategy when he arrived on the scene. His team created a strategy to make information more readily available to their business users to reduce analysis time from months to weeks. His strategy was based upon the creation of a service-oriented architecture using XML and Web services using best-of-breed technology. At the core of the strategy is an enterprise metadata repository that maps the physical-data dictionary of each database into a business-data dictionary. Users access the business-data dictionary to determine the data they want to use for their analysis and the data is retrieved from the physical systems, abstracting the user from the arcane aspects of accessing data from relational database systems. This strategy could be directly tied to their business objectives of improving risk analysis and reducing the time to perform an analysis. As a result, CompuCredit's IT department is able to demonstrate that they are adding significant value to the company's business through its business integration strategy.

a return on investment. Early failures were due to the immaturity of the technology and the gap between what vendors were promising and what they were delivering, the proprietary nature of the technology, the high costs, and the lack of suitably trained individuals. The purpose of an enterprise integration strategy is to enable the company to work smarter. Companies like CompuCredit are rethinking their integration strategies and tying them directly to their business strategies, resulting in a real impact on the business and greater satisfaction with IT. Case Study 3.1 describes the CompuCredit experience as related by Guido Sacchi. It provides a coherent and consistent approach to integration that will guide implementation decisions and reduce costs on tactical projects, while laying the groundwork for business agility and future projects. What will make the results different this time is that technology is finally catching up to support enterprise integration. Similar to networking in the early to mid 1990s, a successful enterprise integration strategy will provide a higher ROI and decrease the total cost of ownership over time.

3.2 Why Has Enterprise-Wide Integration Failed in the Past?

The state of integration technology today mirrors that of local area networks a dozen years ago. Throughout the 1980s, analysts were proclaiming "the year of the network." It was not difficult to predict that network technology would transform organizations by connecting employees and enabling sharing of documents and information far more efficiently than exchanging floppy disks, as well as expensive resources such as laser printers. However, it took almost a decade for networks to become ubiquitous and transform corporate communications. The limiting factor was proprietary technology. Vendors had their own proprietary protocols. The protocols did not interoperate. Network implementations tended to be departmental solutions. When the use of e-mail began to grow, companies realized that their networks didn't interoperate, and enterprise-wide communication across different network technologies required complex and expensive integration. The answer to this problem was standards. Ethernet and TCP/IP have become standard network protocols in virtually all organizations, solving the problem of network interoperability, and finally unleashing the full potential of networks to increase corporate efficiency of all types of communication and file sharing. What seems obvious to us today was anything but back then, when the winners were supposed to be OSI, SNA, and other proprietary protocols from Novell or Microsoft.

Enterprise integration is the next evolutionary stage of enterprise computing. Therefore, to succeed, it is important to understand the lessons of the past so we don't repeat the failures. The success of networking was due to the wide adoption of standards. The success of increasing access to data likewise revolved around the ascent of SQL combined with the emergence of the browser, HTML, and HTTP for improving human access to information. In each case there is an architectural construct, a process that has been absorbed into the IT organization, and standards that support it. In each case costs have declined dramatically and acceptance has become universal. In each case the winner was in doubt for a long time and today it has become intuitively obvious. Although few standards have really succeeded, these five (Ethernet, TCP/IP, SQL, HTML, and HTTP) are the foundations of enterprise architecture in business today. They each erased any proprietary or competing standards from the marketplace. Enterprise architectures that did not accommodate these standards were replaced over time due to marketplace realities.

We are now at a similar juncture with integration technology. Despite the plethora of technology now available, integration has yet to achieve the full potential of enabling straight-through processing and real-time visibility of transactions across applications and business units. Maximizing enterprise efficiency and competitiveness requires much more. But the answer is not to retreat to tactical solutions and give up on the goal of enterprise-wide integration. As with network technology, the answer lies in the emerging integration standards, centering on XML and Web services, which are poised to enable the widespread adoption and success of enterprise integration.

Enterprise-wide integration efforts of the past have not been fully successful because they were largely based on integrating proprietary technologies that were difficult to configure and implement, and difficult to change. It is clear that standards-based approaches are required to resolve that problem. However, simply deploying tactical solutions without an overall enterprise strategy of how they will all fit together in the future will doom companies to repeat the failures of the past.

Unfortunately, standards alone will not guarantee success and the current state of standards does not yet solve all integration solutions. Creating an enterprise integration strategy will help companies speed implementation and reduce costs by defining standards and approaches so that each project does not have to re-create the wheel for each new business initiative. Over time the architectures and process will come to be intuitively obvious, but given the nascent state of enterprise integration, some early guidance is required to be successful. The enterprise integration strategy will provide this guidance to the architectures and processes that are used to develop applications and systems. Creating an agile infrastructure that will meet current and future business needs requires an ongoing commitment. Competitive advantage requires an ongoing strategy that aligns technical solutions to business goals and drivers.

3.3 How to Succeed with an Integration Strategy

Although there have been a lot of early enterprise-level integration failures, many companies have succeeded in achieving an extremely high ROI from enterprise-wide integration. The models, techniques, and templates provided here are based on processes, methods, and techniques that are common best practices used in successful companies that have gained competitive advantage or significant ROI

Case Study 3.2
A Large Retail Bank: Reducing the Complexity of Changing an Address

Throughout the 1990s, the strategy of the leading retail banks was to grow through acquisition. Many regional banks disappeared during this time, swallowed up into larger institutions. During this process, many of these banks ended up with a diversity of information systems. It is not uncommon even today to find 30, 40, or even 50 systems that contain customer information. Checking, savings, personal loans, auto loans, mortgages, credit cards, and every other product provided by the bank would have a separate information system. During acquisitions there would be several systems supporting each product. As a result, getting a single view of a customer was not possible. Furthermore, just changing an address could be a long and dreary process to any bank who maintained several business relationships with a client. Checking and savings information might be changed, but mortgages would require a different process for changing address. This is a perplexing experience to banking customers. Why should something as simple as a change of address require a complex set of actions on their part to get it right? Customer service representatives for the bank could only forward the customer to the next department for service. In one case, a large bank in the

Case Study 3.2 *(cont.)*

southeast had over 30 systems where customers' address information might be contained. When a client had more than two products he or she would be forced to deal with different parts of the bank to get his or her address correct. Inside of the IT organization, each system would have thousands of lines of code (LOC) to manage and update a change of address. This would include the user interface for input, the verification and validation of the information, and the actual update to the database. The update was the smallest portion of the code and usually less than a hundred lines. In this organization there were over 150,000 lines of code associated with changing an address across well over 30 systems—none of it integrated and all of it maintained. Not only were customers not happy, but the cost of the code involved was high. This situation exists in many forms in most large organizations. Through a strategy of improving customer service including change of address, a single service was developed to manage the update to all systems with less than 15,000 LOC, and it provided improved customer support. The business integration strategy led to higher customer satisfaction, reduced complexity and cost of maintenance, and made future integration easier. An application such as this can be a big win for any organization and it demonstrates the value of the business integration strategy.

or both from their ability to leverage integration. They should be applied as a part of the enterprise integration strategy.

- **Create a road map.** The road map should outline a strategy to make enterprise integration a successful and efficient process for the IT organization. This includes the culture, knowledge, processes, and architecture. An effective road map should cover a period of two to three years, never less than one year and never more than five years.
- **Create metrics for measuring the effectiveness of the strategy.** There is an old business adage that you cannot manage what you cannot measure. We consistently see this theme at all levels of enterprise integration, from strategy through implementation. Although there are some common metrics like ROI and cost/benefit ratio, the best metrics at this level are those tied directly to the Business Strategies and Initiatives Specification.

- **Minimize redundancy.** Redundancy is something that is never planned, occurs over time, is justifiable on a case-by-case basis, and is the cause of many major problems in IT organizations. Costs increase on a linear or worse basis, the ability to retain and find staff with the required diverse knowledge and skills leads to a lack of core competency in any one area, and any change results in a cascading of effort across all redundant elements, which often hampers the ability to meet business needs. The cost and complexity of redundancy is often not understood. Furthermore, it can have an enormous negative business impact. Case Study 3.2 (page 42) looks at the author's experiences working in a retail bank and the redundancy related to changing an address.
- **Minimize required skill sets.** Maintaining multiple technologies requires maintaining skills in each. People are always the most expensive part of any system. Minimizing skill sets reduces personnel costs and maximizes investment in skills development. Defining technology standards at an enterprise level is the most effective way to minimize required skill sets.
- **Invest in reuse.** 10% to 20% investment over the cost of a tactical solution can provide a much higher ROI in the future through reuse and business agility; the second usage of a solution can result in reductions in costs of 50% to 80% when the appropriate design is put into place. However, technology is not the core problem with reuse. Culture and processes need to support the idea of a system that supports reusability. Two key enterprise integration strategies that maximize reuse are service-oriented architectures (SOAs) and process-driven integration. (In this chapter we discuss the relevance of SOA and process-driven architectures to the integration strategy. In Chapter 7 and Chapter 9 we discuss them in more detail.)
- **Revisit and revise as business strategies change.** Making enterprise integration a part of the normal way that business is conducted can be daunting. It often goes against the grain of the organization. It requires cutting across organizational boundaries and can add a coordination level that staff may not buy into in the beginning. As a result, the senior executives of the IT organization must lead change.

Each of these elements should be considered in the context of the enterprise integration strategy. They represent characteristics of the best companies in the industry. If we return to our Case Study of General Motors, we can see how they addressed each of these elements in Case Study 3.3 (Dragoon 1998; Moozakis 2001).

Case Study 3.3
General Motors: Strategy Is a Leadership Issue

When Ralph Szygenda took over the role of CIO at GM, he created a strategy that included bringing the strategy into the organization after it had been outsourced to Electronic Data Systems Corporation (EDS). His strategy included organizing his staff, reducing redundant systems, and focusing his skill sets and sourcing on a limited number of technologies and vendors. His strategy is directly opposite of what had been in place, in many ways. For example, GM's financial systems were reduced by 70% from a high of 1,800 separate systems. But this wasn't done just for the sake of change. His philosophy has been that if it doesn't change the business, it is a failure. The success of the business integration strategy is directly proportional to the direction and support that it gets from the CIO. In the case of GM, it was set and managed by the CIO—leading to extraordinary results.

3.4 Key Architectural Best Practices: SOA and Process-Driven Integration

Service-oriented architecture (SOA) and process-driven integration are key strategic integration directions currently considered to be best practices in integration strategy. They are included here because they require an enterprise-wide strategic approach in order to be successful. If companies wish to reap the full benefits Web services, SOA, and process management have to offer, an enterprise strategy is required; technology alone will not provide the business benefits companies are seeking. This section defines these strategies and describes the benefits of adopting them.

3.4.1 Service-Oriented Architecture

Service-oriented architectures are not a new concept. They have been considered best practice for three decades. In a service-oriented architecture, business functionality is packaged as reusable services that can be accessed through standard interfaces independent of platform or programming language. However, SOAs were previously difficult to build. First, there was no consistent component model everyone could agree on. Companies would need to stake the enterprise architecture on choosing among COM, CORBA, and Java J2EE. In fact, these "standards" all competed in the marketplace, ensuring that no one would dominate or become ubiquitous, like TCP/IP is in networking. However, finally there is one standard everyone seems to be supporting—Web services. The Web service standard defines a standardized interface (WSDL), a standardized communication protocol (SOAP), a standardized message format (XML), and a standardized repository for registering and discovering Web services (UDDI). These standards enable a Web service to reside anywhere and be accessed from everywhere. Existing mission-critical applications currently on the mainframe and other platforms can be wrapped in Web services interfaces and then accessed from other applications or Web browsers. This enables business to create business services out of existing systems, and rapidly implement and integrate new functionality. Web services may finally unleash the full potential of SOA. The real benefit of Web services is creating an SOA based on the first universally accepted application-interface standard the industry has offered.

However, creating an SOA is the antithesis of the hype that surrounded the introduction of Web service technology. SOA requires enterprise commitment, planning, and hard work. It is a strategy—not a magic bullet. It is one of the cornerstones on which the architecture concepts of enterprise integration will be built.

3.4.2 Process-Driven Integration

The real-time enterprise needs to respond rapidly to business change, opportunities, and threats. This requires proactive management—responding in real-time to developments as they unfold. To accelerate business processes, reduce inefficiencies, and provide real competitive advantage, companies need to optimize, automate, and manage end-to-end business processes across applications, business units, and even enterprises.

Increasing the velocity of business processes across the enterprise requires real-time visibility into those processes. You can't manage and improve what you can't measure. Furthermore, different constituents require different levels of visibility into the process at each stage of the process. Line of business managers require a business view of the process, and IT managers require a systems view. All constituents need to see the progress of the business process in real time, so the process can be managed effectively and proactively.

However, providing this visibility is a challenge because an end-to-end business process may cross multiple organizational units, applications, and even business entities. For example, an order placed on the Web may need to touch multiple back-end systems, such as a customer-management system, inventory-management system, product-management system, billing system, and external systems, such as FedEx, for product shipping and tracking. The systems typically reside on disparate platforms, including mainframes, AS400, UNIX, and Web application servers.

Process-driven integration provides end-to-end business process visibility and management. It is one of the fastest growing areas of integration because it provides direct value to the business rather than just technical connectivity. BPM solutions typically include the following:

- Process-modeling capabilities for business analysts to define the business process
- Process automation, which enables process routing to be defined by events or content or other relevant business rules
- Workflow for routing and managing manual tasks
- Process monitoring and alerts when a process rule is violated
- Some level of application integration, either through Web services, adapters, a full integration broker, or integration with another vendor's broker.

Advanced features include process simulation, optimizing processes, and running "what if" scenarios based on time and/or cost factors, and a business analytics dashboard that displays key performance indicators for the business manager based on process statistics. Business activity monitoring (BAM), which can send real-time alerts along with analytical and historical information, can help decision makers make faster and better-informed decisions. Gartner predicts that BAM will be a key spending initiative beginning in 2004, and it will become a requirement for future survival and competitive advantage (McCoy and Lheureux 2003).

BPM is also being touted as the solution for orchestrating and managing the flow of information across business services. They are highly compatible strategies and companies will want to investigate and fully evaluate both. These architectural concepts will also form the basis for the enterprise integration strategy.

3.5 How Long Should a Strategy Take?

The enterprise integration strategy does not end with a document produced by a committee. It is an ongoing process that must remain aligned with changing business strategies. Therefore, creating an enterprise integration strategy is not a one-time event—it is an ongoing process. Realizing this should prevent you from getting bogged down in analysis paralysis.

Creating a competency center will reduce the time it takes to create an integration strategy based on business strategies. A competency center is an organizational structure populated with in-depth expertise and processes focused on a specific topic or operational need that can be leveraged across an organization to achieve greater efficiency and improved results. An integration competency center is a centralized resource staffed with skilled personnel who perform on-going research and analysis into the possible technology options and promote integration best practices. This group is in the best position to compare and contrast alternative strategies, and can reduce the time this process takes for individual implementation projects. Although important, creating the integration strategy need not be a large task. Even for a large enterprise, several staff-weeks should suffice. The schedule depends not so much on the time required to create the strategy specification, as on the time required to present it to various stakeholders and secure their approval. Depending on the scope of the enterprise, this process can take from one to three months.

3.6 Business Integration Strategy Specification

The Business Integration Strategy Specification is the document that maps business requirements, strategies, and initiatives to integration strategies and projects. The integration strategy specification can be created on either an enterprise level or a project level. As stated previously, companies will be able to leverage work and investments done on each project if the work is at least owned and managed by an enterprise group. To see the complete Enterprise Integration Strategy Specification, see Appendix B.

3.6.1 Introduction

The introduction should be a short executive overview of the specification. It should begin with a tie back to the business strategies and initiatives and how this will support these needs. In addition, any major constraints, such as limitations imposed by legacy systems or the requirements for high security, should be addressed if they are major factors in the integration strategy. Some background on integration within the organization and any major benefits that would occur as a result of the strategy would be helpful. To create the introduction, answer the following questions:

- How will the integration strategy support business needs?
- Are there any major constraints, such as limitations imposed by legacy systems, or requirements, such as the need for high security, that are a major factor in the integration strategy?
- What are the anticipated benefits of the strategy?

At the end of the introduction the reader should have an understanding of what, why, and how the integration strategy evolved.

3.6.2 Scope

The scope defines whether this strategy covers integration across the entire enterprise, a division, a line of business, or some other scope. The scope of the integration strategy is determined by the business initiatives defined in the business strategy. For maximum ROI and long-term agility, we recommend that the scope of the enterprise integration strategy be enterprise-wide. However, we also recognize that each individual business initiative has a unique scope relative to the business units, applications, data sources, and system user roles. For each type of initiative, different methods of integration and technologies are required. These include data synchronization, application integration, legacy integration, desktop integration (portals and mobile applications), and business-to-business (B2B), including traditional EDI, to XML point-to-point messaging, to complex supply chain integration. The later chapters of this book discuss integration strategies for different types of business solutions.

3.6.3 Key Participants

This section identifies the key stakeholders of the plan, including business managers and executives who contributed information, and team members who created the strategy. Key participants in the integration strategy should include all those responsible for defining infrastructure requirements and standards. Companies seeking to maximize leverage in infrastructure investments have an integration competency center and/or central architecture group. However, in the majority of companies, currently this task is most often distributed among development groups. Without a centralized strategy the likelihood of redundant components is high, raising the cost of both infrastructure maintenance and business change.

As previously stated, a successful business integration strategy does not end with a document produced by a committee. It is an ongoing process that must remain aligned with changing business strategies. Therefore, the process of creating an integration strategy is not a one-time event—it is an ongoing process. It is best to have a centralized group create the integration strategy with heavy involvement with business managers responsible for the business strategy. Different companies implement the function in different ways. In some companies a virtual team "revisits" the strategy periodically. Other companies put it in the domain of the enterprise architecture group. Due to the high number of integration failures in the past, it is becoming a recommended best practice to create an integration competency center.

Although this group can be a part of the enterprise architecture group, integration is a complex technical discipline in itself, and the breadth and depth of emerging technologies and standards warrants specialization. The competency center is responsible for defining standards for communication transport, application interfaces, message formats, messaging models (publish/subscribe, message queuing, request/reply), message routing (workflow, content-based routing, event-based routing), data translation, and transformation. By centralizing the responsibility for data translation and transformation, the company can leverage and reuse one of the most expensive and time consuming and complex tasks of integration—understanding and mapping semantic meaning of data between and among applications.

However an organization decides to implement the role of making these critical integration decisions and recommendations, the group charged with creating the strategy is responsible for ensuring that all IT decisions meet the strategic goals of the organization, with an eye to providing a return on investment. It must be noted here that when the group charged with creating the strategy has no power to ensure compliance of implementations across the organization, they tend to be less successful. When they have a seat on the board that controls the budget, and establishes or approves business metrics for each IT project funded, they are more successful, because they can enforce enterprise standards and strategies. The competency center or strategy group should be a catalyst for business innovation by making the business aware of the opportunities technology creates.

The template defines three types of participants that should be identified in this section:

- The team responsible for the creation of the strategy in its initial form, as well as for any on going improvements. Anyone that provided information or review should be included in this list.

- The group that will implement and apply the strategy.
- Approvers of the strategy.

3.6.4 Integration Strategies

This section identifies key possible strategies based on best practices, testing, and experience. These strategies are listed in the Integration Strategies Table (Figure 3-1). Strategies the company should consider are how to manage redundancy in both technology and skill sets and how to manage reuse. Although the cost savings are high for doing so, technology alone will not deliver any of these savings—it requires an enterprise approach. In fact, the purpose of defining an enterprise strategy and managing and updating the strategy over time, is to maximize IT investments and increase business agility. For example, an SOA strategy is highly recommended as a best practice and can deliver big pay offs over time, but success depends upon a strategy for reuse and an enterprise commitment to the approach. Although process-driven integration has the potential to deliver a very high ROI, the true value will come from optimizing and automating cross-organizational processes. These are the processes that are most difficult to manage. Therefore, again, an enterprise-wide approach will achieve the best results. You should also define how the integration infrastructure will be implemented. Will the company take a utilities approach to building an enterprise infrastructure that will enable interaction between all systems, or will it take a tactical approach for achieving the strategic vision? Lastly, the long-term benefits of creating the strategy depend upon periodically updating it to keep it aligned with the business strategy as it evolves. To ensure that this happens, the company

<Redundancy management strategies>	<strategy>	<rationale>
<Skill set management strategies>	<strategy>	<rationale>
<Reusabilitiy strategies>	<strategy>	<rationale>
<Process driven integration strategies>	<strategy>	<rationale>
<SOA strategies>	<strategy>	<rationale>
<Implementation strategies>	<strategy>	<rationale>
<Business integration strategy lifecycle>	<strategy>	<rationale>

Figure 3-1 Integration Strategies Table

should define the strategy life cycle and determine whether to perform regular periodic reviews (every 6 to 12 months), whether changes in the business strategy will trigger a review of the integration strategy, or whether funding of major projects will trigger the review.

3.6.5 Mapping to Business Strategies and Initiatives

The purpose of the business integration strategy is to provide a tie between the needs of the business and the implementations by IT. It ensures that there is a match between what is desired and what is provided. This section provides a mapping between business initiatives defined in the Business Strategies and Initiatives Specification and integration strategies in the form of a matrix, shown in Figure 3-2.

Discuss nonobvious points of support. If any row or column is blank (i.e., a business strategy has no integration strategy to support it or an integration strategy supports no business strategy), discuss the implications. Any budgeting for projects that has been done to date or expected allocations should be included at this point. This budget figure reflects the IT organization's portion of the budget allocated to this initiative.

By following matrix relationships between the business strategies defined in Chapter 2 and the IS strategies presented here, you can map business requirements to integration requirements. You can also prioritize infrastructure investments by ranking projects based on importance to the company.

3.6.6 Strategic Sourcing

This section describes the approach that the organization feels will be most effective in acquiring any technology. It should set the philosophy, constraints, and

Priority	Business Strategy/Initiative	Scope	Integration Strategy	Budget
1	Regulatory compliance (ex. Sarbanes-Oxley)	Certification of revenue reporting process	Process management	$xxx
2	Increase business efficiency and competitiveness	Tactical initiative to reduce time to process an order	Application integration	$yyy
<priority>	<business strategy>	<scope>	<integration strategy>	<budget>

Figure 3-2 Mapping Business and Integration Strategies

approach to sourcing. Issues to be dealt with are the existing relationships and current use of technology, vendor preferences, best-of-breed versus single vendor, and responsibilities for identifying, selecting, and negotiating contracts. It should define the following:

- **Preference for sourcing approach.** This can include best-of-breed, single vendor, or platform approach, or choosing two or three preferred vendors. The benefit of a best-of-breed approach is that companies can easily take advantage of evolving technologies. The disadvantage is that it increases the training and skills required to implement and maintain the solution. The advantage of a single vendor strategy is that the company will have the greatest leverage in negotiating enterprise purchases. The disadvantage is that a single-source strategy puts you at the mercy of one vendor. Some companies mitigate this risk by choosing a limited number of strategic sources, between one and three, for each type of technology component. The sourcing approach may relate back to the strategy for minimizing skill sets, defined previously in the integration strategies section.
- **Preferred vendors.** This includes preferred vendors for each type of technology or for the entire platform, depending upon the approach defined previously.
- **Procurement process.** This part of the specification may point to another internal document.

3.6.7 Standards

The standards section (Figure 3-3) is arguably one of the most important sections of the integration strategy. Standards reduce costs and increase reusability and agility. They prevent dependence on a specific vendor or technology. Standards are able to accomplish this because they are available for any vendor or organization to implement. By using the standards, organizations can rip out one product and bring in another that supports the same standard. The reality is that this is possible, but there is almost always some rework required. However, this rework is significantly less than if standards were not applied. Standards help preserve IT investments. This is also one of the hardest sections to develop in the integration strategy specification.

Standards often get either too much attention or not enough. The intention of this section is to define an enterprise strategy for how different types of stan-

	Proposed Usage	References
Communication protocols	<Example: B2B communications>	<Web site for JCA or Web service interface specification>
Application interfaces	<Example: packaged application interfaces>	<Web site for JCA or Web service interface specification>
Message formats	<Example: internal messages, external messages, EDI messages>	<Links to appropriate Web sites or internal specification documents>
Process models	<Example: enterprise processes—standard on tool or standard such as BPEL>	<Links to internal documents or appropriate Web site>
Metadata	<Example: metadata about interfaces, Web services, data transformation, etc.>	<Links to internal documents or appropriate Web site>

Figure 3-3 Standards Strategy Table

dards will be used in the architecture. This strategy forms the basis for the integration architecture.

The standards that can be defined in an integration strategy include the following:

- **Standard communication protocols and technology.** These may also be defined for different types of integration projects. For example, for internal application integration the standard communication protocol will most likely be TCP/IP or other network protocols prevalent in the organization. Messaging lies at the heart of the application integration infrastructure. Companies may choose to standardize on vendor solutions such as IBM MQ Series, Software AG EntireX Communicator, or Tibco Rendezvous, or on a messaging standard such as JMS (which most vendors also support). For B2B integration, EDI may be standard for larger partners communicating via a virtual private network (VPN), and Simple Object Access Protocol (SOAP) may be standard for smaller vendors communicating over the Internet. Defining and documenting these decisions as part of the strategy will prevent companies from repeating the mistakes of history and having to integrate different messaging systems across the company.
- **Standard Application Interfaces.** One of the early benefits of EAI technology was the prepackaged application adapter that provided faster connectivity to applications. However, each of these adapters was specific to the

vendor. Moreover, some of the larger EAI vendors grew by acquisition, and their process integration server required different adapters than their application integration server or their B2B server. Companies looking to implement enterprise solutions were finding they needed to install and configure multiple adapters for each system, which quickly eroded the benefits of "packaged" adapters. The Java Connector Architecture (JCA) is a standard specification for creating adapters that can be accessed from any Java application. Alternatively, many companies are choosing to create Web service interfaces to existing applications as part of a strategy for creating a standards-based SOA. This is the approach the authors highly recommend.

- **Standard Message Formats.** This is an area where history is repeating itself in a positive way. In the early days of networking, TCP/IP was considered too "heavy" a protocol for general use. However, the benefits of having a single protocol capable of communication across platforms soon outstripped the negative impact of larger packets. Besides, the networks just got faster to accommodate them. The same is true of XML. Although some say it is overly verbose for some applications, the benefits of having a standard message format that can be interpreted by any system that supports the standard outweighs any reasons not to use it. For this reason, XML is fast becoming the de facto message standard for both internal and external communications.
- **Standard Process Models.** A business process model represents the knowledge of how the business operates. In the case of end-to-end business processes that cut across organizational boundaries involving multiple line-of-business managers responsible for different parts of the process, the model may in fact be the only documentation of how the process is managed across the organization. The time and money invested in creating, automating, managing, and optimizing the model is significant. Companies need to retain the value of that investment by maintaining the models and knowledge within the models. These long-term benefits will provide significant payback to companies in the future. This means the models should not be dependent upon a particular technology or vendor. The benefit of standards-based modeling is that it makes it easier to maintain and change the information in the model over time, and it makes the model more technology independent.

  There have been a number of competing process-model specifications, but various process-standard groups and vendors are coming together behind BPEL, which stands for business process execution language. BPEL is an amalgamation of XLANG from Microsoft and WSFL from IBM, and supersedes both. Microsoft, IBM, and BEA joined to submit BPEL to OASIS, the international standards body. A competing specification has been proposed—Web Service Choreography Interface (WSCI), created by SAP, Sun and BEA; but BPEL seems to be emerging as the clear front-runner. The good news is that agreement on a unified process model also has important implications for companies currently building composite applications using Web services. Composite applications require process orchestration among the different application components or services. For these applications to be portable across technologies, a primary benefit of Web services, the process definition should also be portable.

A process standard will enable companies to retain and reuse the business knowledge represented in the model, including the process rules, flow of control, and management metrics. The standard will also enable organizations to consistently manage and optimize business processes, and implement business change rapidly.

- **Metadata Standards.** One of the most difficult and time consuming integration tasks that cannot be automated by any technology is determining the semantic meaning of data within applications to enable data translation and transformation between systems. For example, System A may have a data entity called Customer. System B may have a data entity called Client. Although a person may be able to easily recognize that these are the same, a computer could not. However, it gets much worse. Understanding semantic meaning of data in some systems may actually require in-depth detective work. For example, financial institutions have many systems that track information about securities. However, each system may track different information about that security. Synchronizing information across these systems is not a mere matter of matching entity names. It requires parsing the information and delivering different data to each target system. Companies need to leverage metadata across systems. This can be accomplished by creating standard metadata definitions—an enterprise vocabulary—and managing them centrally. This is one of the central roles of an integration competency center.

3.6.8 Metrics

The time, effort, and cost of creating an integration strategy should deliver a high return on investment to the company by maximizing reuse of existing systems, process models, and data definitions. Defining standards reduces the cost of creating system interfaces; minimizes redundancy, which lowers the total cost

Integration Strategy	Metric Name	Metric Value	How to Collect	Frequency	Owner
<goal>	<metric>	<value>	<collection>	<frequency>	<owner>
Example: Increase reuse	Component reuse	Number of times component is reused	Number of business processes or composite apps component is used in; alternatively, # of times it's checked out from reuse repository	Monthly	Repository owner, central architecture group, or competency center (different component types may have different owners)

Figure 3-4 Integration Strategy Metrics

of ownership; and lowers the cost of maintaining systems by reducing the skill sets required. The integration strategy should also increase business agility by enabling rapid change within the company.

All of these benefits and goals can be tracked and measured, and the metrics used to measure the success of an integration competency center or strategy group. Metrics should be defined that measure the success and relative value of an integration strategy, tracked over time, and used as input when refining the strategy and determining future infrastructure investments. To be of use, each metric must be measurable and manageable. The effort to collect and track a metric cannot exceed the value of the information it provides. Owners are responsible for tracking and reporting on metrics. Specific metrics that can be employed include tracking reuse, tracking the time needed to implement new solutions or implement changes to existing systems, tracking savings resulting from reducing redundancy, and monitoring Total Cost of Ownership (TCO) of a system, as shown in Figure 3-4.

3.6.9 Risks

The risk section defines everything that can or might go wrong. It may also include a list of assumptions that might be wrong or need further information to

Significant Unknown			
	<issue>	<description>	<mitigation>
Organizational Issues			
	<issue>	<description>	<mitigation>
Cultural Issues			
	<issue>	<description>	<mitigation>
Technical Issues			
	<issue>	<description>	<mitigation>
Management Issues			
	<issue>	<description>	<mitigation>
Ability to Achieve Results			
	<issue>	<description>	<mitigation>

Figure 3-5 Strategy Risks

be validated. This includes the organizational, cultural, technical, or management challenges and ability to achieve the desired business results, as shown in Figure 3-5. Each risk should be associated with a plan to mitigate the risk.

3.6.10 Conclusions and Recommended Next Steps

The goal of the integration strategy is to reduce long-term TCO and increase business agility and competitive advantage. This requires a strategy that does more than simply react to current business needs. Companies must identify the strategies by which the enterprise can use technology to maximize competitive advantage. The key questions addressed in the integration strategy include

- What are the best and most innovative practices in the enterprise's industry?
- What are the best and most innovative practices of successful agile enterprises?
- What are the potential benefits and costs of a specific integration strategy?
- What are the technical and marketplace risks associated with the integration strategy?
- How do we measure success and improve the strategy?

A successful business integration strategy must be tightly aligned with key business strategies and requirements. Management buy-in is essential. Most importantly, to be of practical value, the business integration strategy must enable a strategic approach to tactical solutions. A metaphor for a solid business integration strategy is, "think globally, act locally."

Ignoring any of the above key questions would pose risk to the success of both the strategy and the company. The approach defined here is designed to largely mitigate these risks, and accelerate tactical solutions while building enterprise agility.

3.7 Next Steps

After creating an integration strategy, the next step is defining the integration architecture, as shown in Figure 3-6. Part II (Chapter 4, Chapter 5, and Chapter 6) describes how to create integration architecture and define an architecture specification.

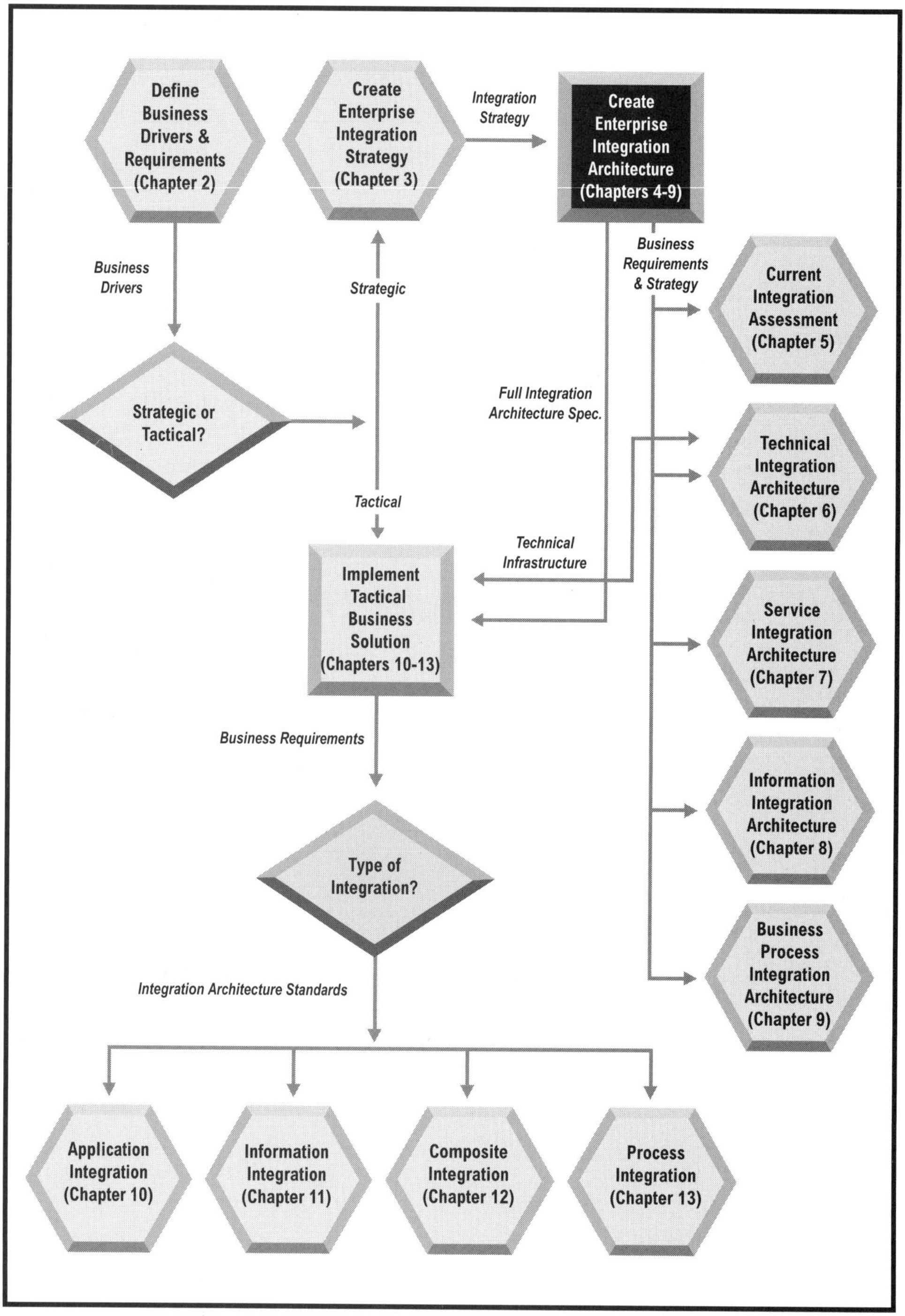

Figure 3-6 Integration Road Map

PART II

Enterprise Integration Architecture

Part II focuses on creating the Enterprise Integration Architecture by applying the results of Part I. Because integration-driven system development requires interplay across a diverse set of enterprise assets, it is important to put an integration architecture in place that can guide each successive implementation. Without this architecture duplication will occur, significant costs will be incurred by each application to develop its own architecture, and reuse will be difficult to achieve. The architecture includes all the services and component technologies needed for different types of integration requirements. This section will provide a structure to guide the design of your architecture.

Chapter 4—Enterprise Integration Architecture Overview

Chapter 4 is an introduction to creating an Enterprise Integration Architecture. It explains the benefits of creating the integration architecture on an enterprise level, as well as different components of the Enterprise Integration Architecture, which include the Current Integration Environment Assessment, the Technical Integration Architecture, the Service Integration Architecture, the Information Integration Architecture, and the Process Integration Architecture. The chapter also includes a discussion of organizational structure and processes for architecture governance, and best practices for creating an Enterprise Integration Architecture.

Chapter 5—Current Integration Environment Assessment

No integration project should start with a clean sheet of paper. Chapter 5 focuses on how to conduct an assessment of the current integration environment. The specification included in the chapter provides an explanation of how to perform and document a current assessment. This current assessment is also used when creating the Technical Integration Architecture Specification, contained in Chapter 6.

Chapter 6—Technical Integration Architecture

The Technical Integration Architecture Specification provides guidelines and standards that constitute the enterprise building code for all integration projects. It is the specification that all projects will reference when choosing integration technology for their particular implementation. Chapter 6 includes the specification template for the technical integration architecture. It includes tables and specifications for defining all integration technologies, integrated applications, and types of integration. It includes conceptual, physical, and development views of the technical integration architecture and a standards profile. The architecture specification template provides an in-depth section on service-level requirements, including availability, integrity and delivery service, scalability, maintainability and manageability, usability, performance, transaction services, persistence services, and directory services. It also defines different levels of security and provides guidelines for capacity planning. Chapter 6 also includes best practices for creating a Technical Integration Architecture.

Chapter 7—Service Integration Architecture

The service integration architecture represents best practice for creating reusable and agile business applications. A service represents a piece of business functionality that can run on platform, and be accessed by other services and applications. Defining services is an essential part of creating a service-oriented architecture (SOA). Chapter 7 defines the benefits of SOA, and provides an event-driven method for defining functionally cohesive and loosely coupled services. Chapter 7 contains the Service Integration Architecture Specification. The specification focuses on the service definitions and interface definitions, and provides a template for using an event-based method for defining services. The chapter includes best practices for creating an SOA.

Chapter 8—Information Integration Architecture

Information integration lies at the heart of all integration projects. However, when information is integrated merely at a tactical level, the semantic mapping of data between systems may be locked in proprietary tools and not reusable across technologies. Chapter 8 defines the importance of managing integrated data as an enterprise resource, and explains the types of metadata that are important to organizations to create an integrated, managed, and reusable information architecture. Chapter 8 includes the Information Integration Architecture Specification that contains a framework for defining information integration patterns and data flows. The specification provides a draft metadata model for integrated information and a relationship model to define integrity rules across applications. Chapter 8 also contains best practices for creating the Information Integration Architecture.

Chapter 9—Process Integration Architecture

The Process Integration Architecture defines end-to-end business processes, which are then automated across existing systems on disparate platforms. The purpose of creating the process architecture is to enable the organization to manage, measure, and improve business processes over time. This requires modeling processes, verifying processes with all stakeholders, perhaps simulating processes to optimize performance, and real-time monitoring of key performance indicators, and continuous process improvement. Chapter 9 contains an overview on why process is important and different methods for defining business process metrics and measuring success, as well as different methods for modeling processes. Chapter 9 contains the Process Integration Architecture Specification. Although we recognize that most of the process specification will be kept in a modeling tool, the specification provides a guide to defining all the important aspects of the process architecture, and best practices for creating it.

The Enterprise Integration Architecture Specifications created in Part II of the book are then used to guide the integration solutions as defined in Part III of the book.

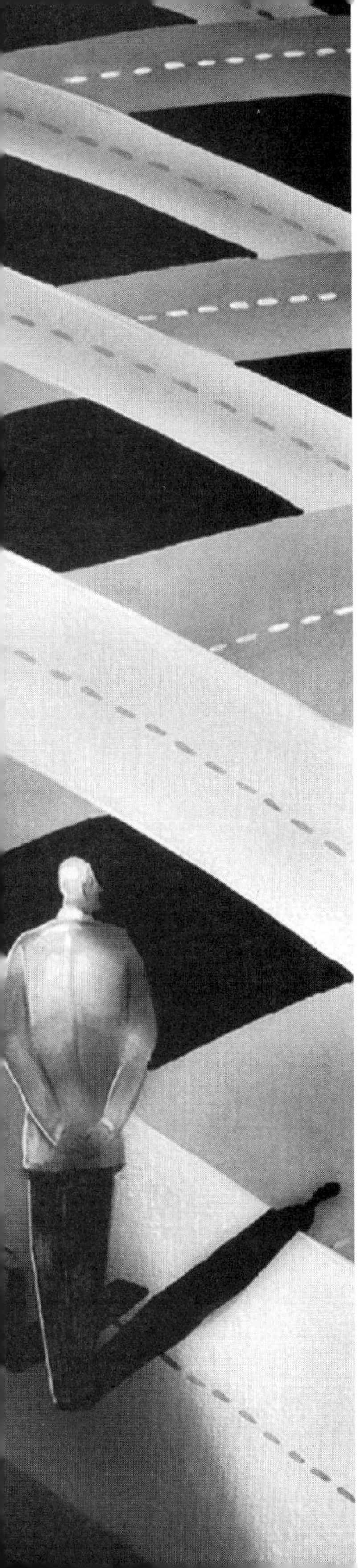

CHAPTER FOUR

Enterprise Integration Architecture Overview

4.1 Executive Overview

The enterprise integration architecture provides a blueprint for both strategic and tactical integration projects. It describes all the components of the architecture. Experience has clearly shown that tactical approaches to building technical infrastructure result in higher maintenance costs and inhibit business agility. Because of this, in the past five years many large organizations and government agencies have established enterprise architecture (EA) frameworks. The enterprise integration architecture fits within the overall framework of the enterprise architecture. Priorities for building the architecture are driven by business requirements and strategies.

A strategic enterprise integration architecture can be compared to city planning. It includes a set of building codes. There is a governance body to ensure that projects meet accepted standards, and there is a process for exceptions. This approach reduces the number of technical configurations and required skill sets, thereby lowering support costs. It also ensures that current and future technology investments are maximized at an enterprise level. In some cases it is not feasible to take a tactical approach. This is especially true in any community of interest that requires the interchange of information. Case Study 4.1 describes how the state of Minnesota started CriMNet as an initiative to provide complete criminal history on

Case Study 4.1
CriMNet: Providing the Right Data in the Hands of the Right People and in the Right Place

Communities of interest are finding it more and more necessary to integrate across the independent organizations in order to achieve significant improvements. However, the nature of being independent makes this integration a monumental challenge because there is no single authority to dictate the result. In these cases, an enterprise integration architecture provides the structure in which these organizations can operate and coordinate without losing their own freedom of movement.

CriMNet is an initiative in the state of Minnesota to provide complete criminal history on suspects and criminals to those involved in public safety and justice systems. Rather than providing a new database of information collected from a vast number of existing systems, it is an enterprise to link together the 1,100 criminal justice jurisdictions in the state.

The architecture is defined as five elements:

- **Vision.** Describes the purpose and goals of the system
- **Organization.** Identifies stakeholders, governance models, and system structure
- **Business Process.** Provides a structure to improve the automation of public safety processes
- **Data.** Describes data standards and dictionary
- **Technology.** Lists of standards, principles, and guidelines for implementation

When completed, the CriMNet system is a secure Internet system that any public safety or justice system can connect into, and it provides the rules for organized and coherent access to information.

In organizations where IT responsibility is highly distributed or in communities of interest with independent organization, enterprise integration architecture becomes the glue that is able to tie the entities together in the sharing of information.

suspects and criminals. It links together 1,100 criminal justice jurisdictions in the state. The whole purpose of an initiative such as CriMNet is to enable enterprise integration.

4.2 The Business Case for a Strategic Enterprise Approach

A strategic approach to building an integration infrastructure is required so the components of the infrastructure seamlessly interoperate to provide integration across business processes and rapid deployment of integrated business solutions. Despite the benefits of the architectural approach, application integration is often viewed as a technical step within an implementation project. Moreover, the integration landscape is expanding and becoming more complex. Different types of business applications require different types of integration technologies. A tactical approach to enterprise integration will result in the coexistence of many technologies that were not necessarily designed to integrate with one another. An enterprise approach enables you to reduce support costs and maximize flexibility.

Enterprise integration does not come in a box. It is a term that covers an array of technology solutions, including: messaging middleware; message brokers/integration servers with data mapping, transformation, and routing tools; portals; information integration; application servers with integration capabilities; business process integration and management (BPM); business-to-business integration (B2Bi); mobile integration; and emerging technologies such as Web services and XML. Each of these technologies has its place in the overall integration architecture. Large companies with broad integration requirements may require most or all of the above. However, the goal of the integration architecture should be to avoid multiples of each. Redundancy in integration technology components increases implementation costs (including the cost of training and maintaining multiple skill sets), maintenance costs, and the cost of change (including costs for integrating and synchronizing redundant functions and technologies).

Contrary to the usual preconception that enterprise initiatives slow you down and cost you more money, an enterprise-wide approach to building an integration infrastructure actually accelerates tactical solutions and can significantly lower maintenance costs and total cost of ownership. Case Study 4.2 is about Keycorp's results from creating strategic enterprise integration architecture (Goldenberg 2003). The results reflect what to expect when enterprise integration architecture is correctly applied in an organization. It is important to

Case Study 4.2
KeyCorp: Developing a Unified Approach to Integration

KeyCorp is a large bank-based financial services company with 3.8 million clients and 21,000 employees. Within the financial-services industry there has been a move to increase client access to account information anywhere, anytime, as well as providing a single, organized view of information that is often collected from a wide array of different systems. KeyCorp has been working on providing client access, integrated views, and multiple channel integration since the mid 1990s. However, it began to see limitations in the architecture beginning in 1999 and decided that it needed to improve the integration platform to better support enterprise-wide applications and platforms.

The IT organization developed KeyServer, an enterprise integration platform that significantly improved the manner in which integration is accomplished. KeyServer provided some amazing results to the organization:

- Reduced development time of applications by 12 to 18 months
- Reduced costs of integration by $2 million within the first year
- Cut costs of integration by 30% to 35% per application

This infrastructure has allowed the business the opportunity to pursue real-time applications related to data mining, cross selling, up selling, and other activities. In the case of their Key Total Treasury application, they created a revenue-generating application that had an ROI of over 200%.

note that major decisions are made at the strategic enterprise level. The enterprise integration architecture defines how new solutions plug into the enterprise resources. Individual projects do not need to spend time and money figuring this out. They can just focus on the functionality of the business solution. As long as they conform to the defined enterprise standards, they can easily and quickly access required information and resources across the company. This is a huge benefit to project groups, and the most efficient, cost effective, and successful way for companies to implement an agile integration infrastructure.

4.3 Components of an Enterprise Integration Architecture

The enterprise integration architecture is multidimensional. The component architectures most relevant to integration each focus on a different domain of the integration architecture. Furthermore, the components interrelate and interact with each other. Figure 4-1 depicts the four component architecture's domains.

4.3.1 Technical Integration Architecture

The technical integration architecture defines the underlying technologies for all integration solutions. This is the basic plumbing that needs to be in place to support the other components of an enterprise integration architecture. This includes messaging, application interfaces, translation and transformation, routing, and process monitoring and management. The technologies that deliver the integration infrastructure services provide an integration grid, similar in concept to the electric grid. When you get a new appliance, you merely have to plug it in

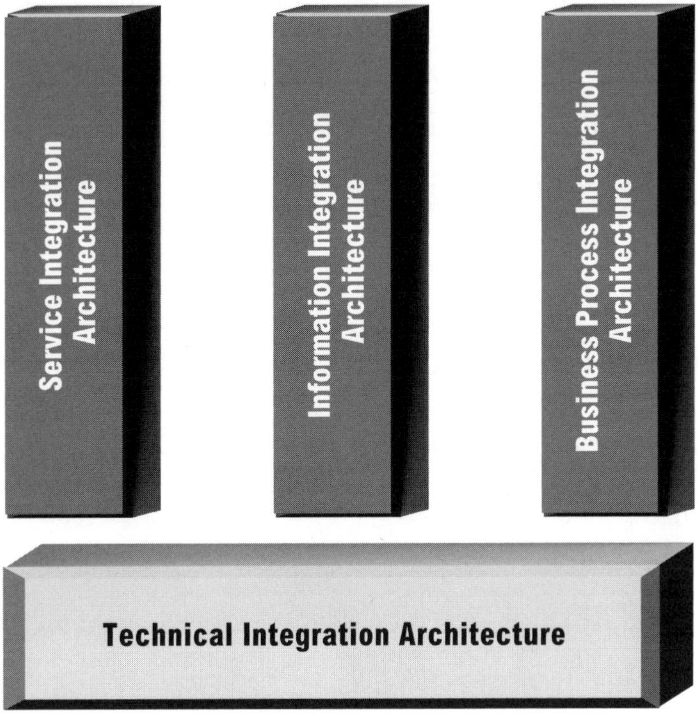

Figure 4-1 Enterprise Integration Architecture Domains

and it works. You don't have to rewire your whole house. Yet in IT, rewiring was the approach most often used. The technologies that deliver the integration infrastructure services comprise the underlying integration grid. In the past, this has been difficult to achieve due to the proprietary nature of the technology, but with the emergence of accepted standards and market pressure to make sure products work together, this has become feasible. Chapter 6 describes the Technical Integration Architecture Specification template and provides guidance for defining infrastructure standards.

4.3.2 Service Integration Architecture

The service integration architecture is a subset of the enterprise application architecture. It defines loosely coupled, reusable business services. This application architecture is the most flexible and adaptable to business change. It enables rapid application integration. Although the benefits of SOAs have been known for over two decades, it is only recently that they are being widely deployed. The reason is Web services, the first universally accepted standard interface. Companies finally feel confident in making the investment in SOA because it does not also require betting on CORBA or J2EE or .NET. The real objective is to enable any programming language, any platform, any data source or target, at any location. Although not yet fully complete or mature, Web services are the clear winner. Chapter 7 describes the Service Integration Architecture Specification template and provides guidance for defining reusable services.

4.3.3 Information Integration Architecture

The information integration architecture provides an enterprise-wide view of data contained in disparate systems. The value of the data itself is dependent on maintaining the integrity of data across systems. There is little value in propagating corruptions throughout multiple systems in a fraction of the time it would have taken with nonintegrated systems. The solution to maintaining the value, meaning, and integrity of data across applications is metadata. Metadata is information about the data. The more descriptive, accurate, and complete the metadata is, the better the integration can be. For the purposes of integration, the metadata is presented in a canonical format so it can easily be mapped back to source systems. XML is becoming the widely accepted standard canonical data format. Chapter 8 describes the Information Integration Architecture Specification template and provides guidance for defining different levels of metadata that enable faster integration.

4.3.4 Business Process Integration Architecture

The business process integration architecture models the business processes that cut across organizational boundaries. The purpose of integration is almost always to improve a business process and increase efficiency. The business process architecture maximizes business agility because it enables changes to business processes to be implemented quickly—at a business process level rather than an infrastructure level. The process architecture includes process models, governance of cut across organizational processes, as well as process metrics that enable the company to track and improve efficiency. Chapter 9 describes the Process Integration Architecture Specification template and provides guidelines and benefits from process-driven integration.

4.4 Organizational Structure and Architecture Governance

Enterprise integration architecture is a journey, not a destination. It needs to be an ongoing effort to continue to support the changing priorities and needs of the organization. Therefore, it requires ongoing support. This means the organization must define the organization structure for defining and managing the integration architecture over time, a governance procedure for ensuring compliance with enterprise standards and managing exceptions, and an enterprise priority-setting process for managing enterprise infrastructure implementation.

4.4.1 Organizational Structure

Because integration requires specialized knowledge and skills, a recommended best practice is to create an integration competency center. The competency center provides integration expertise and coordination across organizational entities. It is responsible for defining the integration architecture, maximizing reuse, ensuring compliance with integration standards, and providing arbitration when organizational issues arise regarding integration.

The success of the competency center requires high-level sponsorship, such as the CIO or CFO. The competency center must be empowered to set and enforce integration standards across the organization if they are to succeed at all. The skill sets required in a competency center include an integration architect, data steward, and business/IT analyst who will act as the liaison between different organizational groups.

4.4.2 Architecture Governance

Integration architecture governance includes processes for ensuring compliance with enterprise standards and a grievance or arbitration process when a project needs to go outside the standards.

Design reviews are an excellent way to ensure project compliance. During the design review the integration architect can act as a consultant to the project, as well as ensure standards are being met. The integration architect is also in the position to help optimize reuse across projects. Integration architecture design reviews are an essential best practice for long-term viability and vitality of the integration infrastructure.

However, sometimes business requirements fall outside the scope of defined standards. Therefore, a grievance process is also an important part of architecture governance. There should be defined procedures for applying for exceptions, as well as guidelines and parameters for granting exceptions to standards.

4.4.3 Enterprise Priority-Setting

Integration projects generally involve multiple organizational groups, each with its own priorities. Therefore, it is essential to establish a formal priority-setting

Integration Project	Reduce Time to Respond to Customer Requests	Reduce Infrastructure Maintenance Costs	Reduce time to Change Business Processes	Reduce Transaction Costs	Total
Customer portal	5	0	0	3	8
B2B integration	5	4	1	4	14
Legacy integration	5	5	3	4	17
Web services	2	3	1	2	8
Information integration	5	5	1	4	15
Business process management	5	2	5	2	14

Figure 4-2 Enterprise Integration Priority Setting

process based on organizational goals and objectives. One method is to create a matrix of integration projects and organizational goals and objectives (from the Statement of Purpose). Rate each integration project according to the number of business goals it will enable. As not all goals are equal, this rating system can be weighted. For example, see Figure 4-2.

4.5 Conclusion

Although a large enterprise is likely to have many integration requirements and require a large variety of integration technologies, no company can implement the entire infrastructure in one fell swoop. Therefore, it will always be necessary to take a tactical approach to integration. However, while meeting the requirements of a funded project, it is important to comply with enterprise building codes, to ensure maximum return on current and future technology investments.

When the enterprise integration architecture is viewed as a strategic initiative, the integration capabilities of the organization can be used more easily across multiple projects. Also, the individual projects do not need to spend the time and expense on researching and choosing technologies, a task that is becoming more daunting as more vendors and technologies are available. The enterprise integration architecture serves as the guide to all implementations and leverages the knowledge and experience of each project across the entire organization.

4.6 Next Steps

A crucial next step is to do a current environment assessment (Chapter 5), as shown in Figure 4-3. It is very important to understand what is already in place when defining enterprise standards or building codes.

Each integration-architecture domain has its own specification template. Companies wishing to maximize business agility, reuse, and ROI will define the architecture for all the integration domains. Companies only interested in tactical solutions may instead decide to skip to Part III of the book: Enterprise Integration Solutions.

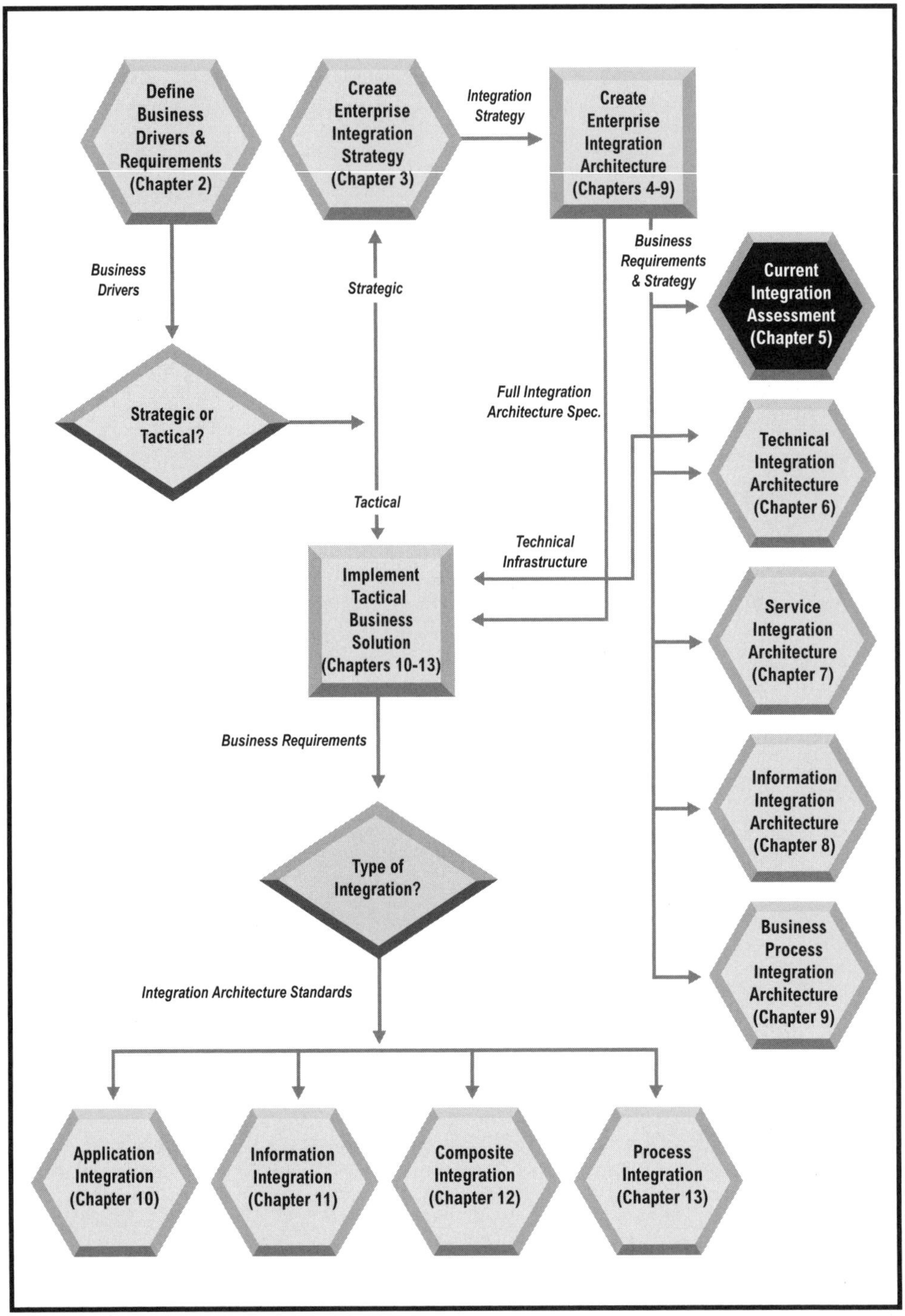

Figure 4-3 Integration Road Map

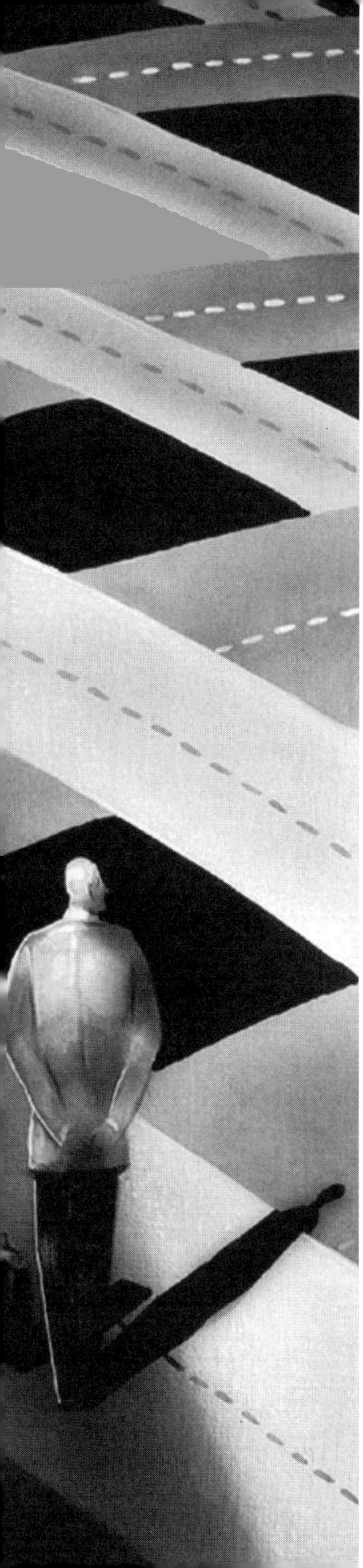

CHAPTER FIVE

Current Integration Environment Assessment

5.1 Executive Overview

A common mistake made in many organizations is to start their enterprise integration architecture activity with a clean sheet of paper. This is neither feasible nor desirable in almost any situation. The current architecture, whether efficient or not, is the starting point for any activity. In fact, the main point of any integration architecture is to allow for reuse of the current IT assets for the use of new business functions. Also, existing software might be employed as part of the overall architecture.

This chapter is about how to structure your assessment of the current environment. It describes the major categories under which integration technology and approaches may exist in the organization. However, the complexity and lack of standards in the world of integration have led to many innovative approaches within organizations, and you may have others that fall outside the norm. These should be captured as well. In addition, the specification described provides a mechanism to take the classifications and document the findings for use in the enterprise integration architecture definition.

The current integration architecture assessment identifies all integration technology currently installed in the organization and applications currently integrated. The current assessment is useful in determining preferred technology components and associated vendors in the final enterprise integration architecture.

5.2 Understanding Integration Technology

Integration vendors typically like to define their solution set in terms of a neatly ordered stack. Although the stacks of each vendor and analyst group differ slightly, a typical stack might look like Figure 5-1.

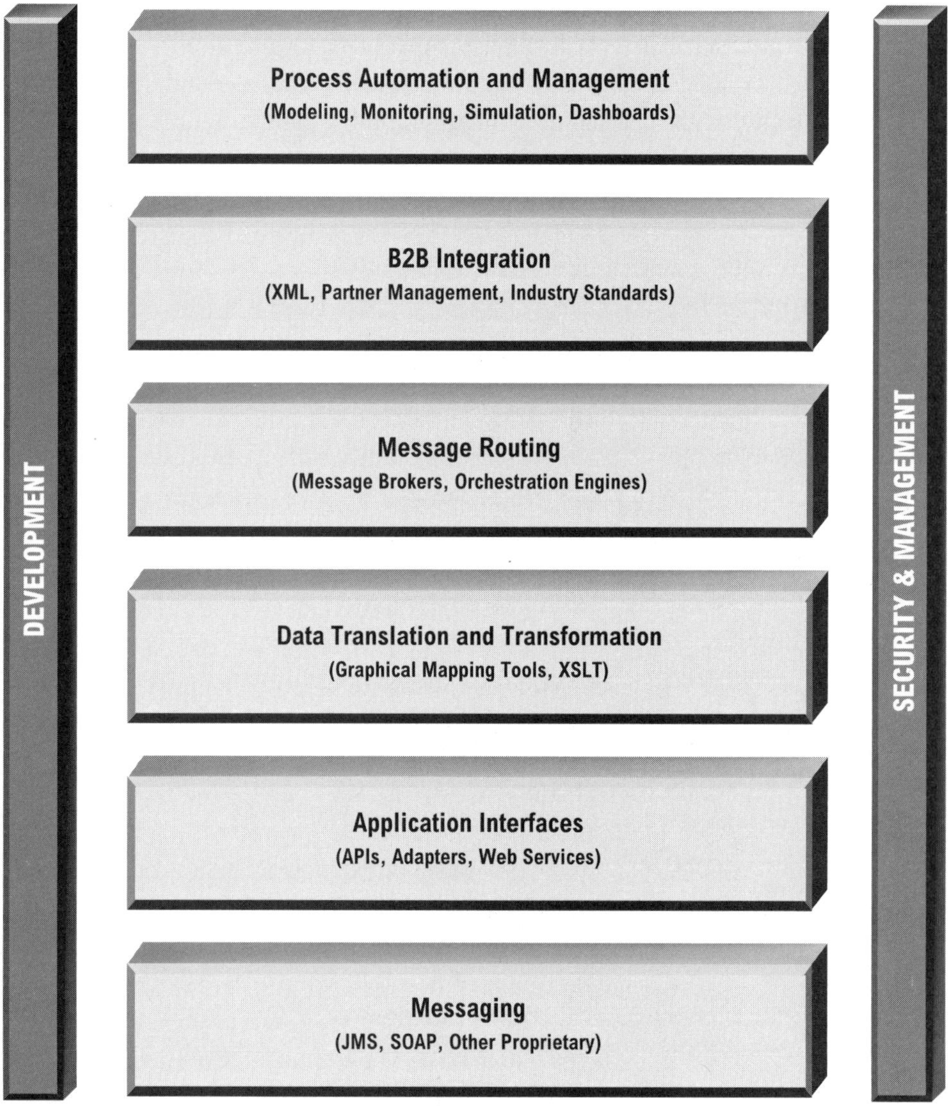

Figure 5-1 Integration Technology Stack

Unfortunately, integration technologies do not actually get deployed in a neat stack. Vendors often do not implement the whole stack and the manner in which they package the offering does not allow it to be used in a plug-and-play approach insinuated by a logical architecture. More often, the pieces of the infrastructure are deployed across the enterprise on different platforms, often coming from multiple vendors, and these technologies need to interact with each other. Figure 5-2 (page 78) depicts the components of enterprise integration architecture as they are more typically implemented in the organization.

At first glance, Figure 5-2 looks jumbled. That is because of the potential and likelihood that each of the components may call upon the services of other components of the infrastructure. In reality, enterprise infrastructures are even far more jumbled and complex than this diagram. This should be a convincing argument for an enterprise approach to an integration infrastructure.

Looking at the current environment with an eye toward the most common categories of integration software is a good way to structure your assessment; it can also accelerate the process. The most typical categories of software used to accomplish integration are messaging systems, integration brokers (also called servers), application servers, packaged application integration, enterprise service buses, data integration tools, adapters and interfaces, information integration technologies including the new enterprise information integration (EII) offerings as well as enterprise content management (ECM) with integration and workflow capabilities, enterprise and Web portals, B2B integration, BPM, and security integration. Point solutions, legacy middleware, and custom coding round out the most common technologies used in integration.

Each organization is different in its current approaches to integration. Although there may be obvious patterns that exist between different organizations, the selection of technology to implement an integration solution is often based on the knowledge and background of the person responsible. A Java developer is likely to select the use of an application server or portal for integration, while a mainframe architect would be more comfortable with a messaging-based approach. An enterprise architect would look at more all-encompassing solutions, like integration brokers, and still others from a business-analyst background might be more comfortable with a business process management toolset. The same problem would be addressed in very different ways in an organization. Capturing this information is important for putting in place a consistent set of guidelines. Chapter 6 through Chapter 9 will help to put in place the architectural framework for enterprise integration architecture. Part III of the book focuses on

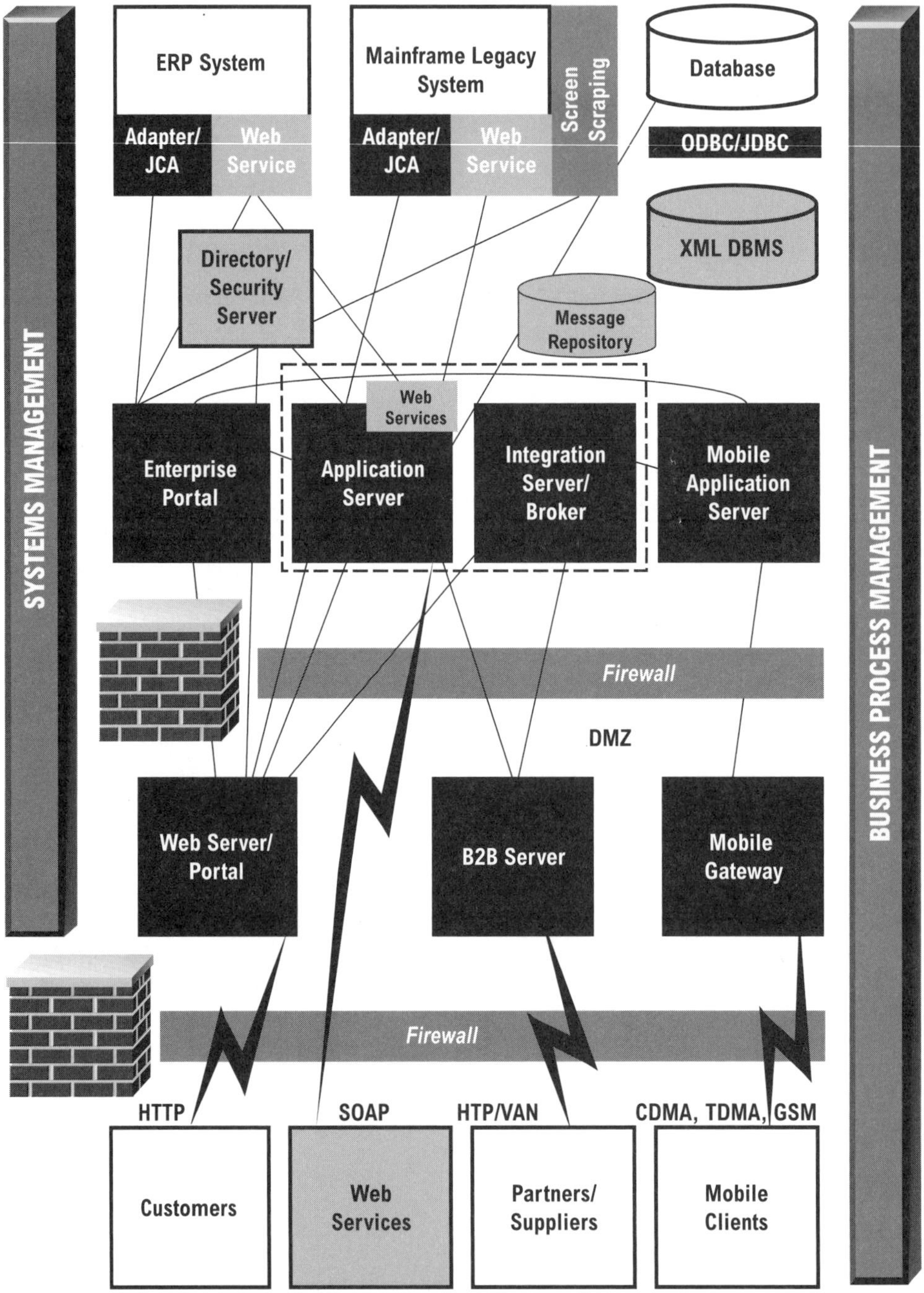

Figure 5-2 Components of Enterprise Integration Architecture

how to choose technologies for a specific integration problem. Patterns are identified and appropriate architectures are described more fully in Chapter 10 through Chapter 13. With this in place, then the organization is guided by an architecture and patterns to efficiently solve integration problems rather than the nuances and backgrounds of the staff assigned to any particular project.

5.3 Current Environment Assessment Specification

The Current Environment Assessment Specification is the document that details the investments and usage of integration technology in the organization. It can have a variety of fundamental uses to the enterprise. First, it helps to understand where the points of investment leverage exist to reduce the costs of the enterprise integration architecture going forward. Second, it can be used in the design of any new application that requires integration to reuse what has already been completed. Finally, it is effective documentation to understand the investment in integration to date and justify any future enterprise-wide investments. See Appendix C for the full Current Environment Assessment Specification Template.

5.3.1 Introduction

The introduction to the Current Environment Assessment should be a short executive overview of the specification. It should define the types of technologies that are being defined and any major constraints in the current environment, such as limitations imposed by legacy systems or the requirements for high security. Also, identify any known issues in the current environment. To create the introduction, answer the follow questions:

- What is the current role of integration technology in the organization?
- How is the current environment meeting business needs?
- How is the current environment failing to meet business needs?

At the end of the introduction, the reader should have an understanding of the current state of integration technology in the organization.

5.3.2 Purpose

The purpose of the Current Environment Assessment is to document and assess the current integration technologies that support the business functions of the enterprise. This assessment will be used when determining recommended technologies and vendors in the Technical Integration Architecture Specification.

5.3.3 Key Participants

The key participants of the Current Environment Assessment include the team responsible for the creation of the current environment assessment in its initial form, as well as for any ongoing improvements. Anyone that provided information or review should be included in this section. Lastly, identify the audience of this document and how they will apply the current environment assessment to their work. The audience includes senior IT managers and those who are responsible for creating the enterprise integration architecture and defining integration standards within the enterprise.

5.3.4 Scope

The scope defines whether the current assessment of integration technology covers the entire enterprise, a division, a line of business, or some other scope. We recommend that the company have a complete inventory of all integration technology and applications currently integrated across the enterprise.

5.3.5 Integration Technologies

Define all integration technologies currently used within the enterprise and all applications that are integrated using the technology. The purpose of this section is to take a complete integration infrastructure inventory.

The categories listed in Figure 5-3 are intended to be a guide to most of the common technologies or approaches. These should be tailored to the organization. For example, we combine data, information, and content integration into a single category. If organizations have developed a highly sophisticated information and content integration portfolio, each of these areas might be broken into separate categories. This is also true of the packaged application integration area where it might be broken up into categories based upon specific Enterprise Resource Planning (ERP) packages such as SAP or PeopleSoft. These decisions should be based upon the complexity of the environment in any category.

Older middleware approaches that are still being used can be captured at the end. An example of this would be the use of the Distributed Computing Environment (DCE). Also, point solutions that solve a specific problem should be identified. Finally, if the organization is using another approach including a fully custom-developed capability or hand-coded interfaces, this should be captured by adding this new category to the list provided.

Integration Technology	Vendor Solutions <Create a separate entry for each currently installed technology.>	Applications
Messaging systems	<Examples are: IBM MQ Series, Tibco Rendevous, JMS, Sonic MQ, SoftwareAG Communicator, etc.>	<List all applications that are connected via this technology.>
Integration brokers/servers	<Examples are: WebSphere Integration Broker, Software AG, Tibco, WebMethods, SeeBeyond, Vitria, Mercator, Sybase Integrator, etc.>	<List all applications that are connected via this technology.>
Application servers with some integration	<List all application server platforms that are also connected to other applications via data integration, messaging, or other application server based integration. Examples are: BEA WebLogic, IBM WebSphere Sybase, Oracle.>	<List all applications that are connected via this technology.>
Packaged application integration	<Examples are: SAP, JD Edwards, Peoplesoft.>	<List all types of packaged applications that are connected and the specific packaged application mechanism that is used.>
Adapters and interfaces	<Examples are: iWays and other packaged adapters.>	<List all types of adapters or interfaces.>
Enterprise service bus and Web services tools	<Examples are: Software AG, Sonic Software, IBM, Microsoft.>	<List all applications that are connected via this technology.>
Data, information and content integration tools	<Examples are: Informatics, IBM, Software AG, Meta Matrix.>	<List all applications or data sources that are connected via this technology.>
Portals	<Examples are: Plum Tree, BEA, IBM.>	<List all applications that are connected via this technology.>
B2B technology	<Examples are: EDI solutions, RosettaNet, HIPAA, XML solutions, and other B2B integration.>	<List all applications that are connected via this technology.> *(continued)*

Figure 5-3 Current Integration Technology Specification

BPM technology	<Examples are: Process modeling and management, process activity monitoring, process simulation.>	<List all applications implemented with this technology.>
Integrated security	<Single sign-on solutions such as LDAP or other directories.>	<Define scope of implementation—enterprise wide, departmental, other.>
Other middleware technologies	<DCE or other middleware.>	<List all applications that are connected via this technology.>
Point solution technology	<Specific products used to solve a specific integration problem.>	<List all applications that are connected via this technology.>
Custom integration solution	<Hand-crafted interfaces or full blown custom integration frameworks.>	<List all applications that are connected via this technology.>

Figure 5-3 *(cont.)*

5.3.6 Application and Data Source Interfaces

The objective of this section is to determine which applications or data sources already have installed adapters or other interfaces (see Figure 5-4). Application and data source interfaces can include hand coded custom interfaces; application APIs; packaged adapters from integration vendors, or other third-party vendors;

Application/Data Source Name	Owner	Platform	Interface	Reusable
<Name of application or data store>	<Department or organization responsible for application>	<Technology used to develop and deploy application>	<API, adapter, Web service or other interface used for integration>	<For adapters, is this adapter only usable with a particular integration technology or is it reusable?>

Figure 5-4 Application and Data Source Interface Specification

Web services; or other component interfaces. This inventory should also determine whether the interface is reusable for other integration projects that may involve that application or data source.

5.3.7 Integration Matrix

After creating an inventory of each application that is integrated, create a matrix of integrations between applications, data sources, or users, as shown in Figure 5-5. This matrix will detail the level of integration between each.

Each of these connections may have been part of a separate tactical integration initiative, so the full scope of integration for each may not have been otherwise documented.

5.3.8 Integration Diagram

This diagram is a graphic representation of the integration matrix. It will graphically depict the scope and complexity of the connections between integrations.

Figure 5-6 (page 84) is a simple example that you can use. However, any notation that you are comfortable with can be used. This simple notation shows the component name and the connectivity with other components as well as the nature of the connection.

	<Application 1>	<Application 2>	<User 1>	<Data Store 1>
<Application 1>	<connection technology>	<connection technology>	<connection technology>	<connection technology>
<Application 2>	<connection technology>	<connection technology>	<connection technology>	<connection technology>
<User 1>	<connection technology>	<connection technology>	<connection technology>	<connection technology>
<Data Store 1>	<connection technology>	<connection technology>	<connection technology>	<connection technology>

Figure 5-5 Integration Matrix

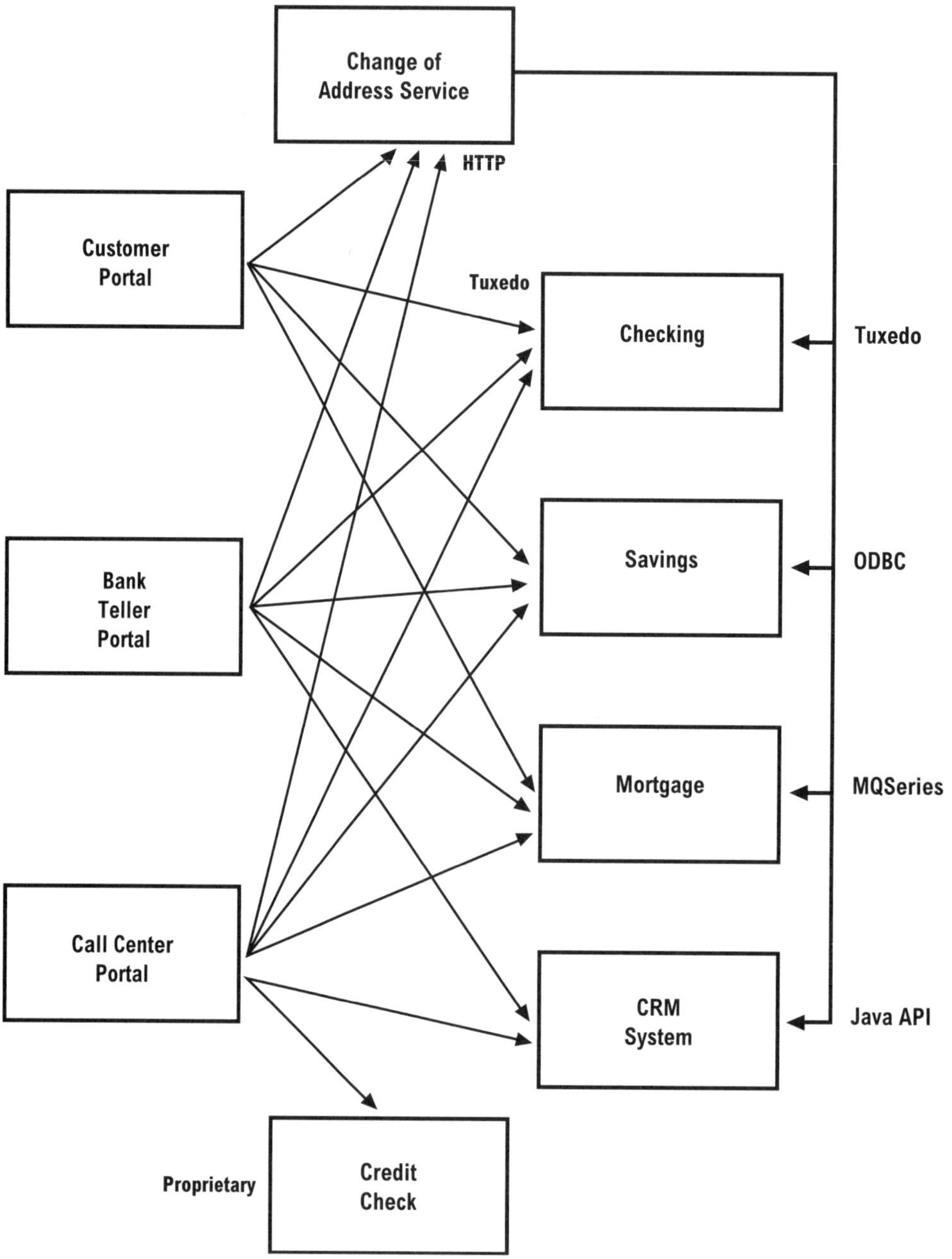

Figure 5-6 Application Integration Diagram

	Authentication	Authorization	Auditing	Confidentiality	Non-repudiation
Internal data		●			
<Application name>		<Technology implemented>			
Partner data	●	●			●
<Application name>	<Technology implemented>	<Technology implemented>			<Technology implemented>
Customer data	●	●	●	●	
<Application name>	<Technology implemented>	<Technology implemented>	<Technology implemented>	<Technology implemented>	
Internal application	●	●			
<Application name>	<Technology implemented>	<Technology implemented>			
Partner application	●	●			●
<Application name>	<Technology implemented>	<Technology implemented>			<Technology implemented>
Customer application	●	●	●	●	●
<Application name>	<Technology implemented>	<Technology implemented>	<Technology implemented>	<Technology implemented>	<Technology implemented>
Internal process		●			
<Application name>		<Technology implemented>			
Partner process	●	●	●		●
<Application name>	<Technology implemented>	<Technology implemented>	<Technology implemented>		<Technology implemented>
Customer process	●	●	●	●	●
<Application name>	<Technology implemented>	<Technology implemented>	<Technology implemented>	<Technology implemented>	<Technology implemented>

Figure 5-7 Security Specification Table

5.3.9 Security

This section defines the security capabilities currently installed and the technology used to deliver the level of security. The specification summarizes the type of security usually required for each type of application, and specifies the current applications in that category and the technology implemented to deliver the required level of security. For example, internal data usually requires authorization. However, for more sensitive data confidentiality (encryption) and authentication might also be required. Figure 5-7 (page 85) is a simple example you can use to document your current security configuration.

5.3.10 Conclusions and Commentary

This section is a summary of all key discoveries found during the assessment process. This should include any areas of risk identified, such as holes in security or hand coded interfaces, and what will not scale and cannot be easily changed. This section should also note any areas of technical redundancy, such as multiple messaging technologies or multiple integration brokers already installed. Finally, any current problems that involve end users' use of the existing systems should also be captured.

5.4 Best Practices and Recommendations

- Aim to minimize redundancy in the infrastructure. Redundant technologies ultimately increase the maintenance costs, personnel costs, and the total cost of ownership.
- Simplify wherever possible. Identify areas of overlap where technologies can be retired.
- Identify system owners while creating the assessment. This is an essential step for both optimizing business processes and improving data quality across the organization. It also helps identify key participants in the architecture process.
- Update the assessment when the architecture changes. The current assessment can be used as inventory of infrastructure technology.

5.5 Next Steps

Although the current assessment can actually be done concurrently with the enterprise integration architecture, it should take far less time to complete. Therefore, the next step is to complete the enterprise integration architecture (see Figure 5-8). The current assessment should provide input into the architecture, especially when defining preferred vendors and technologies.

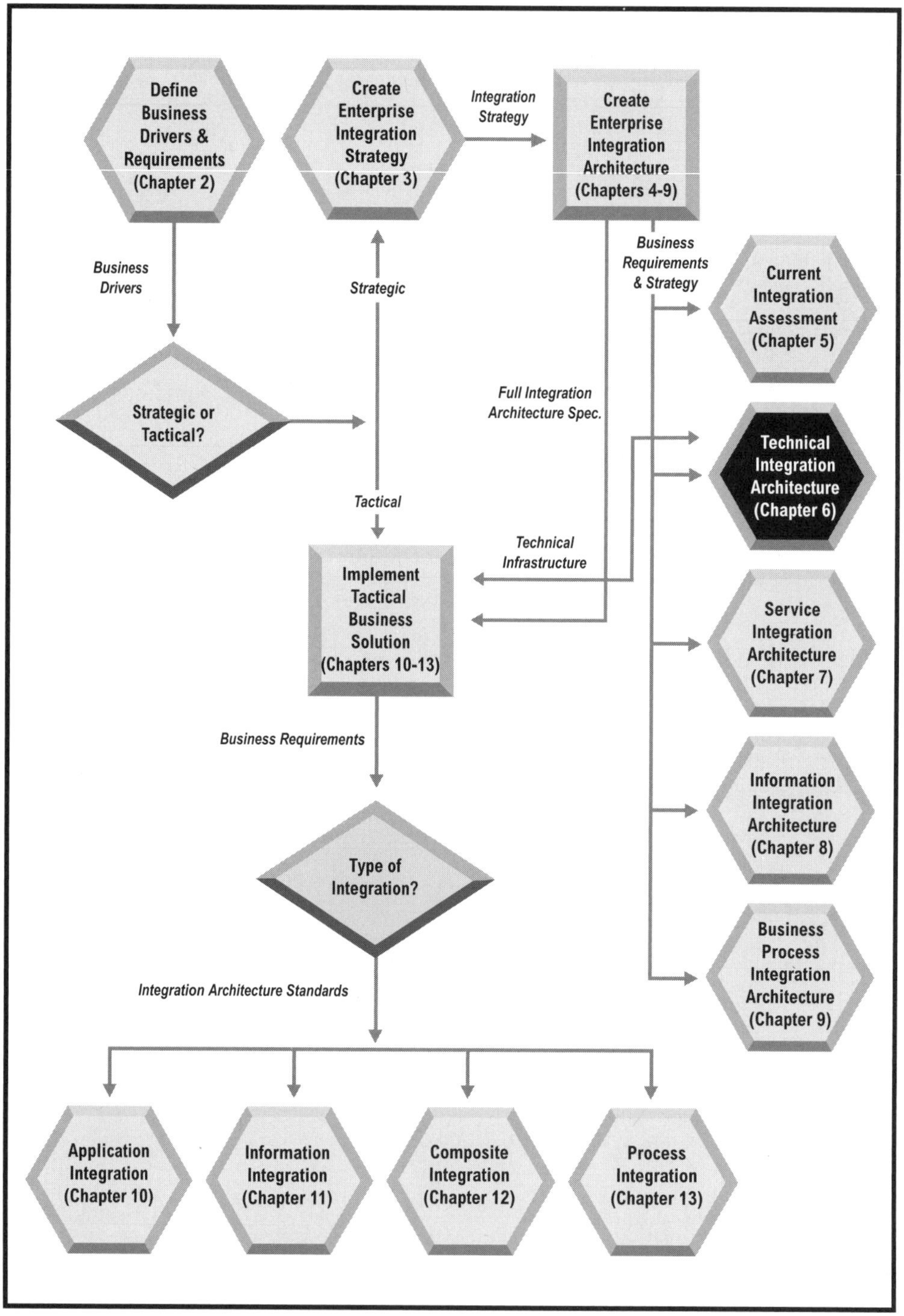

Figure 5-8 Integration Road Map

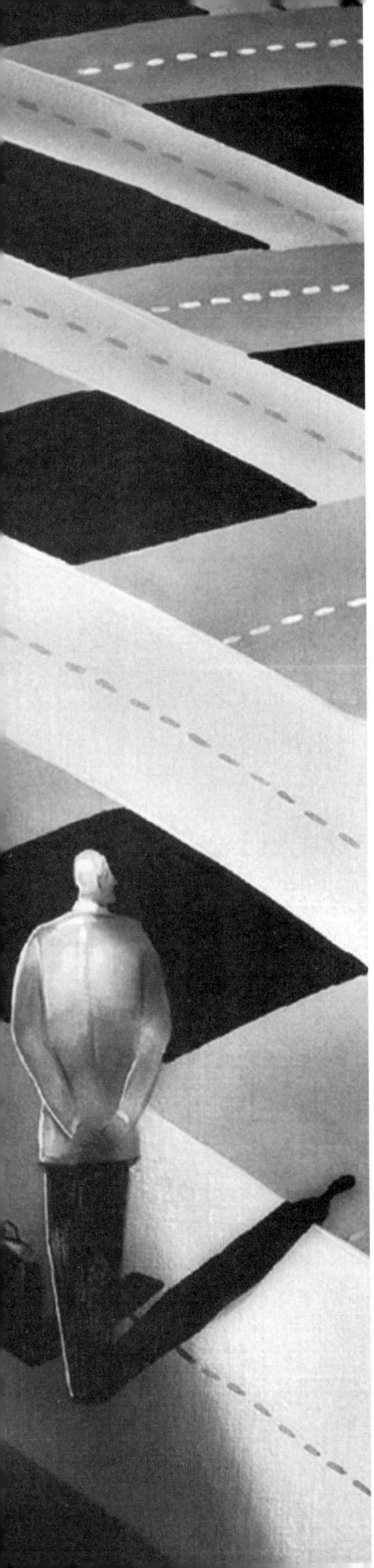

CHAPTER SIX

Technical Integration Architecture

6.1 Executive Overview

The Technical Integration Architecture represents the enterprise building codes for all integration projects. It is the specification that all projects will reference when choosing integration technology for their particular implementation. The architecture includes guidance and design restrictions on how applications should be developed.

Therefore, the specification must be both thorough to define all aspects of the integration architecture, and easily accessible, so that the information can be easily found and understood. While in many cases detailed descriptions are necessary and appropriate, we also recommend the use of summary charts and tables for presenting information. Each of the solution architectures presented in Part III of this book is based on this architecture specification, and is a subset of this specification. Creating an Integration Architecture Specification will guide many IT implementation solutions to ensure interoperability and leverage reuse. For example, the State of Florida has created a set of guidelines for their integration architecture, described in Case Study 6.1 (State of Florida State Technology Office 2003).

The Technical Integration Architecture should be driven by business requirements. Over time, a large organization may need one of everything. While current business needs should drive infrastructure requirements and

Case Study 6.1
State of Florida: Guiding Enterprise Integration Architectures

The complexity of any state government is often not understood by those on the outside. However, with multiple departments, large budgets, changes in budgets, new laws, changes in politicians, and competing priorities it is one of the most complex IT environments that can be imagined. Even with the advent of state CIOs, there is still a highly distributed IT environment in states leading to incompatible architectures, difficulty in sharing information, and duplication of efforts.

The State of Florida has been a leader in organizing the state's IT functions and assets. It has recognized the need to improve the approach to enterprise integration architecture within the state. Its strategy relies on design patterns and reuse of components, coupled with a practical approach. Guidance has been given to incorporate the following approach into any project seeking approval:

- **Demonstrate understanding of the problem domain in context of the State's goals.** Baseline of what the system will do and why it is necessary.
- **Make sense of the data.** Identify data location, flows, and metadata.
- **Make sense of the processes.** Create process models.
- **Identify application interfaces.** Identify or create interfaces.
- **Identify events.** Identify business events that trigger actions.
- **Identify data transformation scenarios.** Map data formats between systems.
- **Map information movement.** Map information flows between systems.
- **Apply technology.** Select technology.
- **Test.** Create a test plan.
- **Consider performance.** Specify performance characteristics.
- **Define the value.** Define ROI.
- **Create maintenance procedures.** Identify operational processes and procedures.

By creating this guidance, they are providing a structure to improve how the state's systems are organized and improving the ability to integrate and reuse components in the future. This is a key step towards achieving an enterprise integration architecture.

implementations, architecture decisions should take future requirements and adaptability into account. It should define the following:

- Common, reusable business-domain services that can support multiple applications
- Common, standardized technical services that can support any style of integration such as service, information, or process oriented
- Service levels that must be supported
- A comprehensive security framework based on a clearly articulated enterprise-wide security policy
- Focus on the ability to leverage existing (legacy) information systems and commercial packaged system products to provide a significant portion of application functionality

In some cases, the technical architecture effort will focus on reducing the number of redundant technologies. The Current Integration Architecture Assessment (Chapter 5) provides a great deal of information that will drive architecture decisions.

6.2 Technical Integration Architecture Specification

As stated above, the Technical Integration Architecture provides the building codes for the integration infrastructure. Project-level adherence to this architecture ensures that there is consistency, reusability, and economic benefit to the organization for investments in integration technology. This adherence can be accomplished through design reviews, as explained in the Architecture Governance section of Chapter 4. See Appendix D for the complete specification template.

6.2.1 Introduction

This specification represents the enterprise technical integration architecture specification. This document will be used to guide all decisions and designs related to integration in the organization. It defines the scope of the integration architecture, preferred vendors and technologies, and enterprise standards. When creating the introduction, outline all enterprise-wide decisions readers of the document should be aware of, and call attention to appendixes, such as references and governance rules.

6.2.2 Scope

Define the scope of the integration architecture. It should address whether it is enterprise-wide or limited to a certain organization or class of applications. Other areas to address include types of integration (data, application, or process), any limitations and reasons for the limitations. The scope must also describe what types of external applications are covered, including whether an application outside the scope of the enterprise is a candidate for connecting to enterprise applications. This will be the case if the organization has any supply chain or e-commerce initiatives planned.

6.2.3 Key Participants

Define the audience and major stakeholders. The audience should include all members of the IT organization; however, it should explicitly list specific roles or titles that are to apply the integration in the normal execution of their jobs. The major stakeholders should include the IT executives and those responsible for maintaining the document.

6.2.4 Integration Architecture Requirements

This section relies on the business requirements captured in Chapter 2 as well as the current integration assessment. The Integration Architecture Requirements section includes requirements for the types of integration services and technologies that will be part of the infrastructure and it defines what services should be utilized for different types of applications, the applications that need to be integrated with each other, and the types or styles of integration that will be used across the enterprise.

6.2.4.1 Types of Integration

The organization needs to begin this specification by identifying the types of the integration that need to be supported (see Figure 6-1). The data from the business strategy and requirements gathered in Chapter 2 and Chapter 3 along with the current assessment described in Chapter 5 guides this activity. It helps to define known requirements for this type of integration to determine scope of investment. For example, if there are a number of applications that require process integration, then the organization should consider an enterprise license for a BPM solution.

6.2.4.2 Integration Services and Technologies

As previously noted, the integration architecture is comprised of a number of different integration services, and these services can be implemented with different

Internal application integration requirements	Simple connectivity, intelligent routing, translation and transformation, application interfaces/adapters	<Applications requiring this level of integration>
Legacy integration requirements	Mainframe, custom or ERP applications	<Applications requiring this level of integration>
Customer, partner, supplier (B2B) integration requirements	EDI, custom or B2B services	<Applications requiring this level of integration>
Composite integration requirements	Composite applications, SOA, new development	<Applications requiring this level of integration>
Portal integration requirements	Integrated portal	<Applications requiring this level of integration>
Information integration requirements	Batch, real-time, volumes, scheduling, structured and unstructured information	<Applications requiring this level of integration>
Process integration requirements	BPM, BAM, and workflow applications	<Applications requiring this level of integration>

Figure 6-1 Types of Integration

technologies. Rather than letting product selection drive architecture, the architecture should be based upon a framework that encompasses all aspects of integration necessary for that organization. The architecture is then constructed using existing or new products. Furthermore, the architecture is constructed on the principles of the organization and not of the products selected. For example, companies embarking on the SOA path can define their architecture as a series of services. Figure 6-2 depicts the different types of integration services, and the technologies that can be used to implement the service. As noted below, there may be a number of technologies used to implement a service because different technologies are suitable for different types of applications. Different technologies implementing the same service doesn't always mean redundancy if the technologies deliver the same service to different types of applications.

Figure 5-3 (page 81), which was constructed during the assessment of the current architecture and shows existing products in the organization, is used as the basis for determining whether the preferred vendor or technology is currently installed.

Integration Service	Integration Technology	Recommended Use	Preferred Vendor/ Technology	Currently Installed?
Adapters and interfaces	Adapters	When a packaged adapter is available for target application	<Vendor name, product name>	<Yes or no>
	Web services	For SOA, composite applications, legacy integration, custom application interfaces, and B2B integration	<Vendor name, product name>	<Yes or no>
	APIs—used with packaged applications	If nothing else is available	<Vendor name, product name>	<Yes or no>
	Screen scraping —used with legacy applications	If nothing else is available, or for fast, tactical solution	<Vendor name, product name>	<Yes or no>
Messaging and connectivity services	JMS messaging	Java applications	<Vendor name, product name>	<Yes or no>
	Proprietary messaging	If already installed, or if function is required	<Vendor name, product name>	<Yes or no>
	SOAP	XML messaging over the Internet	<Vendor name, product name>	<Yes or no>
	FTP	If nothing else is available	<Vendor name, product name>	<Yes or no>
	VAN	EDI, other B2B electronic services	<Vendor name, product name>	<Yes or no>
Routing	Integration servers/brokers	Used for one-to-many or many-to-many routing, hub and spoke architecture	<Vendor name, product name>	<Yes or no>
	Enterprise Service Bus (ESB)	Used for one-to-one, one-to-many or many-to-many routing, bus architecture, can plug in other integration services	<Vendor name, product name>	<Yes or no>
	BPM	High level routing and management of business processes	<Vendor name, product name>	<Yes or no>

Figure 6-2 Integration Services

Integration Service	Integration Technology	Recommended Use	Preferred Vendor/ Technology	Currently Installed?
Translation and transformation	Integration servers—usually have graphical mapping tools	Used for one-to-many or many-to-many integrations	<Vendor name, product name>	<Yes or no>
	Intelligent adapters—translation and transformation occur at the adapter	Scalable distributed computing model; mapping metadata kept in centralized repository	<Vendor name, product name>	<Yes or no>
	XSLT	XML transformation	<Vendor name, product name>	<Yes or No>
Information integration	EII	For aggregated data, such as presenting a single view of customer, or federating data across organizational units	<Vendor name, product name>	<Yes or no>
	(ECM)	For integrating unstructured data including documents, graphics, voice, video, etc.	<Vendor name, product name>	<Yes or no>
	Metadata repository	For creating a canonical format for shared enterprise information	<Vendor name, product name>	<Yes or no>
Portal integration	Enterprise and Web portals	Providing unified interface to disparate information and applications	<Vendor name, product name>	<Yes or no>
Composite applications	Application and Web servers	Used for building new applications or application components or business services	<Vendor name, product name>	<Yes or no>
	Web service orchestration	Used for "assembling" component-based applications	<Vendor name, product name>	<Yes or no>
	Web services	Used for creating application services to be used in the composite application	<Vendor name, product name>	<Yes or no>

(continued)

Figure 6-2 *(cont.)*

Integration Service	Integration Technology	Recommended Use	Preferred Vendor/ Technology	Currently Installed?
Process integration	BPM	Modeling, implementation and management of integrated business processes	<Vendor name, product name>	<Yes or no>
	BAM	Real-time monitoring of processes and dash-boards; may be part of BAM tool	<Vendor name, product name>	<Yes or no>
B2B integration	B2B servers	Used for integration with partners and suppliers, build on-line community. Integrates with back-end applications via adapters or EAI servers	<Vendor name, product name>	<Yes or no>
	EDI	Used for large partners, existing EDI solutions. Used with VAN	<Vendor name, product name>	<Yes or no>
	XML	Used for sending messages to partners via the Internet	<Vendor name, product name>	<Yes or no>
	Web services	Used as a standardized interface	<Vendor name, product name>	<Yes or no>
Mobile integration	Mobile integration servers	Delivers information to different mobile devices from common information and business rules	<Vendor name, product name>	<Yes or no>
Security integration	Security integration servers	Integrates disparate security systems	<Vendor name, product name>	<Yes or no>

Figure 6-2 *(cont.)*

6.2.5 Integration Architecture Description

The Architecture Description contains two different views: the conceptual view and the development view. The conceptual view provides the big picture of the enterprise integration infrastructure and the types of services that will be provided. The development view contains information relevant to developers who will utilize the architecture. In Part III of this book we will describe specific integration patterns and how they utilize the services of the Technical Integration Architecture.

6.2.5.1 Conceptual View

The conceptual architecture is intended to give the big picture of the integration architecture. There is no right way or one way to develop this diagram. It is a conceptual drawing. It needs to convey all of the components of the infrastructure, how they interrelate, and how they relate to the other components of the enterprise. In fact, there may be multiple conceptual views to illustrate a variety of points on the architecture.

The conceptual architecture should include the types of applications or systems that will connect using the integration architecture, what technologies are used for integration, how the technical architecture will be used by portals and on the corporate network and external connectivity as well as how users interact with the resulting applications. The conceptual architecture should be a diagram that can be used to explain the architecture to both management and staff. It will not be satisfying to the technically deep personnel, but it can be used to explain to the business users how the infrastructure is used.

Part III of the book contains patterns and architecture reference diagrams for different integration solutions. However, large companies are likely to have a combination of integration requirements. Below are two examples of diagrams. Figure 6-3 represents a simplified view of the layering of integration services offered. Figure 6-4 (page 99) represents an alternative view of all the integration services that can be part of the Technical Integration Architecture.

The diagram should be accompanied by an overall description of the conceptual architecture, descriptions of each component and the relationships between each.

6.2.5.2 Development View

The development view is a description of how and when each of the different tools and interfaces is used to guide the development team utilizing the integration architecture. An integration architecture is put in place to support developers in the rapid development of new applications that require heavy integration. Many different tools and approaches might be employed by developers to use the architecture. For each and every aspect of the integration architecture there must be a description of how a developer may utilize the integration services in an application. This would include the languages supported and the manner in which services and capabilities are accessed, tools for developing any integrations, and tools for configuration and administration. Also standard interfaces available for use should be defined. (See Figure 6-5, page 100.)

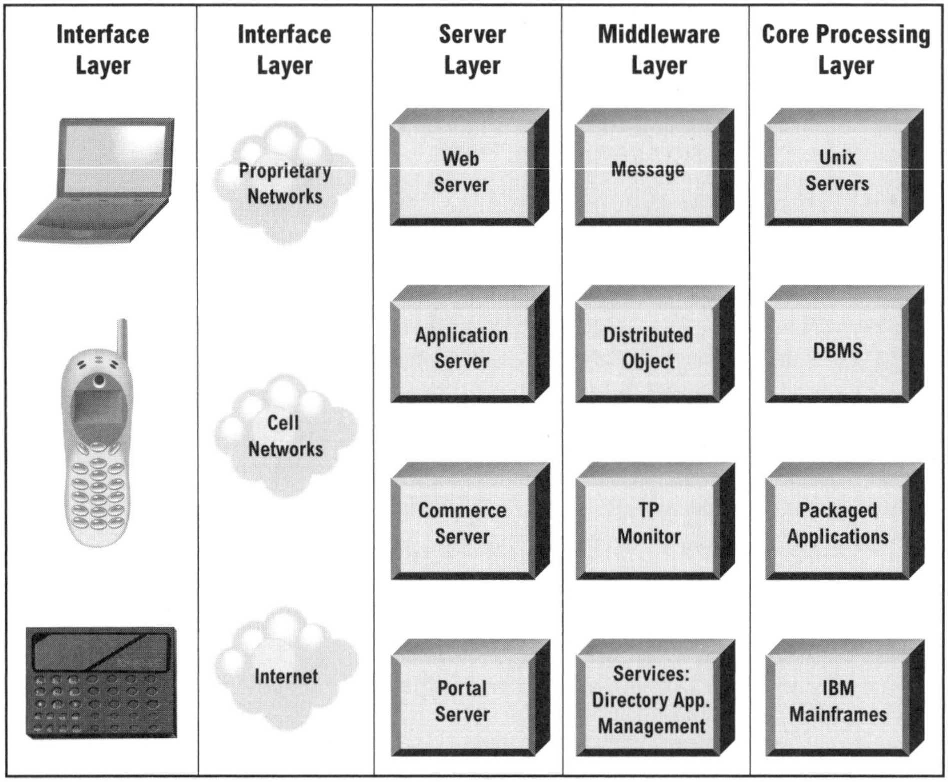

Figure 6-3 Conceptual Architecture Depicted as Layered Services

6.2.6 Standards Profile

This section specifies all standards that have been adopted by the organization that are relevant to the integration architecture. The full specification should also include a governance policy that defines how compliance to standards will be managed, and the process and guidelines for approving solutions that do not comply with standards. Most of these standards are related to interfaces, formats, or communications mechanisms. Architectural standards are beginning to appear that may have a larger impact in the future on an enterprise integration architecture. One key standard to watch is the Model Driven Architecture (MDA) standard from the Object Management Group. Case Study 6.2 describes the activities of MDA (Soley n.d.).

Types of standards to be addressed in the specification are listed in Figure 6–6, (page 100).

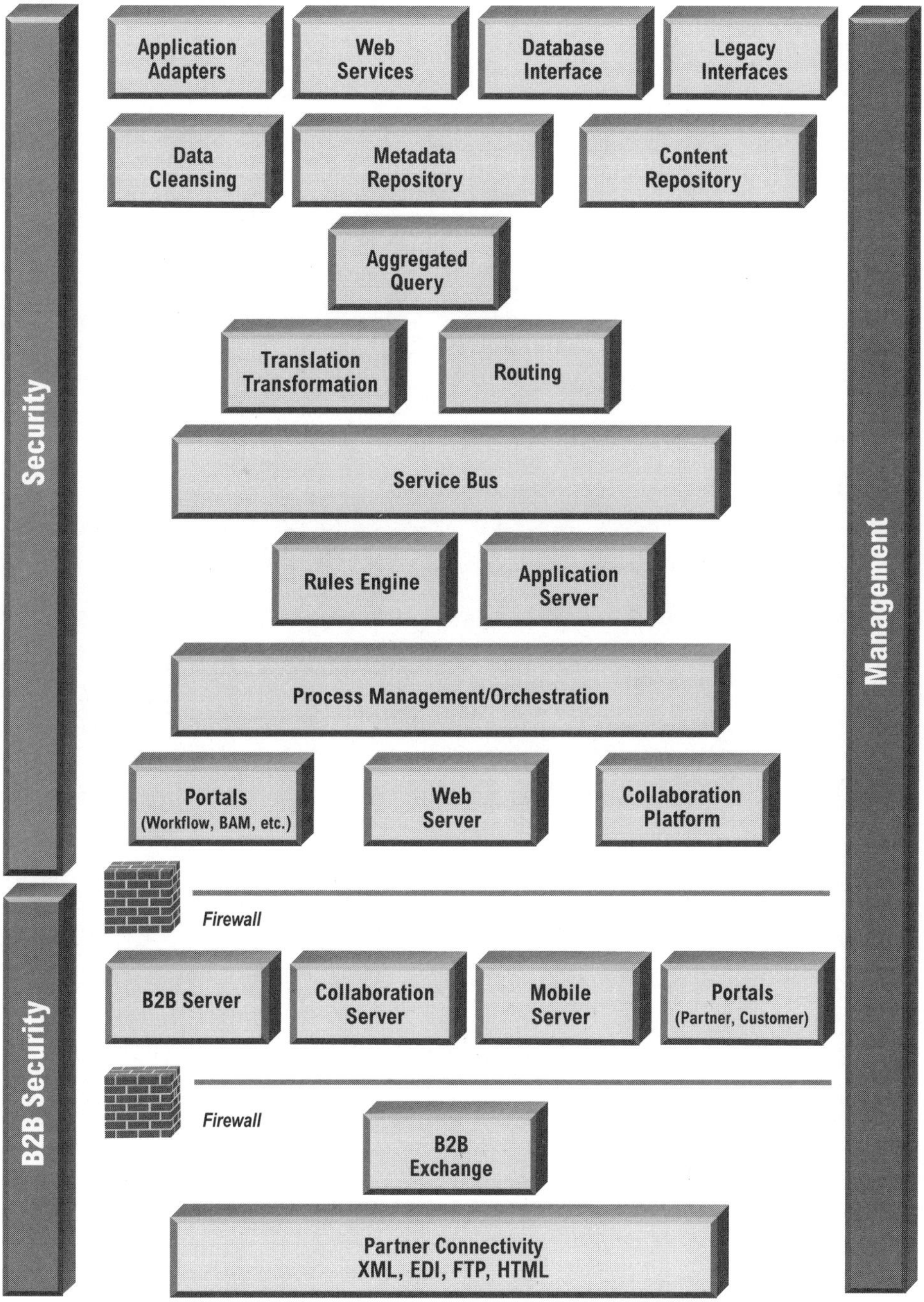

Figure 6-4 Enterprise Integration Architecture

Language support	<List how each language is supported. Describe the form of the access>
Integration definition tools	<List any tools used to create and manage an integration definition>
Integration support tools	<List any tools used to support management and configuration of integrations>
Open interfaces	<List any open interfaces that can be used independent of languages or development tools>

Figure 6-5 Development View Table

Communication protocols	<Industry standard or technology for each type of communication>
	<Example: RosettaNet; JMS; etc.>
Application interfaces	<Industry standard or technology for each type of application>
	<Example: Web services for x types of applications, packaged adapters for y type of applications, JCA for z type of applications>
Message formats	<Industry standard or technology for each type of message>
	<Example: XML for most types of messages, EDI for transactions with large partners, etc.>
Process models	<Industry standard or technology>
	<Example: standardize on a tool or a modeling standard such as BPEL>
Metadata	<Standards for different types of metadata>
	<Example: metadata about interfaces, Web services, data transformation, etc.>

Figure 6-6 Integration Standards

Case Study 6.2
Model Driven Architecture: Improving How Integration Is Accomplished

The Object Management Group has embarked upon the creation of standards related to Model Driven Architecture (MDA). This activity was driven by a desire to protect software investment by integrating what has been built with what you will build. The goal is the specification of an architecture that can last for the next twenty years. Development is accomplished by developing models of the systems to be built that are testable and can be simulated. Once the model is validated, code is generated in the target environment that integrates legacy applications and off-the-shelf products with generated code.

The process for developing an MDA application is:

1. Develop a platform-independent model that describes functionality and behavior.
2. Map the model to target middleware technology and create a platform specific model.
3. Generate code from the platform-specific model for deployment.

Through this approach, systems that are heavily based upon integration can be developed faster and easier than is typical today. In addition, the OMG envisions that through MDA tools will be developed for reverse engineering—to generate models from existing systems for use in new applications. In addition, it will be easier to generate bridging between applications both within and across the enterprise by sharing the platform-independent models between organizations that need to integrate to other systems.

6.2.7 Service-Level Requirements

Service-level requirements include availability, integrity and delivery service, scalability, maintainability, manageability, usability, and performance. Transaction, persistence, and directory services may also be required to support the necessary level of service. These requirements can be derived from the application requirements section or they may be imposed by the organization based upon needs of the business.

Each section will most likely need to break down the requirements by application as well as type or span of integration. These requirements are intended to be a guide for the design and implementation of the integration architecture. Many of these requirements will be at a high level and not at a detailed level that will occur with the application design. Specific application requirements may necessitate adjustments to the high-level specification. It is important that the organization treat the Enterprise Integration Architecture as an ongoing process rather than a finished product.

6.2.7.1 Availability

This section captures the availability requirements, such as when the integration will take place (real time or batch), expectations on the access to the service, and any specific metrics that the integration architecture needs to meet. There are two types of metrics to be defined regarding availability: system availability and availability of integration. Typical system availability measurements are working hour availability, usually defined as 8 hours per day, 5 days per week (8×5), or full time availability, defined as 24 hours per day, 7 days per week (24×7). Availability of integration can be defined as real time or other, such as periodic or batch. This metric defines when the information that has been integrated is available for use.

6.2.7.2 Integrity and Delivery Service

The integrity of integrated information rests on the integrity of the transmission as well as the integrity of the information being processed. Transmission integrity is ensured by transmission services such as guaranteed delivery, once and only once delivery, and persistent message stores. The integrity of the information processes is dependent upon the validity of the translation and transformation process, and the processing of the information by the target system. This metric can be measured in error rates, and relates to both the quality and cost of the system.

6.2.7.3 Scalability

Scalability is a large factor in capacity planning and purchasing. The scalability requirements must be defined for the expected needs of the organization in both the short term and the longer term. Scalability requirements can be defined by the following parameters:

- Amount of information to be passed
- Transaction rates (time/volume)

- Number of applications to be integrated
- Simultaneous end user connections

These requirements determine the type of architecture as well as the technologies selected for implementation.

6.2.7.4 Maintainability and Manageability

Maintainability and manageability refer to the operational characteristics of the architecture. This part of the specification defines the specific services required. Also, define any requirements to integrate with the existing operational environment. Lastly, identify all related maintainability constraints, such as applications that are migrating to different platforms, or are being "sunsetted."

Maintainability and management requirements can be defined by the following services:

- Monitoring and alerting
- Startup, shutdown, and restart
- Troubleshooting and level of support
- Maintainability of code and use of tools
- Installation and managing release of updates and ability to rollback
- Scheduling
- Integration with existing tools

After determining requirements, we recommend summarizing them for the purposes of enterprise planning. Assigning a manageability requirement rating to each application or project can do this. This rating provides a summary view of all manageability requirements. The following rating can be used:

- **Level 1.** Startup, shutdown and restart, troubleshooting, scheduling remote installation
- **Level 2.** Level 1 plus updates and rollbacks, integrated application repository
- **Level 3.** Level 2 plus real-time monitoring and alerts, full integration of development and management tools

6.2.7.5 Usability

Usability refers to how easily each type of user will use the system. Defining all types of system users, along with the type of access and usability they require, helps determine tools and application requirements. Figure 6-7 (page 104) provides a

Type of User	Usability Requirements
Developers <J2EE, .NET, Web services, legacy, integration specialist>	<J2EE and/or .NET programming, Web service programming interfaces>
Analyst	<Modeling interface>
Designer	<Modeling and configuration interface>
Line of business managers	<Browser-based portal or dashboard, real-time alerts>
Other business user	<Browser-based portal, real-time alerts>
Operational managers	<Interface to management tools, portal interface of operational status, real-time alerts>

Figure 6-7 Usability Requirement Table

template for determining usability requirements. This table can be modified or expanded as needed.

6.2.7.6 Performance

Performance requirements define the level of service the infrastructure needs to provide to support business users, processes, and transactions. Performance requirements are also used in the capacity planning view (see Figure 6-8).

A number of different types of measurements may be included in performance requirements. Response time is the expected or acceptable time for

Response time	<Real-time, minutes, hours, days>
Throughput	<Number of transactions, data volumes>
Turnaround time	<Seconds, minutes, hours, days>
Number of simultaneous users	<Subtotals by types of users defined in usability>
Number of connected applications	<Name all applications that will be integrated>

Figure 6-8 Performance Requirement Table

users or applications to wait for a response from the system. It can be measured in sub-seconds or seconds (real time), minutes, hours, or days. Throughput is the amount of information that can be sent through the system within a certain amount of time. It can be measured in number of transactions or volume of data. Turnaround time is the amount of time it takes for the entire process to complete. It can be measured in seconds, minutes, hours, or days. Number of simultaneous users determines the number of live connections or sessions the system must support. Number of connected applications refers to the number of integrated applications that could send or receive information through the system.

6.2.7.7 Transaction Services

Transaction services include distributed transaction support and XA standard transaction compliance. This information determines how transactions will be managed and how transactional integrity will be maintained. This section also defines requirements for supporting industry and regulatory standards such as RosettaNet, HIPAA, or other industry-standard transactions.

6.2.7.8 Persistence Services

Often it is necessary to persist or store data for future use during an integration process. Persistence is required for improved reliability when recovering from a failure. Being able to restart a failed system without losing any in process integrations is the most basic use of a persistence service. However, there are numerous other uses for this type of service. Other types of uses for persisted data include the ability to rollback any actions, perform audits of activity, or use the collected data to analyze activity on the infrastructure. This section defines the requirements to provide storage of the integration data and state information during and after any use of the integration infrastructure.

6.2.7.9 Directory Services

It has become a best practice in modern distributed systems to provide the ability for directory services. Directories provide several fundamental capabilities for the infrastructure. They can provide location transparency by allowing applications to "find" other applications for integration. This reduces the need to hard code location information into the application, and increases adaptability because a location change would not require changes in other applications. In addition, directories can be used to store configuration information on resources or users that can be used by any application or integration process. Finally, a directory can be used to store security information. This use will be examined in closer detail in the section on security.

In this section, define the requirements for directory services. This includes the ability to register any "component" of the system including servers, interfaces, service, schemas, or other types of information.

Figure 6-9 is an example of a simple setup for a directory that might exist. The mandatory fields are the name and location. The type and description are helpful in an operational system. Other fields might be added for specific components.

6.2.7.10 Service Level Summary Table

The Service Level Summary Table (Figure 6-10) is useful for displaying an aggregate view of service-level requirements.

6.2.8 Security

Security is a type of service-level requirement, but it is such an important topic and a highly specialized topic that it is dealt with separately. The specification should start by summarizing the top-level security requirements by the categories or types of applications that will be utilizing the architecture. This can be done in a general manner as shown in Figure 6-11 (page 108), but is more effective if it can be specifically defined.

Component Name	Component Type	Location	Description	Other Fields
<Component name>	<Component type>	<Location>	<Description>	<Value>
<Component name>	<Component type>	<Location>	<Description>	<Value>

Figure 6-9 Directory Services Table

	<Application Type or Name>	<Application2 Name>	<ApplicationN Name>
Availability	<Real time or batch; 8x5 or 24x7>	...	...
Integrity and delivery service	<Guaranteed; once and only once; message stores>	...	...
Scalability	<Connections, locations transactions, data volumes>	...	...
Maintainability and manageability	<Level 1, Level 2, Level 3>	...	...
Usability	<Developers, analysts, designers, LOB managers, other business users, operational managers>	...	...
Performance	<Response time, throughput, simultaneous users>	...	...
Transaction services	<Distributed transactions, XA compliant, HIPAA, other?>	...	...
Persistence	<Storage of data and integration information for recovery, playback and analysis>	...	...
Directory services	<Information about all of the components of the integration infrastructure>	...	...

Figure 6-10 Service Level Summary Table

	Authentication	Authorization	Auditing	Confidentiality	Nonrepudiation
Internal data		■			
Partner data	■	■			■
Customer data	■	■	■	■	
Internal application	■	■			
Partner application	■	■			■
Customer application	■	■	■	■	■
Internal process		■			
Partner process	■	■	■		■
Customer process	■	■	■	■	■

Figure 6-11 Security Table

6.2.8.1 Authentication

Authentication services confirm the identity of a user. A detailed specification of authorization service requirements includes the following:

- **List of user types.** User types should correlate to the types of applications or services a group would access. Examples include: designers, programmers, managers, line of business users, customers, and partners.
- **Level of authentication for each type of user or role.** Levels of authentication may include: password, password with public/private key encryption, digital certificate, and biometrics.
- **Whether unitary login will be supported.** Unitary logic defines whether authentication can be performed once for all applications and services. This requires a centralized directory for all services.
- **Definition of how user accounts will be managed.** User accounts must be constantly created and updated based on the changes that occur in the business. It is important to have a formal process defined on how this information will be kept synchronized.

6.2.8.2 Authorization

Authorization levels determine what operations a user or process is authorized to perform on a set of data or within an application. This section defines categories for authorization, based on application and/or sensitivity of data (see Figure 6-12). Authorization is usually defined in a CRUD matrix that defines rights to Create, Read, Update, or Delete information.

6.2.8.3 Perimeter Security

This section should address how the integration architecture will work with perimeter security and the types or categories of integration that will be required to use the perimeter security features. Perimeter security is the combination of firewalls, encryption, authentication services, and architecture used to protect the enterprise from the outside world. The configuration of the perimeter security will dictate the design of the integration architecture as it relates to external usage.

6.2.8.4 Auditing

This section defines categories for auditing based on the type of application and the sensitivity of the data being processed. Basic categories of auditing are:

- **Level 0. Maintain no information**
  In cases where there is no worry about the interactions because of other factors related to trust, Level 0 can be used, and no auditing would be performed.
- **Level 1. Maintain information on type of interaction and participants**
  In cases where the details are not required and only the knowledge that an interaction has taken place is required, Level 1 would be applicable. This would be used in instances where a rollback is not feasible or necessary, but only the fact that an interaction took place is required.

	<Application 1>	**<Application 2>**	**<Application 3>**	**<Application 4>**
User Role #1	<C, R, U, D>	<R, U>	<R, U>	<R>
User Role #2	<R>	<C, R, U, D>	<R, U>	<R, U>
User Role #3	<R>	<R>	<C, R, U, D>	<R>
User Role #4	<R>	<R, U>	<R, U>	<C, R, U, D>

Figure 6-12 Application Authorization Table

- **Level 2. Maintain only instructions for each interaction**
  Level 2 is used to examine the types of interactions that have occurred and look for odd behavior or verify that an interaction occurred. This may be used to verify that an employee has performed an unauthorized operation on the system and have the information to rollback the action.
- **Level 3. Maintain a complete set of information on every interaction**
  Level 3 is used in cases where the interactions are extremely sensitive and either proof of the interaction or the need to fully audit every interaction is required. Full audit may be required in cases of significant financial transactions, for example.

Performance and resource requirements are the tradeoffs in making a distinction between each level. Otherwise, if performance and resources were free, then level four would always be applied. In many instances, this may not be feasible.

6.2.8.5 Confidentiality

Confidentiality refers to the level of privacy that a transmission requires. Confidentiality usually applies to the level of encryption that is applied. However, it also could be reflected in the communications path that is used. For example, if a high degree of confidentiality is required, then the interaction could be directed onto a higher cost dedicated line rather than following a path that uses an Internet connection. Generally speaking, when using encryption, the higher the level of confidentiality, the slower the response time. However, when considering communications channels, the higher degree of confidentiality, the more expensive the communications. Performance, cost, and security are often tradeoffs.

6.2.8.6 Nonrepudiation

Nonrepudiation is extremely important for B2B transactions. It ensures that a request or an order cannot be repudiated later on. Nonrepudiation services are required to ensure the validity and enforceability of electronic contracts. The specification should define the level of nonrepudiation service required, and which types and categories of applications require it (Figure 6-13).

Types of nonrepudiation include:

- **Nonrepudiated communications sessions.** The endpoints in the communication session, such as an SSL session, exchange tokens that uniquely identify them. This type of nonrepudiation validates that a session took place, but does

Type of Nonrepudiation	Type of Application
Nonrepudiated communications sessions	Simple integrations of applications or the exchange of data between applications.
Nonrepudiated middleware services	Integrations where the interactions are with an middleware infrastructure.
Nonrepudiated transactions	Transaction processing.
Nonrepudiated application actions consisting of multiple transactions	Complex business processes.

Figure 6-13 Nonrepudiation Table

not validate that specific information was exchanged in the session, as it does not permanently bind the session contents to the originator or the recipient.

- **Nonrepudiated middleware services.** Interactions between middleware services, include a token that validates the service's authenticity. Interactions are securely time-stamped and logged. This type of nonrepudiation validates that an interaction took place, but not that specific information was exchanged in the interaction.
- **Nonrepudiated transactions.** The transaction is accompanied with a token that validates its authenticity and the transaction is time-stamped and logged. This type of nonrepudiation validates that a transaction took place, but not what specific data was processed in the transaction.
- **Nonrepudiated application actions consisting of multiple transactions.** The end-user's intent to take the action is recorded, the application actions are uniquely and irrefutably traceable to the user, and the actions are securely time-stamped and securely logged. This validates that the participants intended to engage in the action, irrefutably validates their identities, irrefutably associates the time of the action with this information, and provides nonrepudiation that the whole process was completed.

6.2.9 Capacity Planning View

This section (Figure 6-14, page 112) specifies the design approaches to achieving application requirements defined in the Service Level section. The goal is to define how all service-level requirements will be met including technologies, policies, and procedures.

Requirement	Design Approach
Availability	<Back-up and recovery plan, redundancy plan, fail-over, disaster site, etc.>
Response time	<Network bandwidth, high-speed access, localized access, optimized human interactions, application performance optimization, database optimization>
Throughput	<Network bandwidth, high-speed access, application performance optimization, database optimization, storage capacity>
Turnaround times	<Network bandwidth, high-speed access, application performance optimization, database optimization, real-time alerts>
Number of users	<Connection management, caching, localizing access through redundant stores, optimizing human interactions, application performance, database optimization>
Number of connected applications	<Point-to-point integration, integration server, distributed integration servers>
Transaction services	<Transaction monitor, transaction services within application, other>
Persistence	<Storage systems, recovery and playback capabilities, analytical tools>
Directory services	<Directory server, administrative tools>

Figure 6-14 Capacity Planning Table

6.2.10 Design Constraints and Guidance

All constraints and specific guidance for architects, designers, and developers should be defined at this point. This is an open topic area that is unbounded. However, some areas to consider in the setting of constraints and guidance are

- Known performance limitations
- Formatting guidelines for data
- Constraints on metadata definitions and registration
- Preference on use of different types of interfaces
- Special cases of security implementations
- Deviations allowed from the integration architecture

This section will most likely be very limited in the beginning, but as the use of the architecture leads to better understanding and knowledge of what does and does not work, it will grow over time.

6.2.11 Conclusions and Commentary

The final section of the Integration Architecture Specification summarizes any particular issues or decisions regarding the integration architecture. These can include unresolved solutions to specific requirements. This might be a good place for executive IT management to provide guidance on the expectations of the integration architecture, how it will impact the organization, and what is expected from the staff. Lastly, it might include discussion on where the architecture is going in the future.

6.3 Best Practices in Technical Integration Architecture

- Make the architecture specification a living document. It should be consulted for each new integration project and revised periodically, or whenever required.
- Don't boil the ocean the first time out. Scope the initial integration architecture definition project to last no more than two to three months.
- Make sure all stakeholders have input to the definition and review the architecture specification. Otherwise, the architecture may be sabotaged.
- Plan globally, implement locally.
- Design for reuse.
- Measure and management reuse.
- Implement quality metrics to justify infrastructure investments.

6.4 Next Steps

The Technical Integration Architecture provides the framework for choosing infrastructure technologies for the solutions discussed in Part III of the book. Those looking to implement tactical solutions will be tempted to jump there immediately. However, companies wishing to maximize business agility, reuse, and return on investment, will wish to complete the Enterprise Integration Architecture by defining the Service Integration Architecture (Chapter 7), Information Integration Architecture (Chapter 8), and the Process Integration Architecture (Chapter 9).

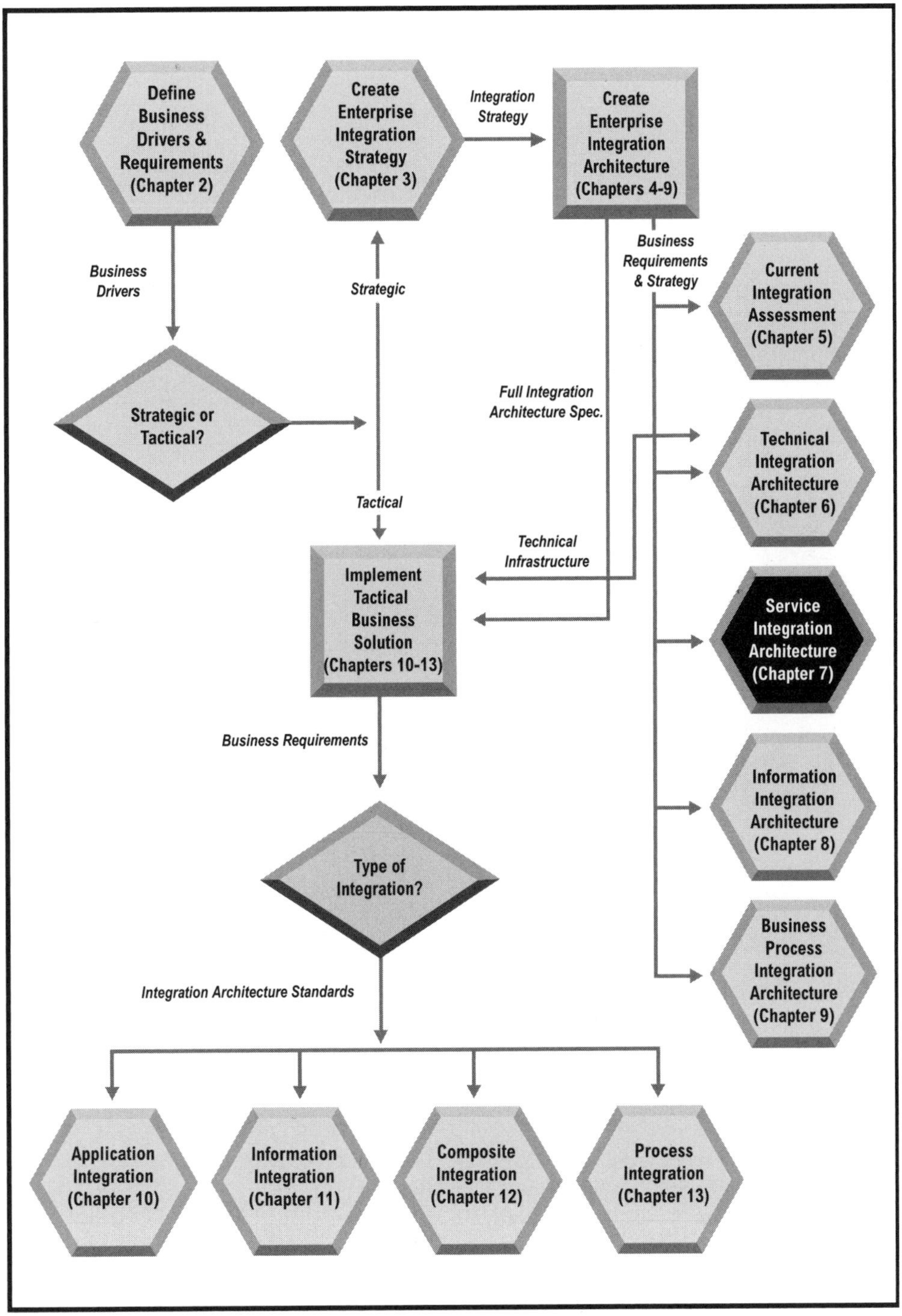

Figure 6-15 Enterprise Integration Roadmap

CHAPTER SEVEN

Service Integration Architecture

7.1 Executive Overview

The Service Integration Architecture defines business applications as reusable, easily changed components of business functionality, and how these components interrelate. This is the concept of a service-oriented architecture (SOA). While SOA has been considered a best practice for over two decades (see sidebar), until recently, very few companies were interested in them. Now SOA is suddenly a hot topic in IT, and at the center of many initiatives aimed at increasing business agility. At this point, if your company is not at least investigating SOA, it should be.

In a SOA, discrete business functions or processes are created as independent components with standard interfaces which can be accessed by other applications, services, or business processes, regardless of the platform or programming language. These services can be flexibly combined to support different or changing business processes and functions. It supports the creation of composite applications, which can be quickly assembled from existing and new services.

In the past, companies had to bet the business on CORBA, J2EE, or .NET to create a SOA. But most large companies use all of the above. The risks and costs of standardizing on one outweighed the potential benefits of SOA. This accounted for the low adoption rate. But Web services have significantly altered the value equation of

The History of Service Oriented Architectures

The concept of SOA began in the early 1980s and was embraced by the networking and object-oriented programming communities. In 1983 the Open Systems Interconnect (OSI) Reference Model was adopted by the International Standards Organization (ISO) as a common reference for the development of data communication standards. It defines the functions of data communications in seven layers. Each layer defines a communication service, and each service has a clearly defined interface with the layer above and below it. This SOA has passed the test of time. While the technology and capabilities in each layer have changed dramatically, the architecture itself stands. As long as the interfaces between services remain the same, the services themselves can be changed easily.

The Open Software Foundation (OSF), the group responsible for the UNIX standard, developed the Distributed Computing Environment (DCE) based on a service-oriented architecture. DCE provides infrastructure services for distributed computing, including authentication and security services (Kerberos), directory services, remote procedure calls, and file and management services.

CORBA is a vendor-independent architecture and infrastructure defined by the Object Management Group (OMG) that enables computer applications to work together over networks using the standard protocol IIOP. CORBA enables interoperability across platforms. CORBA applications are component-based.

The most current component technologies are J2EE and .NET. J2EE is a component-based platform that manages the distributed infrastructure and supports Web services to enable interoperable business applications. It is currently the most widely deployed component model.

.NET is Microsoft's implementation of a Web services architecture, which enables the legions of Microsoft programmers to create Web services in the programming languages they are most familiar with. This preserves a very large investment in existing skill sets. J2EE programmers are usually more expensive than Microsoft programmers.

SOAs. Web services are the first universally accepted standard because all the major vendors can, in theory, support it. They work with .NET, J2EE, and CORBA (as long as everyone sticks to the same version of the standard). Despite some areas of the standard that are still immature, Web services and XML have significantly removed the risk barriers for adopting SOA, making the benefits far outweigh the risks.

Existing mission critical applications currently on the mainframe and other platforms can be wrapped in Web services interfaces and then accessed from other applications or Web browsers. This enables businesses to create business services out of existing systems, and rapidly implement and integrate new functionality. Using Web services, companies can begin creating an SOA by leveraging existing investments and incrementally adding new functionality. SOA is the architecture that will best enable long-term business agility because it supports reuse, and rapid deployment of new solutions.

7.2 Benefits of SOA

- **Enable business agility.** SOA is the best way to enable business agility. It maximizes leverage of existing resources while minimizing the time and cost of deploying new applications. Rather than developing applications from scratch, companies can utilize exiting functionality and create new solutions by assembling component applications from existing and new functionality. This enables rapid deployment of new solutions.
- **Provide higher return on investment.** Companies that define reusable business services and create or wrap business functionality as standard services will maximize their IT investments, through reuse and leveraging existing assets.
- **Enable IT agility.** Standard service definitions can provide a layer of abstraction for business services. A service can run anywhere and be accessed from anywhere. Therefore, a company can easily change location or technology of the underlying code.
- **Reduce training costs.** Business services can be encapsulated and abstracted in a way that makes them easy to utilize and assemble into component applications with minimal programming. Companies can utilize more skilled programmers for creating the underlying functionality and service definitions, which can then be reused by less technical programmers and visual application assembly tools.

- **Reduce the cost of testing and bug fixing.** Each service is like a black box that performs a specific function and has a published interface that accepts defined inputs and produces defined outputs. Each service can be tested individually, then reused over and over again. Interface testing is fairly straightforward, and can be automated using testing tools.
- **Support multiple client types and platforms.** The SOA offers a layer of abstraction from the underlying platforms. This makes it possible for multiple types of end-user devices, including browsers and mobile devices such as pagers, cell phones, PDAs, and other specialized devices to utilize the same business functionality and have information communicated to different devices. This platform independence provides great savings for large companies that have a myriad of technologies in use.
- **Speed development time through parallel development.** Different programmers can independently work on different services because each service is self-contained and does not depend upon the state of another service. As long as the service interfaces are well-defined at the beginning of the project, and programmers know what to expect from other services, they can easily define and create services independently. It used to be said that past a certain point adding more programmers to a project increases development time. This is no longer true with SOAs.
- **Increase scalability and availability.** Because SOA offers location transparency, there is the potential to increase scalability by adding multiple instances of a service. Load-balancing technology would dynamically find and route the request to the appropriate service instance. Likewise, if there are multiple instances of a service on the network, and one becomes available, software can transparently route the request to another instance, thereby providing better availability. This is more the case for new services built on application services, and not legacy functionality that has been wrapped in Web service interfaces.

What makes SOA so compelling is that it can be done on both a large and small scale with the same benefits. Texas A&M University was able to demonstrate these principles in the development of their online class-registration system described in Case Study 7.1 (Software AG n.d.). This application was a small step in the application of SOA with a big impact.

Ultimately, SOAs will become the way most organizations build their IT infrastructures, because it is the best and only proven way to provide long-term

Case Study 7.1
Improving Student Services at Texas A&M

Texas A&M University has been a real leader in the application of technology to supporting the mission of the university. As one of the world's largest educational institutions, improving services to the students—especially during registration—remains a high priority.

A service-oriented architecture using Web services is well suited to provide improved registration and ancillary services to students that expect more electronic services and less time standing in lines. So a decision was made to implement an online service. The IT department developed their class-registration system using Web services and two staff and was able to deliver a system in three months. Most of the service was provided by the existing Cobol and Natural programs running on the mainframe. They were tied together into Web services using EntireX Communicator. It was estimated that using this approach and technology there was a saving of over 50% in development time compared to prior similar efforts in the department.

During registration, thousands of students were served simultaneously and efficiently. The impact to the university was a higher degree of satisfaction by students and a significant reduction in phone calls for the university staff.

agility. However, it will take some time and investment to get there. To date, most of the industry focus has been on solving the considerable technical connectivity problems. However, the larger hurdles to truly enabling business agility through SOA are in defining, building, and managing reusable business services.

7.3 Defining Services—Bottom-Up or Top-Down?

To date, the majority of the focus on SOA and Web services has been on the technical details of defining interfaces. While the standard interface definition is the critical enabler of the system, the bottom-up approach has its limitations. If the focus is only on the interface specification, and not on how to define what functionality to expose as a service, companies will not reap the full benefits of an SOA. Increased business agility and decreased costs are dependent upon well-defined, well-managed, reusable services that are fast and easy to connect to. Unfortunately, there is no mathematical theory or methodology that can tell a developer whether the component or service is at the correct level of granularity to maximize reuse. The most commonly used method of creating business services is the trial-and-error approach. This usually means defining services in the context of a particular business process, then revising for reuse in the next solution.

A top-down business approach to defining services will enable companies to better meet the current and future needs of the business. It starts with the business requirements. Each service should provide the functionality to meet one or more business requirements, and the set of functions should be closely related. This is called functional cohesion. However, the services should be loosely coupled. The processing within one service should not be dependent upon the state of processing in another. A service abstracts the functionality from the underlying technology.

In truth, to get the job done, both bottom-up and top-down methods are necessary. The top-down approach yields a level of abstraction that is necessary to create business agility. However, at some point the model needs to meet the technology, and the services need to be implemented as components or collections of components. Companies will continue to build components from the bottom-up to encapsulate business services. The key is to make these components functionally cohesive to avoid overlapping functionality and loosely coupled to enable rapid change and to minimize the impact of change.

7.4 Event-Driven Service Design

In this chapter we offer a top-down event-driven method for defining discrete business services that can be used on a project or enterprise basis. Defining business requirements in terms of business events offers a number of advantages. First, event-driven service-oriented architectures provide the most agile systems. In the ebizQ webinar, "Creating the New Enterprise Agility: Service-Oriented and Event-Driven" *(http://www.ebizq.net/expoq/events/event39.html),* Roy Schulte, VP Gartner, stated, "agility generally involves event-driven business practices, facilitated by service-oriented architectures." He used the analogy of trains and trucks to describe the agility of SOA. "Changing a truck's direction is easier than making a train go where the tracks don't. If you want the train to move over one foot, you have to do an immense amount of work tearing up and re-laying tracks," Schulte said. "On the other hand, all you need to do to turn the more agile truck is move the steering wheel." SOA is the architecture that provides the wheels for the agile enterprise.

Second, business events are a good way to design services because they are easy for business users to understand, identify, and verify in a design. They represent the essential activities of the business. One of the best ways to ensure maximum reuse of a service is to have an interface design review, so all stakeholders can evaluate whether the service will meet their needs. This is the process used by OASIS to develop standards. When companies adopt this practice, the services are more likely to meet a wider range of needs. Business stakeholders are better able to define and verify business events and required system responses, than technical interfaces. The event responses define the requirements for the interface design.

Finally, defining the business events the system will capture and respond to clearly defines the boundaries of the system. This is essential for ensuring successful and rapid implementations. The event responses are further decomposed into sets of functionally cohesive system responses. These responses may be supplied by exiting systems or new development. The service may be an integrated interface to a set of responses supplied by different systems that need to be coordinated. A service can itself provide different levels of abstraction. The service can also be a single function provided by a component or application. Focusing on business events and required responses provides a business-oriented approach to defining the SOA. This method is described in the Service Integration Specification.

7.5 Service Integration Architecture Specification

Some have called the process of creating reusable business services similar to cooking waffles. You need to throw the first one out, and it gets better over time. While it is certainly an iterative process, this specification will provide guidelines for creating reusable services. A full copy of the specifications is in Appendix E.

7.5.1 Introduction

This SOA Specification provides architecture and design guidance for applying a service-oriented architecture approach to integration. This document defines the events, services, and components. It is the design and architecture specification for the development of the services and components.

7.5.2 Scope

The scope of this specification is defined by the scope of the project. It documents the architecture and design for an SOA approach to an integrated solution. The scope of this specification should describe the scope of the application or system that is being designed.

7.5.3 Key Participants

This section should define the stakeholders who can verify the business events, services, and interfaces; the development team who will execute the implementation of the design; and the team responsible for the architecture and design. Any other participants or stakeholders should also be identified, including their roles.

7.5.4 Business Events

The Business Events section defines the business activities that the system must support. A business event is something that

- Occurs in the business environment
- Occurs at a given point in time
- Must be responded to by the system

The Event Table describes the relevant activities that happen in the business and the required system responses. There are two types of events: business events and temporal events. Business events are activities that occur in the business, and are detected by defining each business activity within the scope of the system. Temporal events occur at a predetermined point in time. Temporal events exist because the business policy demands that certain system activities occur at certain times, or because the system produces its outputs on a timed basis. Case Study 7.2 describes how managing business events more efficiently at Delta Airlines can have significant impact on its business (Tillett and Schwartz 2001).

The business requirements are defined in the Statement of Purpose (Chapter 2, page 30). From that list, create a list of business events within the scope of the system, and define the responses to each event (see Figure 7-1, page 126). In the Event Description column, include how the event is initiated, or detected. When defining Responses, give descriptive names that unambiguously define what the system response is, such as "Verify existing customer," "Enter New Customer," "Check Credit."

Case Study 7.2
Delta Airlines—Managing Business Events Through the Delta Nervous System

The Delta Nervous System (DNS) represents an investment of $1 billion "to deliver timely data to customers, employees, and partners." However, it is not the delivery of the information, but the use of that data in handling business events that is the major benefit of the DNS. For example, an initial application of the system is aimed at baggage handlers and ensuring that they have an accurate picture of gate changes and flight delays so they can better plan the movement of luggage on and off planes. The change in status of a flight is a business event that has repercussions across the airline system. Whenever an event occurs, the change in status can be acted upon by providing the key participants of that event with information and services to react to these changes.

The DNS is turning Delta into a real-time enterprise with the ability to better serve its customers. However, it also has enormous revenue-generation and cost-saving implications. For example, having real-time information allows Delta to increase the number of flights per day by moving planes in and out faster. Overtime of idle ground crews can be reduced through better planning. Costs associated with the mishandling of bags can be eliminated.

While the focus is on making information available, the value will be in identifying meaningful events and then taking appropriate action as a result of the events. It is not necessary for a business to create a new source of information. Rather, it is important to create an architecture that is able to act upon business events and flow those through the system efficiently as a service. Delta has put such a system in place with its DNS.

7.5.5 Services

The system responses defined in the Events Table are used to determine the essential services the system must provide. Some of these services or functions already exist in other systems, and other functionality will be new and must be developed then integrated. The service descriptions define the scope of functionality required to perform a specific business service.

Event Number	Business Event	Event Description	Response
<Event number>	<Name of event>	<Description of the event>	<List containing descriptions of potential actions>
E1	Customer places Web order	This event is kicked off by an external event when a customer makes an order request. It ensures a valid order is placed into the system.	R1.1 Verify existing customer R1.2 Enter new customer R1.3 Check credit R1.4 Check inventory stock
E2	Order is processed	This event is kicked off when an order enters the system. It ensures that the order is ready to ship.	R2.1 Enter accounts payable R2.2 Fulfill order
E3	Order is shipped	This event is kicked off when an order has been processed. It ensures that the order is shipped and all parties are made aware of the results.	R3.1 Tracking number assigned R3.2 E-mail notification to customer
E4	Order is returned	This event is kicked off by an external event when a customer returns an order. It ensures that the returned order is processed correctly.	R4.1 Return authorization issued R4.2 Credit customer account R4.3 Credit inventory

Figure 7-1 Event Table

To maximize business agility and IT investment, business services should be defined at the level of granularity that will optimize reuse. Tight cohesion—grouping closely related functions together into business services—and loose coupling between services are the design metrics that will yield more reusable design.

Three parts of the specification fully define each service: the Service Category Table, the Service Definition Table, and the Service Interface Table.

This level of description is sufficient for developing a new Web service or wrapping existing functionality as a business service.

Service Category Table

The Service Category Table lists all required responses to business events, and defines whether the function already exists in one or more systems, or if it is new functionality. The table also defines likely services to provide the functionality. The service at this point is a first best guess at a services definition and will be refined further in the next step. When defining services, think of modules within an existing application that may perform the service or likely component modules for development (Figure 7-2, page 128).

Service Definition Table

The Service Definition Table fully describes each service at a level sufficient for creating Web services or other integration interfaces. Each service should be described in terms of its functions and systems used to create the service. In creating this table, group all functions and responses together that will form a cohesive module. For example, the service should manage a particular set of data, such as customer information, or product information, or should perform a specific service that might be used in other applications, such as credit checking or pricing. There should be loose coupling between services. Each service should interact with any other service through the defined interface. Changes in one service should not impact functioning of other services.

The description defines how the service will be implemented, such as Web service, application adapter, or application module interface (Figure 7-3, page 129). This is the place in the specification that brings the top-down design down to the technology-specification level.

Response	Description	Service Category	Existing/New Systems
<Response>	<Description>	<Category>	<Systems>
R1.1 Verify existing customer	Verify the existence of the customer in the system	Customer maintenance	Customer database
R1.2 Enter new customer/change customer data	Update customer records with new information	Customer maintenance	Customer management—SAP
R1.3 Check credit	Check the credit rating of customer for proposed order amount	Risk management	Financials
R1.4 Check inventory stock	Check availability of stock to fulfill order	Inventory management	Warehouse system
R2.1 Enter order	Enter all order information via web interface; send to appropriate systems	Order management	Financial A/R; order fulfillment
R2.2 Fulfill order	Pick, package and ship all order items, report on backorders	Order fulfillment	Warehouse system
R3.1 Tracking number assigned	Assign an on-line tracking number to shipment	Shipping management	New—FedEx Web service
R3.2 E-mail notification to customer	Send E-mail to customer when order has been shipped	Shipping management	New—Web component
R4.1 Return authorization issued	Issue return authorization number	Customer management	Customer management
R4.2 Credit customer account	Issue credit to customer account when order is returned	Accounts receivable	Financials
R4.3 Credit inventory	Add returned merchandise to inventory	Inventory management	Warehouse system

Figure 7-2 Service Category Table

Service	Functions	Description	Existing/ New Systems
Customer record maintenance	Check existence/ add/delete/modify	Web service abstracts, database connections and lookups, manages customer records	New—Web service, interfaces with customer management
Credit check	Check credit	Interface to credit check module of ERP system.	Financials
Inventory management	Debit/credit inventory stock	Interface to warehouse management system	Warehouse system
Accounts receivable	Credit/debit customer account	Interface to A/R module of ERP system	Financials
Order management	Workflow management of a manual service	Interface to warehouse management system	Warehouse system
Shipping management	Integrate with FedEx system; send notification to customer	Integrate FedEx tracking Web service into customer web interface; create e-mail notification component	New—FedEx Web service
Customer management	Process returns; call center support	Web portal for call center, providing unified interface to customer and order info	New—Web component

Figure 7-3 Service Definition Table

Service Interface Table

While the Web services standard defines how to specify an interface, it does not define the data and functionality that the interface needs to contain. The Service Interface Specification provides the information necessary for creating Web services or other application or component interfaces. Using the Service Definition Table, list all inputs, outputs, and methods that the interface needs to support, and determine how the interface will be implemented (Figure 7-4).

Service:	Customer maintenance
Inputs	Customer ID; name, telephone number; address; shipping information; e-mail; credit; discount
Outputs	Customer ID; name, telephone number; address; shipping information; e-mail; credit; discount
Methods	MCRUD data operations
Implementation	Portal based interface with data access service that controls connectivity to back-end data sources. Will either build Web service or install vendor data connectivity solution

Figure 7-4 Service Interface Table

The goal of defining standard interfaces is to maximize business agility. The standardized interface enables applications and services built on different platforms with different languages and technology to interoperate. It enables services to change internal functionality and rules or underlying technology without impacting other applications or components, as long as the interface remains the same. Therefore, getting the interface right is essential to maximizing reuse and agility. It is highly recommended that companies follow best practices of the standards committees when defining interfaces by having design reviews that include all stakeholders. It is also recommended that you create a glossary of terminology that is meaningful and consistent across all stakeholders. The purpose of the Interface Specification is to enable such design reviews, and to fully describe the interface so it can be implemented correctly and optimally.

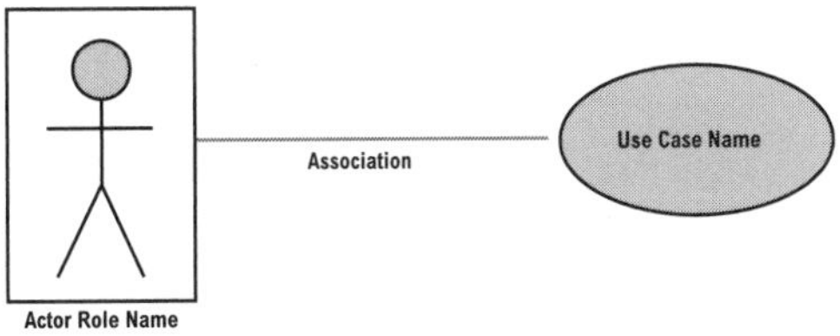

Figure 7-5 Components of a Use Case Diagram

7.5.6 Use Case Diagram and Specification

A use case diagram can be used to depict the relationships between users, events, and services. It is the final piece of the puzzle for the specification. It integrates all of the information from the previous sections.

Use cases define actors and how they interact with the system services. Actors represent a role, and can be humans, other computers, pieces of hardware, or even other software systems. They must supply stimuli to initiate the event that in turn requires a system response (or service). Use cases describe the behavior of the system when one of these actors sends one particular stimulus. It depicts the business events and system responses in terms of the event stimulus that triggers the use case, the inputs from and outputs to other actors, and the behaviors that convert the inputs to the outputs.

The basic components of use case diagrams are the actor, the use case, and the association (see Figure 7-5). An actor is depicted using a stick figure, and the role of the user is written beneath the icon. Actors can be humans, other computers, pieces of hardware, or even other software systems. A use case is depicted with an ellipse, and the name of the use case is written inside. Associations are lines between actors and use cases, and they indicate that an actor participates in the use case.

To support the analysis of nonfunctional requirements (e.g., reliability, maintainability, and performance), use cases should be created to support scenarios in which these nonfunctional requirements will be tested. Examples include: 1) creating a use case that tests performance across a distributed component interface, and 2) creating a use case that tests the adaptiveness of a component by extending it (i.e., adding classes) and examining it to determine if the architectural design principles still hold. These system-level use cases may be implemented in a stand-alone fashion whereby a part or slice of the architecture is being tested independently from the business domain functionality it will need to support.

To create the use case, first identify the primary actors in the system. Then prioritize the services to be implemented. We recommend creating a use case for each proposed service. As an example, see Figure 7-6 (page 132).

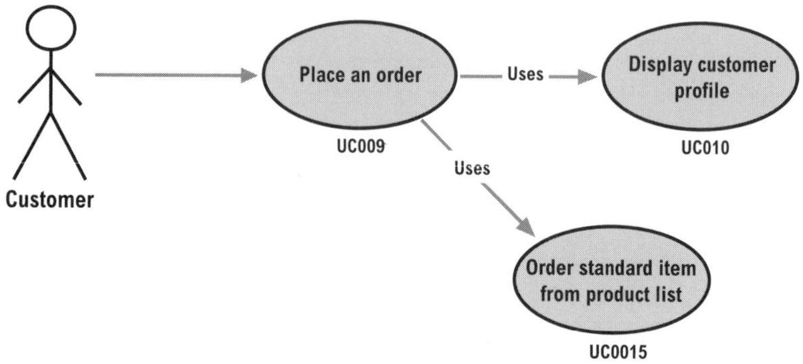

Figure 7-6 Use Case Diagram

The Use Case Specification contains text that further describes the use case (Figure 7-7). The text specification also usually describes everything that can go wrong during the course of the specified behavior, and what remedial action the system will take. This specification can be customized or expanded to handle particular issues within an implementation or organization.

7.5.7 Conclusions and Commentary

This section should provide any final comments on the system, the design, or the usage of the system. It should include any known issues, constraints, or extenuating factors that contributed to decisions, or could affect the system in the future.

Use Case	Use Case 009—Place an Order
Primary actors	Customer
Abstract	This use case allows the customer to create a purchase order using/updating existing customer information or by creating information for a new customer. If the customer has initiated a purchase order directly (without accessing an online catalog), he or she can select the items from a product list for this use case.
Goal	To allow customers to create and submit an order
Focus classes	Customer, item configuration, purchase order, standard item
Preconditions	Customer has user ID and valid password on customer extranet
Trigger	User decides to place an order online

Figure 7-7 Use Case Specification

General scenario	1. Customer clicks the "order" button—**Initiating Event** 2. Screen appears displaying or requesting customer information (UC010—Display Customer Information, UC011—Customer not Found) 3. Customer completes purchase order information including payment type, "Bill to" and "Ship to" addresses 4. Customer selects item from item list (UC017—Order Standard Item from Product List) 5. Customer selects item from online catalog (UC007—Order Standard Item from Online Catalog) 6. Customer clicks on "clear" button 7. Customer clicks on "submit" button 8. Customer clicks on "end" button—**Post Condition (goal achieved)**
Successful operation responses/output	1. User provided visual confirmation of order and confirmation number 2. Order entry system updated with order
Extensions/ alternative paths/ unsuccessful operation responses/outputs	4a. This step may be omitted 7a. This step may be omitted 6a. This step may be omitted
Variations	None
Dependencies	UC007—Initiate Session
Requirements reference	Requirements 4.1, 4.2, 4.3, 4.7
Screen reference	Screen 8
Backend reference	Web Services 2, 7, 9
Notes	None
Issues	Need to verify how "product list" will be displayed, stored, and updated Need to determine how to link submitting the PO when the customer is using the online catalog

Figure 7-7 *(cont.)*

7.6 Best Practices in Service Integration Architecture

A successful service-oriented architecture enables companies to rapidly implement new business solutions or change existing ones and can deliver a substantial ROI. However, SOA is not necessarily easy to accomplish. The following best practices will help you reap the full benefits of SOA.

- **Provide high-level organizational structure and support.** Success with SOA requires ongoing enterprise commitment and investment. SOA cannot be accomplished with a single project. There needs to be a group of experts, such as the competency center, that focuses on the definition, growth, and reuse of the SOA. There need to be organizational processes and policies governing enterprise integration. As integration crosses organizational boundaries, it can also cause territorial disputes. Companies need processes and policies for managing these disputes (described in more detail in section 4.4, Organizational Structure and Architecture Governance).
- **Implement standards-based architecture.** Standards help ensure both interoperability and portability. They prevent technology lock-in, and help preserve value in IT investments. Web service standards are enabling the widespread adoption of SOA, despite the fact that it has been a known best architectural practice for three decades. XML enabling your systems is one way to provide a standards-based transport, management, and storage format for all structured data and unstructured content within the organization.
- **Implement a standards-based approach.** Follow the example of the standards committees that have long experience with creating processes that are successful in creating interoperable standards. Perform design reviews for service interfaces, and include all stakeholders. Stakeholders can be identified through the use cases.
- **Think big, start small.** When planning for an SOA implementation, consider the enterprise-wide impact in order to maximize reuse and agility. But start with a project that has a limited scope and a high probability of success. Nothing succeeds like success. You will learn a lot from each implementation, so wait until you have a couple of smaller implementations under your belt before tackling the most difficult challenges.
- **Invest in training.** You will have a higher probability of success if your employees know what they're doing. Few designers and programmers have experience with SOAs built on standards such as Web services and XML. It's

all too new. All stakeholders, including business and IT managers, architects, designers, programmers, and operational support personnel need to understand the overall concepts of SOA and what their role in the process is. Architects and designers need to understand the design parameters and best practices for creating agile and reusable systems. Programmers need to understand the new technology, and how to implement services and infrastructure components. Operational support personnel need to understand the implications of managing a distributed SOA.

- **Use tools to save time and money.** Don't try to handcraft everything. A wide variety of tools are available that can reduce time and skill sets required to implement the solution. Invest in tools when the advantages clearly outweigh the cost.

The Vanguard Group is an interesting case study where each of these best practices came into play (Case Study 7.3) (Dragoon 2003).

Case Study 7.3
The Vanguard Group's "Brilliantly Simple Solution"

It had been described as a "brilliantly simple solution" when the Vanguard Group made a decision in the late 1990s to align their customers Web portal with their customer service system. In retrospect, it is surprising that more organizations have not come to the same conclusion, because the benefits seem so apparent:

- Parity between the customer interface channels in functionality
- Reduction of complexity in maintaining multiple systems
- An architecture that can be leveraged and reused for other purposes

The actual results have been impressive. Training of internal employees was significantly reduced, virtually eliminating four to six weeks of training. Retiring a large number of databases and applications reduced the complexity of the underlying architecture. Almost 10% fewer staff was required to maintain the systems. User response times were reduced by 60% to 70%, increasing the efficiency of the staff. Furthermore, the architecture supported the development of applications that improved several key business processes, resulting in straight-through processing of transactions. Savings from

Case Study 7.3 *(cont.)*

these changes were expected to result in annual savings of $30 million. The investment to achieve this was significant, but the expected ROI is an internal rate of return of over 20%.

While investments in architecture are often thought of as costs that have no apparent benefit, Vanguard demonstrates that the implementation of an architecture that supports reusability can have significant impact on a business. A well-designed service-oriented architecture is the key to achieving these benefits. Web services are not required, as we see with what Vanguard accomplished, but should help lower the costs that were borne in this project by reducing the amount of custom infrastructure work that is now provided through the Web services technology.

7.7 Next Steps

Services are the building blocks for composite applications and process-driven integration. Defining reusable enterprise services, as well as managing and measuring reuse, requires ongoing enterprise commitment and investment. Success with SOA is as much a matter of management as it is technology. Companies interested in long-term business agility will invest in all aspects of the enterprise integration architecture, including information and process integration architectures (Chapter 8 and Chapter 9, respectively). Companies focused on pressing tactical needs, will define only what is absolutely necessary and move on to implementation (Part III). See Figure 7-8.

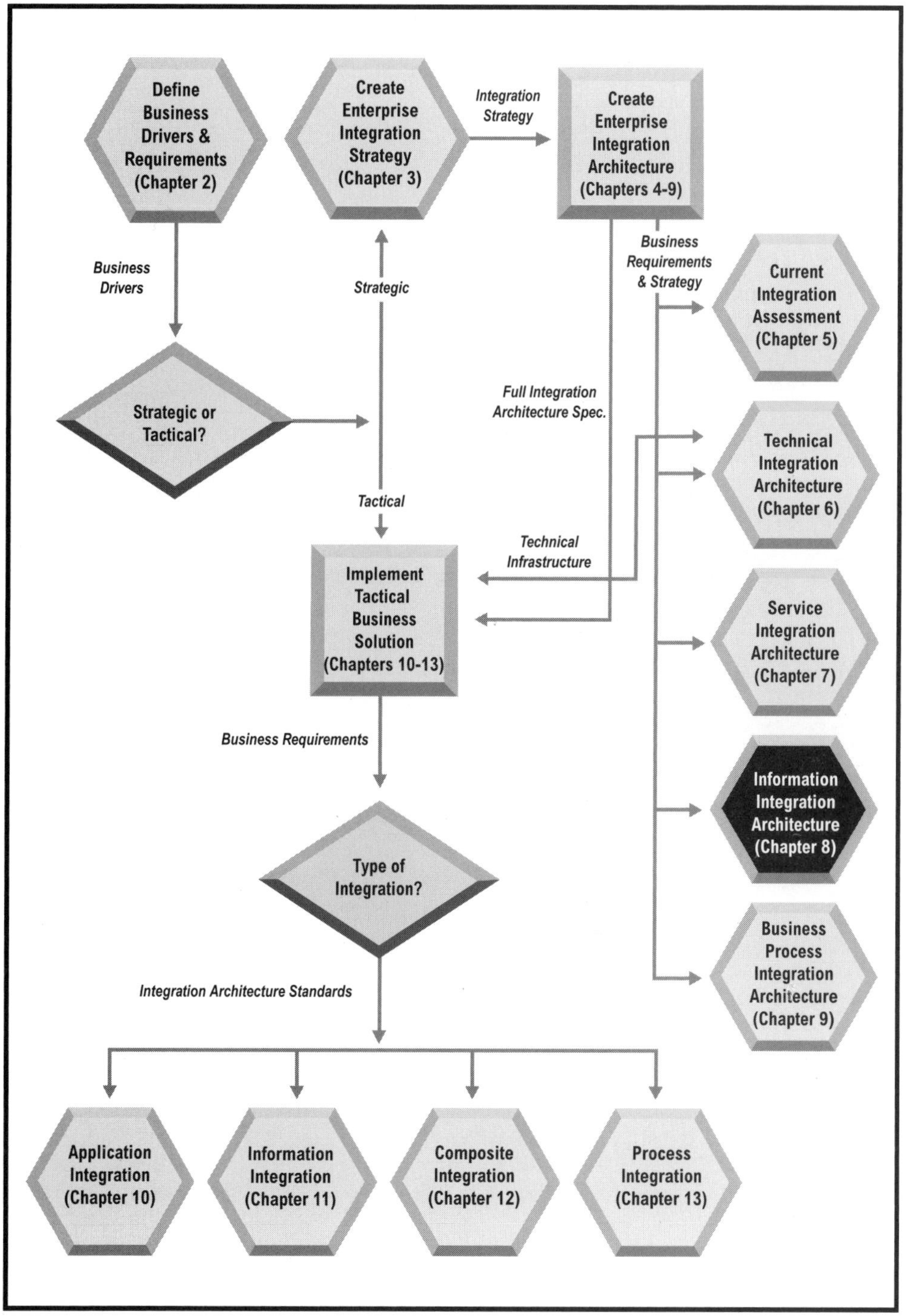

Figure 7-8 Integration Roadmap

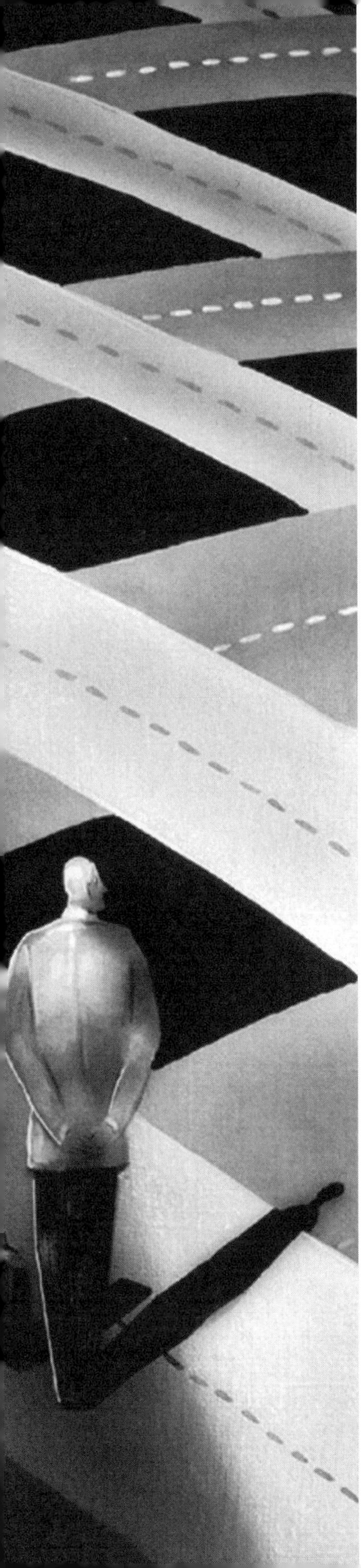

CHAPTER EIGHT

Information Integration Architecture

8.1 Executive Overview

Approaches and practices in integration have changed over the last decade, but what was old is new again. Integration technology and techniques related to both unstructured information in reports and digital media, and structured data in databases, are becoming an important part of the integration landscape once again. This is due to a variety of factors, including the emergence of XML as a data format standard, a realization that there will not be a single approach to solve all integration requirements, and the fact that at the heart of every integration project is a need to access, aggregate, propagate, and publish information. Lastly, organizations are realizing that their data is their business and they need to get more control of and use out of this asset to improve their business.

Information and data are at the heart of every integration project. Ultimately, integration is about different types of data exchange, in many different formats. The problem that lies at the heart of all integration projects is how to enable interoperability among systems with data in different structures and formats. The Information Integration Architecture defines the infrastructure and processes for enabling information to be accessible across systems.

The EAI solution to this problem is to represent data in a canonical format. The canonical format greatly increases reusability and decreases implementation and operational costs and time. Each system needs to be mapped only once into the canonical format; then it can interoperate with other systems in the same canonical format. While there are a number of benefits to a canonical format, most of these benefits are lost if the format is proprietary and can't interoperate with other vendor solutions.

That is the reason XML is so important today. The widespread acceptance and adoption of XML has been largely due to the tremendous need to describe data in a common format to reduce the time and cost of integration, and the fact that there really is no other alternative. XML is the best and only. (See sidebar on XML.)

However, while XML provides a standards-based canonical format, the real value of the data is dependent on maintaining the integrity of data across systems. Propagating incorrect data throughout multiple systems in a fraction of the time it would have taken with nonintegrated systems provides little value to the enterprise. The solution to maintaining the value, meaning, and integrity of data across applications is metadata. Metadata is information about the data. The more descriptive, accurate, and complete the metadata is, the better the integration can be. While a great deal of metadata already exists in systems, and there are a number of tools on the market that can automatically extract metadata from source systems, the quality of the metadata the tool can produce depends very much on what is available in the source system. To achieve the full benefits of metadata, organizations must ensure that all metadata is accurate and complete. This will likely require significant investment. However, down the line, the investment will pay off through increased quality and reuse of data, and decreased implementation time and cost.

Metadata is not just a nice-to-have in the enterprise architecture. It is an absolute necessity. It is how the information in and about systems can be represented independently from all systems, enabling interoperability between and among systems. Good metadata is the foundation for long-term successful integration.

The Information Integration Architecture defines enterprise metadata independent of technologies or platforms, in a manner usable by all integration projects.

The eXtensible Markup Language (XML)

XML has become one of the most important standards to be developed in the past decade. It has become the industry standard for metadata. As a result, it is the critical standard for data definition and document markup. It is a part of the Web services standards, the core standard for Microsoft's .NET platform and the most widely used format for interchange of data. It is arguably the most important standard for any integration architecture.

XML began as an effort to create a "better" HTML by the World Wide Web Consortium (W3C). It was completed in early 1998. Where HTML was a language used to render documents, XML would be a metamarkup language—a language to create markup languages. A markup language is a language that is used to describe the content or format of a document. Markup languages, such as HTML, use tags embedded into the document to express the description of the content and format. The tags used in HTML were found to be limiting for the types of applications that were being developed for the Web. Rather than continue to extend HTML, the decision was made to create a language that could be used to develop markup languages to improve the extensibility, structure, and validation of data formatting.

XML is based upon the Standard Generalized Markup Language (SGML). SGML is the creation of Charles Goldfarb of IBM who created the Generalized Markup Language in 1969 to enhance text editing, broaden formatting capabilities, and improve information retrieval. Goldfarb's work became the basis for the ISO SGML standard that was approved in 1986. HTML is in fact a simplified SGML document type created by Tim Berners-Lee and Anders Berglund.

The W3C viewed SGML as too complex to be used as the basis for any improvement to HTML. The consortium decided to create a group that would pare down SGML to something that had the power of SGML with the simplicity of HTML. As a result the 500+ page SGML specification was reduced to the initial 26-page XML specification.

The XML specification is a language for creating markup languages. Tags are defined in the language and can then be used to markup a

(continued)

The eXtensible Markup Language (XML) *(cont.)*

document or data. A document type definition (DTD) is one method for defining the markup language. Another is XML Schema, which allows for semantic constraints to be added on elements of a document. XML Schema is becoming more popular everyday.

Every document that uses XML must be "well-formed." This means that all the rules of the markup language defined in XML must be met. These rules include:

- There must be an open and close tag for each markup, for example, <para>, </para>.
- Tags must be nested, for example, <para> <sentence> </sentence> </para>.
- Attributes are values of a tag and use a set of single or double quotes, for example, <para sp='double'>.
- There must be one tag that contains all other tags: <html>, </html>.

While it was thought to be a better HTML, XML has not replaced HTML. This is ironic, given the reason that it was created. In fact, it has found its place in improving content management and application integration. In content management, it is being used as SGML was envisioned twenty years ago. More importantly, it has become the lingua franca for interchange of information in business. Existing standards such as HL7 in healthcare and EDI in supply-chain integration have been adapted to use XML. New standards such as the extensible Business Reporting Language (XBRL) are appearing that are based on XML.

Whether you do application, process, or information integration XML will be at the heart of the architecture that you develop. This is one of the most critical standards to understand in order to perform quality integration.

8.2 Understanding Metadata

Data in systems represents business entities, such as customers, employees, products, etc., and provides a persistent record of business events. Metadata, the information describing this data, enables the information to be queried, reported on, consolidated, synchronized, and integrated.

However, as the saying goes, garbage in—garbage out. For integration to provide any business value at all, the information needs to be accurate, and correctly applied in different applications. The long-term value of the data to the enterprise depends on ensuring the integrity of systems information. This requires both semantic and syntactic validation. Semantic validation ensures the information makes sense. Syntactic validation ensures that data is correctly formatted. Data integrity requires both.

A standard metadata model includes information to enable syntactic validation, and enables automation of translation, transformation, and delivery of data to the target systems in the native format. However, it does not include metadata that defines the semantic meaning, including the context, relationships, and dependencies. Entity-Relationship (E-R) diagrams are often used for this purpose. However, E-R diagrams are used in the discovery and design phase. The integrity rules revealed by the E-R diagram need to be added as code in the application or triggers and stored procedures in the database. The semantic meaning has not traditionally been part of the metadata, and this limitation has had a number of implications, especially when data transactions cross applications. There are no built-in cross-application integrity rules. That means that for transaction level integration, additional processing rules will need to be custom coded. This significantly slows the implementation of Web commerce solutions.

Because of the great importance and value in maintaining and communicating the semantic meaning of data in a portable and reusable manner, there are a number of efforts underway to define a semantic metadata model. While many of these efforts are still in the early stages, it is important to know they exist, if only to understand that the metadata created to aggregate data for data and application integration is only the beginning of the Information Integration Architecture. Over time, organizations will need to create richly layered metadata architectures to fully express and protect the meaning and value of business information.

8.3 Metadata Architecture

There are different types of metadata for describing different aspects of the system. Most system developers are familiar with metadata that describes the information in the system. However, this type of metadata does not define transaction and processing rules. These must be defined in the application itself. But in enterprise integration solutions, transactions often cross multiple systems. It would be better to capture the integrity requirements in the metadata so it is available to all systems, rather than coding it in each system. Then, when distributed transaction rules are changed, they only need to be changed in the enterprise metadata, rather then each system. Business agility requires different types of metadata to fully represent the business meaning of data, transactions, and system interactions.

A useful framework for understanding the different possible layers of metadata is the Object Management Group (OMG) Four Layer Metadata Architecture. The Metadata Architecture definition is part of the OMG Model Driven Architecture (MDA), a framework for designing systems that can run on any platform with native look and feel, without any recoding or recompiling. Each layer of the Metadata Architecture provides a higher level of functionality. (For more information, see OMG Meta Object Facility (MOF) Specification, *http://www.omg.org/cwm/.*)

The bottom layer, Layer 0, is the actual information and data values. Level 1 is the metadata layer that is comprised of information describing this data. A data integration model supports the aggregation of data from disparate back-end systems and defines the attributes of the data to enable automatic validation and cleansing. The metadata about each business entity is aggregated into a metadata model, which is about a system and the information in the system. The OMG examples of metadata models include Unified Modeling Language (UML) models and interface definition language (IDL) interfaces.

Level 2, the metamodel layer, is where semantic meaning is added. The metamodel is an abstract language that defines both the structure and semantics of the metadata. Adding semantics to the model means that integrity and business rules do not need to be coded in proprietary triggers and stored procedures, or in application code. At the metadata level, the business rules and meaning of the data are contained in the metadata and are available to all systems. The OMG lists UML metamodels and IDL metamodels as examples.

Level 3 is the meta-metamodel, an abstract language for defining different kinds of metadata. This is equivalent to the metadata repository. The OMG example is the Meta Object Facility (MOF). MOF defines an abstract language and framework for specifying, constructing, and managing technology neutral metamodels, and a framework for implementing metadata repositories.

Each layer in the OMG metadata architecture increases the level of reuse and efficiency, and makes integration an easier task. While the OMG metadata framework is part of the MOF Specification, it is also useful for understanding the metadata standards being developed by other standards bodies.

As the metadata architecture becomes more complete, the cost, time, and complexity of integrating systems will decrease. Metadata is the key to the future integration of automation and management.

8.4 Metadata Standards

Standards are extremely important for enabling metadata interoperability. However, there are so many of them it is difficult to understand how they relate to each other. Different metadata standards are being defined by standards organizations, including: the World Wide Web Consortium (W3C), leading the way for XML and Web-related standards; the Organization for the Advancement of Structured Information Standards (OASIS), an international consortium focused on e-business standards; the Object Management Group (OMG), focusing on design and development; and the Open Application Group (OAG), creating industry-focused metadata models. This section presents an overview of the standards each of these organizations is responsible for, and provides guidelines for which standards may be most important to your organization.

8.4.1 World Wide Web Consortium (W3C)

The W3C is responsible for a number of Web standards. Here we focus on evolving metadata standards for the Semantic Web. The Semantic Web ensures that Web information makes sense by providing a representation of data on the Web that includes the meaning. "The Semantic Web is an extension of the current Web in which information is given well-defined meaning, better enabling computers and people to work in cooperation" (Berners-Lee, Hendler, and Lassila 2001). Part of the Semantic Web is the notion of an **ontology**. An ontology defines a common set of terms to describe and represent a particular domain—a specific subject or knowledge area such as retail, manufacturing, or medicine. Ontologies include computer-usable definitions of business entities, relationships, and properties or attributes. They capture valuable business knowledge in a reusable and adaptable format, and are the framework for implementing the Semantic Web. Ontologies represent Level 2 metadata. They contain both the structure and semantics of the metadata. Ontologies are usually expressed in a logic-based language to provide detailed, consistent, and meaningful distinctions among the classes, properties, and relations. The languages being specified by the W3C are RDF and OWL (see sidebar). Companies interested in advanced Web

W3C Languages for Defining Ontologies: RDF and Owl

The Resource Description Framework (RDF) provides a lightweight ontology system to support the exchange of knowledge on the Web. It's a foundation for processing metadata. RDF enables applications to exchange information on the Web and automatically process it through machine-understandable information. RDF has many uses, including: resource discovery to provide better search engine capabilities; describing the content and relationships for a Web site, page, or digital library; enabling knowledge acquisition through intelligent software agents; describing intellectual property rights as well as privacy policies of Web sites. RDF is an example of Level 2 metadata. It provides semantic meaning.

While RDF is good for describing Web information, the Web Ontology Language (OWL) provides greater machine interpretability of Web content than that supported by XML, RDF, and RDF Schema (RDF-S) by providing additional vocabulary along with a formal semantics. It is an ontology language that can formally describe the meaning of terminology. OWL represents Level 3 metadata. It is a language for describing metadata.

development and functionality will want to look more closely into ontologies and the metadata standards being proposed by the W3C.

8.4.2 The Organization for the Advancement of Structured Information Standards (OASIS)

OASIS is a not-for-profit, worldwide consortium focused on e-business standards for "security, Web services, XML conformance, business transactions, electronic publishing, topic maps, and interoperability within and between marketplaces" *(http://www.oasis-open.org)*. OASIS has more than 600 corporate and individual members in 100 countries around the world. For that reason, ebXML is an important B2B metadata standard. OASIS and the United Nations jointly sponsor ebXML. Companies engaging in global e-commerce will want to pay attention to the ebXML standard.

OASIS (The Organization for the Advancement of Structured Information Standards) ebXML

Electronic Business Extensible Markup Language (ebXML) is an international initiative to research and identify the technical basis upon which the global implementation of XML can be standardized. The goal is to provide an XML-based open technical framework to enable XML to be used in a consistent and uniform manner for the exchange of electronic business data in application-to-application, application-to-human, and human-to-application environments. The ultimate goal of ebXML is to create a single global electronic market.

ebXML specifications include a Collaborative Partner Profile Agreement, a Message Service Specification, a Registry Information Model (RIM), and a Registry Services Specification. RIM provides Level 3 metadata for the implementation of ebXML registries. It provides implementers with information on the type of metadata that is stored in the registry as well as the relationships among metadata classes.

8.4.3 Object Management Group (OMG)

The OMG Metadata Architecture described above is part of the Model Driven Architecture (MDA) initiative. The goal of MDA is to enable complete technology independence from systems design and implementation. An application developed using MDA could be deployed on multiple platforms without changing the code. The OMG is also responsible for the UML standard, which is widely used for application development. The two OMG metadata standards to watch are XMI, which will enable portability of UML design models, and the Common Warehouse MetaModel (CWM). (See sidebar.) Companies that have adopted UML as a development standard will be interested in XMI and CWM.

8.4.4 Open Applications Group (OAG)

The OAG is a not-for-profit industry consortium focused on promoting interoperability among business applications and creating business language standards to support this goal. According to the website (http://www.openapplications.org),

OMG (Object Management Group) XMI and CWM

XMI defines an XML-based interchange format for UML and models through standardized XML document formats and DTDs. In so doing, it also defines a mapping from UML to XML. This is important for enabling the portability of design models as well as the interchange of information across models. There is a specification that will extend XMI to support W3C-standard XML schema in addition to the already-supported MOF metamodel.

The CWM standardizes a metamodel that enables data mining across databases. It forms the MDA mapping to database schemas.

it is the largest publisher of XML-based content for business software interoperability in the world. It has published numerous industry schemas and the OAGIS, which contains a standards-based canonical business language. (see sidebar). The OAG will be of importance to companies in industries heavily involved in implementing industry-specific B2B transactions through the OAGIS framework.

Open Applictions Group Integration Specification (OAGIS), and Business Object Documents (BODS)

The focus of OAGIS is enabling the communication of the information required to do business electronically. Using Web services standards, it provides a canonical message architecture that vertical industries can use to "plug-in" their industry specific information, terminology, content, and constraints. One of the goals is to preserve the terminology for each vertical industry to leverage existing investments in industry standards.

BODs are horizontally defined messages that are common within most industries. Examples include purchase orders, invoices, and shipments, to name a few. BODs can be extended by industry vertical groups to provide additional fields, compounds, components, nouns, constraints, and context. In the OMG Four-Layer Architecture, BODs represent Level 1 metadata. However, there is a Semantic Integration working group in the OAG, seeking to enhance the meaning and usability of the information model.

Metadata management is becoming essential for business agility and enabling rapid integration and systems interoperability. Standards-based solutions help maximize reuse and decrease operational costs. While most companies will begin by focusing on the first two layers of the metadata architecture, it is important to understand the evolving standards in other areas. These efforts will eventually transform the way we build and implement applications, enabling rapid integration and automation. The creation of metadata models represents both a considerable investment and a valuable corporate asset. Ultimately, good metadata will decrease implementation time and cost, increase reuse, and maximize ROI for integration investments.

8.5 Information Integration Patterns

There are two types of information integration: aggregation and publishing. Information aggregation is bringing together information for multiple sources into a single metadata model that provides a single view of the data across systems. A good example of a need for aggregation is the creation of a call-center application that provides a unified view of the relationship with a customer rather than requiring the operators to use a variety of systems and interfaces coupled with their own innate ability to aggregate the information together to perform the same task.

Information publishing is pushing information into multiple back-end systems. There are multiple different models for publishing including one-to-one publishing, one-to-many publishing. and multiple-step publishing. One-to-one publishing is the most simplistic. Allowing a customer to change his or her address online and updating a system with this information is a common example. One-to-many publishing may require transactional support across systems if there are dependencies that must be maintained. However there are instances where there is no dependency and failure to publish with one node does not impact the other nodes. For example, if a customer has several different relationships with a business, such as having a checking account and loan through a bank, it is reasonable to assume that each system is updated with the address information. This may not require transactional integrity. However, if money were transferred from a checking account to pay off a loan then transactional integrity would be required. The final model is a multiple-step publishing where the information is published to nodes in a series of steps. Each step occurs only after a successful conclusion to a prior step. For example, updating an address followed by sending a written confirmation could be done as two-step publishing.

8.6 Enterprise Information Integration Technology

Enterprise information integration (EII) technology is one of the fastest growing sectors in the integration market. EII technology provides a faster and easier way to consolidate information from multiple sources into a single interface, as if all the information came from a single database. EII creates an aggregated and federated information architecture.

Customer and self-service solutions can be made much more user friendly from a single view of customers, patients, or other business entities. The consolidated metadata enables real-time feeds to management dashboards and analytical tools. It provides a virtual data warehouse for real-time reporting. EII allows all back-end information to be seen as if it came from one unified database. Unified access to data in disparate databases simplifies many applications, providing faster, cheaper integration for a number of different business solutions.

EII is focused on Levels 0 and 1 of the OMG Four Layer Metadata Architecture. At this level, semantic meaning needs to be represented and preserved through integrity rules. Integrity rules would need to include cross-application relationships. Level 1 metadata is appropriate for information-driven integration, but less so for transaction-driven integration.

EII solutions typically contain a metadata repository—a data aggregation service that can pull data from multiple back-end systems and aggregate it according to the common metadata model, querying disparate data as if it came from a single source—and management capabilities including data lineage and impact analysis. Data lineage provides the ability to trace back the data values to the source systems they came from. This is very helpful for maintaining data quality across systems. Impact analysis helps determine how downstream systems are affected by any changes. This is very helpful for optimizing systems and performing systems maintenance. The metadata repository and management capabilities of EII are important for all types of integrated data management. Therefore, we expect EII to become an important part of the integrated architecture.

8.7 Information Integration Architecture Specification

A full copy of the specification is in Appendix F.

8.7.1 Introduction

This document is a guide to creating the information integration architecture specification for information-driven business solutions.

8.7.2 Scope

The scope of the Information Architecture Specification can be enterprise-wide or limited to a single integration project. The document should define the business information needs, the relevant metadata, and the underlying integration architecture. The scope should describe the breath of business information covered as well as the systems and data sources involved in the process.

8.7.3 Key Participants

This section identifies all stakeholders in the business information being integrated, including business managers who control all or part of the information, system designers and architect(s), and the development team who will execute the implementation. Any other participants or stakeholders should also be identified, including their roles.

8.7.4 Mapping Requirements to Information Integration Design Patterns

This section is used to identify and map all of the requirements to the design patterns for information integration (see Figure 8-1, page 152). The two basic design patterns are information aggregation and publishing. To identify the business information requirements that need to be defined as part of this specification, start with the Statement of Purpose and the scope of responsibilities defined in the Business Strategies and Initiatives Specification. Then use the design patterns to identify the best approach for implementation.

Examples of requirements that are suited for information integration include creation of management dashboards, single views of customers or other business resources, propagation of information to reduce the retyping of information into systems, virtual-data warehouse, real-time feeding of analytical tools, or automating the use of Microsoft Office documents (or other desktop tools). These types of requirements focus on the real-time aggregation of sources where information is collected and combined together to feed the creation of new bundles of information or the ability to publish a document into several information sources to provide a single update across data sources.

8.7.5 Data Flow Diagram

The Data Flow Diagram (Figure 8-2, page 153) depicts the flow of information. Usually the flow of information is depicted within a single system between processes and one or more data stores, with external systems depicted outside the

Application Name	Business Owner	Description of Information Application	Aggregation or Publishing	Data Sources Involved	Outcome of the Flow of Information
Management dashboard	Head of sales	Daily sales order volumes on a world-wide basis	Aggregation	Order entry systems across the world	Graphical display of sales orders daily, weekly, monthly, and quarterly
Call center customer support system	Head of customer support	Single view of a relationship of a customer for the call center	Aggregation	All systems containing customer information	Single screen unifying all customer information
Online customer change of address	CIO	Update all addresses for a customer self service change of address	Publishing	All systems containing customer addresses	Update to all systems with customer address
<Application name>	<Owner>	<Description>	<Information pattern>	<Source>	<Outcome>

Figure 8-1 Information Integration Patterns Table

circle. In integration, we are primarily interested in the flow of information between systems, so essentially all systems are external. Therefore, we have adapted the traditional data-flow diagram for the purpose of identifying systems sharing a type of information. External systems (depicted as shaded boxes) are systems outside of the enterprise.

The purpose of creating the data flow diagram is to determine which systems are involved in the data flow in order to later determine the integrity rules across systems (which is done in the Relationship Model shown in Figure 8-4).

8.7.6 Metadata Model

Effective metadata management is critical to information-driven architecture. Each application will require a metadata model that combines the new model for

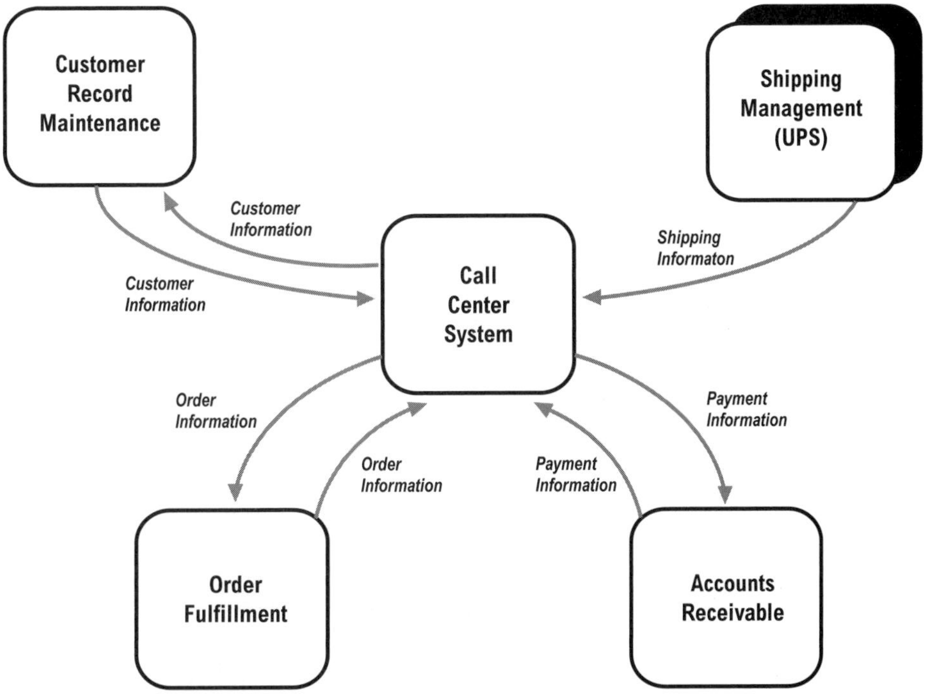

Figure 8-2 Data Flow Diagram Across Systems

the application with the existing models of each of the data sources that is used. The Metadata Model is used to define access and transformation rules. It establishes data lineage and enables impact analysis.

The model can also be used as a strategic asset, lowering the cost of operational management and new implementations. It helps ensure data quality by managing data access and integrity. It helps maximize the investment in systems knowledge.

Metadata for existing data sources must be captured for each element. The model shown in Figure 8-3 (page 154) can be used as a starting point. Many of the enterprise information integration tools currently on the market include metadata repositories that provide their own metadata models. Additionally, if you are using a standards-based approach or an industry-specific ontology model, that will also have its own metadata. Figure 8-3 defines the types of metadata you might consider as part of the overall information-integration architecture.

Basic metadata	Data element name	<Source system data name>
	Data source	<Source>
	Description	<Description>
	Format and data type	<Source system format and type>
	Canonical name	<Enterprise canonical name>
	Canonical format	<XML or other—name format>
	Transformation rules	<From source to canonical format>
	Interface	<Web service, adapter, API, SQL>
Semantic metadata	Integrity rules	<Relationships across applications>
Added security	Security parameters	<Access Control Lists, Directory>
Added management	Platform	<Hardware platform>
	OS	<Operating system and version>
	DBMS	<Database>
	Application platform	<Application server, other>
	Owner of the system	<Company, department, manager>
	Location of the system	<Directory>
	Service information	<Web services directory>
	Message schema information	<Message repository>
	Communication protocol	<SOAP, HTTP, TCP/IP, VAN>
	Access mechanism	<Enterprise message bus, message broker, JMS call, EDI VAN>

Figure 8-3 Integration Metadata Model

8.7.7 Relationship Model

The Relationship Model defines the integrity rules across data objects and systems. If implementing a Level 1 metadata model, the integrity rules will need to be explicitly defined in routing logic or database triggers and procedures. Level 2 metadata models contain semantic meaning within the model itself.

Cannonical name	<Cannonical name>
Source system/service data element name	<Data element name>
Source system/service	<System/service name>
Business rules	<Aggregation and parsing rules>
Target system or service data element name	<Target data element name>
Target system or service	<Service or system name>
Integrity rules	<Rollback and compensation rules>
Security requirements	<Encryption, nonrepudiation, and access rules>

Figure 8-4 Relationship Model

The Relationship Model defines dependencies and rules for cascading deletes, roll backs, and compensating transactions; defines data lineage; and enables impact analysis. Figure 8-4 describes the type of information required. As previously stated, evolving metadata standards will more fully describe these relationships.

8.7.8 Information Design Reviews

Information design reviews are critical to the overall success and agility of the system. The design reviews should include all relevant stakeholders, defined above in the Key Participants section (8.7.3). All parts of the model need to be reviewed and verified. Participants need to verify the portions of the information they are responsible for, including the definition of all elements, how they are created and updated, the formats, and access mechanisms. The business users need to provide the definitions for the information required in the new application. In addition, it will be critical for the stakeholders to ensure they deal with discrepancies on which data source contains the "gold standard" for the organization when there are conflicts or duplications. This is often the most difficult task that the group will face. The overall process should be reviewed for opportunities to improve consistency and quality of information across the organization.

Use the following guidelines for successful design reviews:

- Make sure all the stakeholders are present.
- Explain the process and ground rules before the design review.
- Criticize the design, not the person.
- Designers may only speak to clarify the design and provide background information. They should not "defend" the design.
- Identify "owners" of information.
- Identify systems of record for information.
- Define a process for data quality.

8.7.9 Conclusions and Commentary

This section should provide any final comments on the information, the design, or the usage of the system.

8.8 Best Practices in Information Design

- **Conduct design reviews.** A metadata model represents an aggregated definition of data from different systems in a canonical format. The only way to ensure the common definition is correct is to have the model verified by all the stakeholders—those who have knowledge of each of the systems, and those who need to utilize and integrate the data.
- **Create a metadata repository.** A metadata repository, based on standards, provides a platform for storing, accessing, and managing metadata, and provides access to information across the organization. It is the Rosetta stone to disparate enterprise data. The repository can grow over time, on a project-by-project basis. However, it needs to be actively managed to ensure integrity and data quality and maximize reuse.
- **Manage the repository in the competency center.** There are different types of integration, and different types of metadata. However, the work of researching, defining, and verifying the intent and meaning of data in systems, which forms the foundation for integration, needs to be managed and leveraged. It represents a considerable investment and a valuable and reusable resource for the organization. While different projects may work with different data or levels of metadata, the competency center can track and manage how the metadata is used across projects, how the different levels of metadata relate, and which standards are most appropriate.

- **Add semantic meaning to the metadata.** The more meaning the metadata contains, the less work the programmers need to do. Semantically rich metadata enables electronic transactions to be implemented across systems without needing to add additional application or database code to ensure the integrity of the data. It is the key to enabling e-commerce faster and cheaper than ever before.

8.9 Next Steps

Information and data are at the heart of all integration projects. Defining the information independent of technology or tools is a much better approach for long-term agility and reuse. It enables the work done on one project to be available for the next. Companies interested in long-term business agility will invest in all aspects of the enterprise integration architecture, including defining the process integration architectures (Chapter 9). Companies focused on pressing tactical needs, will define only what is absolutely necessary and move on to implementation (Part III). See Figure 8-5.

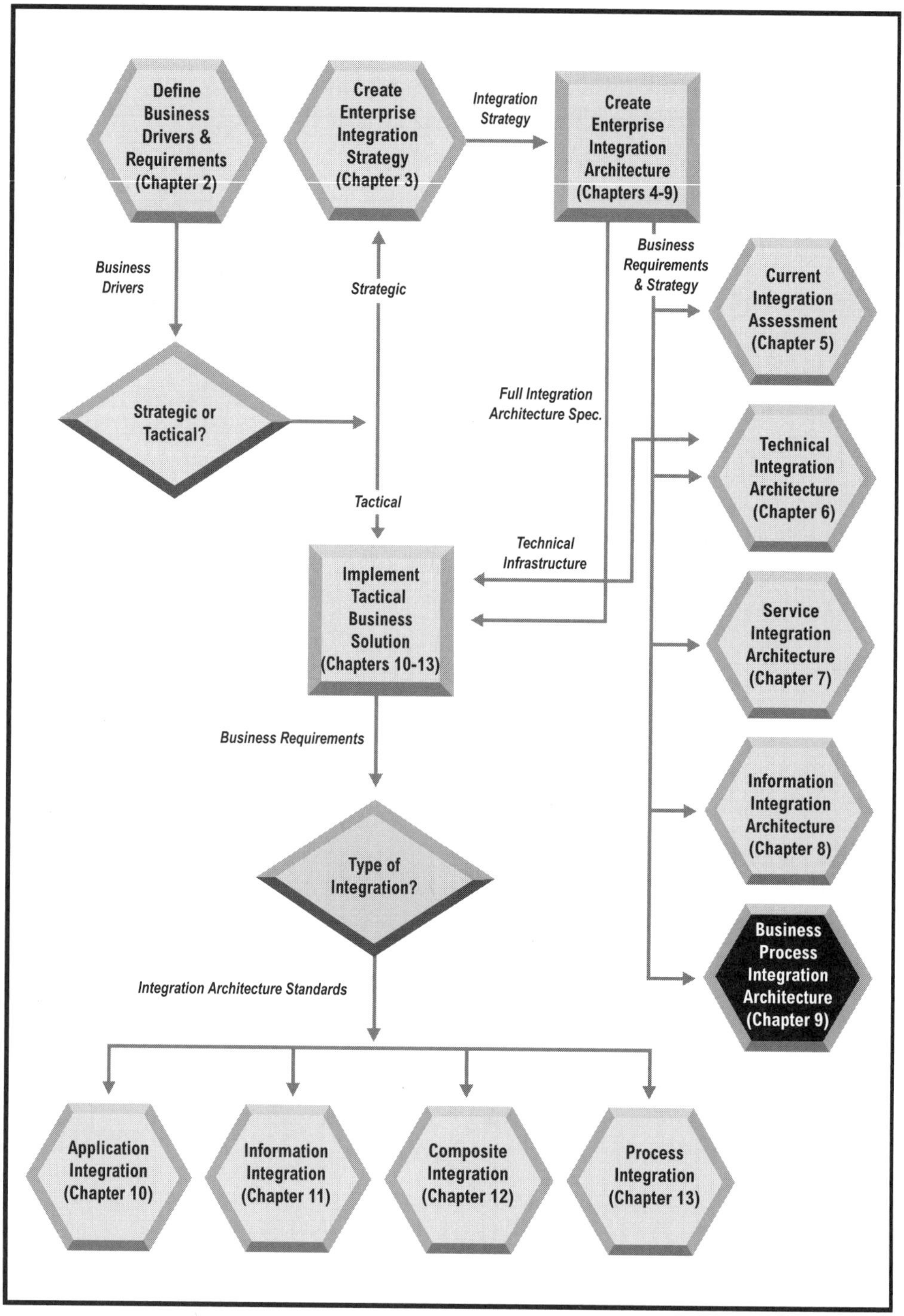

Figure 8-5 Integration Roadmap

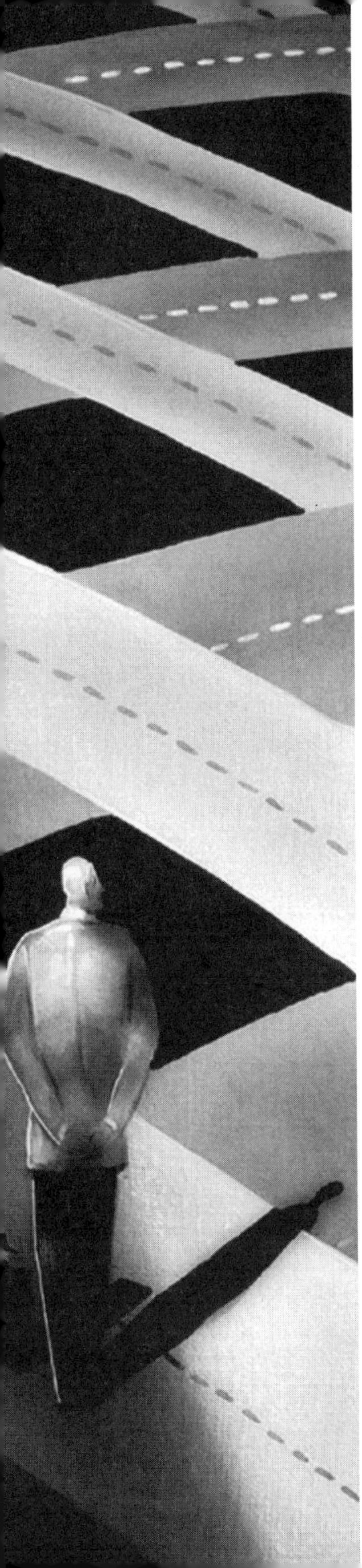

CHAPTER NINE

Process Integration Architecture

9.1 Executive Overview

The purpose of integration is almost always to support improving a business process to increase business efficiency. Process-level integration defines the interactions among systems through business workflow definitions. The instructions for the integration are defined at the business-process level rather than the technical-interface level. Although a technical integration infrastructure is still a necessity to implement process integration, the processes themselves are technology independent. This enables change to be made quickly and easily, increasing business agility.

The role of the Process Integration Architecture is to create process models and definitions as managed entities that can be easily viewed and changed in response to changes in a business. The Process Integration Architecture defines end-to-end business processes, which are then automated across existing systems on disparate platforms.

The key benefit of the Business Integration Architecture is the business level view it provides of the end-to-end process. Process integration technology includes dashboards that enable business managers to track key performance indicators in near real time. Process simulation and analytics provide feedback to help companies optimize business processes, reduce cost, and achieve competitive advantage through better processes. Case Study 9.1 describes how General Electric has achieved significant business process improvement with amazing operational results (Lindorff 2002).

Case Study 9.1

Real Time Process Improvement at General Electric

General Electric is well known as an organization that has a maniacal focus on process improvement. This focus has moved beyond just management practices to the digitization of their business described by their CIO, Gary Reiner, as an "e-buy, e-make, and e-sell" strategy. GE, like other leading companies, is realizing that the future of process improvement is closely associated with the ability to harness their information and automate their processes.

An example of how GE has implemented process improvement is the use of digital dashboards that allow mission-critical operations such as sales, daily order rates, and inventory levels to be monitored in near real time. With this data in hand, automated notifications and status changes can be noted, allowing management and staff to react quicker to changes in their environment. A digital dashboard is critical to any process-improvement activity, because you cannot manage what you do not measure. Without measuring in real time you cannot react in real time. Every process-improvement program should include the use of digital dashboards as a best practice.

General Electric has always been a pioneer in the area of process improvement. By adopting the real-time enterprise philosophy coined by the Gartner Group, they have seen impacts both enterprise wide and at the business unit level. Some examples are:

- 5% improvement in Power Systems' inventory turns
- 10% improvement in Power Systems' receivable turnover
- $680 million cut from purchasing costs through online auctions
- $3 million saved in Plastics Division on payroll
- Twice as many customers handled per sales person

Process automation is one of the key business functions that organizations must master as a core competency to be able to effectively compete. As in the past, GE will be a leader blazing a trail that others must follow.

The Process Integration Architecture also improves alignment between IT and business. It starts with business process models that business people can understand and review. These models depict the shared understanding between the business and IT staff of the end-to-end business process. The process can then be automated directly from the model. This significantly reduces the chance of misinterpreting the business requirement or getting the process wrong. As the process can span multiple business units and managers, there may not be one manager who owns or even understands the complete end-to-end process. The process models represent a shared understanding of how business is conducted across the enterprise, and should be managed as valuable assets.

This chapter appears last in the Enterprise Integration Architecture section because most companies implement it last (if at all). Companies have not been historically strong on process management and improvement—although those that focus on process tend to be the market leaders in their industry. The next section defines why it is so important for companies to pay attention to process.

Companies that do implement a process integration architecture and infrastructure will start their integration projects by modeling the business process and drill down from there, defining which applications, services, and information is required to complete the process. This tends to be a faster and more efficient approach than a bottom-up integration connectivity approach, and is far more responsive to change.

9.2 Why Process Is Important to Business

The benefits of business process management are not a new revelation. It has been known for over half of this century that optimizing business processes yields measurable results. In the 1950s Dr. W. Edward Deming, a mathematician and statistician, proved that improvements in managing business processes lead to improvements in overall business and significant competitive advantage. As a result of Dr. Deming's work, Japanese manufacturing companies were able to produce higher quality products at a lower cost and gain competitive advantage. For his efforts, in May 1960, the Emperor of Japan decorated him with the Second Order Medal of the Sacred Treasure and Japanese manufacturers created the annual Deming Prize in his honor.

Deming taught that variation is created at every step in a production process, and variations have the potential to cause defects. Therefore, the causes of variation need to be identified and reduced and companies need to practice continuous product and process improvement to improve quality and productivity, and decrease costs. Deming proposed a continuous feedback and measurement cycle to reduce defects and improve product quality, usually referred to as the Plan-Do-Check-Act cycle.

- **PLAN.** Design or revise business process components to improve results
- **DO.** Implement the plan and measure its performance
- **CHECK.** Assess the measurements and report the results to decision makers
- **ACT.** Decide on changes needed to improve the process

The Plan-Do-Check-Act cycle is a continuous cycle. To achieve measurable results and business benefit, companies must practice continuous process improvement. Wal-Mart, the world's largest company, is able to require its suppliers to support its process improvement in a manner remarkably similar to the Deming cycle. Case Study 9.2 details the Levi Strauss & Co. experience (Girard 2003).

Dr. Deming's work gave rise to a number of initiatives to manage and measure the efficiency and effectiveness of business, including Total Quality Management (TQM), balanced scorecard, Six Sigma, and ISO 9001. These initiatives can help companies understand how to define key performance indicators to measure their business (see sidebar—How to Measure Success, page 164). These metrics can then be used on a management dashboard.

Despite half a century of research and proven success, few companies have optimized their business processes. In the early 1990s, based on Dr. Michael Hammer's best-selling book *Reengineering the Corporation,* corporations began systematic efforts to improve their business processes. Unfortunately, those initiatives were often less than successful. A key inhibitor to the success of business process reengineering (BPR) was a lack of technology to support the focus on radical reengineering of business processes. The logic for business processes was either buried in the code for each application or was manually performed, requiring significant custom coding and integration efforts to achieve results. This led to great organizational upheaval. In contrast, emerging process integration technology enables companies to leverage existing IT investments and automate new processes that use them.

Process integration supports the Plan-Do-Check-Act cycle to enable process optimization. The business process integration tools provide process modeling, to "Plan" the process, automation and integration to implement or "Do" the process, monitoring tools and dashboards to "Check" processes, and simulation and analytical tools to help companies "Act" to improve processes.

Case Study 9.2
Improving the Supply Chain at Levi Strauss & Co.

Levi Strauss & Co. is one of the most recognizable brand names and popular products in the world. However, like all companies, they must be constantly changing with the needs of market. An important part of their strategy going forward was to distribute their products through Wal-Mart. The implications of this decision were profound to the IT organization. According to Bain Consulting, a key attribute to successfully doing business with Wal-Mart is "the ability to use technology and better business practices to control costs and reduce prices." Furthermore, Wal-Mart sets the bar very high in terms of their requirements for the supply-chain support necessary from their vendors. These facts required a transformation of the supply-chains process and supporting technology in order to execute Levi Strauss & Co.'s strategy to do business with Wal-Mart.

Levi Strauss & Co. embarked on an initiative to improve its supply chain, including efforts aimed at tracking product as it moved through the supply chain. This allowed greater ability to forecast and improved the ability to replenish as well as manage inventory. Before the changes, product was delivered at a low mark of 65%; after the changes, this improved to 95%. One key aspect of the system improvements was the addition of dashboards as the mechanism to monitor and react to the improvements in the supply chain.

Dashboards are a view into a diversity of information that represents the state of a set of processes that must be integrated together. Good process integration incorporates the concept of dashboards into the design to allow the process to be monitored and acted upon by the appropriate personnel.

The supply chain at Levi Strauss & Co. is one area of focus for process improvement that every manufacturing company will need to address. Central to these initiatives is the ability to unlock the information across the system, synthesize and communicate it, and allow actions to be taken either by people or by systems.

How to Measure Success

Each of the process management and measurement initiatives below defines metrics for measuring the efficiency, effectiveness, and quality of business processes. There are no clear guidelines for choosing a particular method. It is more a matter of whether the origins and goals of the method resonate with the organization, or what others in your industry are using, or even what your BPM tool supports.

Total Quality Management (TQM). Directly inspired by Dr. Deming's ideas, TQM was initiated by the US Department of Defense in 1987, and provided a new focus on total ownership cost in acquisitions. TQM includes eight key elements: ethics, integrity, trust, training, teamwork, leadership, recognition, and communication.

Baldrige Award. The civilian equivalent of TQM, this award is a measurement of excellence and is highly prestigious for a company to win, requiring significant investment in time, money, and commitment. Seven categories are evaluated: leadership; strategic planning; customer and market focus; measurement, analysis, and knowledge management; human resource focus; process management; and business results.

Balanced Scorecard. Balanced scorecard defines what to measure beyond traditional financial numbers. It is an approach to aligning strategy with action, and measures the effectiveness of strategies. Categories of measurement include: process redesign and improvement, work group productivity, management support, and competitive advantage. Some business process management (BPM) tools provide balanced scorecard dashboards.

Six Sigma. The objective of this methodology rooted in mathematics and statistics is to reduce process output variation to allow no more than 3.4 defects per million. The method includes sub-methodologies for improving existing processes and creating new processes. Six Sigma can be and is often used in combination with balanced scorecard.

ISO 9001. ISO is a worldwide federation of national standards bodies from more than 140 countries. ISO 9001 is a certification process to

How to Measure Success *(cont.)*

measure excellence; it includes a process model based on the Plan-Do-Check-Act cycle. ISO 9001 criteria includes the following:

- Management responsibility
- Design control
- Document and data control
- Control of customer supplied product
- Process control
- Internal quality audits
- Inspection and test status
- Product identification and traceability
- Control of nonconforming product
- Corrective and preventative action
- Quality system
- Contract review
- Purchasing
- Control of test equipment
- Handling, storage, delivery, etc.
- Servicing
- Control of quality records
- Training
- Inspection and testing
- Statistical techniques

9.3 Understanding Process Integration Technology

Just as there are many Eskimo words for snow, there are multiple terms that describe different types of process-based tools. Each of these is best suited to a particular type of process solution. This section discusses the different types of process-integration technologies, including Business Process Management (BPM), Business Process Integration (BPI), Business Process Automation (BPA), Workflow Automation (WA), Business Activity Monitoring (BAM), and Web Service Orchestration (WSO).

9.3.1 Business Process Management (BPM)

We view BPM as the broadest implementation of process management functionality. It includes support for all aspects of designing, implementing, monitoring, and managing both automated and manual business processes. This includes process modeling, process automation and integration, workflow integration (for manual processes), real-time monitoring and alerts, operational and business dashboards, analytics including key performance indicators, and process simulation for enabling process optimization.

BPM solutions are recommended for companies looking to implement business dashboards, practice proactive process management, and work towards

Case Study 9.3
Improving Margins Through Process Improvement at General Motors Corporation

General Motors Corporation's IT department has demonstrated that process integration can bring substantial business value to an organization. The CIO, Ralph Szygenda, enhanced a variety of core processes in the past few years with significant results in several areas.

Supply chain and logistics processes are core to many enterprises and are a good place to look for opportunities in process integration. At GM they are trying to create a virtual factory by tying together engineering, procurement, and manufacturing processes to cut the time it takes to assemble an automobile. By focusing on this at GM, the results have been staggering; the average time to assemble a car was cut down from 32 hours in 1998 to 26 hours today. In an operation the size of GM, this converts to a savings of $1 billion.

However, at any large organization the opportunities for process improvement are abundant. GM has added online capabilities for dealers that allow them to submit customer-financing applications. These applications are forwarded to the General Motors Acceptance Corp, or GMAC, for processing. A small process improvement like this was able to save $500,000 for GMAC.

Process improvements are core to the CIO's strategy at GM, with a focus on making rapid, incremental improvements that are delivered in short time frames. This best practice can be applied to any size organization.

process optimization. Alternatively, companies looking for compliance or industry solutions may find the solutions are implemented in (and come with) BPM technology. The company then has the infrastructure necessary for continuous process improvement. General Motors Corporation has mastered the art of BPM with results that are nothing less than incredible (Bacheldor 2003). Case Study 9.3 describes its results.

9.3.2 Business Process Integration (BPI)

BPI refers to process-level integration, as opposed to message-level or point-to-point integration. BPI includes the ability to design and model the process, integrate it with the underlying applications, and monitor the process on an end-to-end basis. The monitoring and management capabilities, however, tend to be on the operational level, not the business management level. BPI does not provide analytics and simulation. In other words, it provides process integration without process management.

BPI is appropriate when your management has little interest in process management and improvement and just wants to get the job done as quickly as possible, but the process is changeable, differs by location or business unit, or the underlying applications are changing. The major benefit of a process abstraction layer provided by BPI is that it adds agility for change.

9.3.3 Business Process Automation (BPA)

BPA refers to automating business processes. These tools tend to be transaction oriented and do not necessarily support long-lived transactions or manual processes. BPA tools generally include process modeling, application integration, and processing rules, and may include a development tool for new development, process monitoring, and operational-level management. Companies looking to automate transaction-based processes that do not involve humans and complete in seconds or nano-seconds rather than hours, days or weeks, should consider a BPA tool.

9.3.4 Workflow Automation

Workflow automation focuses on reducing the lag time in manual business processes. It includes a workflow engine that controls the flow of work across workers and departments according to a set of business rules. Managers can assign work to different types of workers. The workflow engine provides load balancing across all workers, accounting for backlogs, vacations, etc. Therefore, work can be automatically and efficiently assigned. Workflow tools provide work portals where employees can see all assignments and report when they're done, to trigger the next part of the processes.

Most business processes include some manual steps. Therefore, most BPM vendors include some support for workflow, but the extent of workflow features differs widely. If your processes have just a few manual steps, such as exceptions and approvals, then minimal workflow features will be sufficient. However if your processes have a significant manual component, then fully investigate the workflow capabilities of any tool you choose, including robust work management features.

9.3.5 Business Activity Monitoring (BAM)

BAM is a term coined by Gartner Group and currently in the cycle Gartner refers to as market push or the start of media infatuation. However, it is more accurately at the stage of vendor infatuation, with each vendor rushing to promote its BAM capability, because Gartner asserted that by 2004 BAM would be one of the four top initiatives driving IT investment, affecting every industry. Although monitoring and analytics are an essential part of BPM, Gartner defined additional BAM capabilities for combining real-time alerts with business intelligence, trend analysis, and data mining. This is the marriage between business integration and business intelligence.

The widespread industry acceptance of BAM is due in part to vendors eagerly looking to define themselves with the next big thing. However, although they all declare they have BAM capabilities, they're at different levels of BAM. Some provide monitoring dashboards that provide notifications, then a person needs to go and do something to react to the alert. The system does not guide the reaction—it only provides the alert. The next stage of BAM integrates business intelligence with near real-time analytics, so when the manager is alerted, he or she also has the information to make a better decision about what to do next to respond to the alert. The next stage of BAM uses business rules based on analytical results and automatically takes action instead of just alerting a person to take action.

This wide variance of capability means there are many types of BAM vendors. The BPM vendors all offer BAM solutions, the EAI vendors have added BAM capabilities or just relabeled what they already had as BAM. There are business intelligence vendors, system management vendors, and pure-play BAM vendors. The BAM market is still in the very early stages.

9.3.6 Web Service Orchestration (WSO)

WSO provides process-level development and coordination among Web services. WSO is used to define and implement the flow of control between the service components of a composite application. Web services can reside on multiple platforms and technologies. They can be components in an application server or legacy applications on a mainframe, and both can participate in a single composite application. The WSO tool includes process modeling, a process engine, and operational-level monitoring and management. Many application server vendors are providing basic WSO tools to enable composite application assembly of application server applications.

WSO is a good fit for composite applications consisting of all Web services. However, if the composite application requires complex integration with multiple platforms and technologies and end-to-end real time process monitoring and management, a BPM solution might be a better fit.

The process integration market is expanding, and buyers will find solutions being offered from a variety of different vendors, including the integration vendors, application-server vendors, and pure-play BPM vendors, as well as workflow and document management vendors, rules engine vendors, and soon, business intelligence vendors. Moreover, companies looking for compliance and industry solutions will find that BPM vendors are offering them, and the technology may come into the enterprise through a packaged solution.

By providing end-to-end, real-time visibility into business processes these tools help companies increase operational efficiency and decrease costs. Because process integration provides a layer of business process abstraction that is physically separated from the applications and implementation technology, it enables rapid business change.

9.4 Process Standards

Although every process tool on the market offers some kind of modeling capability, most are proprietary tools. They may do a fine job modeling your process, but offer no portability or long-term protection of the models. A process model represents valuable corporate knowledge and a significant corporate investment. Portions of the end-to-end process may be known and managed by different people in different parts of the organization. The process model captures the knowledge from across the organization and enables the company to optimize at an enterprise level to maximize ROI. For this reason, process models should be managed over time as valuable corporate assets.

Process modeling standards help companies protect their process investment by enabling portability across tools. This prevents technology lock-in. A standard process execution notation that can be exported and imported by all tools effectively solves the most important problem of technology lock-in. The process modeling standards companies will want to consider include BPEL, UML, and IDEF.

9.4.1 Business Process Execution Language for Web Services (BPEL4WS)

Often known as BPEL, Business Process Execution Language for Web Services is the emerging leader for standard process representation. BPEL is an amalgamation of XLANG from Microsoft and WSFL from IBM, and supersedes both approaches. Microsoft, IBM, and BEA, along with others, joined together to submit the BPEL specification to the international standards body OASIS.

BPEL is a standard execution language, not a standard notation. This means that tools will implement their own styles of models and produce BPEL code from the models. A number of vendors of existing modeling tools have announced support for BPEL. The BPEL standard enables portability of models among tools. Although BPEL is becoming an important process-modeling standard to pay attention to, there are also some others companies may want to consider.

9.4.2 Unified Modeling Language (UML)

The Object Management Group's (OMG) UML is also a relevant process modeling standard, especially for companies focused on new development, and who already use UML. Furthermore, the OMG's Model Driven Architecture (MDA) is a generic approach that can be applied to a wide variety of business problems, including process management. MDA creates a metamodel in UML that abstracts the definition from the implementation. Using this approach, the same model can be used to generate code for multiple platforms. MDA provides the framework to integrate different standards, languages, technologies, and platforms.

Companies implementing composite applications that include new development will be interested in a UML-based approach to process modeling. Developers are usually the ones to define the flow of control in the composite application, and UML has wide acceptance for systems development and among system developers.

9.4.3 Business Process Management Initiative (BPMI) and the Workflow Management Coalition (WfMC)

BPMI and WfMC are two other noteworthy process organizations. BPMI (*http://www.bpmi.org/index.esp*) was established to create specifications to "standardize the management of business processes that span multiple applications, corporate departments, and business partners, behind the firewall and over the Internet." BPMI is working on notation standards as well as process query language. WfMC is an organization focusing on the human component of business processes, including processes for assigning work, sharing documents, and managing task lists. Both BPMI and WfMC support and are contributing to the BPEL standard.

9.4.4 Integration Definition for Function Modeling (IDEF0)

IDEF is based on the Structured Analysis and Design Technique (SADT) introduced by Douglas T. Ross in the early 1970s. In 1981, the US Air Force Program for Integrated Computer-Aided Manufacturing (ICAM) standardized and adopted it as a Federal Information Processing Standard (FIPS), and made public a subset of SADT, called IDEF0. This standard is still in widespread use today, and is an extremely important modeling standard for organizations doing business with the federal government.

Companies should pay attention to the evolution of process standards to ensure the portability of their business models and maximize their process investment over time.

9.5 Process Integration Architecture Specification

See Appendix G for the complete Process Integration Architecture Specification.

9.5.1 Introduction

The Process Specification provides guidance for applying a process-driven approach to integration. This document is a guide to creating the process specification for the composite applications or process-driven business solutions.

9.5.2 Scope

The scope of a Process Specification is usually limited to a set of business processes associated with an integration project. The document should define the business processes and underlying applications to be integrated. We recommend not boiling the ocean. Start with a few business processes that will deliver measurable impact to the business.

9.5.3 Key Participants

This section identifies all stakeholders in the business process(es) being integrated, including business managers who control all or part of the process, system designers and architect(s), and the development team who will execute the implementation. Because the end-to-end process may cross multiple business domains, it may be difficult initially to define all business stakeholders. The process design, review, and verification may, therefore, be an iterative process, with new stakeholders and roles identified along the way.

9.5.4 Business Process Descriptions

This section describes the business processes that have been identified in the requirements. To identify the business processes that need to be defined as part of this specification, start with the Statement of Purpose and the scope of responsibilities defined in the Business Strategies and Initiatives Specification. (Figure 9-1). An alternative way to identify business processes is a bottom up approach (see the process flow models and sequence diagram, section 9.5.5).

Business Initiative

- Online ordering

Business Drivers

- Reduce the order delivery time
- Increase accuracy and decrease time of information provided to other systems and decision makers

Business Strategy

- Automate business processes to improve efficiency

Functional Scope

- Automate the online order process by integrating transactions with back-end systems
- Automate flow of orders to third party suppliers
- Provide real-time visibility and management of the end-to-end order process
- Provide online order tracking

Business Goals

- Decrease time between order and delivery
- Decrease error rates of transactions

Organizational Impact

- Will decrease headcount for order entry department
- Will change phone order process

Figure 9-1 Statement of Purpose

Description of Business Process	Business Process Owner	Kickoff Event	Services Involved in the Process	Outcome of the Business Process
<Description>	<Owner>	<Event>	<Service names>	<Outcome>
Online ordering	Jane Doe, North American Sales Department	Customer creates order form from Web site	Customer portal, sales order system, sales tax system, order fulfillment system, inventory system	Order is placed and customer is notified of order status

Figure 9-2 Business Process Description Table

The Process Description Table can be used to identify each process that will be modeled and implemented (Figure 9-2). A name and a business owner identify each business process. A description of the process is provided along with the event that kicks off the process, the business services that are part of the process and the outcome expected which ends the process. If no services have been defined, then define the functions to be performed as part of the process.

9.5.5 Process Flow Models

A process flow model is a combination of the event(s) that start the process, actors involved throughout the process, services provided by software components, the messages passed between and among services, and the business rules controlling the flow of the process. Each process flow model should have a description of each of these entities as well as a process diagram.

The best way to keep models up-to-date is to do it in software. Paper documentation requires changes to be made and distributed in print. It makes keeping the specification up-to-date with the real process far more difficult. It is easier, cheaper, faster, and better to manage models in software. Therefore, this part of the specification may actually have a reference to the process model stored in software. If your modeling tool provides browser-based access to models, then the URL would be part of the process-specification document. Copies of the model may be included in this specification to distribute printed documentation to be used in the verification process. However, it must be recognized that these models can quickly become out of date as the processes change. Therefore, it is important to include the date and version number of all printed process models.

The process model, including the diagram and all associated specifications, should include the following information:

- The kickoff event(s) of the process. There could be more than one starting point, depending on the purpose and the operation of the process. If a process contains more than one starting point, include all of them.
- All tasks/functions/services to be performed during the execution of the process.
- The order in which the tasks/functions/services should be accomplished, including any tasks that may be performed in parallel.
- All decision points, both those having to do with choosing a path through the process and those that determine whether or not the process should continue.
- The business rules that determine the path of the process.
- Any points at which the process path may split or merge.
- The messages input to and output from each task/function/service.
- The completion point of the process. As a process may have multiple starting points, it can also have multiple completion points.

In order to bridge the gap between IT and business and have a seamless handoff between process design and implementation it is important to hand off a business-process model to programmers in a manner they will recognize and use. As noted in section 9.4, there are a number of different modeling methods and systems of notation. The evolving process standards are likely to impact future adoption of a particular modeling method (see Figure 9-3). In the meantime, each tool either supports its own proprietary notation or it supports one of the more widely used methods, such as activity diagrams (usually modified) (Figure 9-4), data flow diagrams (DFD) (Figure 9-5), or IDEF (Figure 9-6). UML is relevant because it has become the most widely applied standard design notation for programmers. The choice of which type of modeling method to use will depend on which industry you're in as well as which tool you use.

Several vendors are now providing different perspectives for different roles in the process. Some are using Eclipse, an open source framework for tools integration, to enable different models for different design perspectives.

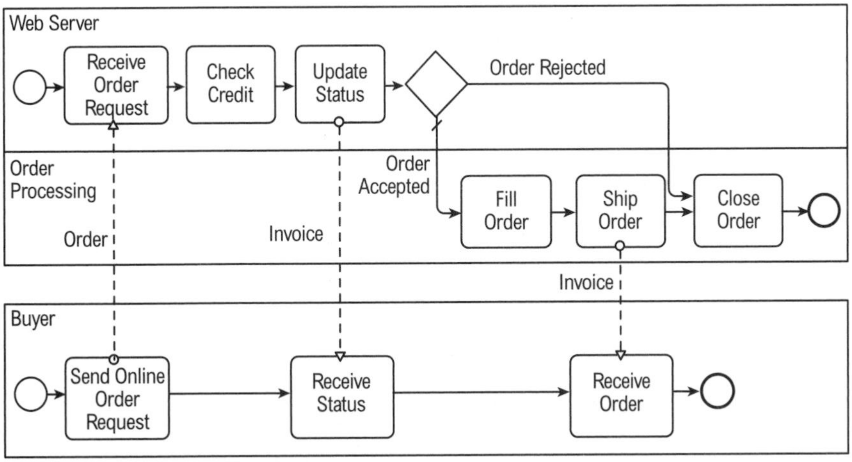

Figure 9-3 BPMI Process Diagram

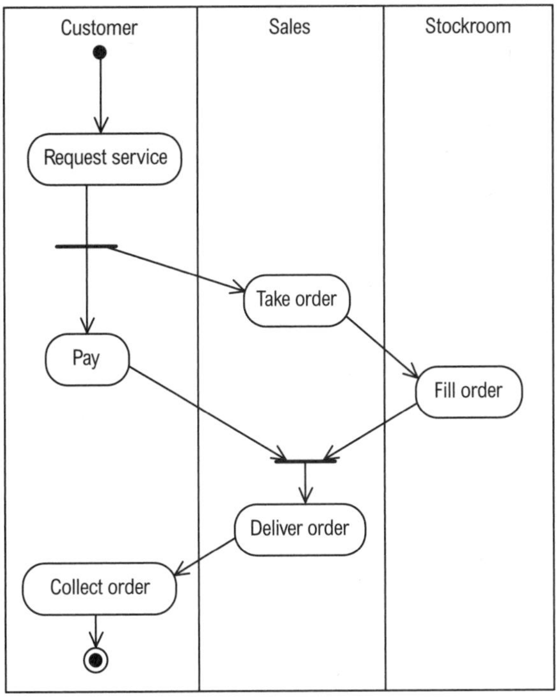

Figure from OMG Unified Modeling Language Specifications, v1.5. Reprinted with permission. Object Management Group, Inc. © OMG 2003. http//:www.omg.org.

Figure 9-4 UML Activity Diagram with Swim Lines

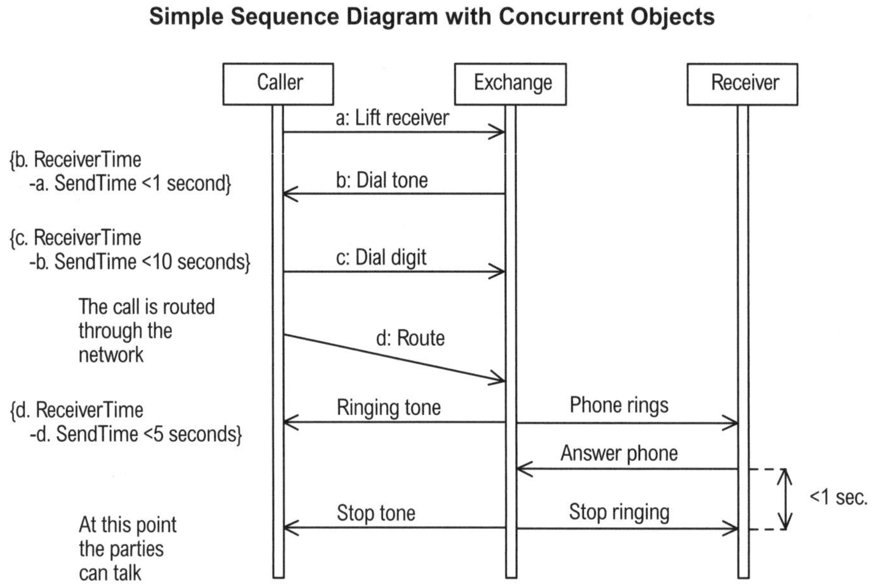

Figure from OMG Unified Modeling Language Specifications, v1.5. Reprinted with permission. Object Management Group, Inc. © OMG 2003. http//:www.omg.org.

Figure 9-5 UML Sequence Diagram

9.5.6 Process Design Reviews

Process design reviews are critical to the overall success and agility of the system. The design reviews should include all relevant stakeholders, defined in the Key Participants section. All parts of the model need to be reviewed and verified. Participants need to verify the portions of the process they are responsible for, including all tasks, functions, and/or services, inputs to and outputs from each service, decision points along the process and business rules that determine the process flow of control, as well as all exception and compensation rules. The overall process should be reviewed for opportunities to decrease time and cost, and increase business flexibility and advantage.

9.5.7 Conclusions and Commentary

This section should provide any final comments on the process, the design, or the usage of the system. It should also include any known issues or upcoming business events, such as a merger or acquisition that might have significant impact on some business processes.

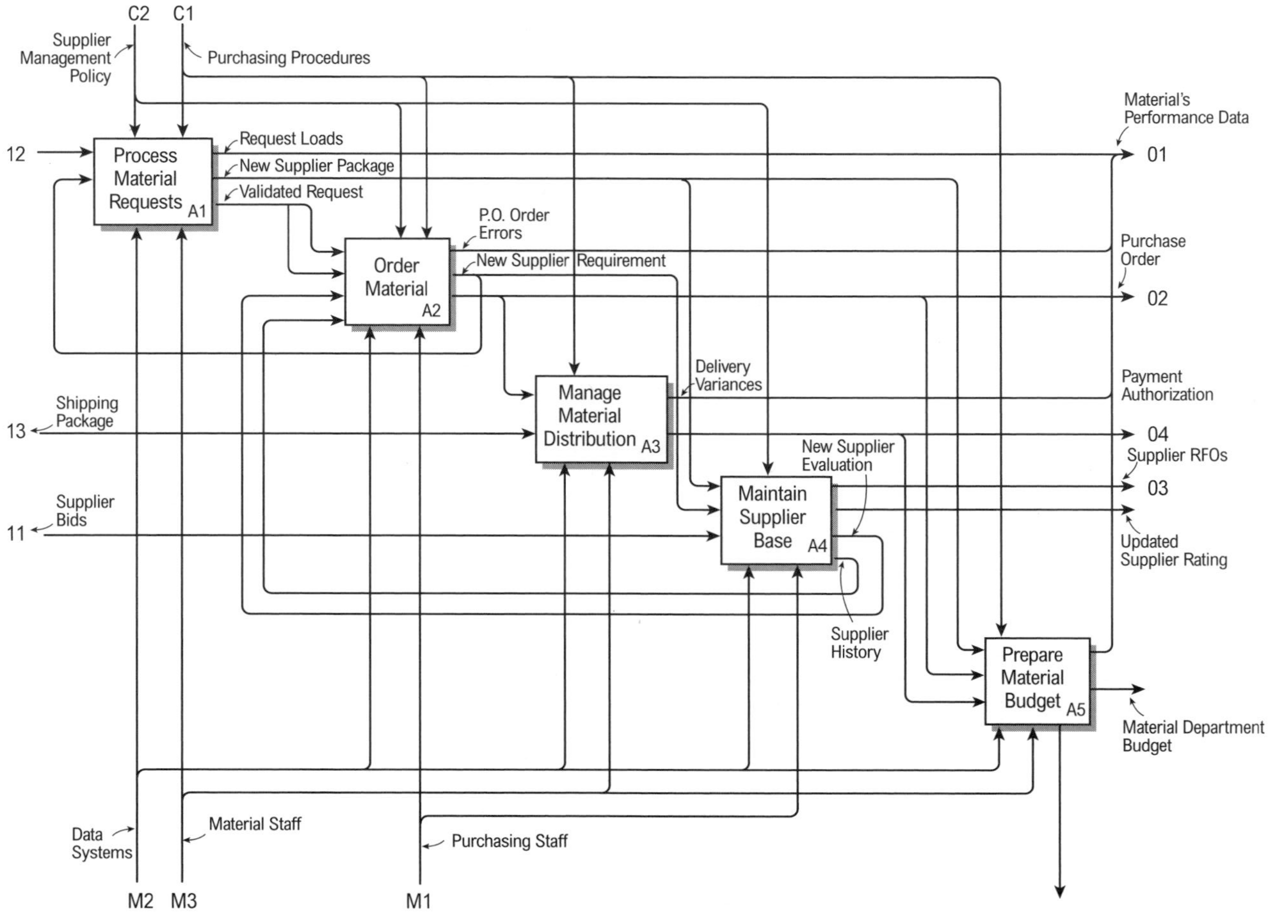

Figure 9-6 IDEF Process Diagram

9.6 Best Practices in Process Integration

- **Plan-Do-Check-Act.** Model and verify business processes with all stakeholders. Automate and integrate processes. Monitor processes on a real-time basis with business and operational dashboards, and practice continuous process improvement.
- **Manage process models as a corporate asset.** The model contains knowledge of the end-to-end business process, which multiple business managers from across the company may have participated in creating. This represents a significant investment. Manage the investment in modeling business processes so that it provides a payoff down the road.
- **Standardize.** Once again, companies should consider the importance and benefits of standards for long-term viability, reuse, and management of business processes. When a company standardizes on a single modeling method, it facilitates communication and verification of process models across different groups and lowers training costs.

Case Study 9.4 describes how Costco applied process integration and these best practices to improve their decision making process and business results (2003).

Case Study 9.4
Process Improvement Is at the Heart of Costco's Electronic Hardware Services Division

The Electronic Hardware Services (EHS) division of Costco is focused on improving the management of returned computers. In-house and third-party resources are used to refurbish the returned items. EHS has applied a process-integration strategy to their operation with goals to improve its internal effectiveness, reduce costs, and improve on the management of third parties. Its strategy requires significant collection of data from a variety of sources to allow

- Automation of the refurbishment processes
- Tracking of costs at each step in the refurbishment process
- Managing warranty claims
- Dashboards to provide management insight into the operations

Through the automation and integration of processes the EHS division has seen results such as identifying a repeat-trouble pattern and removing the item from sale. This resulted in a strong case for full cost recovery from the vendor rather than having to sell at salvage, plus the removal of future returns. In this one instance it resulted in an increase in cost recovery of $212,000. In addition, through the efforts of process automation the EHS organization became more efficient than third parties. The result was a cost reduction of 66%.

EHS was able to significantly reduce its costs by focusing on the core business process and applying technology. Three lessons learned from this are: focus on the core process, have a point of comparison to judge progress and adjust accordingly, and provide insight through the use of dashboards.

9.7 Next Steps

The Enterprise Integration Architecture provides guidelines and standards for all integration projects. Although the Process Integration Architecture is often last to be defined in the integration adoption cycle, once the infrastructure is in place it should become the starting place for integration solutions. Part III of the book describes technologies and reference architectures for specific types of integration solutions (see Figure 9-7). It must be noted that some integration projects require a combination of integration styles. Chapter 14 provides a reference architecture for a completely integrated enterprise that combines all styles of integration.

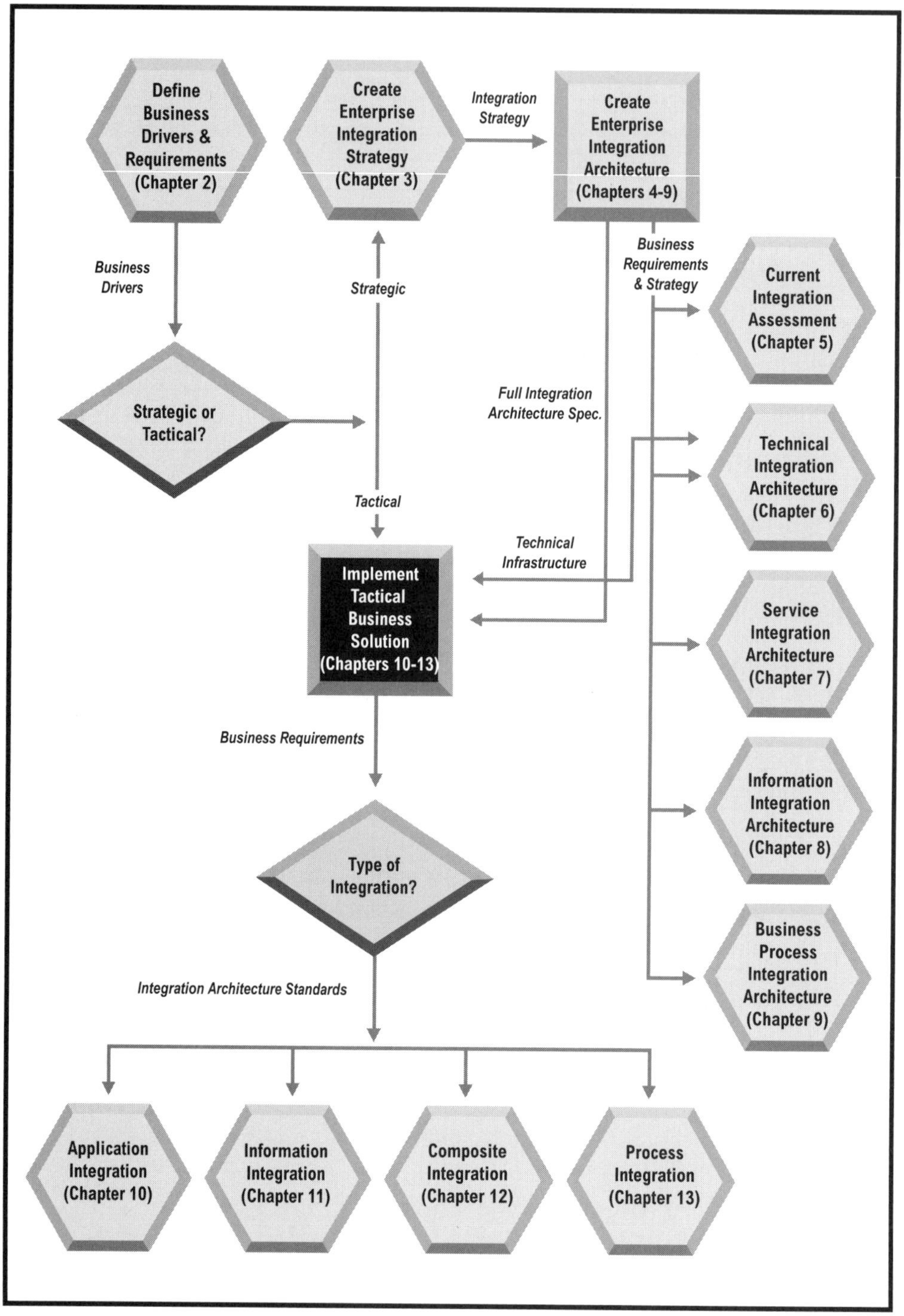

Figure 9-7 Integration Roadmap

PART III

Enterprise Integration Solutions

Part III of the book focuses on implementing different types of integration solutions. With so many different types of integration technologies to choose from, it is extremely difficult and confusing to understand what is needed to implement a specific integration solution. Part III provides reference architectures for each type of solution. Using the reference architecture as a starting point, you can then more quickly evaluate the most appropriate alternative solutions.

A comparison of all the reference architectures reveals a great deal of overlap among them. Companies will maximize their return on infrastructure investment by minimizing redundancy of integration technologies and services.

The ebizQ Roadmap to Integration Technology was used as the model for defining types of integration solutions. The Roadmap is part of the ebizQ Buyer's Guide that includes a vendor directory organized by map categories.

Each type of solution on the roadmap represents a chapter in Part III. Each chapter contains reference architectures and best practices. Readers of this book looking for vendor solutions based on the reference architectures should refer to the online Buyers Guide *(http://www.ebizQ.net)*.

Chapter 10—Application Integration

Application Integration includes a broad array of business integration scenarios. The reference architectures included are hub and spoke message broker, Enterprise Service Bus, legacy integration, B2B Integration, Portals, and Mobile Integration. Application integration includes all technologies that might be used to connect disparate applications both inside and outside the firewall, at a messaging level.

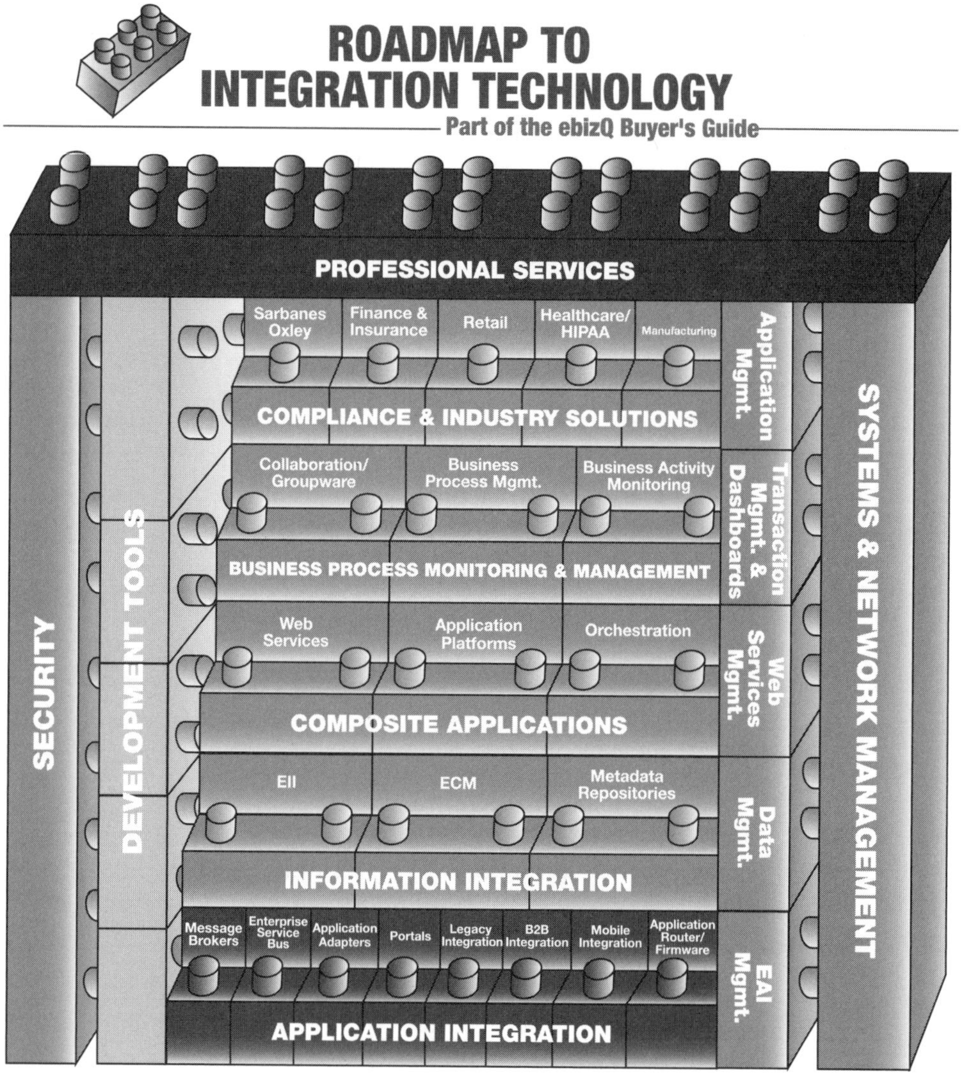

Chapter 11—Information Integration

Chapter 11 focuses on Information Integration and explains one old and two growing segments of the industry. Extract, transform, and load (ETL) is the workhorse of information integration but is beginning to fall short of the needs of most organizations. ETL is batch oriented and aimed at moving large files between applications for processing. The need for real-time access to information across an enterprise has brought about the emergence of enterprise information integration (EII) and enterprise content management (ECM). This chapter will deal with each of these areas as well as addressing the topics of enterprise metadata management and data aggregation.

Chapter 12—Composite Application Integration

Composite applications combine new functionality with existing data and applications. One of the major benefits of a service-oriented architecture (SOA) is the ability to quickly assemble new composite applications. The infrastructure for composite applications may include both EAI and EII, but because new development is involved, the tools as well as the implementers tend to be different.

Chapter 13—Process-Driven Integration

Process-driven integration provides a business-level approach to integration. Companies seeking to optimize business processes, reduce operational costs, and gain real-time visibility into key performance indicators will be interested in business process management (BPM) software, business activity monitoring (BAM), and collaboration software (also called groupware).

Chapter 14—Conclusion: Best Practices for Enterprise Integration

Large companies are likely to have a wide variety of integration needs. A single complex integration solution may require a combination of integration styles and technologies. To increase business agility while reducing implementation and maintenance costs, companies will need to take a strategic approach to integration, even while implementing tactical solutions. This chapter provides a final look at the completely integrated enterprise.

CHAPTER TEN

Application Integration

10.1 Executive Overview

Application integration covers a broad array of business integration scenarios. Many companies start by connecting just a few applications point-to-point, and synchronizing some data and transactions across them. However, as the number of applications and platforms increases, and the complexity of the data structures and transformations grows, the integration requirements and technical solutions change. The business integration scope is also an important factor. When integrating with applications external to the organization or to a myriad of mobile devices, additional integration requirements, technologies, and security are involved.

Despite the attempts of integration vendors to build end-to-end integration platforms, there is no one-size-fits-all integration solution. Each business scenario will have unique requirements, and the optimal solution will most often depend on implementing not one integration technology, but the right set of technologies, and getting them all to work together seamlessly.

This chapter identifies different application integration scenarios, and provides reference architecture models for each. Application integration includes all technologies that might be used to connect disparate applications both inside and outside the firewall, including communication and messaging, translation and transformation, routing, application access, data access, presentation-level integration, B2B integration, and technology integration. This chapter will help you determine the right set of integration services required to implement your solution.

10.2 Application Integration Scenarios

Application integration enables two or more applications to communicate together to perform a business function. Types of problems that are well suited to application integration include

- Replicating transactions across multiple applications
- Extending legacy systems to the Web
- Business-to-business transactions across the Web
- Publishing information and request replies to mobile devices

If the solution requires integrating information from disparate sources to present in a unified interface to a human, such as self-service applications or customer management, or an aggregated view of data is required, such as a single view of the customer across systems, see Chapter 11 on enterprise information integration.

If the solution is focused primarily on new functionality, but needs to be integrated with existing applications, or the enterprise has developed a service-oriented architecture (SOA) and is in a position to create new applications from new and existing services, see Chapter 12 on composite applications.

If the solution requires a combination of automated and manual processes, and the purpose of the solution is to monitor, manage, and optimize end-to-end business processes, see Chapter 13 on process-driven integration.

It is also quite possible to have a combination of integration needs in a single project. The reference architectures in each Chapter in Part III of the book will help you identify overlapping functionality required for the combination of integration requirements. Redundancy in integration technologies is the result of implementing a variety of tactical solutions in isolation. Proliferation of redundant technologies increases maintenance costs and over time, decreases business agility. The enterprise integration architecture helps control redundancy and guides specific implementation decisions.

The next section defines the types of integration technologies specific to application integration. Section 10.4 defines application integration patterns for different types of application integration solutions, and provides reference architectures for each pattern.

10.3 Choosing Application Integration Technology

The value of taking a service-oriented approach to building the integration infrastructure becomes more apparent when considering the collection of technologies for application integration. These include technology for connecting applications, doing data translation and transformation, intelligent routing, application access including legacy integration, B2B Integration, portals, and mobile integration. (For a listing of vendors offering each of these technologies, please refer to the ebizQ Buyer's Guide, *http://www.ebizq.net.*)

10.3.1 Messaging and Connectivity

Every integration solution includes underlying connectivity. Asynchronous communications are usually most appropriate for integration solutions because of the high probability that not all applications are available at the same time. Communication technologies include proprietary message queuing (such as IBM MQ Series, TIBCO Rendevous, and Software AG EntireX). There are also solutions based on the Java Messaging Service (JMS) standard. A number of the EAI vendors also provide messaging as part of their platform. Additionally, application servers also support JMS as well as other messaging solutions. For some integration solutions, such as connecting a few applications using a point-to-point approach, messaging may be the only integration technology needed. If possible, choose just one messaging solution throughout the enterprise. When this is not possible, you will need to integrate the different messaging solutions. Message bridges and message system adapters are available to accomplish this.

10.3.2 Data Transformation

Applications developed for different purposes by different vendors and developers inevitably define similar business entities differently. A customer can be identified in one system as CustID, in another system as Customer, in another system as Name. Furthermore, the definition will most likely be formatted differently in each of these systems; the field can be 20 characters in one system and 30 characters in another. Synchronizing data across applications requires translation and transformation. There are a number of graphical tools for mapping and transforming data from EAI vendors, from data warehousing vendors, and from a new emerging sector of Enterprise Information Integration (EII) vendors (described in Chapter 11). Traditional solutions have been proprietary. As XML has emerged as the lingua franca for the canonical data format, XSLT is emerging as a standards-based transformation solution. The newest products are based upon these standards.

10.3.3 Message Brokers and Enterprise Service Buses

Routing messages between systems is an essential integration service. Routing can be simple, based on headers with destination addresses, or intelligent and based on the content of the message and business rules. Messages need to be parsed and then sent to the target systems in a format they can understand: either a canonical format or an application-specific format. The latter requires data transformation. There are two technologies that provide this functionality, each with different architectures: message brokers and Enterprise Server Buses (ESB).

Message brokers are the original EAI tools, created for the purpose of providing intelligent routing and data transformation. They have a hub and spoke architecture. All routing and transformation is done in the hub. The hub connects to the spoke applications through a standardized interface, which can be an application adapter that works specifically with that broker, a standard adapter based on the Java Connector Architecture (JCA), or most likely these days, a Web service, which can work with any technology or platform. A slight variation on the message broker architecture includes the use of intelligent adapters, where the transformation is done at the target. This increases scalability. Most of the broker vendors have also added a process management layer to their platforms. Case Study 10.1 looks at the use of message brokers to help Central Hudson Gas & Electric Corp. solve a variety of integration problems (Software AG n.d.)

Case Study 10.1
Central Hudson Gas & Electric Corp.: Using a Message Broker to Increase Operational Productivity and Customer Self Service

Central Hudson provides gas and electricity to nearly 350,000 customers in the mid-Hudson Valley in upstate New York. Their choice of an application integration architecture was driven by a need to meet two very different business requirements. The first was to integrate outage report data between core systems. This is a traditional application integration problem that could have been handled in a variety of manners. The second was to provide an improved customer experience through a customer self-service Web site.

The diversity of requirements made it imperative for Central Hudson to create an integration architecture that could be reused across each project.

The architecture that was implemented was based upon a message broker pattern. The message broker provided an efficient way to direct outage reports between the customer information system and the outage management system. Reports are received from call centers, automated voice response systems, the customer self-service portal and devices that send alerts when a problem is detected. This ability to manage the flow of critical information meant that it took hours instead of days to analyze outage information leading to faster restoration of service.

The second major initiative that used the architecture was the customer self-service Web site. This site enables customers to review account status, check payment history, pay bills, and report outages. In addition, customers can self-report their monthly meter reading offering a faster, less expensive alternative to the use of postcards. All of the information necessary to support this application resided in their customer information system (CIS) and needed to be provided in a real-time mode. The message broker was used to direct requests from the self-service Web site to the CIS. This offloaded some of the burden from the call center resulting in a savings of $6 to $7 for every customer inquiry through the site.

An application integration strategy was most relevant because of the need to:

- Route similar information from a multitude of systems
- Synchronize information between two critical applications
- Develop a new customer portal application
- Focus on opening up and reusing existing legacy systems

The result is a reusable framework that has been proven and is available for solving the next application integration problem.

ESB essentially provides the same services as a message broker, but has a very different architecture. The integration services such as routing and translation, plug into the bus, and execution of services is distributed instead of at a central hub. The architecture is extremely flexible and scalable because the options for deploying services are pretty limitless. This makes it easier for companies to perform incremental implementations and tactical solutions. Only the services necessary to do the job are "plugged into" the bus. However, this is also what makes it more complex. Because it provides great flexibility in how services can be implemented, it requires many more decisions, such as where services are located, which technologies are used, which vendors are used, which programmers are involved. However, the ESB vendors are building out their platforms, much as the message broker vendors have done, to provide a full range of integration services, including business process management, to enable a single source solution. Until recently there were no widely accepted standards in the industry. Web services make the service bus a more viable commercial approach to application integration.

The bottom line may be that the ESB is easier for a company to afford and implement tactically and provides increased flexibility and scalability. However, to achieve long-term ROI from ESB architecture, it is necessary to manage the implementation of services on an enterprise level, to reduce redundancy across projects. The problem is that companies most interested in tactical implementations are generally least interested in investing in developing the enterprise integration architecture. Those who skip this step may end up paying more in the end.

10.3.4 Application Interfaces

Once a message gets routed to an application, the application itself needs to be able to accept and process the message. This requires a special application interface to accept external messages. The options for application interfaces include application programming interfaces (APIs), adapters, and Web services. There are also database interfaces, including open database connectivity standard (ODBC) and Java database connectivity (JDBC).

APIs are application-specific, proprietary interfaces that require the sending application to use the function calls specific to the API. This means that the application would need to be hard coded for the API of each application it is integrating within a point-to-point configuration, greatly increasing time and cost for integrating systems and decreasing agility. Any changes to an API ripples out to all applications that utilize it. **Adapters** are generalized APIs that provide a common set of function calls across different applications. Intelligent adapters perform the data translation and transformation at the target, thereby distributing the processing and increasing the scalability of the solution. Nonintelligent adapters provide basic connectivity, and the translation and transformation is done at the hub. It should also be noted that there are technology adapters for connecting to messaging systems, transaction monitors, and application servers.

Adapters are generally specific to a particular vendor's integration broker or ESB. While JCA has been proposed as a standard adapter architecture, the clear market winner seems to be Web services, which provide a standard interface specification. The benefit of Web services is they decrease the cost of application connectivity by obviating the need to install and configure adapters. But while they replace adapters, they do not replace the rest of the integration stack. They do not provide translation and transformation, routing, or process management.

10.3.5 Legacy Integration

Legacy systems typically do not have APIs, and are usually the most challenging applications to integrate. Legacy integration can consume a disproportionate percentage of the time and cost of application integration. Legacy application access is a specialized area of application integration, and there are vendors that specialize in it. Legacy integration solutions are typically used with other integration software and are often part of the integration platform. Legacy integration technology should be selected for the unique set of legacy code that is to be accessed. Emphasis should be placed upon the method that is used to connect into the legacy code. Specifically the operational and performance aspects should receive significant attention. Often too much emphasis is placed on the ease of making the connection. While this is important the long-term viability of a tool is based on how it will impact the stability of the application. It may be that the tool that requires the most work to setup and use provides the best operational characteristics.

10.3.6 Portals

While many EAI solutions focus on automating transactions across systems, portals aggregate information from multiple sources to present a unified interface to the end user. Portals provide a set of information and services for a specific user role or business service. They provide integration "at the glass," giving end users a single graphical interface to disparate systems, including legacy systems. The user is unaware of where the information is coming from. Portals are used for self-service applications, management dashboards, kiosks, registration systems, and many other Web applications. Portal technology is most often focused on portal interface development. The integration with systems fueling the portal can be through adapters provided by the portal vendor or through integration with brokers or ESBs. This will continue to be necessary when the portal includes business transactions as well as presenting aggregated information. However, it must be pointed out here that the emerging EII solutions provide unique capabilities for aggregating disparate information (see Chapter 11).

10.3.7 Mobile Integration

While mobile integration is still in the early stage of adoption, the proliferation of mobile devices throughout organizations provides an opportunity for providing enterprise information to a variety to devices. Mobile devices such as personal digital assistants (PDAs) and cell phones can browse the Internet and receive text messages. For many years, logistics companies have used mobile devices to enter information about shipments and deliveries. Mobile integration offers the possibility of also presenting information on mobile devices. Mobile integration aggregates information and functions from back-end systems and presents it to different mobile devices based on the target display characteristics. There are many challenges in mobile integration, including the number and variety of mobile interfaces, and the fact that it is inherently insecure and unreliable technology. Mobile integration is a specialized market segment with only a few vendors offering solutions. However, as demand increases, the available solutions undoubtedly will also increase.

10.3.8 B2B Integration

When integrating with applications beyond the firewall, including suppliers, partners, and customers, B2B integration services are required. While backend application integration is also required for B2B solutions, additional integration services are also required including support for multiple types of connectivity and messaging including EDI, HTTP, SOAP, and Web services as well as FTP. B2B solutions typically include partner management and different levels of partner software for different size partners. Web services are also an important standard for B2B integration.

B2B integration exchanges are becoming viable alternatives for essentially outsourcing the B2B solution. Each partner only needs to connect with the exchange and doesn't need to manage the details of connecting with every other partner, which reduces the burden on the company for connecting to multiple partners that all have different technology infrastructures. Case Study 10.2 is about northAmerican Logistics's success with transitioning to a modern B2B

Case Study 10.2
northAmerican Logistics: Transitioning to Next Generation B2B

northAmerican Logistics (nAL) is a division of the SIRVA Corporation and focuses on specialized distribution and logistic services. Like many organizations, they have been employing the use of electronic data interchange (EDI) to communicate with their customers and supply chain partners. EDI is the most widely employed form of B2B integration, but it is coming under increasing pressures due to competition from Internet-based solutions. The driver for change is the high costs that result from sending EDI messages across traditional Value-Added Networks (VANs), which prevents small partners from participating in electronic data exchange. nAL and its customers wanted to move to a more open approach that employed XML messages. This is a common trend across many industries, because the cost of an electronic transaction is significantly lower than one that must be manually processed

Without the use of a VAN, an organization needs a B2B integration server to manage the communications between internal and external systems. The server can be located in-house, or the B2B connectivity function can be outsourced. nAL created a B2B gateway using an XML server and messaging software to replace the EDI processes. nAL found XML more powerful than the EDI formats for creating their B2B messages and more suitable to integrating with legacy systems. XML allowed nAL to specify the business language, communicate it to all participants inexpensively over the Internet, and quickly and easily adjust it over time. The solution lowered their costs while providing greater flexibility.

An application integration strategy based upon a B2B design pattern was most relevant because of the need to communicate messages between systems where the messages relate to supply-chain activities between business partners.

By moving to a more open B2B platform, nAL was able to achieve a 549% ROI and provides greater flexibility and agility in communication between nAL and its customers.

integration architecture from a legacy EDI approach (Vijayan 2002 and Software AG n.d.).

10.3.9 Application Integration Platforms

As stated previously, the message broker and ESB vendors have added services to support a wide range of integration requirements. Similarly, the application server vendors have added integration technology. The goal is to create a complete enterprise integration platform. The platform can include all or a combination of the following integration services: messaging, adapters, support for Web services, legacy integration, translation and transformation, B2B integration, business process automation, monitoring and management, workflow management, mobile integration, and portals. With this wide range of technologies, it is not unusual for the integration platform to include a collection of technologies, some of which are licensed from different vendors. Some of these integration platforms are more integrated than others. Few have common interfaces or development tools across all integration capabilities. Some have proprietary development environments that require specialized skills and training. When it comes to integration platforms, a single vendor solution rarely means a single technology and the integration platform may require integration.

Integration platforms are expensive, heavy weight infrastructure solutions. Maximizing the value of an investment in this all-encompassing solution requires that the organization commit all of its resources to this single platform. Taken at face value, this may seem easy. However, while these solutions are wide ranging, they cannot provide everything no matter how complete. Legacy integration is one area where they will generally fall short. Furthermore, they often have one or two areas that they excel in while having mediocre capabilities in other areas. Finally, not all of the capabilities may be of use to the organization, thereby adding costs that may not make sense. For this reason, the Enterprise Application Integration Specification identifies application integration patterns to provide guidance for companies wishing to implement only the integration services they need for a particular solution. Furthermore, this approach supports a service oriented integration architecture, where integration services can be reused and flexibly deployed for different solutions.

10.4 Application Integration Implementation Specification

This specification provides implementation guidance for the development of an application-integration based solution. Application integration includes a number of different services, and applies to a broad range of business solutions requiring integration. When two or more applications need to communicate together to accomplish a given task and the level of integration is passing information and messages between and among applications, then application integration is the appropriate solution. See Appendix H for the complete Enterprise Application Integration Implementation Template.

10.4.1 Introduction

This section describes the specific technical problems that are being addressed in the implementation, and provides context for the specific implementation.

10.4.2 Scope

The scope of an application integration specification is limited to the specifics of the applications that are being integrated. This section of the specification includes organizational units, external organizations, users, and applications involved. It should also define the expected time frames and end result.

10.4.3 Key Participants

This section identifies all stakeholders in the implementation. Very often, once the project goes into implementation, business managers only participate in design reviews (if at all). However, when there is both a business manager and an IT manager responsible for implementation success, the rate of success is statistically much higher. Other key participants include the system designers and architect(s) and the development team who will execute the implementation. Business managers who are responsible for any applications or services included in the solution should be part of all design reviews relevant to their systems. Any other participants or stakeholders should also be identified, including their roles.

10.4.4 Application Integration Implementation Patterns and Services

As stated many times in this book, integration is not a single technology or solution. Choosing the right set of technologies or integration services to meet a specific integration requirement is not an easy task. We have often seen short lists that were comparing very different types of integration technologies.

Understanding different integration implementation patterns will help you identify the right technologies to meet the business requirements.

There are several basic application integration implementation patterns that relate to different types of business solutions.

These patterns are:

- Message broker
- Enterprise service bus
- Legacy integration
- B2B integration
- Portals
- Mobile integration

10.4.4.1 Message Broker

Message brokers are well suited to coordinating and replicating transactions across multiple applications, as well as providing back-end integration to B2B applications and other integration solutions. When more than a couple of applications are involved, or when complex data translation and transformation is required, the message broker is a good implementation choice. For example, when a transaction is entered into one system and the organization wants to update a number of other systems with the same information for other purposes, then a message broker would make sense. When a new employee is hired, his or her information is entered into the human resource system. With this information in hand, messages would be sent outside the company to enter the employee into the health benefits provider and 401(k) system. Inside the organization, messages may be sent to the payroll, security, and e-mail system to initiate business processes to establish these services for the new employee.

The message broker implements an integration hub that provides transformation and routing services (see Figure 10-1). Adapters or Web services provide interfaces to the applications. Note that adapters can be open, meaning they are accessible by different vendor solutions, or are specific to the message broker. Without standard interfaces, if different integration technologies are used multiple adapters on a single application will be required. For this reason, Web services are gaining popularity as standard application interfaces that can be used by multiple vendor technologies.

The message broker implementation is focused on defining message routing rules, configuring adapters, and mapping data sources to each other or a

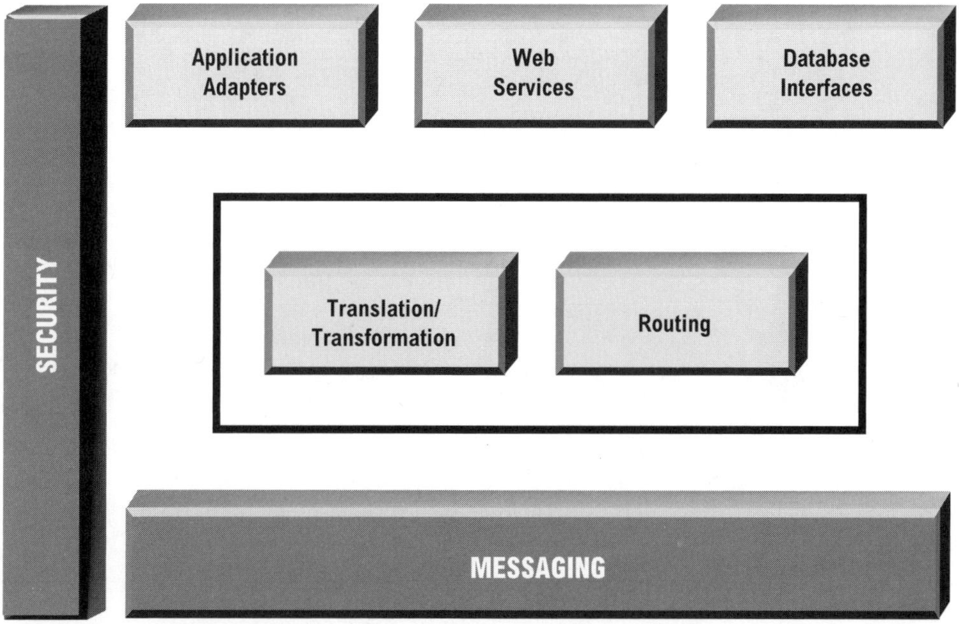

Figure 10-1 Simple Message Broker Reference Architecture

canonical format. While the architecture is primarily hub and spoke, when intelligent adapters are used, transformation and routing can be distributed to the adapters. This increases scalability. The disadvantage is that "intelligent adapters" are proprietary, and the market is moving towards standardized interfaces including JCA and Web services.

It should be noted that the message broker vendors have added other levels of integration to their platforms, including B2B integration, business process management, mobile integration, and portals. These products continue to evolve into broader integration platforms that will handle multiple integration patterns.

The Implementation Table (Figure 10-2, page 198) further defines the services identified in the implementation architecture. The broker can provide messaging, or the broker may integrate with and use the messaging system already in place.

10.4.4.2 Enterprise Service Bus (ESB)

The ESB is beginning to gain more popularity as a viable option to a message broker. The ESB provides connectivity services, including transport protocol, message protocol, and message routing; some provide guaranteed message delivery through a light weight message repository. ESBs also usually provide some

Integration Service	Vendor/Product	Implementation Notes
Message broker	<Vendor name/ product name>	<Technology platform>
Messaging	<Vendor name/product name if different than broker vendor>	<Technology platform>
Application interface	<Vendor name/product name or deployment technology>	<Specify: integration broker adapter; Web service; JCA interface; data interface (ODBC, JDBC, OLE DB, ADO).>
Security	<Vendor name/product name or deployment technology>	<Specify how security is implemented, including integration with LDAP or other repository or product.>

Figure 10-2 Message Broker Implementation Table

basic data transformation, such as XML translation via XSLT style sheets. However, for more complex data transformation requirements, an additional data transformation tool might be required. The big advantage of the ESB is that other integration services can easily be plugged in when needed. The ESB provides a very flexible and scalable architecture. The ESB is better suited when using Web services as the method of connectivity to applications. It provides the infrastructure for the development and management of these services. While a message broker might use the Web service interface, it is not intended to provide the infrastructure for the interface. For example, if a company wants to create a Web service to update a change of address, then an ESB would make more sense than the message broker. This type of Web service would be useful in an environment where the change can come into the organization through multiple channels. In a banking environment where the customer might go to a branch, talk to a call center or interact with a portal it would be useful to have this type of Web service. The Web service would not only have the connectivity element but the interface elements that could be integrated into the teller, call center, or portal applications. The ESB would provide all of the infrastructure support to manage this Web service, including the directory, routing, translation, and operational management.

The ESB Reference Architecture (Figure 10-3) and Implementation Table (Figure 10-4, page 200) help manage redundancy by documenting reusable services and technology in the infrastructure.

The ESB Implementation Table further defines the services identified in the ESB Reference Architecture. As stated previously, the ESB architecture supports a best-of-breed approach in implementing integration services. Therefore, the implementation table calls out all the services separately. In contrast, the message broker implementation assumes all these services come from the message broker vendor.

10.4.4.3 Legacy Integration

Legacy integration provides a number of ways to extract and insert information or invoke processing on mainframe systems. There is no generic approach or set of standards in legacy integration implementations. The systems were never designed to be accessible to other systems—quite the contrary. They were designed not to let anyone in.

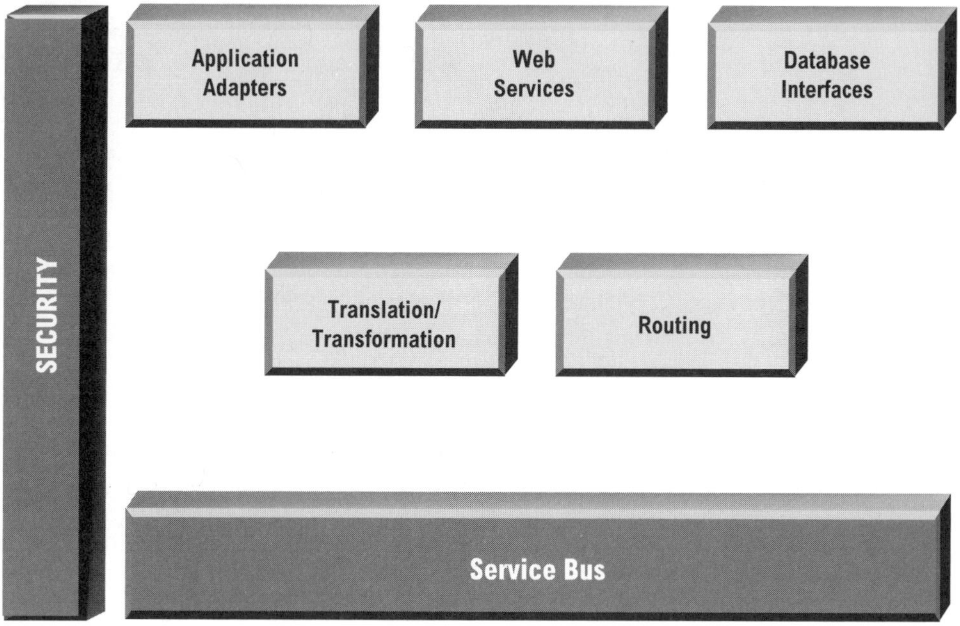

Figure 10-3 ESB Reference Architecture

Integration Service	Vendor/Product	Implementation Notes
Enterprise service bus (ESB)	<Vendor name/product name>	<Technology platform>
Translation and transformation	<Vendor name/product name>	<Transformation at hub or target>
Application interface	<Vendor name/product name or deployment technology>	<Specify: integration broker adapter; Web service; JCA interface; data interface (ODBC, JDBC, OLE DB, ADO).>
Security	<Vendor name/product name or deployment technology>	<Specify how security is implemented, including integration with LDAP or other repository or product.>

Figure 10-4 ESB Implementation Table

The goal is to integrate with the legacy data, application, or process noninvasively, without changing the legacy application. Creating a new interface to the legacy system can do this. There are different types of interfaces that can be used.

- **Database interfaces.** These data level adapters allow front-end applications access mainframe data through the database calls native to the requesting application, including JDBC, ODBC, ActiveX Data Objects (ADO), and OLE-DB (a set of COM-based interfaces that provide uniform access to data in diverse data or information sources). Data interfaces are appropriate for nontransactional systems, such as information aggregation and publishing to the Web.
- **Messaging interfaces.** If the integration includes transaction processing, a message interface can provide better integrity and manageability than a data interface. Vendors provide connectors for JCA and SOAP messaging. There is also a number of proprietary messaging systems available for the mainframe, including IBM MQ Series, TIBCO Rendezvous, and Software AG EntireX.
- **Screen/report interface.** Sometimes, the only way to access mainframe data is through the screen or report interface, also called screen and report scraping.

They both work the same way. The 3270 screen or report provides a defined interface to legacy systems for extracting information to the screen or report. The interface technology captures those data bits, and redirects them to a Web browser. The available technology adds the ability to combine data from several screens and/or reports. This is the least adaptable and reusable of solutions, but it is widely used because in many cases it is still much better than having to crack mainframe code; in which case you don't know what you might break.

- **Service interface.** The service level interface, also called legacy wrapping, is the most adaptable and reusable method of legacy integration, but it also requires the highest initial investment. The technology enables mainframe processes and functions to be wrapped with a Web service, .NET, Java, or CORBA interface. .NET, Java, and CORBA components can also be expressed as Web services. The industry-wide acceptance of Web services has taken the risk out of investing in creating service-level interfaces to mainframe functionality. Originally created to enable B2B integration, the initial adoption of Web services has been in mainframe integration.

Typically, legacy integration is focused on the mainframe because this is the source of most legacy applications. However, legacy systems on UNIX platforms, especially those implemented more than five years ago, may also present challenges to integration. Figure 10-5 (page 202) depicts the different interfaces to mainframe applications, but they may also be applied to legacy systems on other platforms. Each of these interfaces can be implemented in a piecemeal fashion, or a legacy integration platform can provide a single solution that provides multiple interface options.

The Legacy Integration Implementation Table (Figure 10-6, page 203) defines what types of interfaces are provided to the mainframe, and what specific technologies are used. This information will serve as a resource in future implementation to define what interfaces have already been implemented on the mainframe. Therefore, in the implementation notes, it is important to include specifically what data, functions, or services are available through the interface.

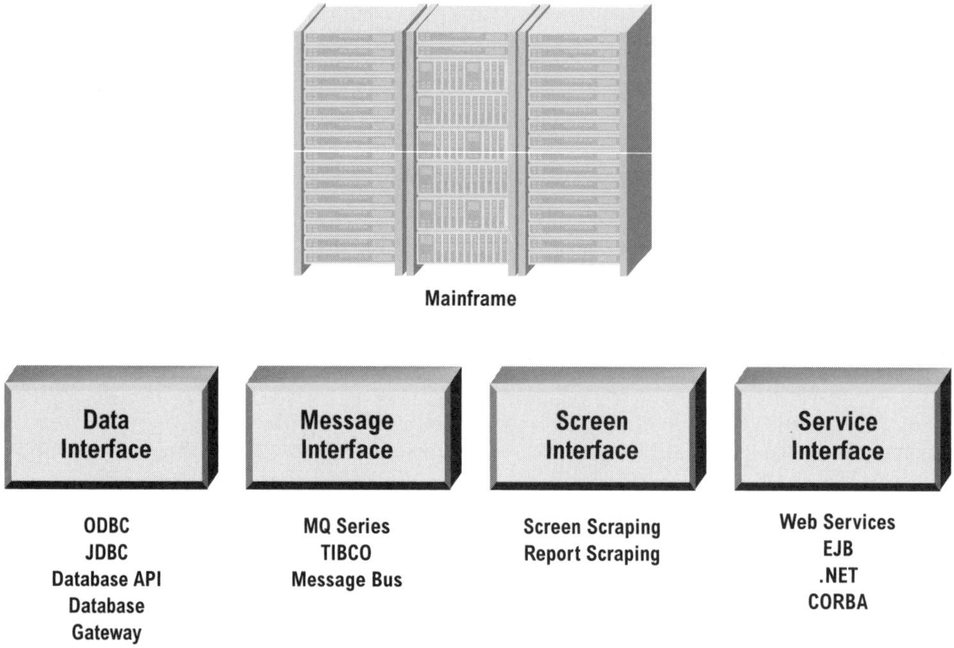

Figure 10-5 Legacy Integration Reference Architecture

10.4.4.4 B2B Integration

B2B integration technology is used whenever business data needs to be communicated among trading partners. EDI has been the workhorse of B2B integration for over a decade. In the past few years, the options for business interconnectivity have exploded, giving organizations a much richer set of choices. While it may seem that a custom development using an ESB or message broker might be simple, it is better to consider the use of a B2B server or service to get some of the critical support services. For example, if an organization desires to setup an online auction capability, then one of the new servers or services would be a logical choice.

B2B integration most often includes application integration services, but also has additional services required when integrating with applications external to the organization. Partners may use a variety of communication mechanisms to communicate, including EDI, HTML, Web services, or even FTP. In some cases, a browser interface is appropriate for small partners. Additional security is sometimes required for encrypting transactions, authenticating the sender, and

Integration Service	Vendor/Product or Custom	Implementation Notes
Legacy integration—data interface	<Vendor, product name>	<JDBC adapter to specific mainframe data source>
Legacy integration—message interface	<Vendor, product name>	<MQ Series on mainframe provides access to CICS transactions>
Legacy integration—screen/report interface	<Vendor, product name>	<Provides all customer order information>
Legacy integration—service interface	<Vendor, product name or custom code>	<Order processing service, customer maintenance service, order tracking service>

Figure 10-6 Legacy Integration Implementation Table

ensuring nonrepudiation of the transaction. Security for accepting external transactions and integrating them with back-end systems is also a consideration for B2B integration. In addition, these B2B solutions usually provide services required for partner management, including defining and managing processes among and between partners, as well as service-level agreements.

Some B2B services integrate directly to back-end systems through adapters and application APIs. Others are part of an EAI solution or integrate with an EAI solution through technology adapters. A growing area for B2B is enabling collaboration between and among partners to negotiate direct supply-chain interactions, such as product specifications and design, so collaboration services may be included.

Another option is to outsource B2B connectivity through an electronic exchange. There are a few vendors offering a B2B hosting platform for outsourcing B2B connectivity. The benefit is that the exchange provider takes care of all partner connectivity. Figure 10-7 (page 204) depicts both options of an internal B2B server and connectivity to an external exchange.

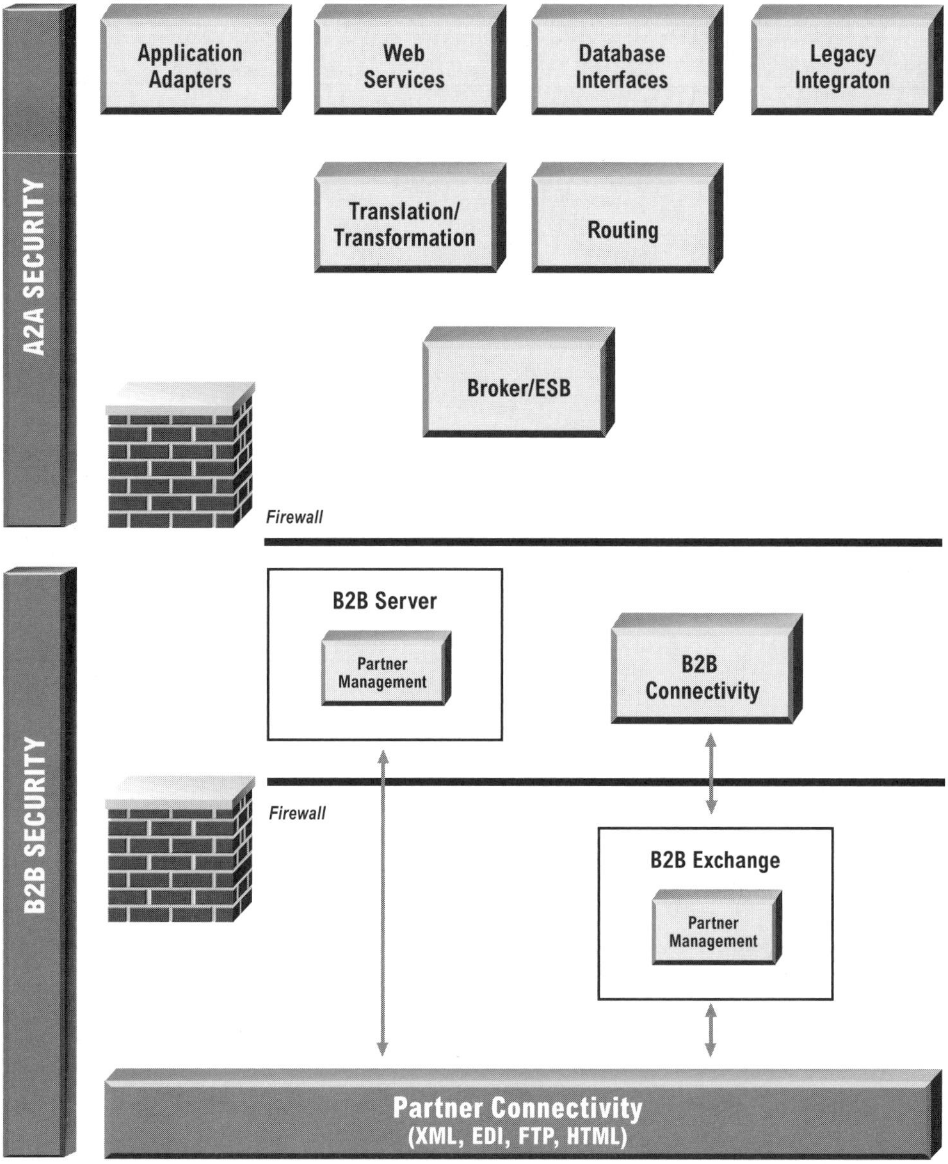

Figure 10-7 B2B Integration Reference Architecture

The B2B Implementation Table (Figure 10-8) specifies all components of the B2B architecture, including how back-end integration will be accomplished. This can be through other integration technology, including message brokers and enterprise service buses, or it may be through application adapters.

Integration Service	Vendor/Product	Implementation Notes
B2B connectivity	<Vendor, product name>	<B2B server or central exchange>
Partner connectivity	<Vendor, product name>	<List all connectivity options including XML messaging, EDI, FTP, browser interfaces, exchange hub, or other.>
Partner management	<Vendor, product name>	<Define services provided including process management, collaboration services, service level agreements, or other.>
B2B security	<Vendor, product name>	<Define all security services provided including encryption, authentication through digital certificates or other authentication, nonrepudiation services.>
Back-End Application Integration		<Include all application integration services included in the B2B solution.>
Broker/enterprise service bus	<Product/protocol>	<Technology platform>
Translation and transformation	<Vendor name/ product name>	<Transformation at hub or target>
Routing	<Vendor, product name or custom code>	<Level of routing supported; content based, business rules, header only info>
Application interface	<Vendor name/ product name or deployment technology>	<Specify: integration broker adapter; Web service; JCA interface; data interface (ODBC, JDBC, OLE DB, ADO).>
Legacy integration	<Vendor, product name>	<Define type of integration.>
A2A security	<Vendor name/ product name or deployment technology>	<Specify how security is implemented, including integration with LDAP or other repository or product.>

Figure 10-8 B2B Integration Implementation Table

10.4.4.5 Portals

Portals provide integration at the glass (or graphical display). By themselves, they are not an integration technology. They are used to represent the results of integration. They can be used to extend mainframe or other internal application functionality to the Web and provide customer-facing applications.

Portals require extensive integration services. There are a number of different ways to provide portal integration. All of the methods described previously are legitimate methods. The portal can have point-to-point connections to each of the applications. APIs, database interfaces, Web services, or adapters can be used. Portals can also be part of an application server solution, and the application server can provide the integration services. Message brokers and ESBs can also provide integration services to the portal. Lastly, when the portal requires real-time access to aggregated enterprise data, EII (discussed in Chapter 11) can be used. Moreover, if the portal supports business transactions as well as data aggregation, a combination of technologies can be used. Figure 10-9 depicts the alternative integration services that can be used in a portal implementation. Each of the services in the dotted box can be implemented as the sole portal

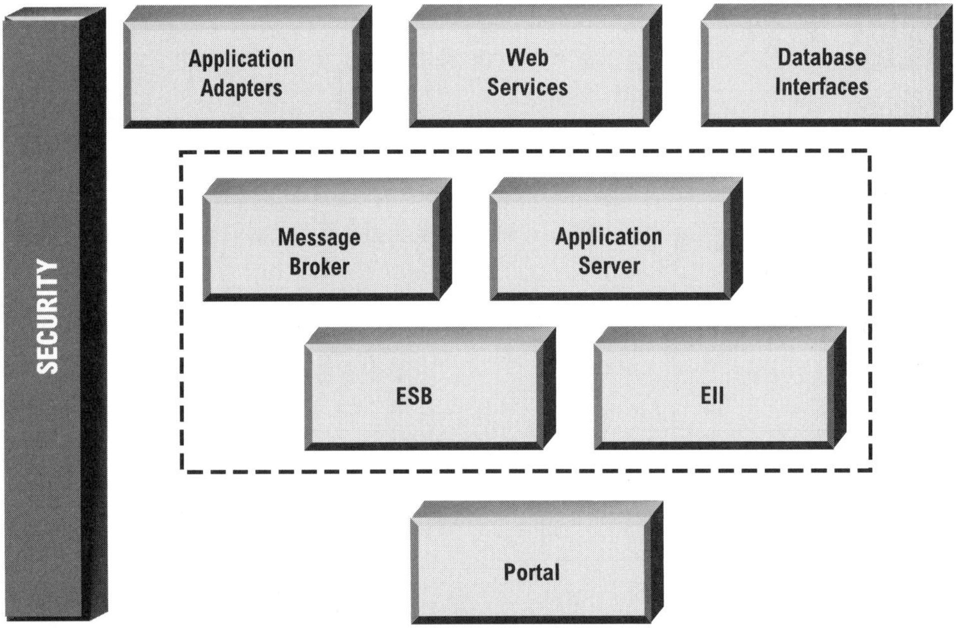

Figure 10-9 Portal Integration Reference Architecture

Integration Service	Vendor/Product	Implementation Notes
Portal	<Vendor, product name>	<Stand alone or part of application server or message broker platform?>
Back-End Application Integration		<Include all application integration services included in the portal solution.>
Message broker/enterprise service bus	<Product/protocol>	<Technology platform>
Application server	<Vendor, product name>	<Technology platform>
EII	<Vendor, product name or custom code>	<Level of routing supported; content based, business rules, header only info>
Application interface	<Vendor name/product name or deployment technology>	<Specify: integration broker adapter; Web service; JCA interface; data interface (ODBC, JDBC, OLE DB, ADO).>
Legacy integration	<Vendor, product name>	<Define type of integration.>

Figure 10-10 Portal Integration Implementation Table

integration solution. Alternatively, EII can be combined with a message broker, or ESB, or application server. Multiple types of interfaces may be used in a single implementation.

The Portal Integration Implementation Table (Figure 10-10) defines all the technologies and services that will be implemented as part of the portal solution.

10.4.4.6 Mobile Integration

If mobile devices are part of the solution, including multiple types of PDAs, cell phones, and other hand-held devices, then mobile integration servers can significantly reduce the time and cost of connecting to these devices. A mobile integration server can take the same information from multiple source systems, and flexibly format it for different target devices.

A number of EAI vendors partner with mobile integration vendors or license the solutions to provide this capability. The mobile integration server sits in between the firewalls in the DMZ, much like a B2B server. Also it can connect to applications through adapters or through other application integration platforms and brokers.

Because wireless connectivity is inherently insecure there are additional services that must be implemented, including additional security, and especially services for guaranteeing delivery. Mobile integration is becoming increasingly popular in business. The two basic uses are providing email and browser access to the mobile employee and the creation of custom mobile applications such as delivery tracking or warehouse logistics operations. The need for this technology is to deal with the unique constraints of bandwidth, screen size, and input mechanisms. In the future, these capabilities will be add-on enhancements to other methods such as an ESB, but the market has not fully matured to this level. Investments into these technologies should be treated as investments for several years since the rate of change here will be very high for the next few years. Figure 10-11 depicts a mobile integration architecture.

The Mobile Integration Specification Table (Figure 10-12, page 210), like B2B integration, may specify how integration to back-end systems will be implemented. This can be through other integration technology, or through application adapters.

10.4.4.7 Other Services

In this section other services are identified. This could include security, transactional, persistence, or other types or services. Integration implementations may involve a number of different patterns defined previously in this chapter and in other chapters in Part III of this book. In this section describe any additional services that will be included in the implementation.

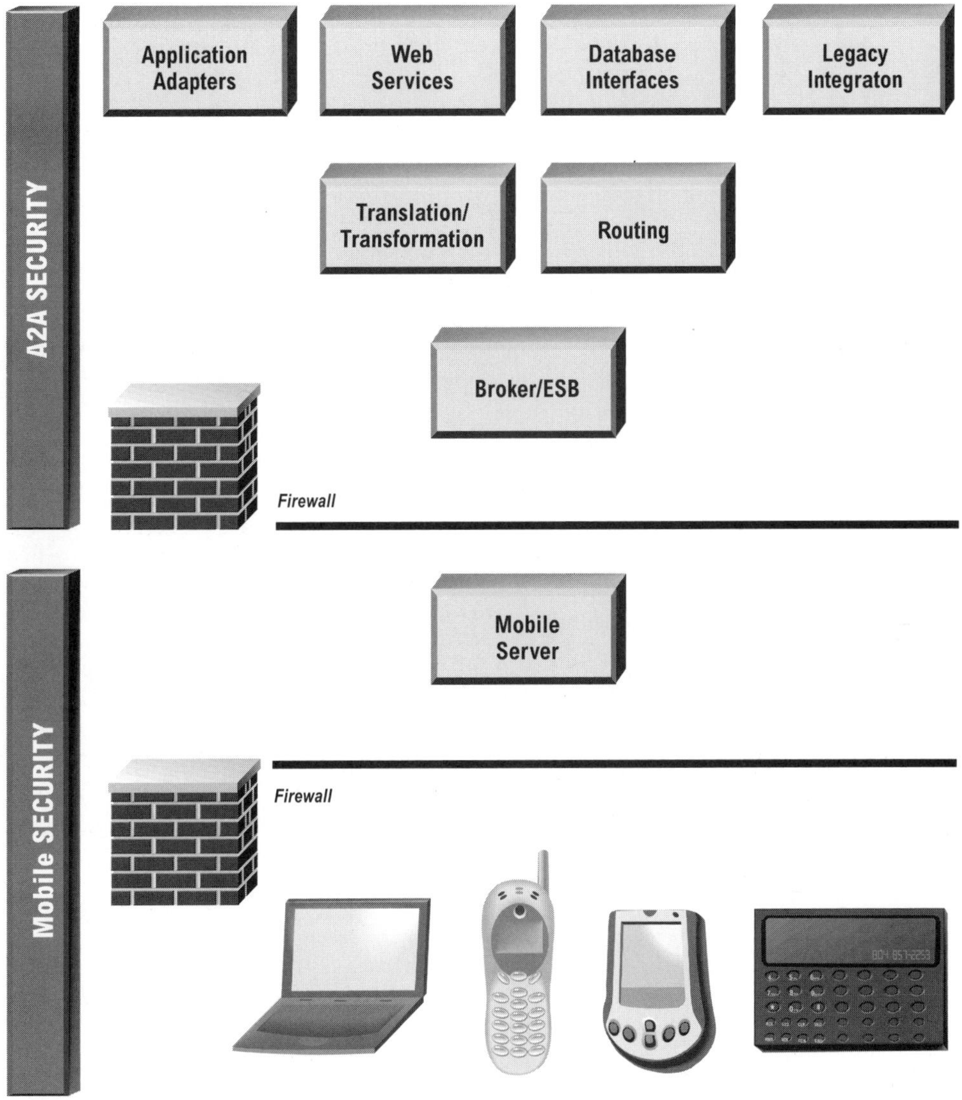

Figure 10-11 Mobile Integration Reference Architecture

Integration Service	Vendor/Product	Implementation Notes
Mobile integration server	<Vendor, product name>	<Define all services provided, including process management, as well as mobile interfaces supported. Also define reliability features.>
Mobile security	<Vendor, product name>	<Define all security services provided including encryption and authentication.>
Back-End Application Integration		<Include all application integration services included in the mobile solutions.>
Broker/enterprise service bus	<Product/protocol>	<Technology platform>
Translation and transformation	<Vendor name/ product name>	<Transformation at hub or target>
Routing	<Vendor, product name or custom code>	<Level of routing supported; content based, business rules, header only info>
Application interface	<Vendor name/ product name or deployment technology>	<Specify: integration broker adapter; Web service; JCA interface; data interface (ODBC, JDBC, OLE DB, ADO).>
Legacy integration	<Vendor, product name>	<Define type of integration.>
A2A security	<Vendor name/ product name or deployment technology>	<Specify how security is implemented, including integration with LDAP or other repository or product.>

Figure 10-12 Mobile Integration Implementation Table

10.4.5 Conclusions and Commentary

This section provides any final comments on implementation.

10.5 Best Practices in Application Integration

- **Invest in reuse.** It may cost a bit more initially, but will decrease implementation time and cost on future projects. Create reusable interfaces that can be leveraged in the next project.
- **Avoid or reduce redundancy.** Redundancy ultimately increases implementation and maintenance costs. One messaging system and one metadata repository for canonical data are a must for enabling enterprise integration.
- **Minimize the impact of change.** Take a service-oriented approach for creating the enterprise integration infrastructure. Design the solution with minimal dependency on particular technologies. Replacing a particular technology or vendor solution for an integration service should cause minimal disruption. This can be accomplished by adding layers of abstraction, such as access services, to the infrastructure.
- **Use standards wherever practical.** XML is currently an appropriate message and canonical data format standard. Web services are evolving as a standard application interface. Where standards are not yet mature, design the solution so that propriety technology can be changed later on with minimal impact to existing applications.

10.6 Next Steps

Large companies are likely to have a diverse set of integration needs, and therefore are likely to implement a number of different integration patterns. All of the patterns included in this chapter can be combined with any or all of the other patterns in this book. The patterns can be used as a guide when implementing tactical solutions. However, when using multiple patterns there is a risk of implementing overlapping technologies and increasing redundancy in the infrastructure. While business requirements dictate what types of integration services are necessary, the technologies used to implement the services, and the enterprise integration architecture should control how they are implemented. When implementation choices are guided by enterprise building codes, redundancy and cost can be controlled.

Each remaining chapter focuses on a different integration pattern, each of which meets a particular set of business requirements (Figure 10-13). Chapter 11 is on information integration, Chapter 12 is on composite integration, and Chapter 13 is on process integration. Some implementations may require a combination of patterns. Over time, a large enterprise can expect to have all types of integration technology. Chapter 14 shows how the patterns can all fit together in an integrated enterprise infrastructure.

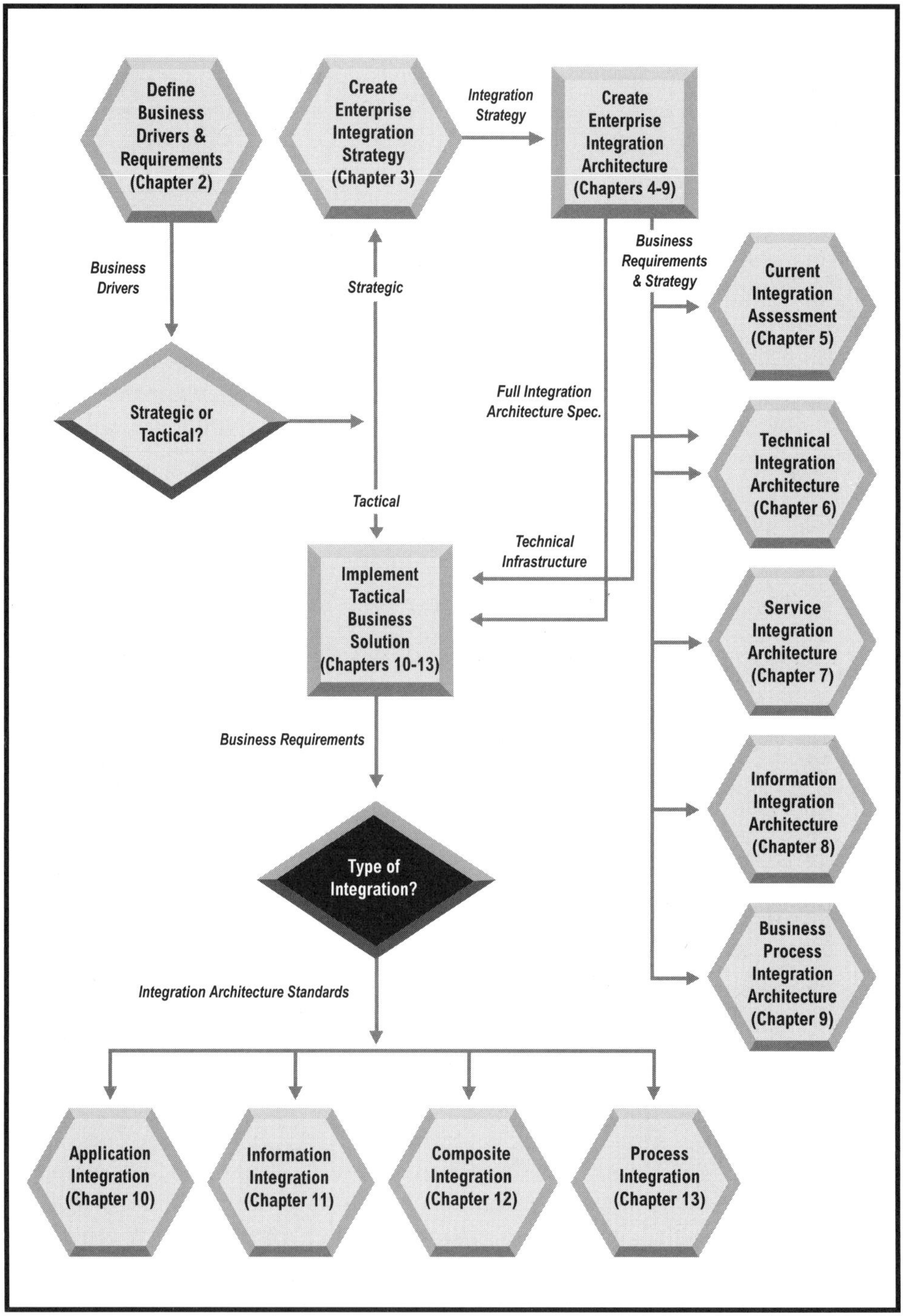

Figure 10-13 Integration Roadmap

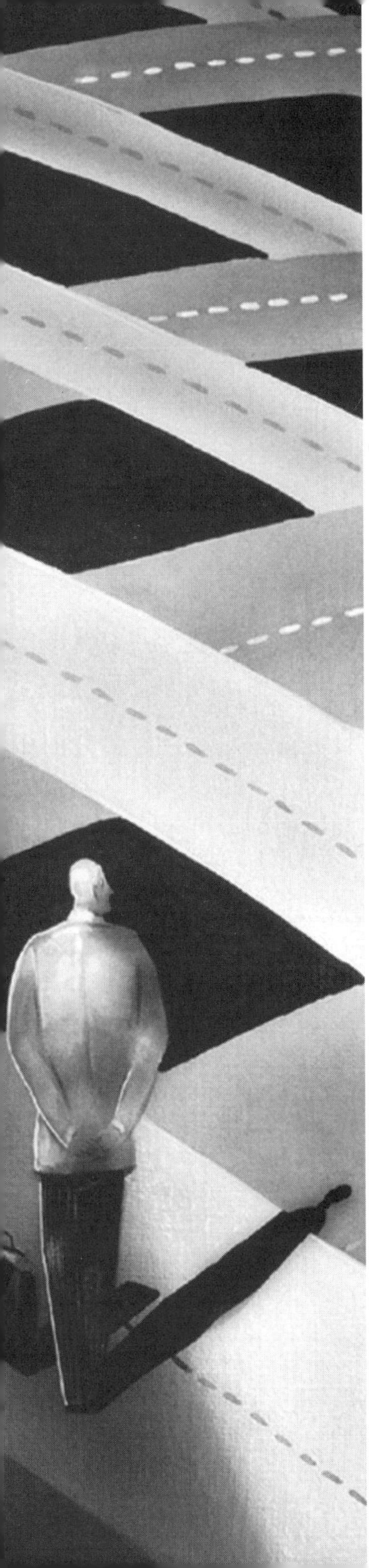

CHAPTER ELEVEN

Information Integration

11.1 Executive Overview

Data integration was the earliest form of integration. Data files were moved between systems in batch mode. Corporate information was consolidated in the form of data warehouses, data marts, and operational data stores. While these physical consolidated data sources continue to be important to organizations, real-time integration technologies became much more attractive solutions.

Data integration has matured dramatically in the last few years. In the past it was a point-to-point solution, strictly focused on moving blocks of information from one system to another. With the movement to real time, a focus on the importance of metadata and the need to integrate all forms of content, we find that data integration is a subset of the larger area of information integration. For the sake of clarity, we define data integration to mean structured data, managed by databases. Information integration includes both the structured data and unstructured information such as documents, graphics, and streaming media. For example, a Web site or portal could aggregate data from multiple databases and synchronize updates to all of them, as well as present other types of unstructured data, such as graphics and audio. Because Web and portal applications are becoming more robust and include multiple capabilities, information integration is likely to become extremely important.

The workhorse of data integration has been ETL tools. They were created to *e*xtract the information, *t*ransform it into a consolidated view, and then *l*oad it into a data warehouse in a batch mode. The data volumes involved were generally large, the load cycles long, and information in the data warehouse typically a day to a week old. For synchronizing data across operational systems, operational data stores were created, which enabled the real-time update of information. But the problem with each of these solutions was the need to physically move large volumes of data from source systems to multiple consolidated data stores including the data warehouse, distributed data marts, operational data stores, and analytical multidimensional databases. Latencies and inconsistencies are pretty much a given with such an architecture.

Enterprise application integration (EAI) resolved the latency problem by synchronizing changes across systems in real time, but less adequately addressed the needs aggregating and consolidating data and information across the enterprise. EAI maps source data to a canonical data format and enables exchanging data among systems, but does not define an aggregated view of the data objects or business entities. However, a customer service representative on the phone wants to be able to ask a question about the customer, and have the response come from the appropriate system—without needing to know what that system is. This requires the ability to make a query across distributed data sources as if they were a single database. EAI does not address this problem at all. Enterprise information integration (EII) does.

EII is simultaneously an old and new idea. It provides the data aggregation capabilities of the old ETL tools, but provides real-time access to accurate information, much like EAI. It also provides an infrastructure for integrated enterprise data management. With EAI, the semantic meaning of data, valuable corporate information required for enterprise data quality management is stored in proprietary mapping tools. These tools are designed to make it easy to map data formats between applications. They were not designed to provide enterprise information management. Metadata repositories are designed for this purpose. Yet the information discovered to enable the transformations is the same information required for the metadata repository. In an ideal world, the metadata repository would manage the data that is used by the transformation engine. In the real world semantic metadata is in multiple places, and not centrally managed. Metadata management is an issue for long-term quality of distributed information (see Chapter 8).

The other pressing need is to integrate and manage unstructured information. Documents, e-mail, graphics, streaming media, and other types of electronic data might be included in Web applications. Enterprise content management (ECM) provides these capabilities. ECM systems may also provide some application integration and workflow capabilities, redundantly providing these integration services also provided by other technologies in the infrastructure. While many large organizations will require ECM, EAI, and EII, there is little integration across these technologies today. They can all be services on an enterprise service bus, but a move toward common metadata will help companies manage both enterprise information and enterprise integration much more easily.

11.2 Information Integration Scenarios

This chapter focuses on technologies and architectures for implementing and operating applications built upon an enterprise information integration infrastructure. Information integration can be used to deploy the following kinds of applications

- Creating a single view of a customer or other business entity
- Enterprise data inventory and management
- Real time reporting and analysis, and creating management dashboards
- Updating a data warehouse
- Creating a virtual data warehouse
- Updating common information across information sources
- Creating portal applications containing both structured and unstructured data from disparate systems
- Integrating unstructured data, including documents, audio, video and other electronic media, into applications.
- Providing an infrastructure for enterprise information management, including all forms of digital media

Information integration simplifies the creation of all these applications by enabling the information so that it can be accessed and managed as if it came from a single data source.

While information integration has tactical benefits for providing a fast and easy way to access back-end data sources, the strategic benefit is the role it can play in long-term data management. An Aberdeen research report states that database administration costs now dominate the total cost of ownership (TCO) of applications below the 500-user level, and they continue to increase in importance for all sizes of applications (Kernochan 2003). Information integration enables a company to take an enterprise approach to managing information.

11.3 Choosing Information Integration Technology

Information integration is an emerging market sector. Currently the major categories of information integration technology are split between structured and unstructured data. Extract, transform, and load (ETL) tools are the most popular method of integration for synchronizing data. However, two areas that seem to be clearly emerging are EII and ECM.

ETL and EII focus on structured data integration. The difference being that ETL is a batch oriented tool and EII is real time. In addition, while EII product offerings focus on consolidating information contained in structured databases, a few also support unstructured content. ECM provides management and integration of unstructured information contained in documents, audio, video, and graphic files. While either EII or ECM may solve your current information integration requirements, in the future, the content managed by these different technologies might need to be integrated into rich media applications. Furthermore, compliance regulations such as Sarbanes-Oxley stipulate storage requirements and management of other enterprise information and communications including e-mail. This has led some BPM vendors to partner with ECM vendors. The information integration market is sure to evolve and consolidate to cover the full range and more solutions that integrate both structured and unstructured information over the next couple of years.

Currently, for the most part these different technologies are not integrated, and each provides overlapping and redundant services including application adapters and metadata repositories. While the current technology choices might make it impossible to avoid redundancy, an integrated enterprise metadata repository will go a long way to enabling rapid information integration in the future. The evolving metadata standards (see Chapter 8) as well as the acceptance of XML as the canonical data format will enable the convergence of different types of metadata into a single enterprise-wide repository. Companies should begin capturing metadata about integrated solutions in a common format on a common platform so this information can be leveraged and reused in the future. Leaving this information in proprietary data mapping tools constrains future business agility.

11.3.1 ETL

ETL tools are broadly available although there are neither standards nor common architecture among ETL solutions. Each product has a different environment where it excels. While most perform very well with modern relational databases, there are very real differences in products in regard to which legacy systems they will support in a mainframe environment. Furthermore, integration with packaged applications will be different among the offerings. ETL tools tend to be stand-alone and batch oriented, focused on the data warehouse market. Some provide additional features and functions to synchronize databases and packaged applications.

11.3.2 EII

The EII market is just emerging. The focus of tools in this market is to access information in real time from across multiple information systems. At the heart of these solutions is a metadata repository that contains the data definitions for all existing systems as well as the access mechanisms for retrieving the information. In most cases, these are a one-way delivery of information. However, new implementations are providing two-way integration. The other major feature of an EII tool is the data aggregation service that allows new data structures to be created from existing structures. Data lineage and impact reporting allows the system to ensure that changes can be evaluated and managed to existing systems. XML and Web services are rapidly becoming the standards on which these products are based. Case Study 11.1 revisits the CompuCredit case study to look at the business benefits of an EII approach (CIO Magazine 2003).

Case Study 11.1
CompuCredit: Creating an Enterprise Data Architecture

In Case Study 3.1 we introduced CompuCredit to illustrate an organization that executed a strategy to make information more readily available to their business users to reduce analysis time from months to weeks. The integration strategy was based on a design pattern that combined data integration with an enterprise metadata repository (EMR). Standards were a key element to the selection of a partner. XML and Web services were a critical factor in

(continued)

Case Study 11.1 *(cont.)*

the architecture and design. The EMR, data integration, and standards were combined together to form CompuCredit's XML Gateway. The XML Gateway provided transparent access to the diversity of internal and external data sources and applications that are required to reduce the time and effort to acquire and manage the credit-card receivables portfolios that are at the heart of the business.

An information integration strategy was the most relevant architectural approach given the need to provide information in real time from multiple sources in an integrated view to users and user driven applications.

CompuCredit used Software AG's XML integration technology as the basis for the Gateway's EMR and data integration components. Although it is not necessary to base this design on standards, the focus on standards by CompuCredit increases the ability for the infrastructure to be used by a variety of tools and technologies, thereby paving the way to solve future problems.

11.3.3 ECM

Most organizations spend their money on managing their structured information while the vast amount of their unstructured information is stored on hard drives of personal computers without any mechanism to find and reuse this information. The ECM market is oriented at providing solutions to solve this problem. There is no common acceptable product architecture or standards under which these are developed. However, a metadata repository is a core of any solution. The architectures often use the same application integration components to access information on disparate platforms and systems. Case Study 11.2 looks at how the State of North Dakota applied an ECM approach to help their legislators (Software AG n.d.).

Case Study 11.2
State of North Dakota: Replacing Volumes of Paper with Instant, Online Access to Bill information

The State of North Dakota legislature meets every other year to pass or amend hundreds of bills in an 80-day session. This is a paper intensive environment, where traditionally a legislator would have a two-foot long rolling binder of bill books, with reams of additional information at the office. Mainframe access to bills was available, but not practical for many staff members.

The Legislative Automated Work Station (LAWS) was built to enable legislators to efficiently access and update bill information from their laptops while Congress is in session. Their content is provided to them in an integrated manner with additional features, like calendar and e-mail, as well as other content from legacy systems, such as hearing schedules and session comparisons, transcripts of constituent phone calls, and roll-call votes from each chamber. All of this information can be searched in seconds.

An information integration strategy based on an enterprise content management pattern was the most relevant architectural approach given the need to provide structured and unstructured information in real time from multiple sources in an integrated view to users and user-driven applications.

The State of North Dakota was able to reduce the burden on their legislators as a result. Information is immediately available, staff are not wasting time copying documents, and this is provided in an easy-to-use interface.

11.4 Information Integration Implementation Specification

11.4.1 Introduction

This specification provides implementation guidance for the development of an information integration-based solution. The information integration architecture from Chapter 8 will form the basis for the implementation. This section describes the specific technical problems that are being addressed in the implementation to give context to the specific implementation. See Appendix I for the full specification.

11.4.2 Scope

The scope of an Information Integration specification is limited to the specifics of the information and systems that are being integrated. It should cover organizations, information, systems, and the expected end result.

11.4.3 Key Participants

This section identifies all stakeholders in the implementation, including business managers who control all or part of the systems, data stewards or those responsible for data quality, system designers and architect(s), and the development team who will execute the implementation. Any other participants or stakeholders should also be identified, including their roles.

11.4.4 Information Integration Patterns and Services

There are several basic implementation patterns for an information integration solution. These information integration patterns are

- Data Integration
- Unstructured Content Integration
- Metadata Repository Integration

This section defines the particular pattern that is being used and provides details on the configuration of the specific components of the implementation.

11.4.4.1 Data Integration

Data integration involves structured data, generally found in different databases across the organization. As previously stated, ETL solutions have given rise to real-time enterprise information integration (EII). Solutions may provide a virtual data warehouse with integrated access across distributed data sources, mid-tier caching, or a physical mid-tier data store for real-time data aggregation and reporting. If batch synchronization is acceptable then the architecture can be simplified by choosing a specific ETL product. However, an EII-based architecture provides a more robust architecture upon which to build an integrated enterprise architecture.

The best examples for the use of simple data integration is to batch-synchronize two databases. For example, setting up a process to take a set of orders entered for a day and load this data into the fulfillment system. This is the traditional use of ETL technology.

EII vendors have technology for providing real-time access to data from multiple operational data stores. This includes optimizing distributed queries through proprietary indexing technology and/or distributed query optimization, caching data, and/or creating a mid-tier data store. In addition, EII provides the ability to aggregate data into a single logical view. The ability to create different views of consolidated information to support different applications increases ease of use. Data cleansing was generally part of the older ETL tools and some EII vendors are including the capability to support enterprise data quality management. A great example of the use of this technology is to create a single view of a customer. Most organizations struggle to understand the relationship they have with a customer. Data exists across multiple systems with conflicting definitions. The desire to create a marketing campaign that is distributed through e-mail is often difficult when there is multiple conflicting e-mail addresses entered into different systems. Trying to value customers is impossible without creating a single view of the information to determine whether clients are profitable and where to spend effort. This single view becomes reusable and can be utilized in portal applications or in call center operations.

Distributed transaction management may be necessary when updates are made to distributed data sources. The EII tool may include transaction management, support the XA transaction management standard, or integrate with a transaction processing (TP) monitor. This becomes critical when the single view is used not only to view, but also to update information. For example, the ability to update customer information from a single aggregated view allows for improved accuracy across systems. It enables updating a customer's address or e-mail information across systems from a single unified view.

While data warehouses will continue to exist to provide summary and historical data, EII can be used to integrate real-time business events with the historical data in warehouses to implement real-time BAM and decision support systems. For example, after a single view has been created, the information can be tied into a business intelligence tool that can operate in real time on data rather than only in a historical mode. The nature of BAM is real time. Any scheduling activity where changes can have significant impacts, such as airlines or delivery operations, can benefit from real time activity monitoring.

The Data Integration Reference Architecture (Figure 11-1) depicts the required and optional services for data integration. The query service represents the ability to access disparate data sources as if they were a single database (including the ability to make a single SQL call across databases) and support

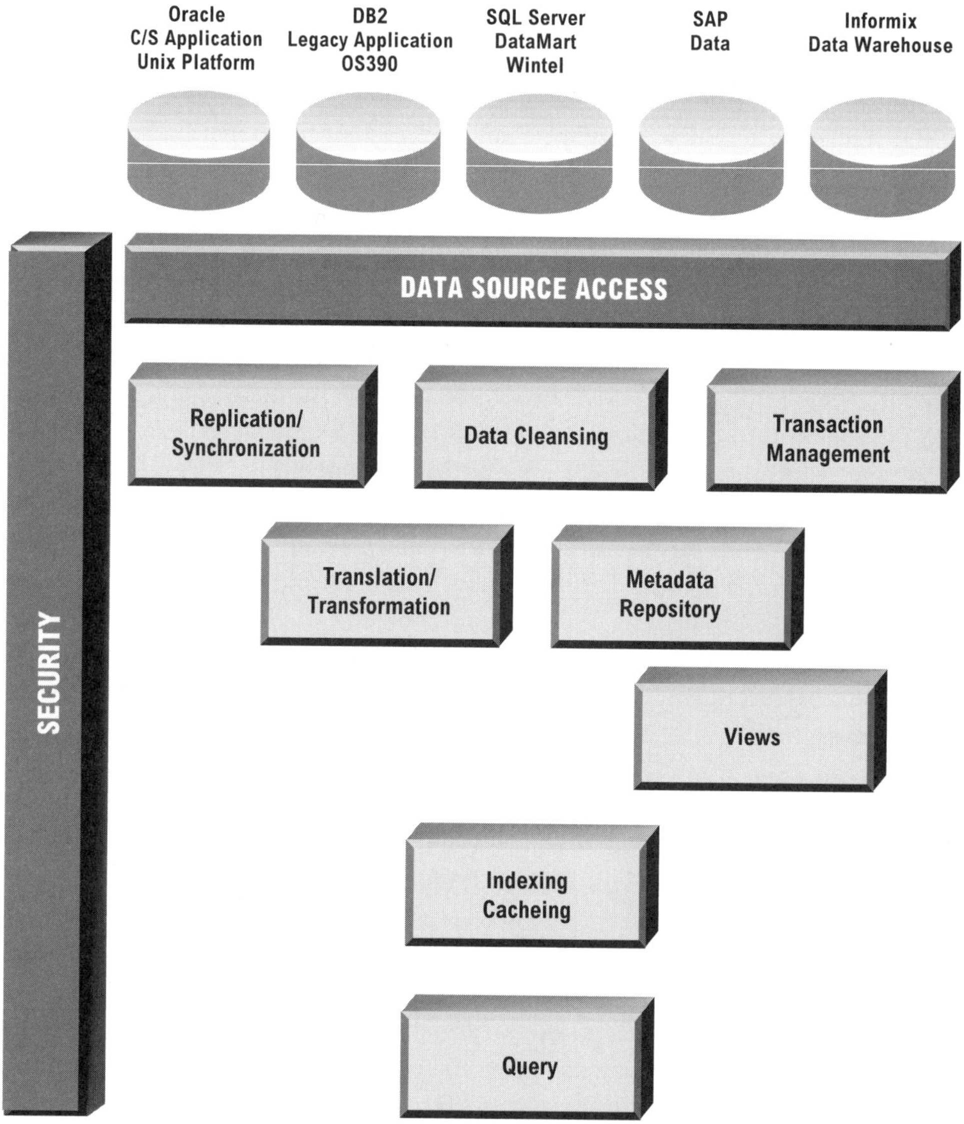

Figure 11-1 Data Integration Reference Architecture

real-time queries of consolidated and federated data. Indexing and caching represents methods to enable fast real time queries. Views represents the ability to create different virtual views of consolidated information to simplify access and support specific applications or users. The metadata repository stores all relevant information about the data objects. Data translation and transformation is required to map information into the consolidated view and make updates to the sources. Data cleansing, often part of a data warehouse, is very important for maintaining the accuracy of integration data. Data replication and synchronization has been available from database vendors for a while, and is a very useful service for data integration. The data source access layer includes application adapters and database gateways such as ODBC and JDBC.

The Implementation Table (Figure 11-2, page 224) specifies all the integration services provided in the Information Integration Architecture, along with relevant implementation details.

11.4.4.2 Unstructured Content Integration

While data integration provides integrated access to information in databases, there is a vast amount of unstructured data that all needs to be integrated with Web portals and applications, including documents, images, photos, audio, video, and other digital media. This unstructured information requires the same management and query capabilities as structured information management and integration. ECM solutions provide this capability.

The services provided by ECM solutions (Figure 11-3, page 225) include content repository, search (query) capability, version control (check in/out), replication of content changes, integration, content rendering (translation/transformation), security, process management, and content delivery. The future direction is to have both unstructured and structured data accessible and managed through one tool. A few EII vendors already offer it. Organizations that create content from existing information assets can benefit from ECM. For example, the creation and management of product labels may seem easy, but when a label needs to be managed for different markets with different regulations with different languages, but with a single brand image, an ECM solution becomes mandatory.

The Unstructured Information Table (Figure 11-4, page 226) details the implementation. All the services may come from a single ECM vendor, or from a combination of vendors. ECM vendors typically have multiple modules and capabilities that can be flexibly deployed, so even when using a single vendor it is useful to specify the services or modules implemented.

11.4.4.3 Metadata Repository Integration

Metadata repositories are often part of both EII and ECM solutions. However, they are also listed separately here to call attention to their importance and to the

Integration Service	Vendor/Product	Implementation Notes
Data integration tool	<Vendor name/ product name>	<Modules deployed, method (virtual DB, mid-tier data store; indexing and retrieval)>
EII	<Vendor name/ product name>	<Modules deployed>
Translation and transformation	<Vendor name/ product name if different EII vendor>	<Formats supported>
Data source access	<Vendor name/ product name if different EII vendor>	<ODBC, JDBC, SOAP, other methods supported>
Metadata repository	<Vendor name/ product name if different EII vendor>	<DBMS technology>
Query	<Vendor name/ product name if different EII vendor>	<Ability to query enterprise information grid as a single data source. Define query language or method.>
Views	<Vendor name/ product name if different EII vendor>	<List views available to simplify use for specific applications or users.>
Data cleansing	<Vendor name/ product name>	<Done by the tool or scripts?>
Replication/data synchronization	<Vendor name/ product name>	<Part of DB or EII server?>
Transaction management	<Vendor name/ product name if different EII vendor>	<Define roll-back or compensation.>
Security	<Vendor name/ product name if 3rd party security vendor used>	<Methods and level of security provided>

Figure 11-2 Data Integration Implementation Table

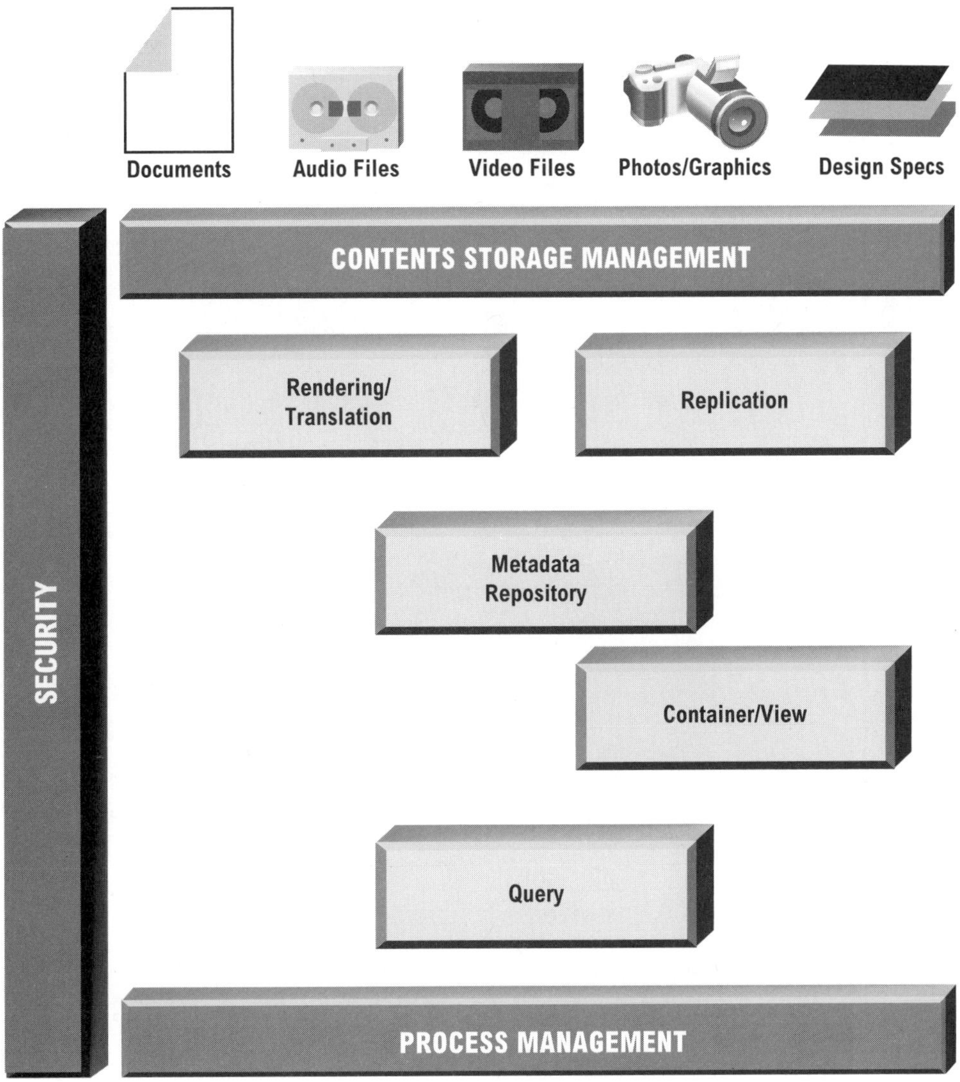

Figure 11-3 Unstructured Information Reference Architecture

fact that common information metadata is an essential part of the integration infrastructure. A metadata repository is essentially a database that contains information about data sources (see Chapter 8 for more information regarding metadata). Unfortunately, much integration metadata is buried in proprietary tools. In order to maximize reuse and business agility, metadata should be managed consistently as a valuable enterprise resource.

Integration Service	Vendor/Product	Implementation Notes
ECM	<Vendor name/ product name>	<Modules deployed>
Rendering (translation and transformation)	<Vendor name/ product name if different ECM vendor>	<Formats supported, including HTML, PDF, MS Word, MS Excel, TIFF, JPEG>
Content repository	<Vendor name/ product name if different ECM vendor>	<Types of content supported including documents, images, photos, audio, and video>
Metadata		<Types of metadata descriptions supported including thumbnails, key words; common information management metadata>
Query capabilities		<Ability to query different types of content with a common method; full text query; scanned text query>
Content objects/ containers (views)		<Define content objects that contain other content objects, for example, Web page.>
Content propagation		<Ability to propagate changes across a variety of sources to ensure content is synchronized>
Process management	<Vendor name/ product name if different ECM vendor>	<Modules deployed, including modeling, management dashboard, etc.>
Security	<Vendor name/ product name if 3rd party security vendor used>	<Model and level of security provided>

Figure 11-4 Unstructured Information Implementation Table

The enterprise metadata repository contains all of the metadata on information and application sources. An active metadata repository contains the access mechanisms as well. The metadata repository also contains new metadata descriptions, such as canonical format, that can be mapped onto the source metadata either directly or applying transformation or calculation rules. Adapters or other integration technologies, including database gateways and Web service interfaces, are used to connect to the existing sources.

Active data access services within a repository provide the capabilities to query the repository in a common way, and access the information source through this abstraction layer. The repository provides a common mechanism for creating a single view of a customer or other resource, enterprise data inventory and management, real-time reporting and analysis, creating a "virtual data warehouse," and updating common information across information sources.

Because EII and ECM solutions could each have their own metadata repositories, a company could wind up with multiple repositories to manage, and metadata that needs to be synchronized and integrated. In principle, the metadata repository should provide a level of abstraction that makes it easier to consolidate, integrate, and manage distributed information. In practice, the company may need to create a multi-tiered metadata architecture to provide the levels of abstraction necessary to deliver this agility. The architecture diagram and specification table should include all metadata sources. Figure 11-5 (page 228) shows how an enterprise metadata repository would work with EII and ECM solutions to provide access to different types of enterprise information.

The Metadata Repository Implementation Table (Figure 11-6, page 229) defines the critical services for supporting real-time distributed data access. While the list below defines a checklist to look for in a solution, the success of the metadata repository will depend more on the processes and culture of the organization. High-level support and commitment are often the defining factors for success.

11.4.5 Conclusions and Commentary

This section should provide any final comments on implementation.

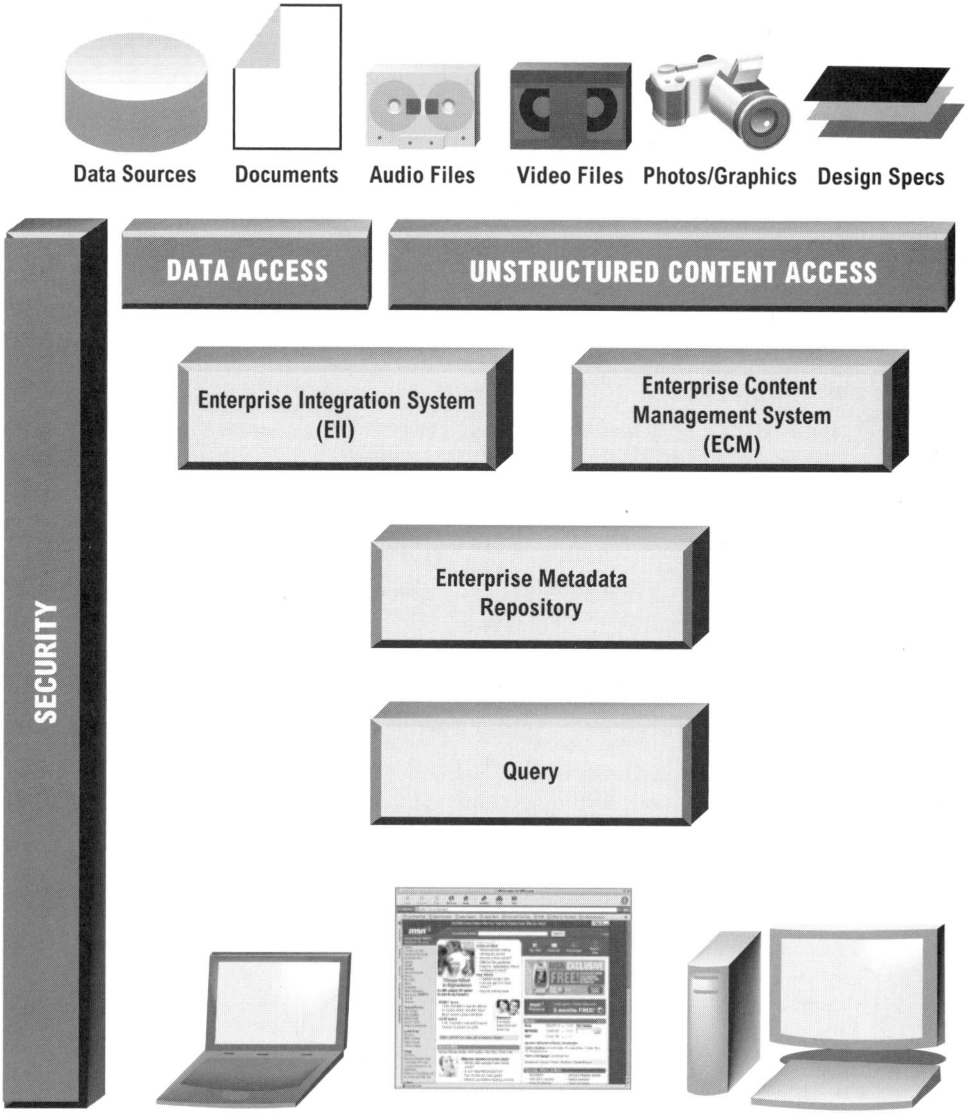

Figure 11-5 Metadata Repository Reference Architecture

Integration Service	Vendor/Product	Implementation Notes
Metadata repository	<Vendor name/ product name>	<Types of content supported including documents, images, photos, audio, and video>
Canonical format		<XML, proprietary, other>
Translation and transformation/ format rendering	<Vendor name/ product name>	<Formats supported, including XML, other data formats, HTML, PDF, MS Word, MS Excel, TIFF, JPEG.>
Query capabilities	<Language(s) supported>	<SQL; key word search, full text query, other>
Access capabilities	<Vendor name/ product name>	<Database API or gateway, adapter, other>
Replication	<Vendor name/ product name>	<Mechanism for synchronizing changes across sources>
Security	<Vendor name/ product name if 3rd party security vendor used>	<Model and level of security provided>

Figure 11-6 Metadata Repository Implementation Table

11.5 Best Practices in Information Integration

- **Create an EMR.** Create a comprehensive enterprise metadata repository that provides information about different types of enterprise information sources.
- **Organize a "center of excellence."** Create an enterprise integration competency center. Creating the metadata repository incrementally, on a project-by-project basis, will work well as long as a centralized group manages it so overlaps and inconsistencies can quickly be identified and resolved.
- **Focus on data quality.** Appoint information stewards who are responsible for the quality of data in source systems. The information stewards are also

responsible for participating in design reviews and ensuring the semantic meaning of data is correctly mapped to the canonical format.

- **Identify "gold standards" for data.** Create an enterprise information architecture that includes information on sources of record (authoritative data sources) for each business entity that must be consistent across the enterprise.
- **Ensure appropriate testing is accomplished.** Create a test plan to ensure that queries to a consolidated data view will return correct responses.

11.6 Next Steps

The next step in information integration is to implement the solution. However many information integration solutions are part of a larger integration initiative. If you are interested in composite applications, see Chapter 12. If you are interested in process management, see Chapter 13. If the project requires real time updates to back-end systems and distributed transaction management across systems, see Chapter 10 on application integration. (See Figure 11-7.)

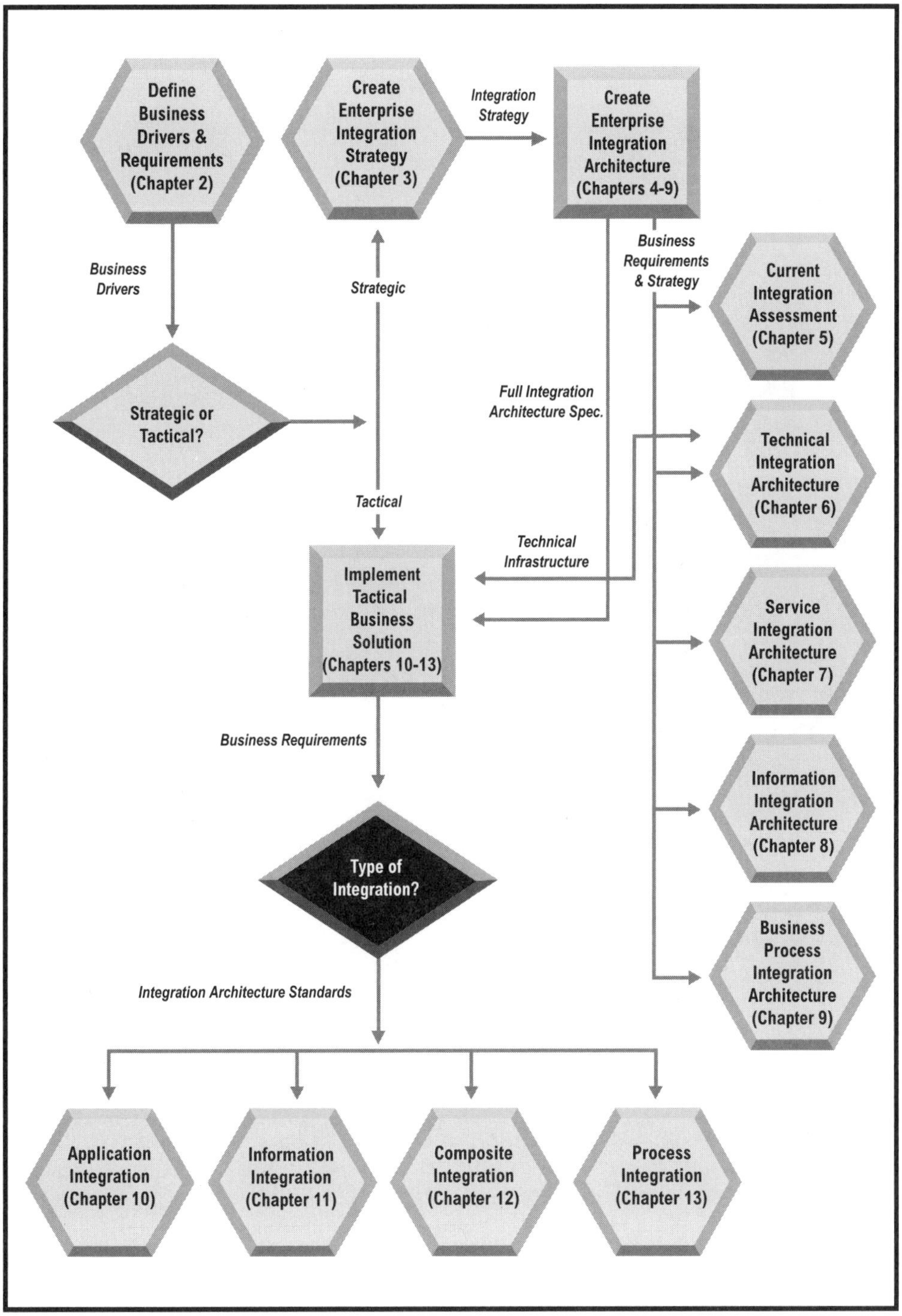

Figure 11-7 Integration Roadmap

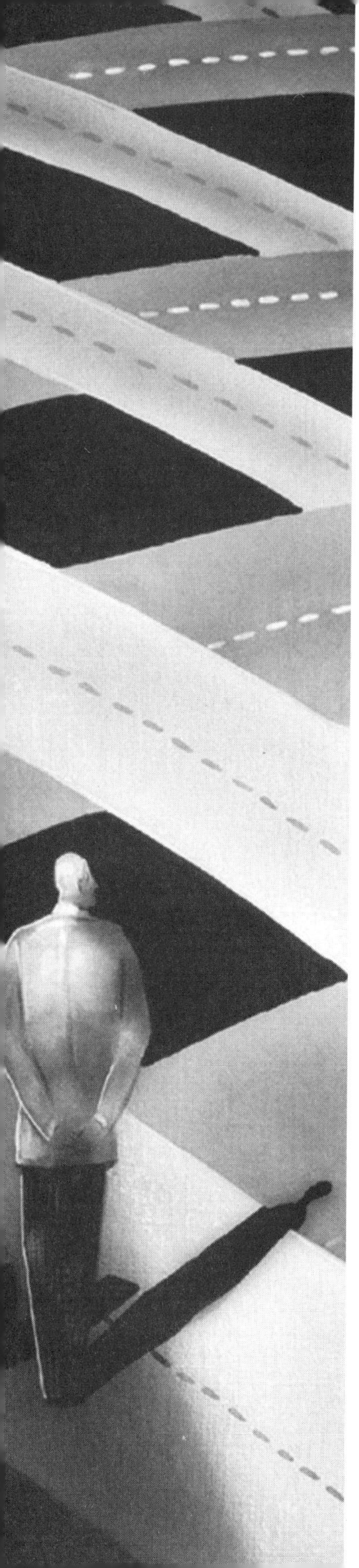

CHAPTER TWELVE

Composite Application Integration

12.1 Executive Overview

Business agility is the new business mantra. The ability to deliver new solutions faster, respond quickly to market changes or emerging opportunities, and manage the enterprise in real-time is the goal of all organizations seeking to gain competitive advantage. Integration is changing the nature of application development from a standalone activity that focuses on the creation of new code to an activity that is centered on using existing applications as the basis for developing new business systems. Rather than creating a new customer database for an application, you can reuse the existing CRM system. Rather than creating code to determine the value of a customer, you can reuse the existing custom application on the mainframe. Rather than creating a new user interface from scratch, you can reuse the portal interface. Achieving this new level of business agility requires the ability to quickly add new functionality or business processes while leveraging existing system and information assets. This is the goal of composite integration.

Composite integration is a form of application assembly. It is not a new idea. The idea of components and application assembly has been discussed for over twenty years going back to the early days of object-oriented programming. Rather than writing the application from scratch, the application is assembled from existing components or business services, and combined with new services. However, what makes it different is that composite integration is accomplished through standardized interfaces for the components representing business services. In the past, it was very difficult to achieve the benefits of composite application assembly unless the enterprise standardized on just one development platform. Due to the lack of standards, integrating across different platform and technologies was difficult, time consuming, and expensive. Web services and application integration technology have now removed this obstacle. Any modern development environment and language can be used to develop these applications.

What makes composite application integration different from application and information integration is the focus on creating new applications through the reuse of existing systems as software components. This is done in a programmatic fashion. Programmers rather than integration specialists perform the integration using the application development tool sets. The end result feels like a custom-developed application and not an integration of existing systems. However, the application is primarily constructed through the integration of existing systems.

Composite application integration helps achieve business agility because it enables companies to develop new functionality and integrate it with existing systems and information sources. It enables an incremental approach to delivering systems and can rapidly deliver new business processes or functions through a modular approach.

Composite application integration presupposes a service-oriented architecture. The components of the composite application are bundles of code implementing a business function, packaged at a level of granularity to maximize reuse, and wrapped in a standard interface. With this architecture, the bundles of code themselves can be written in any programming language as long as it adheres to a standardized interface, and Web services have become an almost universally supported interface. A Web service can physically reside on any platform, and be accessed by any program or service that can call a Web service. A composite application can include services or components running on different platforms, and written in different programming languages. Integration technology is an essential enabler of composite applications.

While integration provides the underpinnings, composite application assembly is a unique style of integration that is more programmatic in nature. The center of the solution is more often the development and deployment platform rather than an integration broker.

The business case for composite applications is clear. However, realizing a 30% to 40% savings first requires a sizeable investment in creating and managing reusable modules of code. But companies can ill afford not to make that investment if they wish to achieve business agility. Case Study 12.1 shows how Miami-Dade County was able to achieve remarkable results through the application of SOA and composite application integration (Morris and Gold-Bernstein 2003).

Case Study 12.1
Miami-Dade County Integrates and Extends the Mainframe Through Web Services

Miami-Dade County is the largest metropolitan area in the State of Florida, with an annual budget of more than $3 billion, and over 2.2 million residents. The county systems are responsible for all aspects of local government, including Life Safety Systems, supporting Police and Fire; Property Tax; Permitting and Licensing; Courts—including criminal, civil and local courts; Finance and Accounting; and Human Services.

The systems supporting the government activities are primarily on mainframes. Miami-Dade needed to keep those systems running, and extend their capabilities for e-government initiatives. The county has adopted a leading-edge mentality towards information technology. Since 1998, Miami-Dade has provided Web-based applications to make it easier for residents to do business with the county. In 1999, it won Computerworld's Top 25 Wireless Innovators Award.

In 2001, Miami-Dade implemented e-Permitting to allow contractors to apply for, pay, and receive building permits online. They can print the permit and hang it up—never needing to go into an office. This is a huge savings in time for contractors and homeowners, while reducing the county's operational costs. Each month e-permitting accounts for hundreds of thousands of dollars worth of transactions.

To continue to improve operational efficiency, Miami-Dade decided to create a service-oriented architecture using Web services to extend the legacy systems. For example, property tax information is required across

(continued)

Case Study 12.1 *(cont.)*

the county. Police on an investigation call to find out who the legal owner of a property is, realtors use the information extensively—in fact, property tax information is required by all 40 county departments for their stand-alone applications. Miami-Dade created a Web service for the Property Tax Appraisal System that provides standardized access to all required information in one reusable service.

The next big project is the answer center that handles all 911 emergency calls and all 311 county information calls through a set of services.

Applying a composite application architecture pattern was the most relevant given the need to:

- Provide new services to a diverse constituency
- Allow access by both users and other applications
- Refresh and leverage legacy systems
- Develop new types of applications on the services

In local government, funding is always an issue. Miami Dade has been able to reduce overall development and maintenance costs through their SOA and composite applications, while improving service to the county residents.

12.2 Composite Application Integration Scenarios

Composite applications can be used to solve the following business requirements:

- Extending the functionality of packaged applications
- Assembling new business solutions from existing modules
- Adding a new functional module to existing applications

In all of these scenarios, the focus is on implementing new business functionality from a combination of new and existing components. It is the building block approach to application development. Integration technology is the primary enabler of this approach.

In each case, a programmer focuses his or her design efforts on the modules that exist or working to establish new interfaces for existing systems. New modules are minimized, and if they need to be developed are done so in a fashion to allow reuse in the future. The bulk of the application is in orchestrating the flow between existing modules. The first few applications using this approach can be challenging, because the Web service interfaces may not exist for a broad enough set of services.

12.3 Choosing Composite Application Integration Technology

The key technologies for composite application integration are application platform suites, Web services that provide the standardized interface, and orchestration technology to control the flow of the business process across all technical components and services.

Composite application integration is a distinct style of integration. It involves different core technologies and the implementers are usually application developers rather than integration specialists. In this chapter we focus on the development aspect of composite applications. However, it must be noted that the technologies discussed under Application Integration (Chapter 10), can also be used to provide the infrastructure for composite applications.

12.3.1 Application Platform Suites

Application platform suites include portals, integration brokers, and application servers. The components of the suite may not share a single platform or common development environment. However, an integrated platform has numerous advantages, including decreasing training and maintenance costs. All the major application server vendors offer platform suites but not all offer solutions on a common platform. There are also some Web service integration suites that offer lighter weight solutions.

12.3.2 Web Services

Web services provide the standardized interface to the components and systems that are part of the composite application. All the integration broker vendors support Web services. Additionally, as stated above, there are also pure play Web service development and deployment suites. When choosing technology for creating Web services, consider the skill sets necessary for implementing the solution. For example, in some implementations the legacy application developers may be the primary implementers because they understand how best to wrap the legacy code, and a tool focused on legacy skill sets might be most appropriate. In other cases, a tool focused on .NET or Java developers might be more appropriate.

12.3.3 Orchestration

Orchestration manages the flow of control across the services in the composite application. While the functionality of the application is delivered by the different services, the overall business process is defined in the orchestration logic. Orchestration is still in the early stages of adoption. There have been a number of different standards proposed by different groups, and at this point BPEL4WS (Business Process Execution Language for Web Services) is the most widely supported. There are currently few tools on the market that are fully BPEL compliant, although vendors are giving much lip service to the standard. The choice of orchestration technology is closely tied to the development and deployment platform and will most likely come from the application platform and integration suite vendors. Business process management tools can also be used to orchestrate composite applications.

12.4 Composite Integration Implementation Specification

12.4.1 Introduction

This specification provides implementation guidance for the implementation of a composite application integration based solution. It is most likely that the Service Integration Architecture Specification from Chapter 7 will form the basis for the implementation.

This section describes the specific technical problems that are being addressed in the implementation, and provides a context for the specific implementation. See Appendix J for the full specification.

12.4.2 Scope

The scope of a Composite Integration Implementation Specification is limited to the specific services, components, and systems that are being integrated. It should cover organizations, information, systems, and the expected end result.

12.4.3 Key Participants

This section identifies all stakeholders in the implementation, including business managers who control all or part of the systems, the development team who will execute the implementation, and any system designers and/or architect(s) who participated. Any other participants or stakeholders should also be identified, including their roles.

12.4.4 Composite Integration Patterns and Services

There is really only one composite integration pattern but there are numerous variations on how it can be implemented. The composite application consists of services and/or components or systems that can be called as services. The services have a standard interface, and are integrated into an application through code logic or an orchestration engine.

A good example of a composite application is the creation of any new channel for product sales. For example, if an organization wants to create a call center to provide a new method for customers to place orders, this would be a good candidate for a composite application. Since all of the processes exist for placing an order, it makes more sense to use this infrastructure rather than build a redundant set of applications that will need to be integrated together to synchronize the information. The same holds for creating a customer portal that can be a duplication of the call center functionality provided in a new user interface with different security controls.

Figure 12-1 depicts the Composite Application Integration Reference Architecture with the services essential for composite applications. The services can be implemented through an application platform suite, message broker, ESB, or adapters.

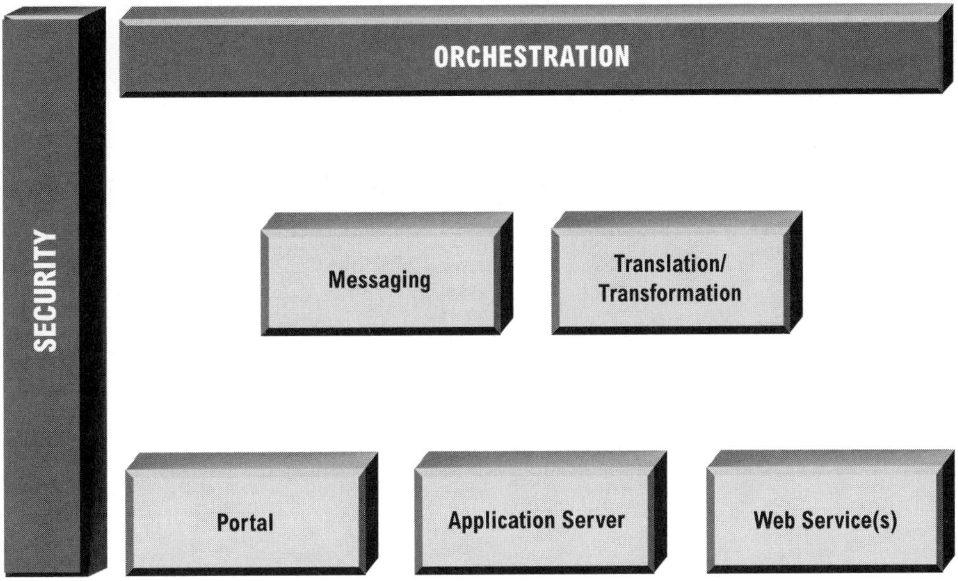

Figure 12-1 Composite Application Integration Reference Architecture

Integration Service	Vendor/Product	Implementation Notes
Development and deployment	<Vendor name/ product name>	<Application server, Web services development tool>
Service interface	<Vendor name/ product name>	<Web services>
Translation and transformation	<Vendor name/ product name>	<Application platform suite, message broker, other service>
Orchestration	<Vendor name/ product name>	<Web service orchestration, workflow, process engine>
Portal	<Vendor name/ product name>	<Portal services provided such as: transactions, workflow, etc.>
Messaging	<Vendor name/ product name>	<Messaging services provided such as: publish/subscribe, guaranteed delivery, etc.>
Security	<Vendor name/ product name if 3rd party security vendor used>	<Level of security provided>

Figure 12-2 Composite Application Implementation Table

The Composite Application Implementation Table (Figure 12-2) defines the alternative technologies that can be used to implement the solution.

12.4.5 Conclusions and Commentary

This section should provide any final comments on implementation.

12.5 Best Practices in Composite Application Integration

- **Invest in creating reusable services.** This may require a higher initial investment, but will decrease cost and implementation time in future implementations. The strategy also increases business agility.
- **Create functionally independent services.** Loose coupling between services makes the infrastructure more adaptable to change.

- **Manage and reward reuse.** Changing programmer behavior involves both the carrot and the stick. The carrot includes rewards for maximizing reuse. The stick is the central architecture group that manages reuse. This can include rewards for minimizing development time that would inspire developers to look for ways to reuse existing assets.
- **Structure design reviews.** Focus design reviews on the definition of interfaces to improve reuse potential.
- **Implement directory services.** Use a directory to register and locate interfaces and components at runtime.

12.6 Next Steps

Composite integration is an on-going journey. The goal is to create reusable business services that can be implemented quickly and inexpensively. While there is a high ROI for reuse, few companies achieve it because it requires ongoing management and investment. Reuse often requires a change of development focus. Programmer productivity is directly disproportionate to the amount of programming done. The less a programmer codes, the more productivity he or she can achieve. Much more can be accomplished through reuse.

The next step in composite integration is to manage and grow the repository. Reward reuse—employees generally focus on where they are being measured. Reward contributions of reusable services, and reward reuse of existing services. This will help build a culture of reuse.

The composite application may include a combination of other patterns as well, including process integration and substantial application integration and/or data integration. If this is the case, you can refer to the appropriate chapters in Part III of this book (Figure 12-3).

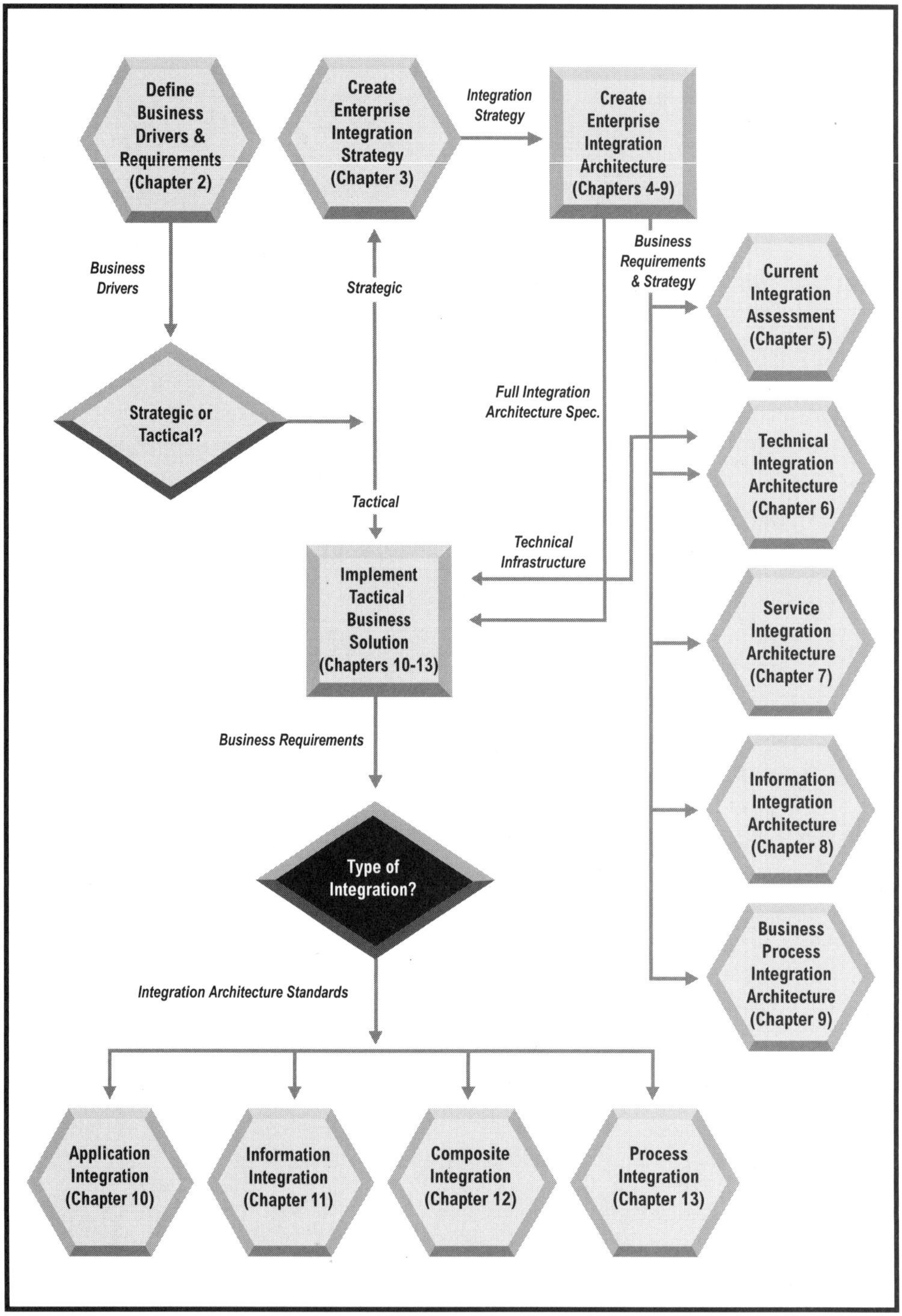

Figure 12-3 Integration Roadmap

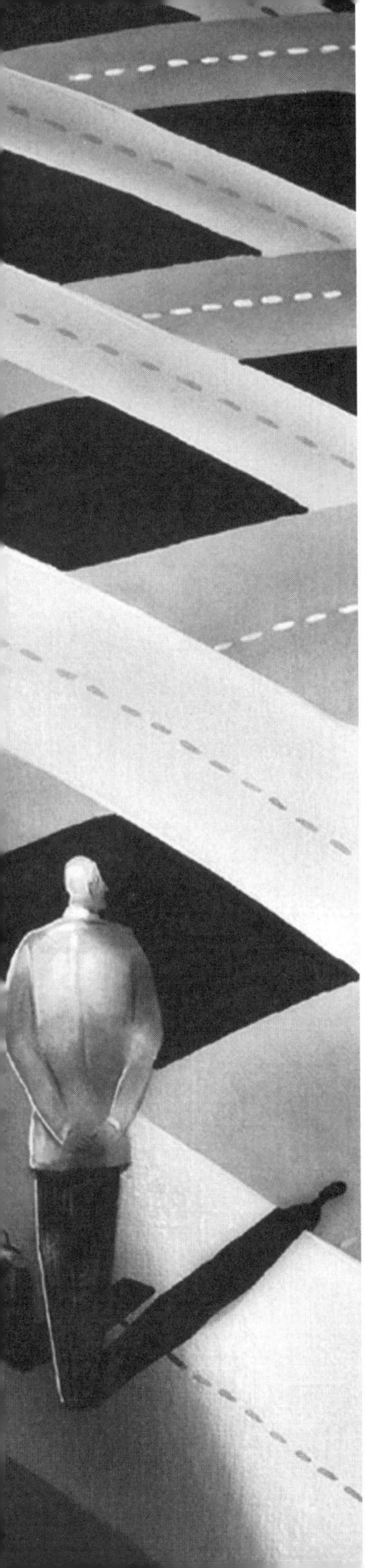

CHAPTER THIRTEEN

Process-Driven Integration

13.1 Executive Overview

Businesses have been focused on process improvement to improve operational efficiency since the era of business process reengineering (BPR). However, BPR failed in many organizations because the supporting information systems did not allow changes without significant rework. Process integration was born out of a need to allow business processes to be quickly automated and adjusted. Furthermore, it has expanded to allow for processes to be managed and monitored in real time providing a feedback loop to business management. Management dashboards provide graphical views of critical business processes, events, and key performance indicators, and are updated in real time.

Process integration is a powerful tool for enabling managers to quickly react to important business events and to be proactive when opportunities arise. However, in order to reap the rewards of process integration, companies need to invest in defining, managing, and optimizing their business processes. This is still a large leap for the majority of companies.

Process integration is an application that sits on top of the underlying applications that actually perform the business functions. The process layer defines, monitors, and manages a business process that spans multiple applications. The difference between process integration and either application or information integration is that the integration is defined as a process rather than as a message between applications or as information. Composite application integration and process integration are similar in many regards. However, the three key differences between process integration and composite integration are that process integration is focused on the definition and creation of business processes rather than code, is aimed at business process analysts versus programmers, and does not presuppose a service-oriented architecture.

Process integration uses a variety of technology in application and information integration including adapters, brokers, etc. to integrate with the underlying applications. Although process integration technology could conceivably be used to create composite applications by tying together business services and components, standardized interfaces and business components and services are not a prerequisite. Furthermore, the objectives and developers of process integration and composite applications are different. As previously stated in Chapter 12, composite applications are usually created by application developers and the goal is rapid application development through reuse. Business analysts more often define process integration solutions and the goal is improving business efficiency by automating business processes and managing them in real time.

The process integration market segment is predicted to grow considerably in the next few years. This growth is likely to be fueled by integration solutions or process templates that provide a large percentage of the solution. Compliance regulations in finance and healthcare are driving adoptions of solutions based on integration technology. Process integration provides an excellent platform for these solutions, because it makes them easy to customize. At best, any packaged solution will meet 75% to 85% of needs. A process-integration template can reduce the time and cost of customizing solutions. Once the technology comes through the door with the industry or compliance solution, then it can be used on other projects. Case Study 13.1 shows how process integration accelerated the integration of business acquisitions and enabled flexible business processes across divisions (Gold-Bernstein 2002).

Process integration can help companies optimize business processes, reduce operational costs, and improve business agility. It provides business and operational managers the tools they need to stay on top of a real-time business environment. But the technology alone does not guarantee success. To achieve sustainable competitive advantage, companies need to commit to process management and continual process improvement.

Case Study 13.1
Nextel International Gains
Business Flexibility through Process Integration

Nextel International is the leading provider of trunking services in Latin America. Nextel's digital subscribers account for roughly 30% of the total corporate mobile subscribers in the countries where it operates.

A few years ago, Nextel International acquired seven companies in six countries across Latin America and the Philippines, and needed to activate the new customers of each of these companies as quickly as possible. This required integrating the customer systems and business processes of each of these companies, each with different local taxation requirements and unique business processes.

Nextel's goal was to integrate the new businesses, combining business practices and assets, while attempting to preserve effective business processes—a large challenge for any company. Using Fuego's BPM solution, Nextel was able to implement standardized company-wide processes, which could also be tailored to each division's unique and effective way of working. Business process integration enabled Nextel to activate customer accounts 2400% faster than they otherwise would have, while completely automating local taxation requirements.

A process-integration strategy is the most relevant architectural approach when there is a need to implement a complex new business process that requires interaction among a diversity of applications, where the processes change frequently, and where the business wishes to gain better efficiency and flexibility through process management.

When this is done correctly, organizations can get more value by looking for best practices within existing processes and driving these best-in-class concepts into other parts of the business.

13.2 Process Integration Scenarios

Process integration technology is well suited to the following business requirements.

- **Process-improvement initiative.** It has been shown that companies that focus on process and continual process improvement outperform their competitors to a very significant degree (see Chapter 9). These companies tend to be the market leaders in their industry. Continual process improvement delivers competitive advantage, but requires high-level commitment and investment.
- **Industry-specific processes.** BPM provides excellent technology for creating templates to implement specific business processes. For example, a risk management system for finance might integrate information from multiple systems to calculate risk. Industry solutions provide the majority of the solution and reduce implementation time and risk of failure. The process integration technology makes it easy to customize the solution.
- **Compliance solution.** Process integration vendors have focused heavily on compliance solutions because they provide a captive market. Healthcare companies are required by law to implement electronic transactions formatted in the HIPAA standard. Although compliance usually represents a cost, healthcare organizations are finding that they are actually achieving an ROI from HIPAA solutions. Electronic transactions, combined with back-end integration, lower transaction errors and costs.

  Sarbanes-Oxley is another compliance solution driving the adopting of process integration technology. It requires executives to certify the process that generated the financial figures, such as how revenue is recognized, and holds executives personally responsible for signing off on the financial statements and criminally liable for any inconsistencies. The image of high-level executives going off to jail in handcuffs is a powerful motivator for executives to be interested in technology solutions that will protect them. Compliance also requires limiting any variance from the proscribed process to ensure the process has been followed. Process automation and integration is well suited to providing these capabilities and providing the platform for compliance solutions.

13.3 Choosing Technology for Process Integration

Process integration technology includes business process management (BPM) tools for automating and managing processes, workflow management for manual processes, and collaboration tools. There is a great deal of convergence in the market. Just about all the EAI vendors include process level integration. There are also a number of pure-play BPM solutions that include adapters for back-end integration or integrate with an integration broker or enterprise service bus. The workflow vendors have entered the market, as well as the enterprise content management (ECM) vendors. A couple of rules development platform vendors have also reinvented themselves as BPM vendors. In fact, just about every vendor with a process or rules engine has entered the market. The different vendors offer solutions optimized for different types of processes.

13.3.1 Business Process Modeling

Business process technology typically includes a modeling tool for defining the business process. The standards for a process modeling and execution language are evolving (see Chapter 9), and most modeling tools are proprietary. However, many vendors are at least giving lip service to the emerging standards, especially BPEL. This will be important for model portability. It enables a company to leverage the investment in defining business processes and exporting the execution code to different tools. At a minimum, if the tool can import and export BPEL, it will prevent technology lock-in, and ensure long-term viability.

13.3.2 Process and Rules Engines

Many process vendors are now offering both process and rules engines. Process engines are designed to manage the state of a process, including long-running processes, which can take hours, days, or even weeks. For example, a cable or DSL line may be installed days or weeks from the initial order, and could involve third-party subcontractors, such as the installers. The system needs to track the state of each task or sub-process in the overall end-to-end process over a period of time. This has implications for transaction management in long running processes. A transaction committed weeks ago cannot necessarily be merely rolled back. It may require a series of compensating transactions to "undo" the action, such as sending a letter out to the customer.

It is becoming more common for vendors to also offer a rules engine to define the parameters that control the process. Rules are much easier to change than code embedded in a process execution language or a process model. Furthermore, rules can be distributed and localized. If the process spans organizational entities, then parts of the process are often managed by different entities. A rules engine enables the rules specific to a part of the process to be managed and changed locally. For example, a rule might say that orders over $1,000 require management approval. In very busy times, this rule might be changed to $2,000. The process does not need to be changed at all. Process rules can be localized by departments or geography. Rules distribution and federation puts control in the hands of the line-of-business managers. Because of the flexibility rules provide, it is becoming more of a necessity for process integration.

13.3.3 Supporting Manual Processes

When choosing process technology you must first determine what type of processes are predominant in the organization. For example, some process tools were built primarily for automated processes, and have limited support for manual processes. If you are attempting to reduce the inefficiencies in manual processes, then look for a solution that offers strong workflow capabilities, including workload balancing among employee roles and an interface to display individual work assignments. It is beneficial to have both manual workflow and automated business processes supported with a single modeling tool as it significantly lowers training and maintenance costs. But processes that predominantly involve people, especially large numbers of people, will require robust and scalable solutions.

13.3.4 Enabling Business Process Improvement

If the implementation is part of a business process improvement initiative, look for strong modeling and simulation capabilities, including time and cost-based analysis of tasks and processes. Simulation tools provide historical analysis based on past process performance along with what if analysis. Success also requires a commitment to process management and continual process improvement. In this case, the tool is only as good as the people who use it.

13.3.5 Business Activity Monitoring (BAM)

When seeking to gain real-time visibility into business processes, BAM is important. The BAM market is still in the very early stages. EAI vendors, BPM vendors, software management vendors, pure-play start-ups, and infrastructure-management vendors are offering BAM solutions.

Gartner, which coined the term, defines different stages of BAM. The first stage is informational. The management dashboard provides real-time visibility into business processes and exception alerts, then a person needs to go and decide how to respond to the alert. When business intelligence is added, the alert includes analytical information to help produce a more informed decision more quickly. The future of BAM is to have the system automatically respond. IBM Research is working on autonomic computing with the goal to create computer systems that regulate themselves, the way our autonomic nervous system works in our bodies. Most of the BAM technology currently available is at the level of providing real-time information in management dashboards.

13.3.6 Supporting Collaborative Processes

Collaboration software, also called groupware, has been around since the mid 1980s. However, it is now starting to become part of the integration infrastructure. Collaborative process integration includes facilities to allow disparate team members to communicate, coordinate, and manage the process, as well as collaborate on documents, models, and other project deliverables. Collaboration solutions are generally network-based solutions, and may integrate with enterprise content-management solutions and desktop tools. Collaboration tools are also being introduced in supply chain and manufacturing environments, where organizations need to collaborate and negotiate on product design and other issues.

13.3.7 Supporting Multiple Types of Processes

Large organizations are likely to have different types of processes to support. The issue is whether the company should choose one process solution and force fit it to all applications, or deploy multiple technologies and optimize each solution. Unfortunately, the latter approach will guarantee redundancy in modeling tools and process engines, which ultimately impacts the bottom line and increases the total cost of ownership. The optimal solution would be to have a complete service-oriented architecture and deploy integration services as needed. The vendors, however, have a vested interest in their own platforms, and this is not yet a reality. Companies may have no alternative but to support several different process integration platforms.

13.4 Process Integration Implementation Specification

13.4.1 Introduction

This specification provides implementation guidance for the development of a process-integration based solution. It is most likely that the process design specification from Chapter 9 will form the basis for the implementation.

Process integration represents a specific style of integration. It manages the integration of an end-to-end business process, as well as processes that span organizations. It is appropriate for business process improvement initiatives, automating interactions between organizational entities, and implementing industry and compliance solutions.

This section describes the specific technical problems that are being addressed in the implementation, and provides context for specific implementation. See Appendix K for the full specification.

13.4.2 Scope

The scope of a process integration specification is limited to the business processes that are being automated and integrated. It can include processes within departments or between departments, divisions, territories, companies, and business customers and partners.

13.4.3 Key Participants

This section identifies all stakeholders in the implementation, including business managers who control all or part of the process, system designers and architect(s), and the development team who will execute the implementation. Because there may be multiple managers responsible for parts of the process, continuous process improvement, and process optimization will be difficult to achieve without a process owner or manager who is responsible for the end-to-end process. Any other participants or stakeholders should also be identified, including their roles.

13.4.4 Process Integration Patterns and Services

Process integration is in the very early stages of adoption, and patterns may emerge over time. This section includes the following patterns:

- Process automation
- Business activity monitoring (BAM)
- Collaborative process integration

This section defines the particular pattern that is being used and provides details on the configuration of the specific components of the implementation.

13.4.4.1 Process Automation

Process automation requires underlying application integration services. The solution may provide integration services such as adapters, or may integrate with an EAI solution. Many BPM tools do both in order to provide implementation flexibility.

The services included in process automation include process modeling, process simulation, process management including support for long-lived processes, business rules management, transaction support including compensating transactions, as well as all necessary application integration services. Because it is important to manage process models as valuable enterprise knowledge and content, Figure 13-1 includes a process repository. However, this can be part of an

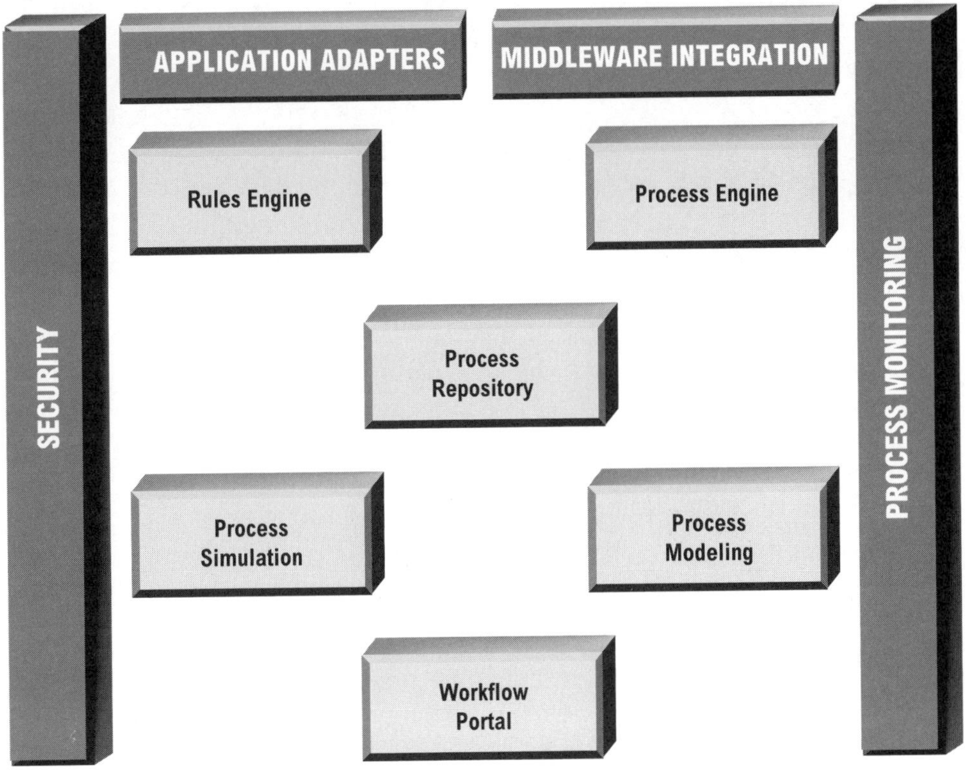

Figure 13-1 Process Automation Reference Architecture

existing repository or content management solution. Note that BAM is on the diagram because process analytics and management dashboards are often part of the process automation solution. However, it can also be a separate implementation. A good example for process integration is an employee review process. This type of process is often difficult to manage, requires integration across a diversity of data sources, involves a lot of people, and is often labor intensive. Business process integration could be kicked off at a time indicated by corporate policy and procedures. The information necessary is collected from a variety of sources and the templates for the review are created and forwarded to the appropriate managers.

The Process Automation Implementation Table (Figure 13-2) specifies the integration services included in a process automation solution, along with relevant implementation details. Customize the following table for your implementation.

13.4.4.2 Business Activity Monitoring (BAM)

BAM provides real-time visibility into business processes. BAM can be part of a business process management solution or it can be a stand-alone solution. Because the BAM market is young and evolving, the current BAM solutions have different focuses and configurations. For example, some solutions focus on analytical information, monitoring data warehouses, and sending alerts when certain events occur or conditions arise. Some are more focused on the tools for graphically building the management dashboard. Some are focused on fast information access. The future direction of BAM includes automated responses and autonomic computing.

The basic services provided by BAM include a management dashboard with key performance indicators relevant to particular roles in the organization, and real-time analytics to populate the dashboard, which include either providing business intelligence capabilities, such as monitoring and aggregating events in data warehouse or integrating with another business intelligence solution. BAM solutions may include information integration capabilities to pull information from analytical data stores in real time. The actual monitoring capabilities can be implemented with application agents, process event logs, or it might be part of the BPM solution. A BAM solution may also contain modeling or development capabilities to define the BAM solution, as each one is likely to be unique. A good example of using BAM is the management of the entire process of admitting patients in hospitals through discharge and might even included the coding and billing process. Hospitals are a complicated environment and by monitoring all

Integration Service	Vendor/Product	Implementation Notes
Process modeling	<Vendor name/ product name>	<State of BPEL or other standard models supported>
Process simulation	<Vendor name/ product name>	<Add-on or integrated?>
Process management	<Vendor name/ product name>	<Support for long-lived processes?>
Rules management	<Vendor name/ product name>	<Rules management may replace process management or may augment it.>
Workflow management	<Vendor name/ product name>	<Is there an additional process modeling and management engine?>
Application interface	<Vendor name/ product name or deployment technology>	<Specify: integration broker adapter; Web service; JCA interface; data interface (ODBC, JDBC, OLE DB, ADO).>
Middleware integration	<Vendor name/ product name>	<Integration with other integration technologies>
Process repository	<Vendor name/ product name>	<Part of enterprise repository or content management systems or separate?>
BAM	<Vendor name/ product name>	<Include monitoring capabilities here if it is part of the BPM solution.>

Figure 13-2 Process Automation Implementation Table

aspects of the process, actions can be taken to deal with especially heavy workloads, dealing with problems in the coding process or managing the accounts receivables and collection processes.

The reference architecture in Figure 13-3 (page 254) depicts the basic services that might be included in a BAM implementation with current technologies. The architecture is likely to evolve significantly as the market matures.

The Implementation Table (Figure 13-4, page 255) specifies all the integration services provided in the BAM solution, along with relevant implementation details. Modify the table on page 255 to depict your implementation.

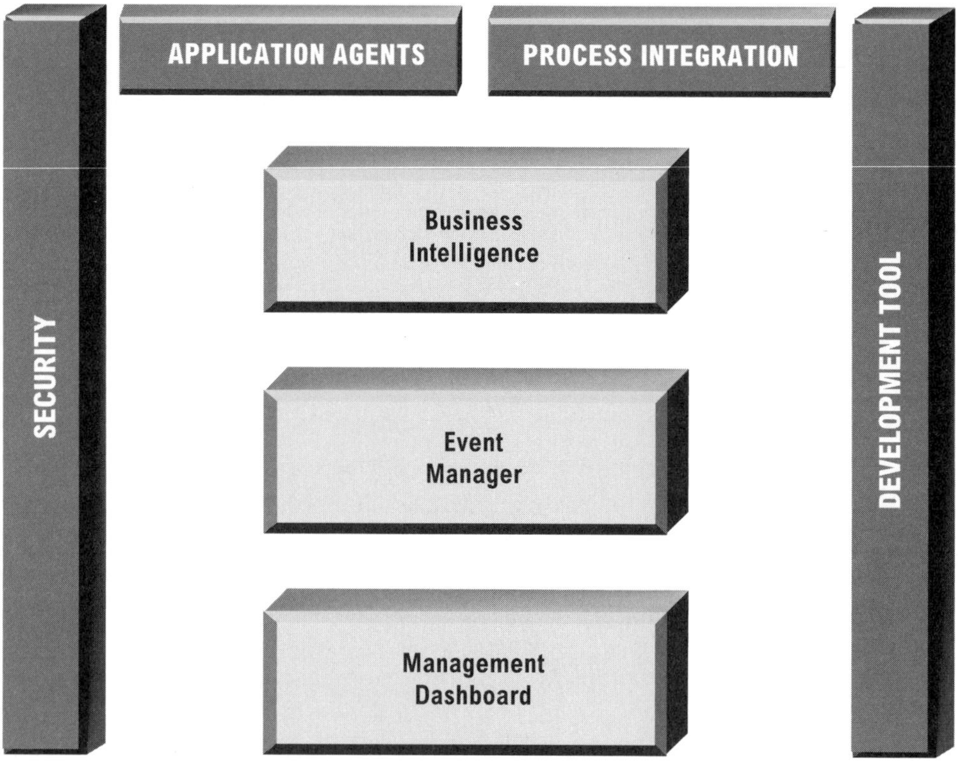

Figure 13-3 BAM Reference Architecture

13.4.4.3 Collaborative Process Integration

Collaborative process integration provides a platform for integrating work from different team members in different locations. It allows team members to manage their work process, communicate, coordinate, and collaborate on documents, models, and other project deliverables.

The heart of the collaborative solution is a collaboration portal that provides access to all information and services supporting the project. This includes artifacts including deliverables, meeting notes, discussions, decisions, etc. A project repository is important for managing project artifacts. The repository can be part of the collaboration platform, or may integrate with a content management solution.

Version control with check in and check out facilities are crucial features for collaboration. Often check in/check out is part of the collaboration platform.

Integration Service	Vendor/Product	Implementation Notes
BAM solution	<Vendor name/ product name>	<Users of the solution>
Management dashboard	<Vendor name/ product name>	<Key performance indicators included for each type of user>
Business intelligence	<Vendor name/ product name>	<Define integration technology and analytical data sources>
Event manager	<Vendor name/ product name>	<Event server, process engine event logs>
Application interface	<Vendor name/ product name>	<BAM agents, process or part of BPM solution>
Development/ modeling	<Vendor name/ product name>	<Graphical development to generate BAM solution>

Figure 13-4 BAM Implementation Table

However, it is also possible for the collaboration portal to integrate with a content management system or a version control system. The latter is important for software development as the code is often managed by an existing version control system. There is no either/or here. A number of different configurations are possible.

Project management may also be provided by the platform, or it can integrate with a project management system, such as Microsoft Project. Workflow is often included as part of the platform to manage the collaborative process. Project coordination is provided with an electronic calendar and meeting scheduling. A facility to support threaded discussions and negotiations, and document decisions is also helpful. Because much project communication is done through e-mail, which is particularly difficult to manage and archive, e-mail integration is becoming more important. The collaboration platform should include role-based security with granular levels of authorization, so access rights can be defined at the artifact level. For example, some documents may require the input from the whole team, and some may be "read only" for most of the team, save a couple of members.

As noted previously, although groupware solutions have been around since the mid 1980s, they are beginning to provide more integration capabilities as they evolve and integrate with other enterprise solutions. Collaboration is also becoming important in some other integration patterns, especially B2B integration, where partners need to collaborate and negotiate on business processes, product designs, and other joint efforts. A good example for collaborative integration is any design process that involves outside vendors. The automotive industry has been a leader in applying this technology. The collaboration tool provides version control on designs, and tracks conversations, feedback, and decisions.

As process collaboration integration becomes more firmly entrenched in organizations, the architecture is likely to evolve. Figure 13-5 is a reference architecture based on a collection of capabilities currently available, although no one vendor may offer all of them.

The Implementation Table (Figure 13-6) specifies all the integration services provided in the collaborative integration solution, along with relevant implementation details. Modify the following table to specify your implementation.

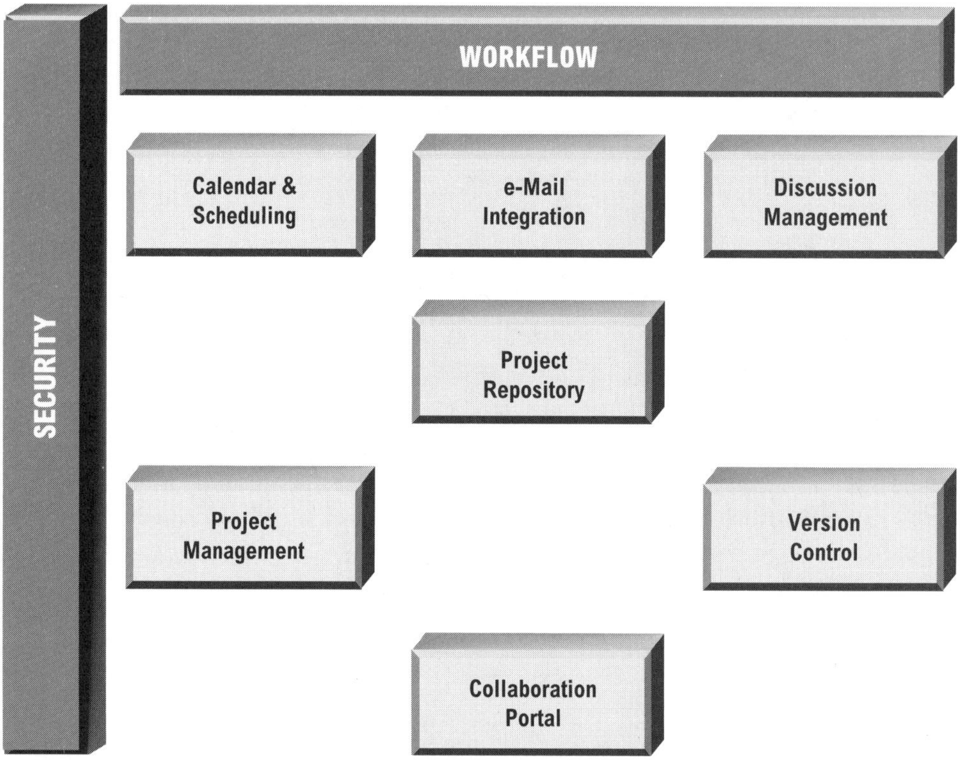

Figure 13-5 Collaborative Process Reference Architecture

Integration Service	Vendor/Product	Implementation Notes
Collaborative platform	<Vendor name/ product name>	<Hosted within organization or by vendor>
Collaboration portal	<Vendor name/ product name>	<Key features provided>
Project repository	<Vendor name/ product name>	<Part of platform or integration with ECM>
Version control	<Vendor name/ product name>	<Part of platform, part of ECM, third party, combination for different types of information>
Project management	<Vendor name/ product name>	<Part of platform and/or integration with project management tool>
Workflow	<Vendor name/ product name>	<Part of platform or integration with workflow tool>
Calendar and scheduling	<Vendor name/ product name>	<Part of platform or integration with calendaring and scheduling tool>
Discussion management	<Vendor name/ product name>	<Tool for threaded discussions that are part of project history>
E-mail integration	<Vendor name/ product name>	<E-mail integration with project repository>
Security	<Vendor name/ product name>	<Role based security>

Figure 13-6 Collaborative Process Implementation Table

13.4.5 Conclusions and Commentary

This section should provide any final comments on implementation.

13.5 Best Practices in Process Integration

- **Make an organizational commitment to continuous process improvement.** Process optimization is a discipline and a journey, not a single software installation. Although it holds the potential to deliver competitive advantage, it requires significant investment. Organizations that create a culture of continuous process improvement will reap the highest rewards (but this requires the highest level of commitment).

- **Measure process performance.** Measurement is essential for process improvement. Process performance can be measured in terms of time and/or cost. It can also be measured in terms of overall business performance with metrics such as profitability, customer satisfaction, or growth in market share. Simulation tools are extremely helpful for calculating performance from actual process statistics, and doing what-if analysis.
- **Reward process improvement.** You can expect employee behavior to be tied to how performance is measured. To create a culture of continuous process improvement, reward process improvement. Otherwise, there will be little incentive to embrace continuous change.
- **Provide real-time management dashboards.** Put business managers in the driver's seat with customized dashboards that display key performance indicators and real-time alerts. Provide business managers with the information they need to proactively manage the business. Give them the ability to easily manage and change the processes and business rules they are responsible for.
- **Manage an automated process as a reusable component.** Automated processes can be reusable just as any component or interface can be reused. By allowing processes to be pieced together in new workflows, a business can quickly optimize its operations as changes occur or insight is gained through activity monitoring.

13.6 Next Steps

The nature of process integration is that it is never done. The first implementation is just a starting point that will be adjusted and changed. The next step is to ensure that the changes are being tracked and managed so that the processes are defined and documented.

In addition, enterprise integration is an ongoing journey. The integration infrastructure will evolve over time and the process integration components are only a part of the overall solution. It needs to be refreshed to stay in step with the overall architecture. The integration roadmap (Figure 13-7, page 260) and life cycle is one you will return to again and again.

Each new project will have its own unique requirements. An implementation may be a combination of integration styles and patterns. Use the patterns and guidelines provided in this chapter and book as a starting point. Available technology choices may constrain the ability to implement the optimal architecture. It is also important to remember that the patterns and technology will change and that process integration is one of the least developed of the forms of integration. To see an example of service-oriented enterprise integration reference architecture that can accommodate any and all integration needs, see Chapter 14, Conclusion: Best Practices for Enterprise Business Integration.

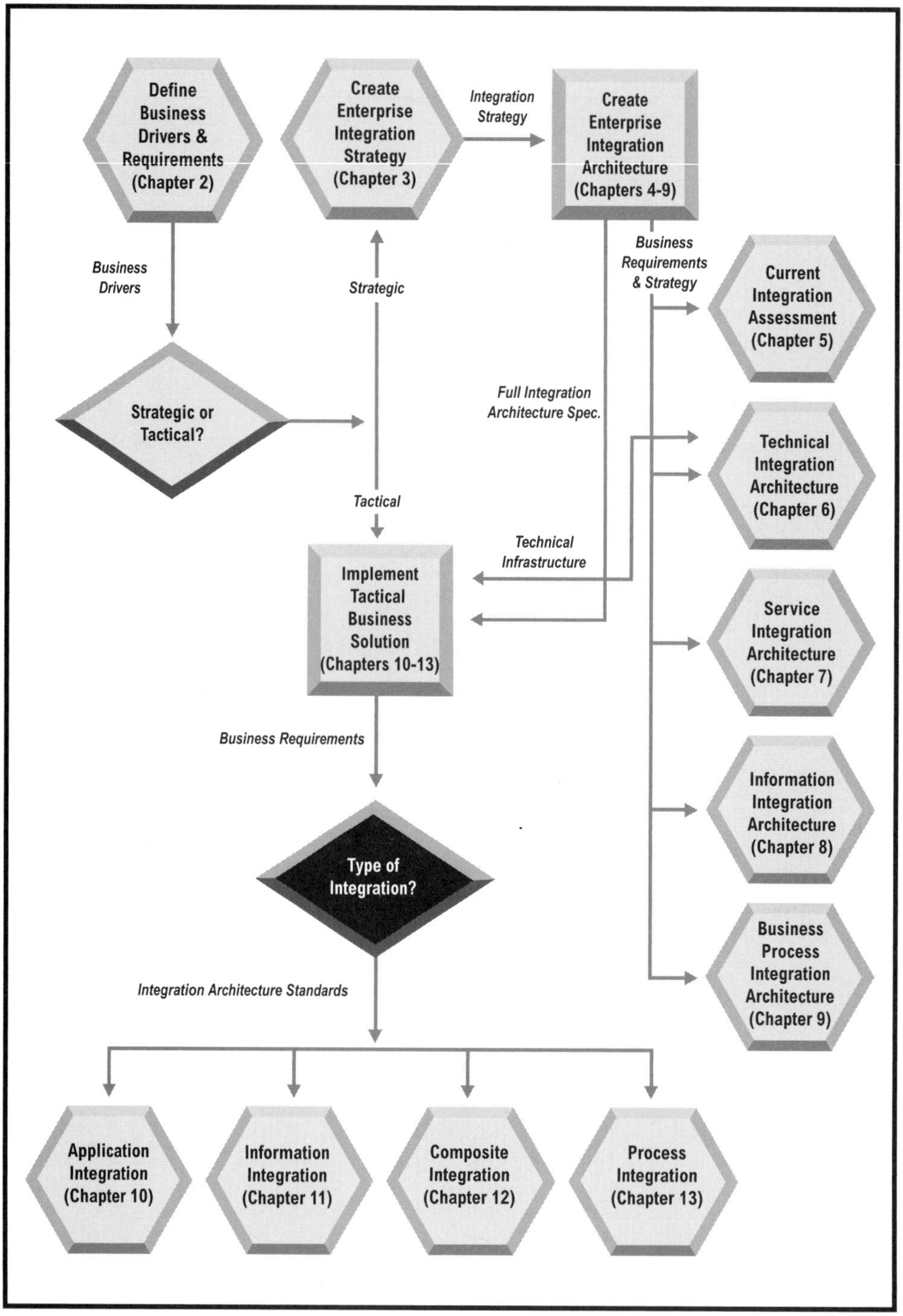

Figure 13-7 The Integration Roadmap

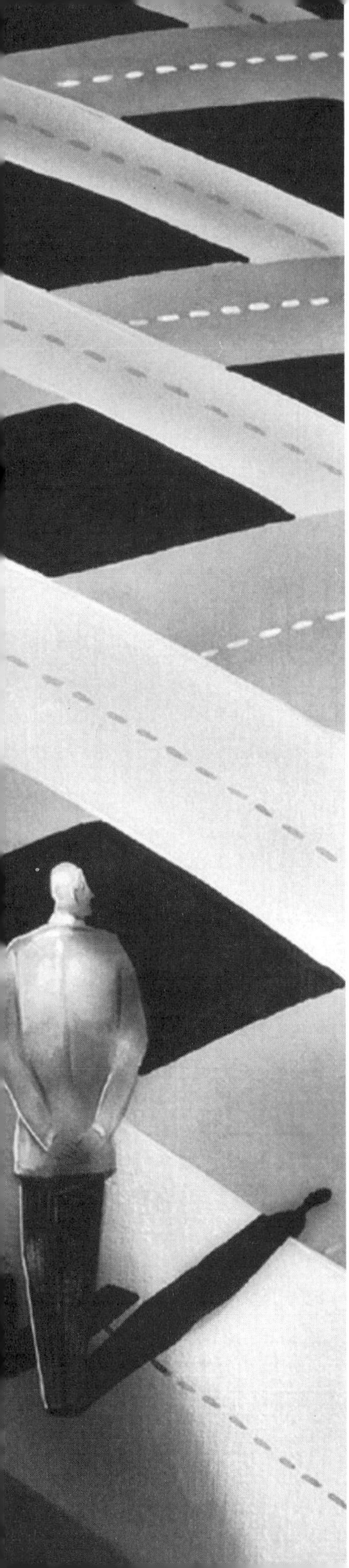

CHAPTER FOURTEEN

Conclusion: Best Practices for Enterprise Integration

14.1 Executive Overview

Integration problems have been with us since the advent of information systems. What has changed is the nature of integration. In the past, it was focused on making information systems work together at a hardware or software level. The consumer of the integration was the technology professional. Today integration is required to directly support an organization's goals and needs.

This book is intended to help organizations deal with this change and align an organization's strategy and tactics with the ability to effectively implement a solution. Given the importance of integration, it is imperative that the IT organization is able to quickly and efficiently implement a solution. The role of an integration architecture is to provide reusable infrastructure services to support the rapid implementation and reduce the cost of new business solutions. The integration infrastructure ultimately enables business agility.

Organizations that recognize the importance of an agile infrastructure and are willing to make the investment will choose to apply the strategic approach. Organizations with more immediate needs and/or tight budgets often follow the tactical approach. In either case, as we have seen with best in class organizations, it will be imperative that an IT organization becomes effective at leveraging their existing assets.

In the end, this book is about return on assets. The critical concepts to getting the most out of your assets are:

- The accelerating rate of business change, combined with the highly competitive global marketplace, has forced organizations to find new ways to respond quickly and effectively. Service-oriented architecture (SOA), considered best practice for decades, is finally being widely adopted. SOA is becoming an architectural imperative for enabling business agility and maximizing ROI of IT assets.
- Reducing redundancy in the infrastructure significantly reduces the total cost of ownership (TCO). A significant amount of energy goes into duplication of effort around the technology used to integrate. As a result, each integration takes longer than necessary, does not build significant competency, and leaves the organization with an operational complexity that makes future integration even more difficult. Ultimately, this impacts the bottom line in higher maintenance costs.
- Many business problems are never addressed because the integration complexity cuts across the entire enterprise and there is no effective mechanism to integrate other than to "boil the ocean." Infrastructure should be built and used to be effective. In many organizations infrastructure is bought but never fully implemented or adopted by the organization. It is critical that the organization embrace the infrastructure to get real business benefit.
- Proprietary technology has been one of the biggest limiting factors that have held back effective enterprise integration. The emergence of standards is paving the way to developing a truly open integration infrastructure that supports all platforms, vendors, and programming languages. XML and Web services standards will do for integration what TCP/IP did for networking. At this point, there is more risk in not adopting and implementing these standards.
- Integration is inherently complex. It involves numerous technologies and organizational entities. Companies need to manage both the technical and organizational complexity in order to ensure success. This includes reducing redundancy in the infrastructure, training personnel in the effective use of the technology, and providing a structure and process for resolving cross-organizational issues and turf wars that may arise during the integration process.
- Although integration technology plays a big role in maximizing IT assets, choosing the right integration technology can be a daunting task, given the

number and variety of available options. As shown in Part Three of this book, each integration pattern represents a unique solution set. Matching the business problem to the right integration pattern will help you identify the appropriate technology, making the implementation of the business solution significantly easier. It will also help control implementation costs and reduce risk.

14.2 Reference Architecture for the Fully Integrated Enterprise

Although each integration pattern has its unique technology requirement, there is also significant overlap across patterns, including translation, transformation and routing services, repositories, adapters, development environments, management, and security. Therefore, although it is helpful on a project level to use the patterns to guide implementation, it is also important at an enterprise level to control redundancy and manage reuse.

The Reference Architecture for the fully integrated enterprise represents an aggregated view of all the integration patterns, into a fully integrated infrastructure (see Figure 14-1, page 264). Companies with multiple integration requirements will inevitably require multiple integration patterns. The purpose of this aggregated view is to minimize redundancy of infrastructure services and maximize reuse and ROI of IT assets.

Although every integration pattern includes translation and transformation, the integrated enterprise reference architecture has only one translation and transformation service. However, every integration pattern discussed in Part III has translation and transformation. Likewise, rules engines may appear in a number of different application patterns, including process automation and composite applications. Ideally, each application will need only one type of adapter; all types of servers could use the same translation and transformation; there would be one repository for all types of metadata, etc.; and all the integration services could be commonly managed by one management console.

This optimized service-oriented integration architecture is not quite possible with the current state of technology. However, companies should strive to minimize redundancy at an enterprise level as much as possible to decrease long-term maintenance costs. This requires a strategic approach to integration.

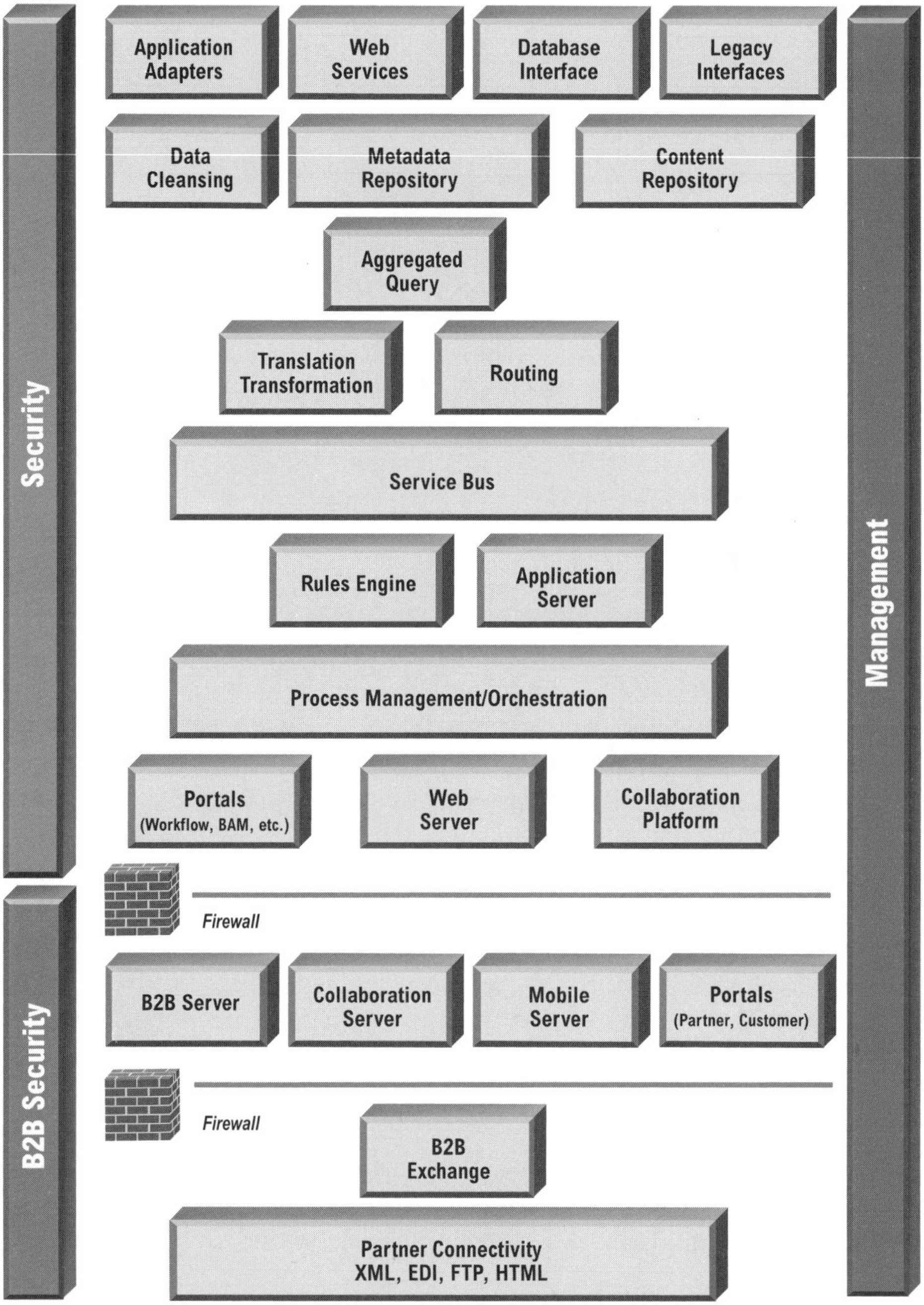

Figure 14-1 Integrated Enterprise Reference Architecture

14.3 Succeeding with Strategic Integration

The fully integrated enterprise can only be achieved through a strategic approach to integration. This statement is made with the full knowledge that the majority of integration projects are tactical implementations. Throughout this book we have attempted to lay out a convincing argument, including supporting case studies, that although the strategic approach requires an initial higher investment, in the long run it significantly reduces the time and cost of implementing new solutions, while increasing business agility. However, the strategic approach requires upper level IT and business management support, as well as a supportive organizational culture.

Although upper level management support is crucial, sometimes an evangelist is required to inspire the commitment. You can use the case studies in this book to help build a compelling argument. If the evangelist route doesn't work in your organization, an initial success can sometimes speak louder than words. A tactical approach can be taken to prove out the underlying concepts and help to convince the organization to move forward strategically.

Even with a mandate to move ahead, a pervasive "not invented here" attitude in the organizational culture could sabotage any potential benefits of the integration infrastructure. Maximizing IT assets requires a culture of reuse. This culture needs to be built both from the top down and the bottom up. From the top down, management needs to invest in resources and processes to maximize reuse, including architects to participate in design reviews to identify opportunities for reuse, and reuse repositories to manage the reusable services. From the bottom up, application developers need to be rewarded for reuse, both when including an existing service in a new implementation, and for contributing reusable services to the repository. Rewards can be a fast and effective way to change behavior and create the desired cultural change.

The relationship between the business and IT organization has a large impact on whether a strategic approach or tactical integration approach is used. The strategic approach requires that there exists a positive working relationship between the IT and business groups. Otherwise, they will not make the initial investment required, even if the tactical approach ends up ultimately costing more. Ironically, a strategic approach helps to build the business and IT relationship. However, without at least some initial business support the strategic approach is difficult to apply.

14.4 Applying This Book

The goal of this book is to help readers understand the different integration approaches and technologies. It provides tools, including templates and reference architectures, to develop requirements and specifications for guiding the approach to integration on both the strategic enterprise level and on tactical projects. This book is not intended to be a full-blown integration methodology. However, it forms the cornerstone for putting a methodology in place.

Apply these tools within the context of your organization's existing methods, to fill any existing gaps. The templates can be applied as is or merged into the organizations existing methodology.

14.5 Final Thoughts

Integration is not a point in time, but a journey that must be taken by any successful IT organization. Just like networking in the late 1980s and early 1990s, integration will have a lot of uncertainty and challenges. However, over the next decade integration technology will become an essential part of the IT infrastructure and will be expected to work 24/7; require very little effort to setup, use, and operate; enable the creation of business services and processes; and connect these services and processes to any desktop and portable device.

No one can predict all of the right choices. This book lays out the landscape that has emerged, the important problems and patterns, and case studies from best-in-class organizations that are living examples of the importance and benefits of integration. This book is a starting point you can use. Your challenge will be to learn as you go and adapt to the specific needs of your organization.

A good mantra for the enterprise integration journey is "think strategically, act tactically." While meeting the tactical integration needs of the organization, incrementally build an infrastructure to accommodate the next implementation, and the next. "In the long run, we only hit what we aim at" (Henry David Thoreau). Create an enterprise architecture plan that will serve as your roadmap, and implement it in a tactical fashion, project by project.

We sincerely hope this book will be a helpful guide on your integration journey.

APPENDIX A

Business Drivers and Requirements Specification

<ENTERPRISE NAME>

<PLACE LOGO HERE>

<author>
<version>
<revision date>

Template Instructions

This is a template for the Business Drivers and Requirements Specification. This page should be removed prior to publication of the specification. The template is a guide for the enterprise and should not be blindly followed. The organization should

- *Review the chapter in the book that refers to the template to understand its use.*
- *Examine the template outline and determine what additions might be necessary based on unique organizational needs.*
- *If absolutely necessary, remove any sections that will not apply. (The authors strongly discourage this practice.)*
- *Save the template for future use.*
- *Begin to develop the document.*

Guidance is given for preparation of the document throughout the template.

- *Text shown as normal text should be used in the document. It may be modified as necessary.*
- *Text shown in pointed brackets is either instructional guidance in the application of the document or a description of the type of information to be added and should be removed prior to publication.*

Headers and footers should be customized as necessary as a final step in the completion of the document.

Business Drivers and Requirements Specification

1. Introduction

The Business Drivers and Requirements Specification is the document that defines the drivers, goals, scope, and metrics that measure success, potential business benefits, and ROI of the investment.

<The introduction should be a short executive overview of the specification. In addition, any special aspects of the project should be addressed, including the sponsoring organizations and business champion. A history of the initiative would be helpful as well. At the end of this section the reader should have an understanding of how the business drivers and requirements evolved.>

2. Scope

<This section defines the scope of the Business Drivers and Requirements Specification, specifically whether it is enterprise wide, or for a specific business unit or business initiative.>

3. Key Participants

<This section identifies all stakeholders in the requirements process, including business managers, the sponsoring organizations and business champions, and the owner of the proposed initiative.>

4. Statement of Purpose

<The Statement of Purpose is a succinct specification used to communicate the business goals and functions of the initiative. It makes the business case for the initiative. It does not include implementation of technology.>

Business Initiative

<Name of business initiative>

Business Drivers

<Include only one or two drivers; keep initiative focused>

Business Strategy

<For example, automate business processes, reduce operational redundancies, etc.>

Functional Scope

<List all business processes included in the scope of the initiative>

Business Goals

<Define the business benefits the initiative will provide, such as decrease business cycle times, decrease errors, etc.>

Organization Impact

<Impact to the organization once the initiative is complete. Large initiatives will have major impacts that will transcend the technology and impact how people work. Many projects fail because the corporate culture was not ready for the change.>

5. Cost Estimates

<This section lists high-level costs and an estimated time frame. Costs at this point should be a rough order of magnitude and used for budgeting purposes and estimating ROI. It must be understood that these will be refined in the follow-on phase with the next level of detail.>

Costs	Total	Description
Project management	$75000	This is the cost of a project manager for the project for nine months
Hardware	<value>	<description>
Software	<value>	<description>
Development	<value>	<description>
Consulting	<value>	<description>
<Category #1>	<value>	<description>
<Category #n>	<value>	<description>

6. ROI

<This section documents the potential or expected ROI for the business initiative under consideration. You can use the template to guide your assessment of an ROI for the integration initiative.>

Reduce Personnel Costs	Reduce head count	<calculation of estimated savings>
	Reduce training costs	<calculation of estimated savings>
	Reduce customer support costs	<calculation of estimated savings>
	Other	<calculation of estimated savings>
Reduce IT Costs	Reduce error rates	<calculation of estimated savings>
	Reduce cost of fixing errors	<calculation of estimated savings>
	Eliminate rekeying of information	<calculation of estimated savings>
	Reduce system support costs through integration	<calculation of estimated savings>
	Other	<calculation of estimated savings>

Reduce Business Costs	Reduce the cost of implementing change	<calculation of estimated savings>
	Reduce costs through optimized business processes	<calculation of estimated savings>
	Other	<calculation of estimated savings>
Increase Revenue	Increase revenue from existing customers	<calculation of estimated increased revenue>
	Attract new customers by rapid response to emerging opportunities	<calculation of estimated increased revenue>
	Create new opportunities through integration with partners and suppliers	<calculation of estimated increased revenue>
	Create new opportunities by bringing products and services to market	<calculation of estimated increased revenue>
	Create new sales or distribution channels	<calculation of estimated increased revenue>
Other	Other	<calculation of estimated increased revenue>

7. Metrics

<Metrics are used to measure the success of the initiative and are created by turning business goals into measurable KPIs. For each goal there can be more than one metric.>

Business Goal	Metric Name	Metric Value	How to Collect	Frequency	Owner
Decrease time between order and shipment	Delivery time	Days	Business activity monitoring solution	On shipment of each order	Line of business manager
Decrease transaction errors	Transaction errors	Number of errors	Exception handling log	Weekly	Operational manager
<goal>	<metric>	<value>	<collection>	<frequency>	<owner>

8. Risks

<The risks are a collection of everything that can or might go wrong. It may also include a list of assumptions that might be wrong or need further information to be validated. With each risk should be associated a plan to mitigate the risk and the owner of the risk.>

Significant unknown			
<issue>	<description>	<mitigation>	<owner>
Organizational issues			
<issue>	<description>	<mitigation>	<owner>
Cultural issues			
<issue>	<description>	<mitigation>	<owner>
Technical issues			
<issue>	<description>	<mitigation>	<owner>
Management issues			
<issue>	<description>	<mitigation>	<owner>
Ability to achieve results			
<issue>	<description>	<mitigation>	<owner>

9. Conclusions and Recommended Next Steps

<This section should provide any final comments on requirements. It should include any known constraints or other business factors that could affect architecture, design, and implementation decisions.>

Appendix A: References

<The appendix should list any reference documents used in the creation of the document so that its contents can be traced back to their sources if necessary. This should be broken down into internal documents and external documents. Internal documents are those that belong to the organization. External documents are items such as articles, whitepapers, Web sites, or product documentation.>

APPENDIX B

Business Integration Strategy Specification

<ENTERPRISE NAME>

<PLACE LOGO HERE>

<author>
<version>
<revision date>

Template Instructions

This is a template for the Business Integration Strategy Specification. This page should be removed prior to publication of the specification. The template is a guide for the enterprise and should not be blindly followed. The organization should

- *Review the chapter in the book that refers to the template to understand its use.*
- *Examine the template outline and determine what additions might be necessary based on unique organizational needs.*
- *If absolutely necessary, remove any sections that will not apply. (The authors strongly discourage this practice.)*
- *Save the template for future use.*
- *Begin to develop the document.*

Guidance is given for preparation of the document throughout the template.

- *Text shown as normal text should be used in the document. It may be modified as necessary.*
- *Text shown in pointed brackets is either instructional guidance in the application of the document or a description of the type of information to be added and should be removed prior to publication.*
- *Text shown in double-pointed brackets is a placeholder for the insertion of text by the authors.*

Headers and footers should be customized as necessary as a final step in the completion of the document.

Enterprise Integration Strategy Specification

1. **Introduction**

   <The introduction should be a short executive overview of the specification. It should answer the following questions:

   - How will the integration strategy support business needs?
   - Are there any major constraints, such as limitations imposed by legacy systems, or requirements, such as the need for high security, that are a major factor in the integration strategy?
   - What are the anticipated benefits of the strategy?>

2. **Scope**

   <The scope defines whether this strategy covers integration across the entire enterprise, a division, a line of business, or some other scope. The types of applications involved determine the scope of the integration strategy, and the methods of integration required. The scope should not be defined in terms of technological boundaries. For example, a strategy for the communication network is inappropriate.>

3. **Key Participants**

   <There are three types of participants that should be identified:

   - The team responsible for the creation of the strategy in its initial form, as well as for any on going improvements. Anyone that provided information or review should be included in this list.
   - The group who will implement and apply the strategy.
   - Approvers of the strategy.>

4. **Integration Strategies**

   <Companies must identify the strategies by which the enterprise can use technology to maximize competitive advantage. Key integration strategies include service-oriented and process-driven architectures. Business goals defined in the Statement of Purpose (Business Drivers and Requirements Specification, page 271) should be front and center when defining integration strategies. The matrix below can be used as a guide for defining your particular set of integration strategies.>

<Redundancy management strategies>	<strategy>	<rationale>
<Skill set management strategies>	<strategy>	<rationale>
<Reusabilitiy strategies>	<strategy>	<rationale>
<Process driven integration strategies>	<strategy>	<rationale>
<SOA strategies>	<strategy>	<rationale>
<Implementation strategies>	<strategy>	<rationale>
<Business integration strategy lifecycle>	<strategy>	<rationale>

5. Mapping to Business Strategies and Initiatives

<This section provides a mapping between business initiatives defined in the Business Strategies and Initiatives Specification and integration strategies in the form of a matrix. Discuss nonobvious points of support. If any row or column is blank (i.e., a business strategy has no integration strategy to support it or an integration strategy supports no business strategy), discuss the implications. Any budgeting for projects that has been done to date or expected allocations should be included at this point. This reflects the IT organization's portion of the budget allocated to this initiative. Rank projects in importance to company, to prioritize infrastructure investments.>

Priority	Business Strategy/Initiative	Scope	Integration Strategy	Budget
1	Regulatory compliance (ex. Sarbanes-Oxley)	Certification of revenue reporting process	Process management	$xxx
2	Increase business efficiency and competitiveness	Tactical initiative to reduce time to process an order	Application integration	$yyy
<priority>	<business strategy>	<scope>	<integration strategy>	<budget>

6. Strategic Sourcing

<This section describes the approach that the organization feels will be most effective to acquiring any technology. It should set the philosophy, constraints, and approach to sourcing. Issues to be dealt with are the existing relationships

and current use of technology, vendor preferences, best-of-breed versus single vendor, responsibilities for identifying and selecting as well as negotiating contracts. It should define the following:

- Preference for best of breed approach versus single vendor or platform approach versus two or three preferred vendors
- Preferred vendors for each type of technology
- Procurement process (this part of the specification may point to another internal document)>

7. Standards

<The intention of this section is to define an enterprise strategy for how different types of standards will be used in the architecture. This strategy forms the basis for the integration architecture.

The standards that can be defined in an integration strategy are shown on the chart. One of the purposes of this section of the strategy is to decide which standards to define at an enterprise level.>

	Proposed Usage	References
Communication protocols	<Example: B2B communications>	<Web site for JCA or Web service interface specification>
Application interfaces	<Example: packaged application interfaces>	<Web site for JCA or Web service interface specification>
Message formats	<Example: internal messages, external messages, EDI messages>	<Links to appropriate Web sites or internal specification documents>
Process models	<Example: enterprise processes—standard on tool or standard such as BPEL>	<Links to internal documents or appropriate Web site>
Metadata	<Example: metadata about interfaces, Web services, data transformation, etc.>	<Links to internal documents or appropriate Web site>

8. Metrics

<Metrics that measure the success and relative value of an integration strategy should be defined. Metrics should be tracked over time and used as input when refining the strategy and determining future infrastructure investments. To be of use, each metric must be measurable and manageable. The effort to collect and track a metric cannot exceed the value of the information it provides. Owners are responsible for tracking and reporting on metrics.

Specific metrics that can be employed are tracking reuse, tracking the time to implement new solutions or implement changes to existing systems, tracking savings from reducing redundancy, and monitoring TCO of a system.>

Integration Strategy	Metric Name	Metric Value	How to Collect	Frequency	Owner
<goal>	<metric>	<value>	<collection>	<frequency>	<owner>
Example: Increase reuse	Component reuse	Number of times component is reused	Number of business processes or composite apps component is used in; alternatively, # of times it's checked out from reuse repository	Monthly	Repository owner, central architecture group, or competency center (different component types may have different owners)

9. Risks

<The risk section defines everything that can or might go wrong. It may also include a list of assumptions that might be wrong or need further information to be validated. This includes the organizational, cultural, technical, or management challenges and ability to achieve the desired business results. Each risk should be associated with a plan to mitigate the risk.>

Significant Unknown			
	<issue>	<description>	<mitigation>
Organizational Issues			
	<issue>	<description>	<mitigation>
Cultural Issues			
	<issue>	<description>	<mitigation>
Technical Issues			
	<issue>	<description>	<mitigation>
Management Issues			
	<issue>	<description>	<mitigation>
Ability to Achieve Results			
	<issue>	<description>	<mitigation>

10. Conclusions and Recommended Next Steps

<This section should complete the document with any major conclusions as well as any recommended next steps or approved management actions. This document will be used throughout the project(s) to guide and evaluate the results.>

Appendix A: References

<The appendix should list any reference documents used in the creation of the document so that its contents can be traced back to their sources if necessary. This should be broken down into internal documents and external documents. Internal documents are those that belong to the organization. External documents are items such as articles, whitepapers, Web sites, or product documentation.>

APPENDIX C

Current Environment Assessment Specification

<ENTERPRISE NAME>

<PLACE LOGO HERE>

<author>
<version>
<revision date>

Template Instructions

This is a template for the Current Environment Assessment Specification. This page should be removed prior to publication of the specification. The template is a guide for the enterprise and should not be blindly followed. The organization should

- *Review the chapter in the book that refers to the template to understand its use.*
- *Examine the template outline and determine what additions might be necessary based on unique organizational needs.*
- *If absolutely necessary, remove any sections that will not apply. (The authors strongly discourage this practice.)*
- *Save the template for future use.*
- *Begin to develop the document.*

Guidance is given for preparation of the document throughout the template.

- *Text shown as normal text should be used in the document. It may be modified as necessary.*
- *Text shown in pointed brackets is either instructional guidance in the application of the document or a description of the type of information to be added and should be removed prior to publication.*
- *Text shown in double pointed brackets is a placeholder for the insertion of text by the authors.*

Headers and footers should be customized as necessary as a final step in the completion of the document.

Current Environment Assessment Specification

1. **Introduction**

This document defines the current information technology environment as it pertains to the business integration strategy and architecture as of <<date>> for <<enterprise>>. <The introduction to the Current Environment Assessment should be a short executive overview of the specification. It should define the types of technologies that are being defined and any major constraints in the current environment, such as limitations imposed by legacy systems or the requirements for high security.>

2. **Purpose**

<The purpose of the Current Environment Assessment is to document and assess the current integration technologies that support the business functions of the enterprise. This assessment will be used when determining recommended technologies and vendors in the Integration Architecture Document.>

3. **Key Participants**

<There are two types of participants that should be identified:

- The team responsible for the creation of the current environment assessment in its initial form as well as for any on going improvements; anyone that provided information or review should be included in this list.
- The audience of this document; include how they will apply it to their work.>

4. **Scope**

<The scope should define the boundaries for the current environment assessment. Does it cover the entire enterprise or only a segment? It should cover internal as well as external assets.>

5. **Integration Technologies**

<This section should identify the integration technologies that are used by the type. It should describe the specific vendor technology and the applications that are connected using the technology. If there are technologies that are purchased but not used (shelfware) this should be identified as well.>

Integration Technology	Vendor Solutions <Create a separate entry for each currently installed technology.>	Applications
Messaging systems	<Examples are: IBM MQ Series, Tibco Rendevous, JMS, Sonic MQ, SoftwareAG Communicator, etc.>	<List all applications that are connected via this technology.>
Integration brokers/servers	<Examples are: WebSphere Integration Broker, Software AG, Tibco, WebMethods, SeeBeyond, Vitria, Mercator, Sybase Integrator, etc.>	<List all applications that are connected via this technology.>
Application servers with some integration	<List all application server platforms that are also connected to other applications via data integration, messaging, or other application server based integration. Examples are: BEA WebLogic, IBM WebSphere Sybase, Oracle.>	<List all applications that are connected via this technology.>
Packaged application integration	<Examples are: SAP, JD Edwards, Peoplesoft.>	<List all types of packaged applications that are connected and the specific packaged application mechanism that is used.>
Adapters and interfaces	<Examples are: iWays and other packaged adapters.>	<List all types of adapters or interfaces.>
Enterprise service bus and Web services tools	<Examples are: Software AG, Sonic Software, IBM, Microsoft.>	<List all applications that are connected via this technology.>
Data, information and content integration tools	<Examples are: Informatics, IBM, Software AG, Meta Matrix.>	<List all applications or data sources that are connected via this technology.>
Portals	<Examples are: Plum Tree, BEA, IBM.>	<List all applications that are connected via this technology.>

(continued)

B2B technology	<Examples are: EDI solutions, RosettaNet, HIPAA, XML solutions, and other B2B integration.>	<List all applications that are connected via this technology.>
BPM technology	<Examples are: Process modeling and management, process activity monitoring, process simulation.>	<List all applications implemented with this technology.>
Integrated security	<Single sign-on solutions such as LDAP or other directories.>	<Define scope of implementation—enterprise wide, departmental, other.>
Other middleware technologies	<DCE or other middleware.>	<List all applications that are connected via this technology.>
Point solution technology	<Specific products used to solve a specific integration problem.>	<List all applications that are connected via this technology.>
Custom integration solution	<Hand-crafted interfaces or full blown custom integration frameworks.>	<List all applications that are connected via this technology.>

6. Application and Data Sources Interfaces

<Using the information on applications or data sources from the prior section's interfaces should be described in detail. This section should list all integrated applications or major data stores and connector information. The objective is to determine which applications or data stores already have installed adapters or other interfaces. An effort should be made to determine the reusability of the interface.>

Application/Data Source Name	**Owner**	**Platform**	**Interface**	**Reusable**
<Name of application or data store>	<Department or organization responsible for application>	<Technology used to develop and deploy application>	<API, adapter, Web service or other interface used for integration>	<For adapters, is this adapter only usable with a particular integration technology or is it reusable?>

7. Integration Matrix

<This section gives a unified view of the current environment's integrations, first by purpose and second by technology. Where there exist multiple integrations between each application, place all the descriptions of the purpose and each individual technology in the cell making sure there is a clear identification between the purpose and technology.>

	<Application 1>	**<Application 2>**	**<User 1>**	**<Data Store 1>**
<Application 1>	<connection technology>	<connection technology>	<connection technology>	<connection technology>
<Application 2>	<connection technology>	<connection technology>	<connection technology>	<connection technology>
<User 1>	<connection technology>	<connection technology>	<connection technology>	<connection technology>
<Data Store 1>	<connection technology>	<connection technology>	<connection technology>	<connection technology>

8. Integration Diagram

<A diagram should be placed here that is a schematic of the current environment, identifying the current configuration including the servers, systems software versions, application software, adapters, databases, integration software, networking, administrative, and security systems. It may not be possible or desirable to have a single diagram; each diagram should be included. For example, there might be a separate physical network diagram and security diagram. There may need to be several diagrams of the applications, due to complexity. All diagrams should be clearly marked. In addition, any supporting diagrams that already exist should be included.>

9. Security

<Security is defined separately because of the complexity and the importance of this topic to integration. In this section, a description of the security requirements and the implementation approach for each type of data, application, or process will need to be identified.>

	Authentication	Authorization	Auditing	Confidentiality	Non-repudiation
Internal data		●			
<Application name>		<Technology implemented>			
Partner data	●	●			●
<Application name>	<Technology implemented>	<Technology implemented>			<Technology implemented>
Customer data	●	●	●	●	
<Application name>	<Technology implemented>	<Technology implemented>	<Technology implemented>	<Technology implemented>	
Internal application	●	●			
<Application name>	<Technology implemented>	<Technology implemented>			
Partner application	●	●			●
<Application name>	<Technology implemented>	<Technology implemented>			<Technology implemented>
Customer application	●	●	●	●	●
<Application name>	<Technology implemented>	<Technology implemented>	<Technology implemented>	<Technology implemented>	<Technology implemented>
Internal process		●			
<Application name>		<Technology implemented>			
Partner process	●	●	●		●
<Application name>	<Technology implemented>	<Technology implemented>	<Technology implemented>		<Technology implemented>
Customer process	●	●	●	●	●
<Application name>	<Technology implemented>	<Technology implemented>	<Technology implemented>	<Technology implemented>	<Technology implemented>

10. Conclusions and Recommended Next Steps

<This section is a summary of all key discoveries found during the assessment process. This should include any areas of risk identified, such as holes in security or hand coded interfaces, and what will not scale and cannot be easily changed. This section should also note any areas of technical redundancy, such as multiple messaging technologies or multiple integration brokers already installed. Finally, any current problems that involve end users' use of the existing systems should also be captured.>

Appendix A: References

<The appendix should list any reference documents used in the creation of the document so that its contents can be traced back to their sources if necessary. This should be broken down into internal documents and external documents. Internal documents are those that belong to the organization. External documents are items such as articles, whitepapers, Web sites, or product documentation.>

APPENDIX D

Technical Integration Architecture Specification

<ENTERPRISE NAME>

<PLACE LOGO HERE>

<author>
<version>
<revision date>

Template Instructions

This is a template for the Technical Integration Architecture specification. This page should be removed prior to publication of the specification. The template is a guide for the enterprise and should not be blindly followed. The organization should

- *Review the chapter in the book that refers to the template to understand its use.*
- *Examine the template outline and determine what additions might be necessary based on unique organizational needs.*
- *If absolutely necessary, remove any sections that will not apply. (The authors strongly discourage this practice.)*
- *Save the template for future use.*
- *Begin to develop the document.*
- *Guidance is given for preparation of the document throughout the template.*
- *Text shown as normal text should be used in the document. It may be modified as necessary.*
- *Text shown in pointed brackets is either instructional guidance in the application of the document or a description of the type of information to be added and should be removed prior to publication.*
- *Text shown in double-pointed brackets is a placeholder for the insertion of text by the authors.*

Headers and footers should be customized as necessary as a final step in the completion of the document.

Technical Integration Architecture Specification

1. Introduction

<This document represents the technical integration architecture specification that will be used to guide the integration of applications for <<enterprise name>>. This document is to guide all decisions and designs related to integration in the organization to ensure that there is consistency, reusability, and economic benefit to the organization.>

2. Scope

<Define the scope of the technical integration architecture. It should address whether it is enterprise-wide or limited to a certain organization or class of applications. Other areas to address include types of integration (data, application, or process), any limitations, and reasons for the limitations. The scope must also describe what types of external applications are covered, for example, applications outside the scope of the enterprise that are candidates for connecting to enterprise applications.>

3. Key Participants

<Define the audience and major stakeholders. The audience should include all members of the IT organization; however, it should explicitly list out specific roles or titles that are to apply the integration in the normal execution of their jobs. The major stakeholders should include the IT executives and those responsible for maintaining the document.>

4. Integration Architecture Requirements

4.1 Types of Integration

<The types of the integration to be performed needs to be defined. The data from the prior section is used to extrapolate the requirements for this section. Define which types of integration to determine scope of investment.>

Internal application integration requirements	Simple connectivity, intelligent routing, translation and transformation, application interfaces/adapters	<Applications requiring this level of integration>
Legacy integration requirements	Mainframe, custom or ERP applications	<Applications requiring this level of integration>
Customer, partner, supplier (B2B) integration requirements	EDI, custom or B2B services	<Applications requiring this level of integration>
Composite integration requirements	Composite applications, SOA, new development	<Applications requiring this level of integration>
Portal integration requirements	Integrated portal	<Applications requiring this level of integration>
Information integration requirements	Batch, real-time, volumes, scheduling, structured and unstructured information	<Applications requiring this level of integration>
Process integration requirements	BPM, BAM, and workflow applications	<Applications requiring this level of integration>

4.2 Integration Services and Technologies

<Discuss the role of different types of components to the overall strategy. This section guides technology selection for specific projects. Include preferred vendors and solutions and any technologies for which the company has enterprise licenses. List the different types of integration services and the technologies that can be used to implement the service.

Figure 5-3, which was constructed during the assessment of the current architecture and shows existing products in the organization, is used as the basis for determining whether the preferred vendor or technology is currently installed.>

Integration Service	Integration Technology	Recommended Use	Preferred Vendor/ Technology	Currently Installed?
Adapters and interfaces	Adapters	When a packaged adapter is available for target application	<Vendor name, product name>	<Yes or no>
	Web services	For SOA, composite applications, legacy integration, custom application interfaces, and B2B integration	<Vendor name, product name>	<Yes or no>
	APIs—used with packaged applications	If nothing else is available	<Vendor name, product name>	<Yes or no>
	Screen scraping—used with legacy applications	If nothing else is available, or for fast, tactical solution	<Vendor name, product name>	<Yes or no>
Messaging and connectivity services	JMS messaging	Java applications	<Vendor name, product name>	<Yes or no>
	Proprietary messaging	If already installed, or if function is required	<Vendor name, product name>	<Yes or no>
	SOAP	XML messaging over the Internet	<Vendor name, product name>	<Yes or no>
	FTP	If nothing else is available	<Vendor name, product name>	<Yes or no>
	VAN	EDI, other B2B electronic services	<Vendor name, product name>	<Yes or no>
Routing	Integration servers/brokers	Used for one-to-many or many-to-many routing, hub and spoke architecture	<Vendor name, product name>	<Yes or no>
	Enterprise Service Bus (ESB)	Used for one-to-one, one-to-many or many-to-many routing, bus architecture, can plug in other integration services	<Vendor name, product name>	<Yes or no>
	BPM	High level routing and management of business processes	<Vendor name, product name>	<Yes or no>

Integration Service	Integration Technology	Recommended Use	Preferred Vendor/ Technology	Currently Installed?
Translation and transformation	Integration servers—usually have graphical mapping tools	Used for one-to-many or many-to-many integrations	<Vendor name, product name>	<Yes or no>
	Intelligent adapters—translation and transformation occur at the adapter	Scalable distributed computing model; mapping metadata kept in centralized repository	<Vendor name, product name>	<Yes or no>
	XSLT	XML transformation	<Vendor name, product name>	<Yes or No>
Information integration	EII	For aggregated data, such as presenting a single view of customer, or federating data across organizational units	<Vendor name, product name>	<Yes or no>
	(ECM)	For integrating unstructured data including documents, graphics, voice, video, etc.	<Vendor name, product name>	<Yes or no>
	Metadata repository	For creating a canonical format for shared enterprise information	<Vendor name, product name>	<Yes or no>
Portal integration	Enterprise and Web portals	Providing unified interface to disparate information and applications	<Vendor name, product name>	<Yes or no>
Composite applications	Application and Web servers	Used for building new applications or application components or business services	<Vendor name, product name>	<Yes or no>
	Web service orchestration	Used for "assembling" component-based applications	<Vendor name, product name>	<Yes or no>
	Web services	Used for creating application services to be used in the composite application	<Vendor name, product name>	<Yes or no>

(continued)

Integration Service	Integration Technology	Recommended Use	Preferred Vendor/ Technology	Currently Installed?
Process integration	BPM	Modeling, implementation and management of integrated business processes	<Vendor name, product name>	<Yes or no>
	BAM	Real-time monitoring of processes and dash-boards; may be part of BAM tool	<Vendor name, product name>	<Yes or no>
B2B integration	B2B servers	Used for integration with partners and suppliers, build on-line community. Integrates with back-end applications via adapters or EAI servers	<Vendor name, product name>	<Yes or no>
	EDI	Used for large partners, existing EDI solutions. Used with VAN	<Vendor name, product name>	<Yes or no>
	XML	Used for sending mes-sages to partners via the Internet	<Vendor name, product name>	<Yes or no>
	Web services	Used as a standardized interface	<Vendor name, product name>	<Yes or no>
Mobile integration	Mobile integra-tion servers	Delivers information to different mobile devices from common informa-tion and business rules	<Vendor name, product name>	<Yes or no>
Security integration	Security inte-gration servers	Integrates disparate security systems	<Vendor name, product name>	<Yes or no>

5. Integration Architecture Description

<The Architecture Description contains two different views: the conceptual view and the development view.>

5.1 Conceptual View

<The conceptual view shows all of the components and their relationships. This conceptual view can be drawn in a number ways. For example, it could be shown

as a layered architecture with the lowest level protocols shown above TCP/IP, and at the highest level the applications and how they connect into the system. Furthermore, the layers could be split to show how the layers fit into the server architecture. For example, the services would be shown on different servers than the adapters or interfaces. Each application would be shown dependent on the servers or mainframes on which they reside. The conceptual view would demonstrate how they fit together and the relationships inside and outside the firewall.>

5.2 Development View

<The development view is a description of how and when each of the different tools and interfaces is used, to guide the development team utilizing the integration architecture. For each and every aspect of the integration architecture, there must be a description of how a developer may apply the architecture. This would include the languages supported and the manner in which services and capabilities are accessed, tools for developing any integrations, and tools for configuration and administration. Additionally, standard interfaces available for use should be defined.>

Language support	<List how each language is supported. Describe the form of the access>
Integration definition tools	<List any tools used to create and manage an integration definition>
Integration support tools	<List any tools used to support management and configuration of integrations>
Open interfaces	<List any open interfaces that can be used independent of languages or development tools>

6. Standards Profile

<This section specifies all standards that have been adopted by the organization that are relevant to the integration architecture. The full specification should also include a governance policy that defines how compliance with standards will be managed, and the process and guidelines for approving solutions that do not comply with standards.>

Communication protocols	<Industry standard or technology for each type of communication>
	<Example: RosettaNet; JMS; etc.>
Application interfaces	<Industry standard or technology for each type of application>
	<Example: Web services for x types of applications, packaged adapters for y type of applications, JCA for z type of applications>
Message formats	<Industry standard or technology for each type of message>
	<Example: XML for most types of messages, EDI for transactions with large partners, etc.>
Process models	<Industry standard or technology>
	<Example: standardize on a tool or a modeling standard such as BPEL>
Metadata	<Standards for different types of metadata>
	<Example: metadata about interfaces, Web services, data transformation, etc.>

7. Service Level Agreements

<Service level requirements include availability, integrity, scalability, maintainability, manageability, usability, performance, transaction services, persistence, and directory services.>

7.1 Availability

<There are two types of availability metric: system availability (8×5, 24×7), and availability of integration (real time, periodic, or batch). This metric defines when the information that has been integrated is available for use.>

7.2 Integrity and Delivery Service

<Integrity of integrated information rests on the integrity of the transmission as well as the integrity of the information being processed. Transmission integrity is

ensured by transmission services such as guaranteed delivery, once-and-only-once delivery, and persistent message stores. The integrity of the information processes is dependent upon the validity of the translation and transformation process and the processing of the information by the target system. This metric can be measured in error rates.>

7.3 Scalability

<Scalability requirements determine the type of architecture as well as the technologies selected for implementation, and are a large factor in capacity planning and purchasing. The scalability requirements must be defined for the expected needs of the organization in the short term as well as the longer term. Scalability requirements can be defined by the following parameters:

- Amount of information to be passed
- Transaction rates (time/volume)
- Number of applications to be integrated
- Simultaneous end-user connections

7.4 Maintainability and Manageability

Maintainability and management requirements can be defined by the following services:

- Monitoring and alerting
- Startup, shutdown, and restart
- Troubleshooting and level of support
- Maintainability of code and use of tools
- Installation and managing release of updates and ability to rollback
- Scheduling
- Integration with existing tools

After determining manageability requirements, we recommend summarizing them for the purposes of enterprise planning. Assigning a manageability requirement rating to each application or project can do this. This rating provides a summary view of all manageability requirements. The following rating can be used:

- **Level 1.** Startup, shutdown and restart, troubleshooting, scheduling remote installation
- **Level 2.** Level 1 plus updates and rollbacks, integrated application repository
- **Level 3.** Level 2 plus real time monitoring and alerts, full integration of development and management tools

7.5 Usability

<Usability refers to how easily each type of user will use the system. Define all types of system users, along with the type of access and usability they require. The table below can be modified or expanded as needed.>

Type of User	**Usability Requirements**
Developers <J2EE, .NET, Web services, legacy, integration specialist>	<J2EE and/or .NET programming, Web service programming interfaces>
Analyst	<Modeling interface>
Designer	<Modeling and configuration interface>
Line of business managers	<Browser-based portal or dashboard, real-time alerts>
Other business user	<Browser-based portal, real-time alerts>
Operational managers	<Interface to management tools, portal interface of operational status, real-time alerts>

7.6 Performance

<Performance requirements define the level of service the infrastructure needs to provide to support business users, processes, and transactions. Performance requirements are also used in the Capacity Planning View (section 9 of this template).>

Response time	<Real-time, minutes, hours, days>
Throughput	<Number of transactions, data volumes>
Turnaround time	<Seconds, minutes, hours, days>
Number of simultaneous users	<Subtotals by types of users defined in usability>
Number of connected applications	<Name all applications that will be integrated>

7.7 Transaction Services

<Transaction services include distributed transaction support and XA standard transaction compliance. This information determines how transactions will be managed and how transactional integrity will be maintained. This section also defines requirements for supporting industry and regulatory standards such as RosettaNet, HIPAA, or other industry standard transactions.>

7.8 Persistence Services

<Persistence is required for improved reliability when recovering from a failure. Being able to re-start a failed system without losing any in-process integrations is the most basic use of a persistence service. Other types of uses for persisted data include the ability to rollback any actions, perform audits of activity, or to use the collected data to analyze activity on the infrastructure. This section defines the requirements to provide storage of the integration data and state information during and after any use of the integration infrastructure.>

7.9 Directory Services

<Directories can provide location transparency by allowing applications to "find" other applications for integration. They can store configuration information on resources or users that can be used by any application or integration process. Finally, a directory can be used to store security information. The table below depicts the types of information to specify for directory services.>

Component Name	**Component Type**	**Location**	**Description**	**Other Fields**
<Component name>	<Component type>	<Location>	<Description>	<Value>
<Component name>	<Component type>	<Location>	<Description>	<Value>

7.10 Service Level Summary Table

<The Service Level Summary Table is useful for displaying an aggregate view of service level requirements.>

	<Application Type or Name>	<Application2 Name>	<ApplicationN Name>
Availability	<Real time or batch; 8x5 or 24x7>	...	...
Integrity and delivery service	<Guaranteed; once and only once; message stores>	...	...
Scalability	<Connections, locations transactions, data volumes>	...	...
Maintainability and manageability	<Level 1, Level 2, Level 3>	...	...
Usability	<Developers, analysts, designers, LOB managers, other business users, operational managers>	...	...
Performance	<Response time, throughput, simultaneous users>	...	...
Transaction services	<Distributed transactions, XA compliant, HIPAA, other?>	...	...
Persistence	<Storage of data and integration information for recovery, playback and analysis>	...	...
Directory services	<Information about all of the components of the integration infrastructure>	...	...

8. Security

<Security is a type of service-level requirement, but it is such an important topic and a highly specialized topic that it is dealt with separately. The specification should start by summarizing the top-level security requirements by the categories or types of applications that will be utilizing the architecture. This can be done in a general manner, as shown in the following table, but it is more effective if it can be specifically defined.>

	Authentication	Authorization	Auditing	Confidentiality	Nonrepudiation
Internal data		■			
Partner data	■	■			■
Customer data	■	■	■	■	
Internal application	■	■			
Partner application	■	■			■
Customer application	■	■	■	■	■
Internal process		■			
Partner process	■	■	■		■
Customer process	■	■	■	■	■

8.1 Authentication

<Authentication services confirm the identity of a user. A detailed specification of authorization service requirements includes the following:

- **List of user types.** User types should correlate to the types of applications or services a group would access. Examples include: designers, programmers, managers, line-of-business users, customers, and partners.
- **Level of authentication for each type of user or role.** Levels of authentication may include: password, password with public/private key encryption, digital certificate, or biometrics.

- **Whether unitary login will be supported.** Unitary logic defines whether authentication can be performed once for all applications and services. This requires a centralized directory for all services.
- **Definition of how user accounts will be managed.** User accounts must be constantly created and updated based on the changes that occur in the business. It is important to have a formal process defined on how this information will be kept synchronized.>

8.2 Authorization

<Authorization levels determine what operations a user or process is authorized to perform on a set of data or within an application. This section defines categories for authorization, based on application and/or sensitivity of data. Authorization is usually defined in a CRUD matrix that defines rights to Create, Read, Update, or Delete information.>

	<Application 1>	**<Application 2>**	**<Application 3>**	**<Application 4>**
User Role #1	<C, R, U, D>	<R, U>	<R, U>	<R>
User Role #2	<R>	<C, R, U, D>	<R, U>	<R, U>
User Role #3	<R>	<R>	<C, R, U, D>	<R>
User Role #4	<R>	<R, U>	<R, U>	<C, R, U, D>

8.3 Perimeter Security

<This section should address how the integration architecture will work with perimeter security and the types or categories of integration that will be required to use the perimeter security features. Perimeter security is the combination of firewalls, encryption, authentication services, and architecture to protect the enterprise from the outside world. The configuration of the perimeter security will dictate the design of the integration architecture as it relates to external usage.>

8.4 Auditing

<This section defines categories for auditing based on the type of application and the sensitivity of the data being processed. Basic categories of auditing are:

- **Level 0.** Maintain no information
- **Level 1.** Maintain information on type of interaction and participants
- **Level 2.** Maintain only instructions for each interaction
- **Level 3.** Maintain a complete set of information on every interaction

Performance and resource requirements are the tradeoffs in making a distinction between each level.>

8.5 Confidentiality

<Confidentiality refers to the level of privacy that a transmission requires. Confidentiality usually applies to the level of encryption that is applied, but could also be reflected in the communications path that is used.>

8.6 Nonrepudiation

<Nonrepudiation is extremely important for B2B transactions. The specification should define the level of nonrepudiation service required, and which types and categories of applications require it.>

Type of Nonrepudiation	**Type of Application**
Nonrepudiated communications sessions	Simple integrations of applications or the exchange of data between applications.
Nonrepudiated middleware services	Integrations where the interactions are with an middleware infrastructure.
Nonrepudiated transactions	Transaction processing.
Nonrepudiated application actions consisting of multiple transactions	Complex business processes.

9. Capacity Planning View

<This section specifies the design approaches to achieving specific application-required responsiveness, throughput, capacity, reliability and availability, and

scalabiliy. The information from Service Level Requirements is the input to capacity planning. The goal is to define how all service level requirements will be met.>

Requirement	Design Approach
Availability	<Back-up and recovery plan, redundancy plan, fail-over, disaster site, etc.>
Response time	<Network bandwidth, high-speed access, localized access, optimized human interactions, application performance optimization, database optimization>
Throughput	<Network bandwidth, high-speed access, application performance optimization, database optimization, storage capacity>
Turnaround times	<Network bandwidth, high-speed access, application performance optimization, database optimization, real-time alerts>
Number of users	<Connection management, caching, localizing access through redundant stores, optimizing human interactions, application performance, database optimization>
Number of connected applications	<Point-to-point integration, integration server, distributed integration servers>
Transaction services	<Transaction monitor, transaction services within application, other>
Persistence	<Storage systems, recovery and playback capabilities, analytical tools>
Directory services	<Directory server, administrative tools>

10. Design Constraints and Guidance

<All constraints and specific guidance for architects, designers, and developers should be defined at this point. Some areas to be considered in the setting of constraints and guidance are

- Known performance limitations
- Formatting guidelines for data
- Constraints on metadata definitions and registration
- Preference on use of different types of interfaces
- Special cases of security implementations
- Deviations allowed from the integration architecture>

11. Conclusions and Recommended Next Steps

<Summarize any particular issues or decisions regarding the integration architecture.>

Appendix A: References

The appendix should list any reference documents used in the creation of the document so that its contents can be traced back to their sources if necessary. This should be broken down into internal documents and external documents. Internal documents are those that belong to the organization. External documents are items such as articles, whitepapers, Web sites, or product documentation.

APPENDIX E

Service Integration Architecture Specification

<ENTERPRISE NAME>

<PLACE LOGO HERE>

<author>
<version>
<revision date>

Template Instructions

This is a template for the Service Integration Architecture Specification. This page should be removed prior to publication of the specification. The template is a guide for the enterprise and should not be blindly followed. The organization should

- *Review the chapter in the book that refers to the template to understand its use.*
- *Examine the template outline and determine what additions might be necessary based on unique organizational needs.*
- *If absolutely necessary, remove any sections that will not apply. (The authors strongly discourage this practice.)*
- *Save the template for future use.*
- *Begin to develop the document.*

Guidance is given for preparation of the document throughout the template.

- *Text shown as normal text should be used in the document. It may be modified as necessary.*
- *Text shown in pointed brackets is either instructional guidance in the application of the document or a description of the type of information to be added and should be removed prior to publication.*
- *Text shown in double-pointed brackets is a placeholder for the insertion of text by the authors.*

Headers and footers should be customized as necessary as a final step in the completion of the document.

Service Integration Architecture Specification

1. **Introduction**

This specification provides architecture and design guidance for applying a service-oriented architecture approach to integration for <<system name>>. This document will be the design and architecture specification for the development of the application.

2. **Scope**

<The scope of this specification is limited to an application or system. The document should define the architecture and design for applying a service-oriented architecture approach. The scope should describe the scope of the application or system that is defined in the architecture and design.>

3. **Key Participants**

<This section should define the users of the application or system, the development team who will execute the implementation of the design, and the team responsible for the architecture and design. Any other participants or stakeholders should also be identified including their roles.>

4. **Business Events**

<Business Events define the business activities that the system must support. A business event

- Occurs in the business environment
- Occurs at a given point in time
- Must be responded to by the system

The Event Table describes the relevant activities that happen in the business and the required system responses. There are two types of events: business events and temporal events. Business events are activities that occur in the business. Business events are detected by defining each business activity within the scope of the system. Temporal events occur at a predetermined point in time. Temporal events exist because the business policy demands that certain system activities occur at certain times, or because the system produces its outputs on a timed basis.

In the Event Description column, include how the event is initiated or detected. When defining Responses, give descriptive names that unambiguously define what the system response is, such as "Verify existing customer," "Enter New Customer," "Check Credit.">

Event Number	Business Event	Event Description	Response
E1	Business event 1	<Description of the event>	R1.1 Response 1 to business event 1 . . . R1.*n* Response n to business event 1
E2	Business event 2	<Description of the event>	R2.1 Response 1 to business event 2 . . . R2.*n* Response n to business event 2
E3	Business event 3	<Description of the event>	R3.1 Response 1 to business event 3 . . . R3.*n* Response n to business event 3
E4	Business event 4	<Description of the event>	R4.1 Response 1 to business event 4 . . . R4.*n* Response n to business event 4

5. Services

<The system responses defined in the Events Table define the essential services the system must provide. Some required functionality already exists and other functionality will be new and must be developed, then integrated. The service descriptions define the scope of functionality required to perform a specific business service.

To maximize business agility and IT investment, business services should be defined at the level of granularity that will optimize reuse. Tight cohesion—grouping closely related functions together into business services, and loose coupling between services are the design metrics that will yield more reusable design. The service description should include the methods to be supported by the service, the inputs and outputs, and the general description. This level of description is sufficient for developing a Web service or other interface. Starting from the business level definition, it drills down to a level sufficient to turn the service description into a Web service.>

5.1 Service Category Table

<The Service Category Table lists all required responses to business events, defines whether the function already exists in one or more systems, or if it is a new functionality. The table also defines likely services to provide the functionality. The service at this point is a first best guess at a services definition and will be refined further in the next step. When defining services, think of modules within an existing application that may perform the service or likely component modules for development.>

Response	Description	Service Category	Existing/New Systems
<Response>	<Description>	<Category>	<Systems>
R1.1 Response name	What are the actions or services performed?	Service category	<Category>
R*n.n* Response name	What are the actions or services performed?	Service category	<Category>

5.2 Service Definition Table

<Each service should be described in terms of its function and systems used to implement the function. In creating this table, group all functions and responses together that will form a cohesive module. For example, the service should manage a particular set of data, such as customer information or product information, or should perform a specific service than might be used in other applications, such as credit checking or pricing. There should be loose coupling between services. Each service should interact with any other service through the defined interface. Changes in one service should not impact functioning of other services.

The description should define how the service would be implemented. For example:

- **Service1 Description.** Web service that abstracts database connections and lookups, and manages customer record maintenance. Supports match, read, create, update, and delete operations.
- **Service2 Description.** Interface to accounts receivable.>

Service	Functions	Description	Existing/ New
Service Name	Response number and name, for responses 1 through *n*.	Implementation description	<Systems>
Service *n*	Response number and name, for responses 1 through *n*.	Implementation description	Example: database, ERP, mainframe, new

5.3 Service Interface Table

<While the Web services standard defines how to specify an interface, it does not define the data and functionality that the interface needs to contain. The Service Interface Specification provides the information necessary for creating Web services or other application or component interfaces. Using the Service Definition Table, list all inputs, outputs, and methods that the interface needs to support, and determine how the interface will be implemented.

Inputs should include all data fields and/or functions the interface must support. Likewise, the outputs should also include all data fields and/or functions the interface must support. For example, a credit check service might define inputs as customer ID, name and telephone number, and amount; and outputs as credit approval or credit disapproval.>

Service:	Service Name
Inputs	<List all inputs>
Outputs	<List all outputs>
Methods	<List all methods>
Implementation	<Web service, packages adapter, custom adapter, application API, other>

6. Use Cases

<Use Cases define actors and how they interact with the system services. Actors represent a role, and can be humans, other computers, pieces of hardware, or other software systems. They must supply stimuli to initiate the event that in turn requires a system response (or service). Use cases describe the behavior of the system when one of these actors sends one particular stimulus. It depicts the business events and system responses in terms of the event stimulus that triggers the use case—the inputs from and outputs to other actors, and the behaviors that convert the inputs to the outputs.>

6.1 Use Case Diagram

<The basic components of use case diagrams are the actor, the use case, and the association. To create the use case, identify the primary actors in the system, then prioritize the services to be implemented. We recommend creating a use case for each proposed service.

Actor	An actor is depicted using a stick figure, and the role of the user is written beneath the icon. Actors can be humans, other computers, pieces of hardware, or other software systems.	
Use Case	A use case is depicted with an ellipse. The name of the use case is written within the ellipse.	
Association	Associations are links between actors and use cases, and indicate that an actor participates in the use case in some form.>	

6.2 Use Case Specification

<The Use Case Specification contains text that further describes the use case. The text specification also usually describes everything that can go wrong during the course of the specified behavior, and what remedial action the system will take. This specification can be customized or expanded to handle particular issues within an implementation or organization.>

Use Case	**Use Case Name**
Primary actors	Actor name/role
Abstract	Textual description of the use case
Goal	What is to be achieved as a result of the actor interacting with the system?
Preconditions	The state of the process before the activities commence; the events that are precursors to the stimulus for this use case
Trigger	Event(s) that triggers the use case
General scenario	Step-by-step description of the flow through the use case
Successful operation responses/outputs	Response number and name, 1. .*n*.
Extensions/ alternative paths/ unsuccessful operation responses/outputs	Response number and name, 1. .*n*.
Dependencies	Any use cases that this use case is dependent upon; functionality that must occur prior to initiation of this use case
Requirements reference	Pointers to any requirements documents that this use case supports for traceability
Screen reference	Pointers to any screens that will be used during the use case
Backend reference	Description of any backend systems accessed during the use case
Notes	Any other comments not covered above

7. Conclusions and Recommended Next Steps

<This section should provide any final comments on the system, the design, or the usage of the system. It should include any known issues, constraints, or extenuating factors that contributed to decisions or could impact the system in the future.>

Appendix A: References

<The appendix should list any reference documents used in the creation of the document so that its contents can be traced back to their sources if necessary. This should be broken down into internal documents and external documents. Internal documents are those that belong to the organization. External documents are items such as articles, whitepapers, Web sites, or product documentation.>

APPENDIX F

Information Integration Architecture Specification

<ENTERPRISE NAME>

<PLACE LOGO HERE>

<author>
<version>
<revision date>

Template Instructions

This is a template for the Information Integration Architecture Specification. This page should be removed prior to publication of the specification. The template is a guide for the enterprise and should not be blindly followed. The organization should

- *Review the chapter in the book that refers to the template to understand its use.*
- *Examine the template outline and determine what additions might be necessary based on unique organizational needs.*
- *If absolutely necessary, remove any sections that will not apply. (The authors strongly discourage this practice.)*
- *Save the template for future use.*
- *Begin to develop the document.*

Guidance is given for preparation of the document throughout the template.

- *Text shown as normal text should be used in the document. It may be modified as necessary.*
- *Text shown in pointed brackets is either instructional guidance in the application of the document or a description of the type of information to be added and should be removed prior to publication.*
- *Text shown in double-pointed brackets is a placeholder for the insertion of text by the authors.*

Headers and footers should be customized as necessary as a final step in the completion of the document.

Information Integration Architecture Specification

1. **Introduction**

   <This specification provides the design guidance for applying an information-driven approach to integration for <<system name>>. This document is a guide to creating the information architecture specification for the enterprise information integration based applications or information driven business solutions.>

2. **Scope**

   <The scope of an information specification is limited to an integration project. The document should define the business information needs and the underlying integration architecture. The scope should describe the breath of business information covered as well as the systems and data sources involved in the process.>

3. **Key Participants**

   <This section identifies all stakeholders in the business information being integrated, including business managers who control all or part of the information; system designers and architect(s); and the development team, who will execute the implementation. Any other participants or stakeholders should also be identified, including their roles.>

4. **Mapping Requirements to Information Integration Design Patterns**

   <This section is used to identify and map all of the requirements to the design patterns for information integration. The two basic design patterns are information aggregation and publishing. To identify the business information requirements that need to be defined as part of this specification start with the Statement of Purpose and the scope of responsibilities defined in the Business Strategies and Initiatives Specification. Then use design patterns to identify the best approach for implementation.>

Application Name	Business Owner	Description of Information Application	Aggregation or Publishing	Data Sources Involved	Outcome of the Flow of Information
Management dashboard	Head of sales	Daily sales order volumes on a world-wide basis	Aggregation	Order entry systems across the world	Graphical display of sales orders daily, weekly, monthly, and quarterly
Call center customer support system	Head of customer support	Single view of a relationship of a customer for the call center	Aggregation	All systems containing customer information	Single screen unifying all customer information
Online customer change of address	CIO	Update all addresses for a customer self service change of address	Publishing	All systems containing customer addresses	Update to all systems with customer address
<Application name>	<Owner>	<Description>	<Information pattern>	<Source>	<Outcome>

5. Data Flow Diagram

<The Data Flow Diagram depicts the flow of information across systems. The purpose of the data flow diagram is to determine which systems are involved in the data exchange, and to later determine the integrity rules across systems (done in the Relationship Model, section 7).

The diagram on page 328 is an adaptation of a traditional data flow model in order to focus on the flow of information across systems. Here external systems (depicted as shaded boxes) are systems outside of the enterprise.>

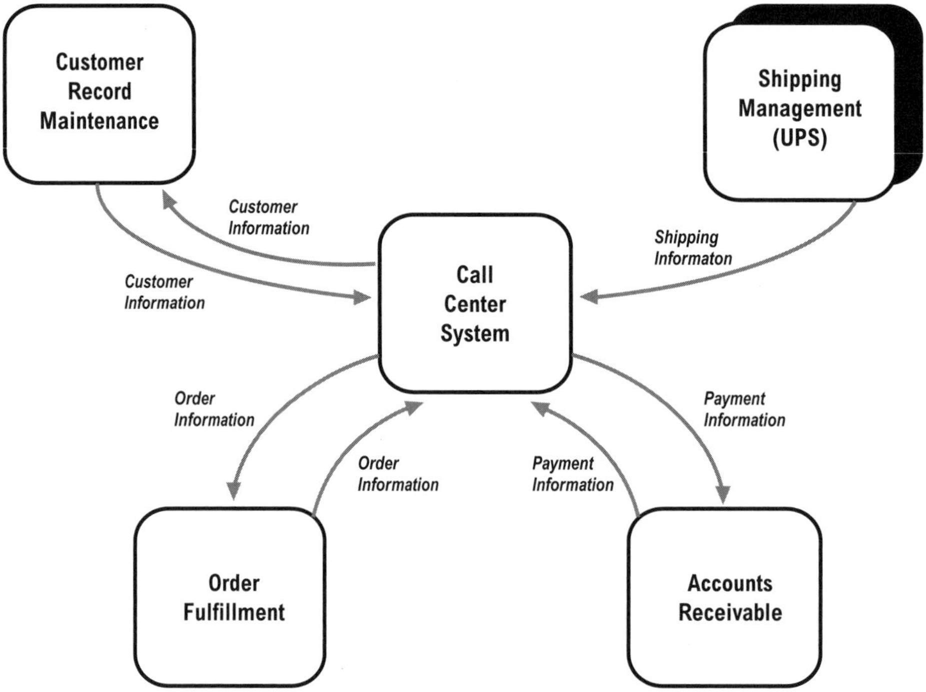

6. Metadata Model

<Each application will require a metadata model that combines the new model for the application with the existing models of each of the data sources used. The Metadata Model is used to define access and transformation rules. It establishes data lineage and enables impact analysis.

Metadata for existing data sources must be captured for each element. The information model can be extended as needed to support the enterprise.>

Basic metadata	Data element name	<Source system data name>
	Data source	<Source>
	Description	<Description>
	Format and data type	<Source system format and type>
	Canonical name	<Enterprise canonical name>
	Canonical format	<XML or other–name format>
	Transformation rules	<From source to canonical format>
	Interface	<Web service, adapter, API, SQL>
Semantic metadata	Integrity rules	<Relationships across applications>
Added security	Security parameters	<Access Control Lists, Directory>
Added management	Platform	<Hardware platform>
	OS	<Operating system and version>
	DBMS	<Database>
	Application platform	<Application server, other>
	Owner of the system	<Company, department, manager>
	Location of the system	<Directory>
	Service information	<Web services directory>
	Message schema information	<Message repository>
	Communication protocol	<SOAP, HTTP, TCP/IP, VAN>
	Access mechanism	<Enterprise message bus, message broker, JMS call, EDI VAN>

7. Relationship Model

<The Relationship Table defines the mapping of the data between the new applications and the existing systems as well as the integrity rules across data objects and systems.

Note that the system/service and source data element name are added here to provide lineage. The target system/service is included to enable impact analysis. The business rules can include aggregation and parsing rules particular to that data flow.>

Cannonical name	<Cannonical name>
Source system/service data element name	<Data element name>
Source system/service	<System/service name>
Business rules	<Aggregation and parsing rules>
Target system or service data element name	<Target data element name>
Target system or service	<Service or system name>
Integrity rules	<Rollback and compensation rules>
Security requirements	<Encryption, nonrepudiation, and access rules>

8. Information Design Reviews

<Information design reviews are critical to the overall success and agility of the system. The design reviews should include all relevant stakeholders, defined above in the key participants section. All parts of the model need to be reviewed and verified. Participants need to verify the portions of the information they are responsible for, including the definition of all elements, how they are created and updated, the formats, and the access mechanisms. The business users need to provide the definitions for the information required in the new application. In addition, it will be critical for the stakeholders to ensure they deal with discrepancies on which data source contains the "gold standard" for the organization when there are conflicts or duplications. This is often the most difficult task that the group will face. The overall process should be reviewed for opportunities to improve consistency and quality of information across the organization.

Use the following guidelines for successful design reviews:

- Make sure all the stakeholders are present.
- Explain the process and ground rules before the design review.
- Criticize the design, not the person.
- Designers may only speak to clarify the design and provide background information. They should not "defend" the design.
- Identify "owners" of information.

- Identify systems of record for information.
- Define a process for data quality.>

9. **Conclusions and Recommended Next Steps**

<This section should provide any final comments on the information, the design, or the usage of the system.>

Appendix A: References

<The appendix should list any reference documents used in the creation of the document so that its contents can be traced back to their sources if necessary. This should be broken down into internal documents and external documents. Internal documents are those that belong to the organization. External documents are items such as articles, whitepapers, Web sites, or product documentation.>

APPENDIX G

Process Integration Architecture Specification

<ENTERPRISE NAME>

<PLACE LOGO HERE>

<author>
<version>
<revision date>

Template Instructions

This is a template for the Process Integration Architecture Specification. This page should be removed prior to publication of the specification. The template is a guide for the enterprise and should not be blindly followed. The organization should

- *Review the chapter in the book that refers to the template to understand its use.*
- *Examine the template outline and determine what additions might be necessary based on unique organizational needs.*
- *If absolutely necessary, remove any sections that will not apply. (The authors strongly discourage this practice).*
- *Save the template for future use.*
- *Begin to develop the document.*

Guidance is given for preparation of the document throughout the template.

- *Text shown as normal text should be used in the document. It may be modified as necessary.*
- *Text shown in pointed brackets is either instructional guidance in the application of the document or a description of the type of information to be added and should be removed prior to publication.*
- *Text shown in double-pointed brackets is a placeholder for the insertion of text by the authors.*

Headers and footers should be customized as necessary as a final step in the completion of the document.

Process Integration Architecture Specification

1. **Introduction**

   <This specification provides the design guidance applying a process-driven approach to integration for <<system name>>. This document is a guide to creating the process specification for the composite applications or process driven business solutions.>

2. **Scope**

   <The scope of a process specification is limited to an integration project. The document should define the business processes and the underlying integration architecture. The scope should describe the breath of business processes covered as well as the systems involved in the process.>

3. **Key Participants**

   <This section identifies all stakeholders in the business process(es) being integrated, including business managers who control all or part of the process, system designers and architect(s), and the development team who will execute the implementation. Any other participants or stakeholders should also be identified including their roles.>

4. **Business Process Descriptions**

   <This section identifies and describes all of the business processes that have been identified in the requirements. A name and a business owner identify each business process. A description of the process is provided along with the event that kicks off the process, the business services that are part of the process, and the outcome expected to end the process. If no services have been defined, then define the functions performed as part of the process. To identify the business processes that need to be defined as part of this specification, start with the Statement of Purpose and the scope of responsibilities defined in the Business Strategies and Initiatives Specification (Chapter 2).>

Business Process Name	Business Process Owner	Description of Business Process	Kickoff Event	Services Involved in the Process	Outcome of the Business Process
<Name>	<owner>	<description>	<event>	<functions>	<outcome>

5. **Process Flow Models**

<A process flow model is a combination of the event(s) that start the process, actors involved throughout the process, services provided by software components in the system, the messages passed between and among services, and the business rules controlling the flow of the process. Each process flow model should have a description of each of these entities, as well as a process diagram.

If a process modeling tool is used to create this part of the specification, add a reference to the tool and file. If your tool provides browser-based access to models, then place the URL here along with a description.

There are many methodologies for designing and depicting process flows, including data flow diagrams and IDEF diagrams.>

6. **Process Design Reviews**

<Process design reviews are critical to the overall success and agility of the system. The design reviews should include all relevant stakeholders, defined above in the key participants section. All parts of the model need to be reviewed and verified. Participants need to verify the portions of the process they are responsible for, including all tasks, functions and/or services, inputs to and outputs from each service, decision points along the process, and business rules that determine the process flow of control, as well as all exception and compensation rules. The overall process should be reviewed for opportunities to decrease time and cost and increase business flexibility and advantage.>

7. **Conclusions and Recommended Next Steps**

<This section should provide any final comments on the process, the design, or the usage of the system.>

Appendix A: References

<The appendix should list any reference documents used in the creation of the document so that its contents can be traced back to their sources if necessary. This should be broken down into internal documents and external documents. Internal documents are those that belong to the organization. External documents are items such as articles, whitepapers, Web sites, or product documentation.>

APPENDIX H

Application Integration Implementation Specification

<ENTERPRISE NAME>

<PLACE LOGO HERE>

<author>
<version>
<revision date>

Template Instructions

This is a template for the Application Integration Implementation Specification. This page should be removed prior to publication of the specification. The template is a guide for the enterprise and should not be blindly followed. The organization should

- *Review the chapter in the book that refers to the template to understand its use.*
- *Examine the template outline and determine what additions might be necessary based on unique organizational needs.*
- *If absolutely necessary, remove any sections that will not apply. (The authors strongly discourage this practice.)*
- *Save the template for future use.*
- *Begin to develop the document.*

Guidance is given for preparation of the document throughout the template.

- *Text shown as normal text should be utilized in the document. It may be modified as necessary.*
- *Text shown in pointed brackets is either instructional guidance in the application of the document or a description of the type of information to be added and should be removed prior to publication.*
- *Text shown in double pointed brackets is a placeholder for the insertion of text by the authors.*

Headers and footers should be customized as necessary as a final step in the completion of the document.

Application Integration Implementation Specification

1. **Introduction**

<This specification provides implementation guidance for the development of an application integration based solution.

Application integration represents a specific style of integration. This style is to solve problems where two or more applications communicate together to accomplish a given task. Types of problems that are well suited to application integration are

- Coordinating actions and replicating transactions across multiple applications
- Opening up legacy systems and extending them to the Web
- Creating new user interfaces
- Business-to-business transactions
- Deploying applications to multiple mobile and hand-held devices

This section describes the specific technical problems that are being addressed in the implementation, and provides context for the specific implementation.>

2. **Scope**

<The scope of an application integration specification is limited to the specifics of the applications that are being integrated. This section of the specification includes organizational units, external organizations, users, and applications involved. It should also define the expected time frames and end result.>

3. **Key Participants**

<This section identifies all stakeholders in the implementation, including business managers who control all or part of the systems, the business manager responsible for implementation, system designers and architect(s), and the development team who will execute the implementation. Any other participants or stakeholders should also be identified, including their roles.>

4. **Application Integration Implementation Patterns and Services**

<There are several basic implementation patterns for an application integration solution. This section should define the particular pattern that is being used and then provide details on the configuration of the specific components of the implementation.

These patterns are

- Message broker
- Enterprise Service Bus (ESB)
- Legacy integration
- B2B integration
- Portals
- Mobile integration>

4.1 Message Brokers

<Message brokers are well suited to coordination across multiple applications, replication of transactions, and B2B applications.

The message broker implementation involves an integration hub that provides transformation services to convert the messages into the correct format for the receiving application. The broker provides intelligent routing to manage the complexity of moving the messages between applications, and translation and transformation, generally through proprietary graphical-mapping tools. Adapters provide interfaces into applications and are the points where applications can send or receive messages.

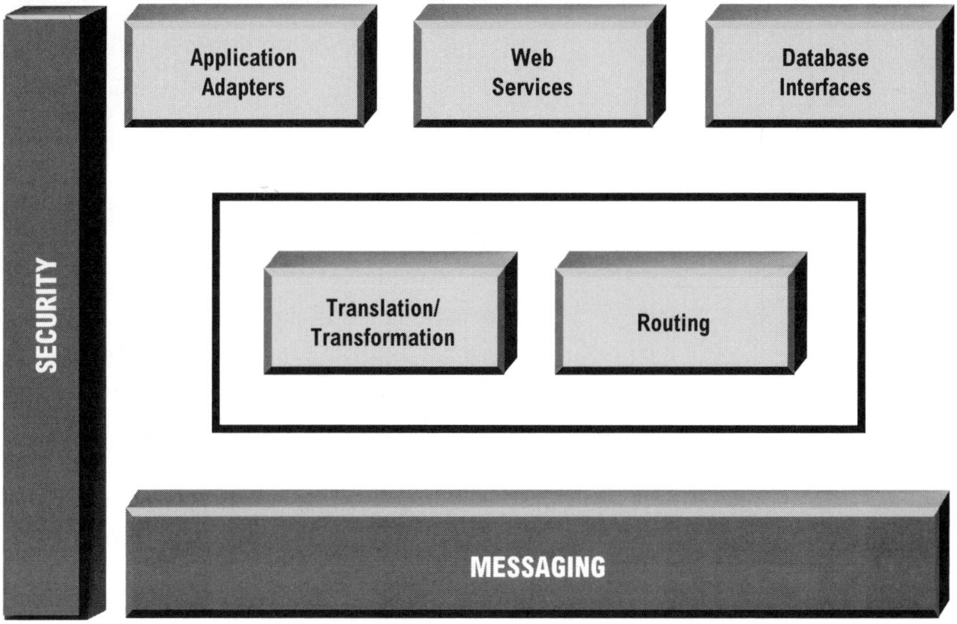

Message Broker Reference Architecture

The implementation table further defines the services identified in the implementation architecture. Revise the following template to define the particular implementation.>

Integration Service	Vendor/Product	Implementation Notes
Message broker	<Vendor name/ product name>	<Technology platform>
Messaging	<Vendor name/product name if different than broker vendor>	<Technology platform>
Application interface	<Vendor name/product name or deployment technology>	<Specify: integration broker adapter; Web service; JCA interface; data interface (ODBC, JDBC, OLE DB, ADO).>
Security	<Vendor name/product name or deployment technology>	<Specify how security is implemented, including integration with LDAP or other repository or product.>

Message Broker Implementation Table

4.2 ESB

<The ESB is more flexible and scalable than the message broker, but also more complex to implement. Until recently, there were no widely accepted standards in the industry. Web services make the service bus a more viable commercial approach to application integration. Essentially, the ESB solves the same set of business problems that a message broker does, but it has a different architecture.

The ESB provides connectivity services, including transport protocol, message protocol, message routing, and guaranteed delivery. ESBs also usually provide some basic data transformation, such as XML translation via XSLT style sheets, but additional translation and transformation tools may be necessary for complex data transformation requirements. The ESB has adapters or connecters into applications that provide interfaces into the application as the method of communication. These interfaces represent services that are provided. The services can be registered into a directory. Requests can be sent to specific locations or routed based upon rules.

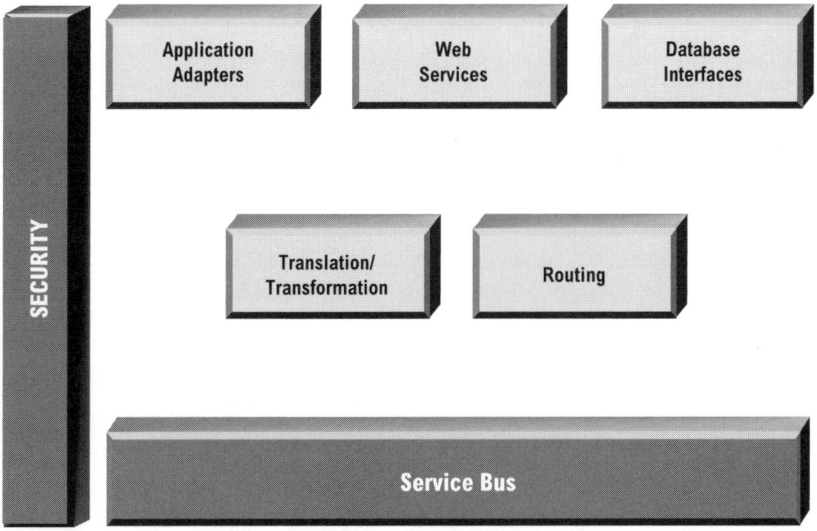

Enterprise Service Bus Reference Architecture

The Enterprise Service Bus Implementation Table further defines the services identified in the ESB reference architecture. Modify the following template to define the specific implementation, adding additional services when needed.>

Integration Service	Vendor/Product	Implementation Notes
Enterprise service bus (ESB)	<Vendor name/product name>	<Technology platform>
Translation and transformation	<Vendor name/product name>	<Transformation at hub or target>
Application interface	<Vendor name/product name or deployment technology>	<Specify: integration broker adapter; Web service; JCA interface; data interface (ODBC, JDBC, OLE DB, ADO).>
Security	<Vendor name/product name or deployment technology>	<Specify how security is implemented, including integration with LDAP or other repository or product.>

Enterprise Service Bus Implementation Table

4.3 Legacy Integration

<The goal is to integrate with the legacy data, application, or process noninvasively, without changing the legacy application. This can be done by creating a new interface to the legacy system. This section defines what type of interfaces will be used.

- **Database interfaces.** Database-level adapters that allow front-end applications access to mainframe data through database calls native to the requesting application, including JDBC, ODBC, and ADO.
- **Messaging interfaces.** If the integration includes transaction processing, a message interface can be used. This includes connectors for JCA and SOAP messaging, or proprietary solutions including IBM MQ Series and TIBCO Rendezvous on the mainframe.
- **Screen/report interface.** Sometimes, the only way to access mainframe data is through the screen or report interface, also called screen and report scraping. They both work the same way. The 3270 screen or report provides a defined interface to legacy systems for extracting information to the screen or report. The interface technology captures those data bits, and redirects them to a Web browser.
- **Service interface.** The service-level interface, also called legacy wrapping, enables mainframe processes and functions to be wrapped with a Web service, .Net, Java, or CORBA interface. Web service interfaces to mainframe processes and services provide the most adaptable and reusable method of legacy integration, but also the highest initial investment.

The Legacy Integration Implementation Table further defines the services identified in the Legacy Integration Reference Architecture. Modify the following template to define the specific implementation. Be sure to define what legacy functions are available.>

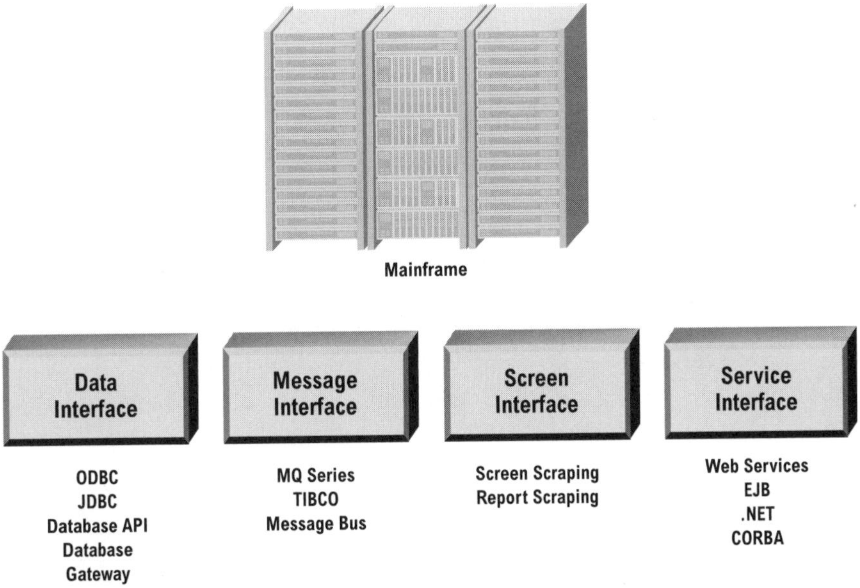

Legacy Integration Reference Architecture

Integration Service	Vendor/Product or Custom	Implementation Notes
Legacy integration—data interface	<Vendor, product name>	<JDBC adapter to specific mainframe data source>
Legacy integration—message interface	<Vendor, product name>	<MQ Series on mainframe provides access to CICS transactions>
Legacy integration—screen/report interface	<Vendor, product name>	<Provides all customer order information>
Legacy integration—service interface	<Vendor, product name or custom code>	<Order processing service, customer maintenance service, order tracking service>

Legacy Integration Implementation Table

4.4 B2B Integration

<B2B integration usually includes application integration services, but also adds additional services required when integrating with applications external to the organization, including

- B2B Connectivity through either a B2B server or an external exchange
- Multiple connectivity options for partners including EDI, HTML, XML, and FTP
- Additional B2B security for encrypting transactions, authenticating the sender, and ensuring nonrepudiation of the transaction.
- Partner management, including processes, business rules, and service-level management.

Use the diagram on the facing page as a reference when defining your B2B implementation.

The B2B Implementation Table specifies all components of the B2B architecture, including how back-end integration will be accomplished. Modify the template on page 350 to define the specific implementation.>

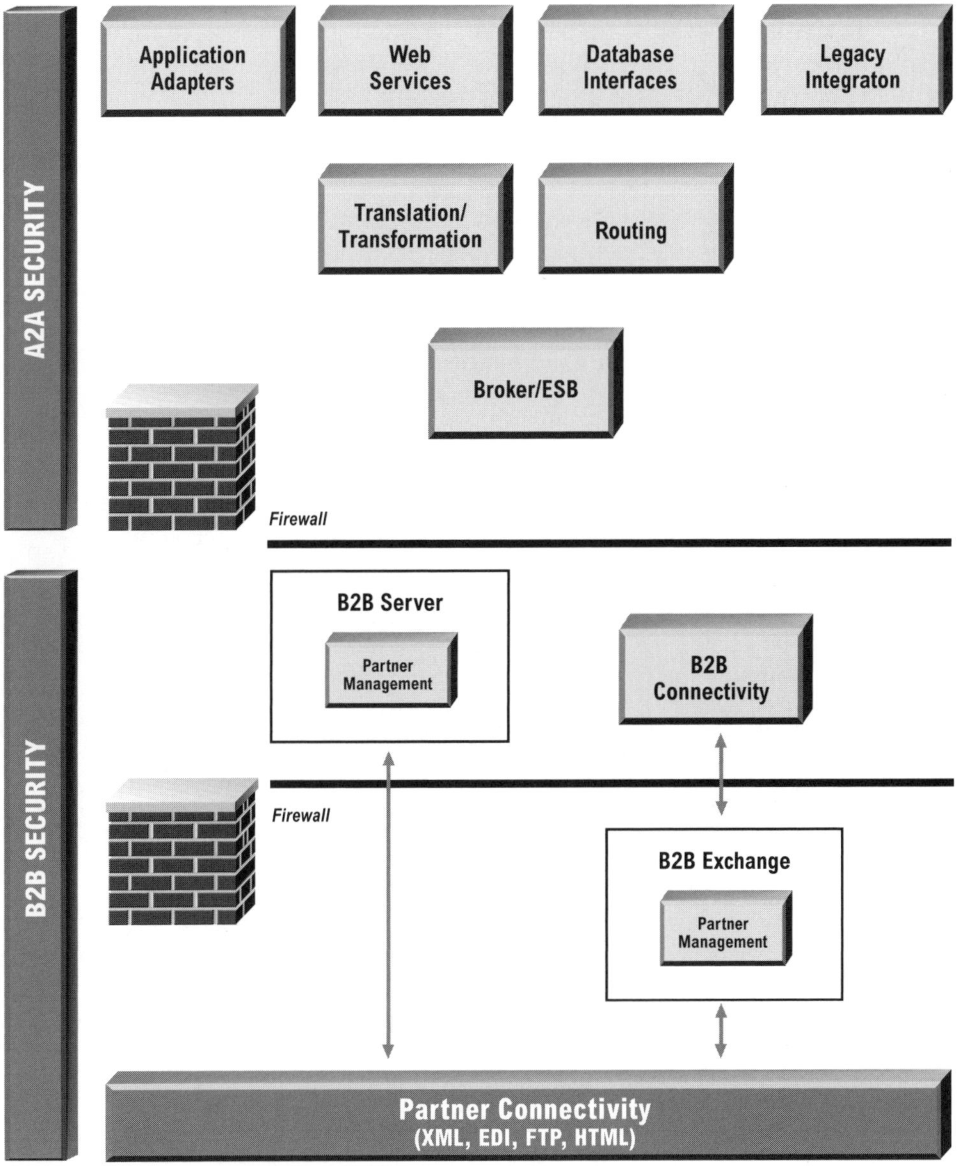

B2B Integration Reference Architecture

Integration Service	Vendor/Product	Implementation Notes
B2B connectivity	<Vendor, product name>	<B2B server or central exchange>
Partner connectivity	<Vendor, product name>	<List all connectivity options including XML messaging, EDI, FTP, browser interfaces, exchange hub, or other.>
Partner management	<Vendor, product name>	<Define services provided including process management, collaboration services, service level agreements, or other.>
B2B security	<Vendor, product name>	<Define all security services provided including encryption, authentication through digital certificates or other authentication, nonrepudiation services.>
Back-End Application Integration		<Include all application integration services included in the B2B solution.>
Broker/enterprise service bus	<Product/protocol>	<Technology platform>
Translation and transformation	<Vendor name/ product name>	<Transformation at hub or target>
Routing	<Vendor, product name or custom code>	<Level of routing supported; content based, business rules, header only info>
Application interface	<Vendor name/ product name or deployment technology>	<Specify: integration broker adapter; Web service; JCA interface; data interface (ODBC, JDBC, OLE DB, ADO).>
Legacy integration	<Vendor, product name>	<Define type of integration.>
A2A security	<Vendor name/ product name or deployment technology>	<Specify how security is implemented, including integration with LDAP or other repository or product.>

B2B Integration Implementation Table

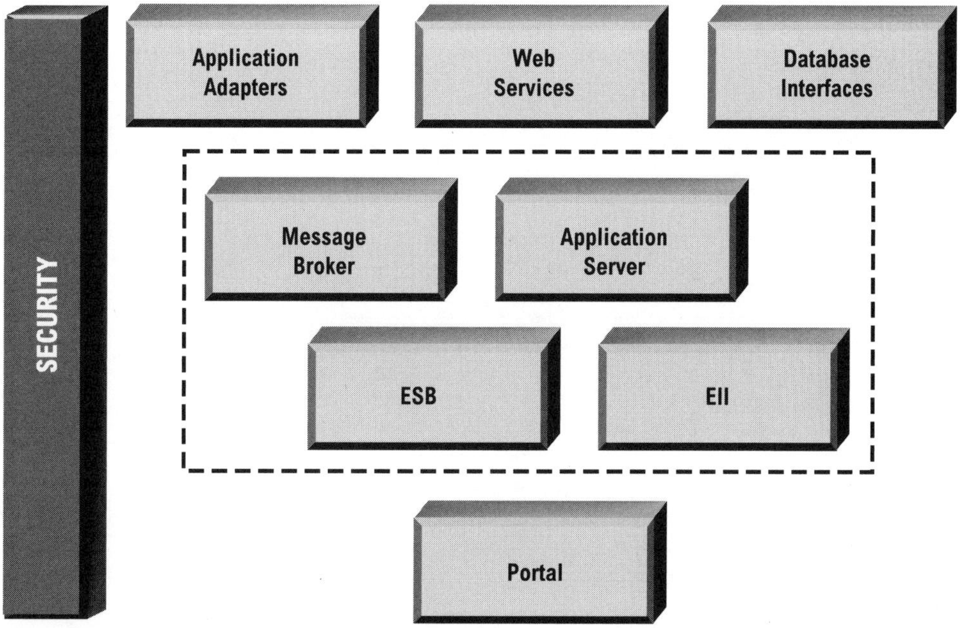

Portal Integration Reference Architecture

4.5 Portals

<Portals provide integration at the glass. They are used to extend mainframe functionality to the Web, and provide customer-facing applications. Portals require extensive integration services. There are a number of different ways to provide portal integration. The portal can have point-to-point connections to each of the applications it integrates with. APIs, database interfaces, Web services, or adapters can be used. Portals can also be part of an application server solution, and the application server can provide the integration services. Message brokers and ESBs can also provide integration services to the portal. Lastly, when the portal requires real-time access to aggregated enterprise data, enterprise information integration (EII) can be used. Moreover, if the portal supports business transactions as well as data aggregation, a combination of technologies can be used. The Portal Integration Reference Architecture depicts the alternative integration services that can be used in a portal implementation. Each of the services in the dotted box can be implemented as the sole portal integration solution. Alternatively, EII can be combined with a message broker, ESB, or application server. Multiple types of interfaces may be used in a single implementation.

The Portal Integration Implementation Table defines all the technologies and services that will be implemented as part of the portal solution.>

Integration Service	**Vendor/Product**	**Implementation Notes**
Portal	<Vendor, product name>	<Stand alone or part of application server or message broker platform?>
Back-End Application Integration		<Include all application integration services included in the portal solution.>
Message broker/enterprise service bus	<Product/protocol>	<Technology platform>
Application server	<Vendor, product name>	<Technology platform>
EII	<Vendor, product name or custom code>	<Level of routing supported; content based, business rules, header only info>
Application interface	<Vendor name/product name or deployment technology>	<Specify: integration broker adapter; Web service; JCA interface; data interface (ODBC, JDBC, OLE DB, ADO).>
Legacy integration	<Vendor, product name>	<Define type of integration.>

Portal Integration Implementation Table

4.6 Mobile Integration

<The mobile integration pattern is similar to B2B integration. It includes back-end application integration, and a mobile integration server can take the same information from multiple source systems and flexibly format it for different target devices. Mobile integration reliability and security are key issues to pay attention to, because the mobile network is inherently unreliable and insecure.

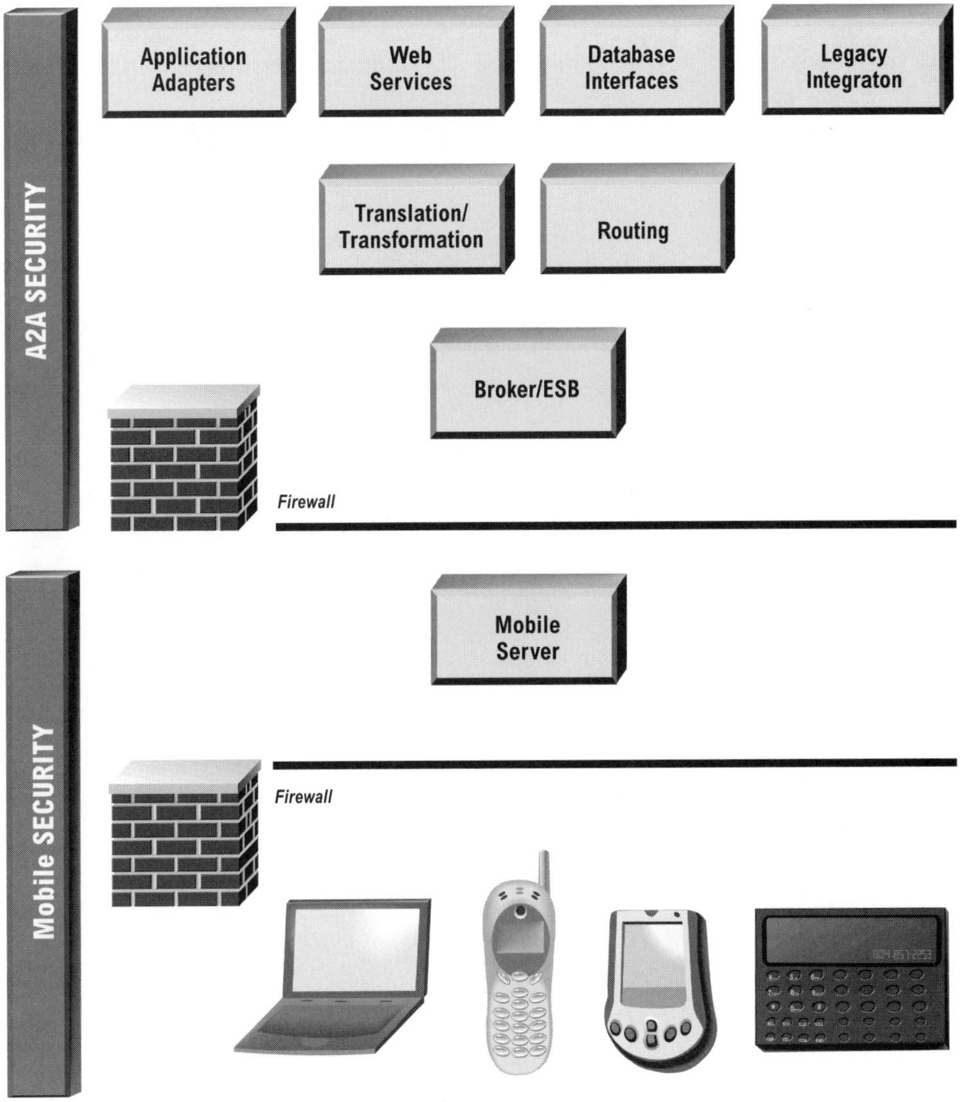

Mobile Integration Reference Architecture

Integration Service	**Vendor/Product**	**Implementation Notes**
Mobile integration server	<Vendor, product name>	<Define all services provided, including process management, as well as mobile interfaces supported. Also define reliability features.>
Mobile security	<Vendor, product name>	<Define all security services provided including encryption and authentication.>
Back-End Application Integration		<Include all application integration services included in the mobile solutions.>
Broker/enterprise service bus	<Product/protocol>	<Technology platform>
Translation and transformation	<Vendor name/ product name>	<Transformation at hub or target>
Routing	<Vendor, product name or custom code>	<Level of routing supported; content based, business rules, header only info>
Application interface	<Vendor name/ product name or deployment technology>	<Specify: integration broker adapter; Web service; JCA interface; data interface (ODBC, JDBC, OLE DB, ADO).>
Legacy integration	<Vendor, product name>	<Define type of integration.>
A2A security	<Vendor name/ product name or deployment technology>	<Specify how security is implemented, including integration with LDAP or other repository or product.>

Mobile Integration Implementation Table

The Mobile Integration Specification Table, like B2B integration, may specify how integration to back-end systems will be implemented. Modify the following template to define the specific implementation. Be sure to include any additional services added for reliability.>

4.7 Other Services

<In this section other services are identified. This could include security, transactional, persistence, or other types of services or rules. Integration implementations may involve a number of different patterns defined above and in other chapters in Part III of this book. In this section, describe any additional services that will be included in the implementation.>

5. Conclusions and Recommended Next Steps

<This section provides any final comments on implementation.>

Appendix A: References

<The appendix should list any reference documents used in the creation of the document so that its contents can be traced back to their sources if necessary. This should be broken down into internal documents and external documents. Internal documents are those that belong to the organization. External documents are items such as articles, whitepapers, Web sites, or product documentation.>

APPENDIX I

Information Integration Implementation Specification

<ENTERPRISE NAME>

<PLACE LOGO HERE>

<author>
<version>
<revision date>

Template Instructions

This is a template for the Information Integration Implementation Specification. This page should be removed prior to publication of the specification. The template is a guide for the enterprise and should not be blindly followed. The organization should

- *Review the chapter in the book that refers to the template to understand its use.*
- *Examine the template outline and determine what additions might be necessary based on unique organizational needs.*
- *If absolutely necessary, remove any sections that will not apply. (The authors strongly discourage this practice.)*
- *Save the template for future use.*
- *Begin to develop the document.*

Guidance is given for preparation of the document throughout the template.

- *Text shown as normal text should be utilized in the document. It may be modified as necessary.*
- *Text shown in pointed brackets is either instructional guidance in the application of the document or a description of the type of information to be added and should be removed prior to publication.*
- *Text shown in double pointed brackets is a placeholder for the insertion of text by the authors.*

Headers and footers should be customized as necessary as a final step in the completion of the document.

Information Integration Implementation Specification

1. **Introduction**

<This specification provides implementation guidance for the development of an information integration solution. It is most likely that the information integration oriented design specification from Chapter 8 will form the basis for the implementation.

Information integration represents a specific style of integration. This style is to solve problems where information from various sources needs to accessed and updated. Types of problems that are well suited to information integration are

- Creating a single view of a customer or other resource
- Enterprise data inventory and management
- Real time reporting and analysis
- Updating a data warehouse
- Creating a virtual data warehouse
- Providing an infrastructure for enterprise information management including all forms of digital media
- Updating common information across information sources
- Creating portal applications containing both structured and unstructured data from disparate systems

This section describes the specific technical problems that are being addressed in the implementation to give context to the specific implementation.>

2. **Scope**

<The scope of an information integration specification is limited to the specifics of the information and systems that are being integrated. It should cover organizations, information, systems, and the expected end result.>

3. **Key Participants**

<This section identifies all stakeholders in the implementation, including business managers who control all or part of the systems, data stewards or those responsible for data quality, system designers and architect(s), and the development team who will execute the implementation. Any other participants or stakeholders should also be identified, including their roles.>

4. **Information Integration Patterns and Services**

<There are several basic implementation patterns for an information integration solution. This section defines the particular pattern that is being used and

provides details on the configuration of the specific components of the implementation.

These patterns are

- Data integration
- Unstructured content integration
- Metadata repository integration>

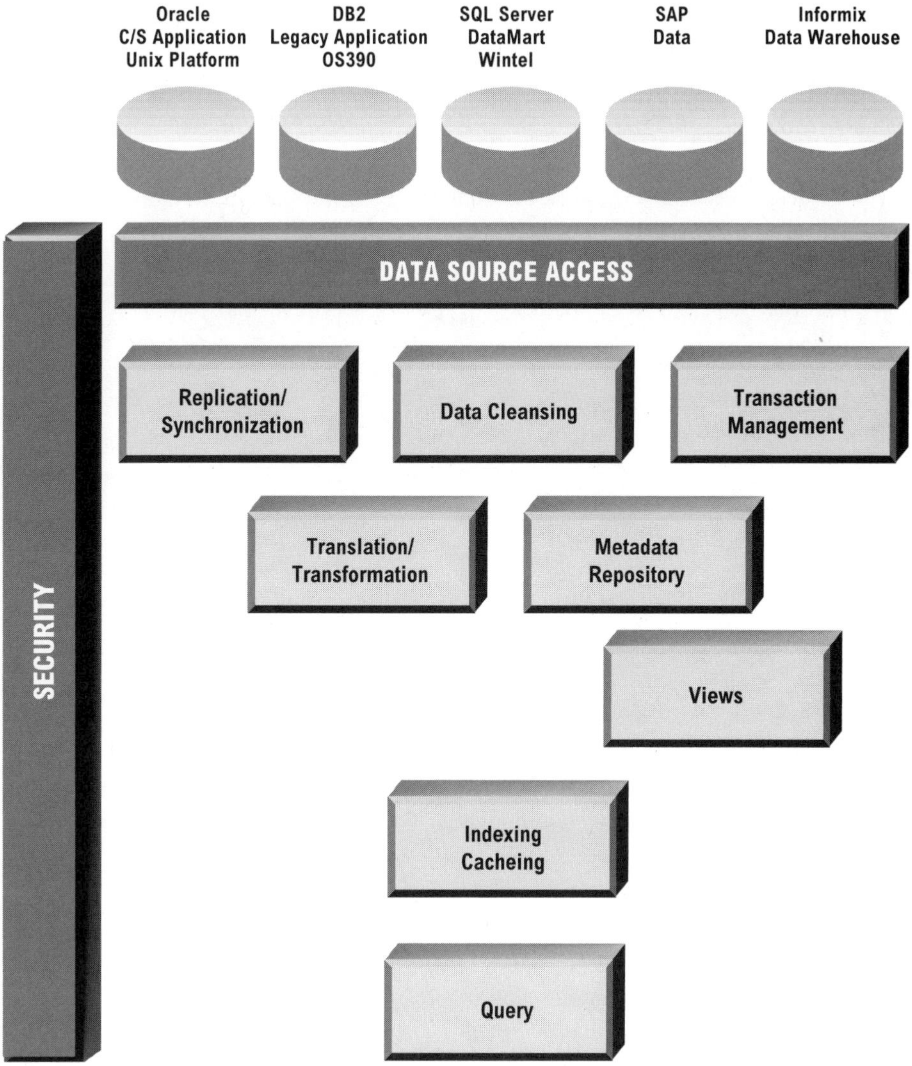

Data Integration Reference Architecture

4.1 Data Integration

<Data integration involves structured data, generally found in different databases across the organization. Data integration and aggregation services include accessing disparate data sources as if they were a single database (including the ability to make a single SQL call across databases), translation and transformation, support for different views (virtual tables) of consolidated information, data cleansing, and transaction management when required for publishing changes to data. (See diagram on page 361.)

The Data Integration Implementation Table specifies all the integration services provided along with relevant implementation details. Modify the following template to define the specific implementation.>

Integration Service	Vendor/Product	Implementation Notes
Data integration tool	<Vendor name/ product name>	<Modules deployed, method (virtual DB, mid-tier data store; indexing and retrieval)>
EII	<Vendor name/ product name>	<Modules deployed>
Translation and transformation	<Vendor name/ product name if different EII vendor>	<Formats supported>
Data source access	<Vendor name/ product name if different EII vendor>	<ODBC, JDBC, SOAP, other methods supported>
Metadata repository	<Vendor name/ product name if different EII vendor>	<DBMS technology>
Query	<Vendor name/ product name if different EII vendor>	<Ability to query enterprise information grid as a single data source. Define query language or method.>
Views	<Vendor name/ product name if different EII vendor>	<List views available to simplify use for specific applications or users.>

Data Integration Implementation Table

Integration Service	Vendor/Product	Implementation Notes
Data cleansing	<Vendor name/ product name>	<Done by the tool or scripts?>
Replication/data synchronization	<Vendor name/ product name>	<Part of DB or EII server?>
Transaction management	<Vendor name/ product name if different EII vendor>	<Define roll-back or compensation.>
Security	<Vendor name/ product name if 3rd party security vendor used>	<Methods and level of security provided>

Data Integration Implementation Table *(cont.)*

4.2 Unstructured Content Integration

<Unstructured data that needs to be integrated with Web portals and applications include documents, images, photos, audio, video, and other digital media. All of this unstructured content requires a common set of services. The services provided by ECM solutions include content repository, search (query) capability, version control (check in/out), replication of content changes, integration, content rendering (translation/transformation), security, process modeling and management, and content delivery.

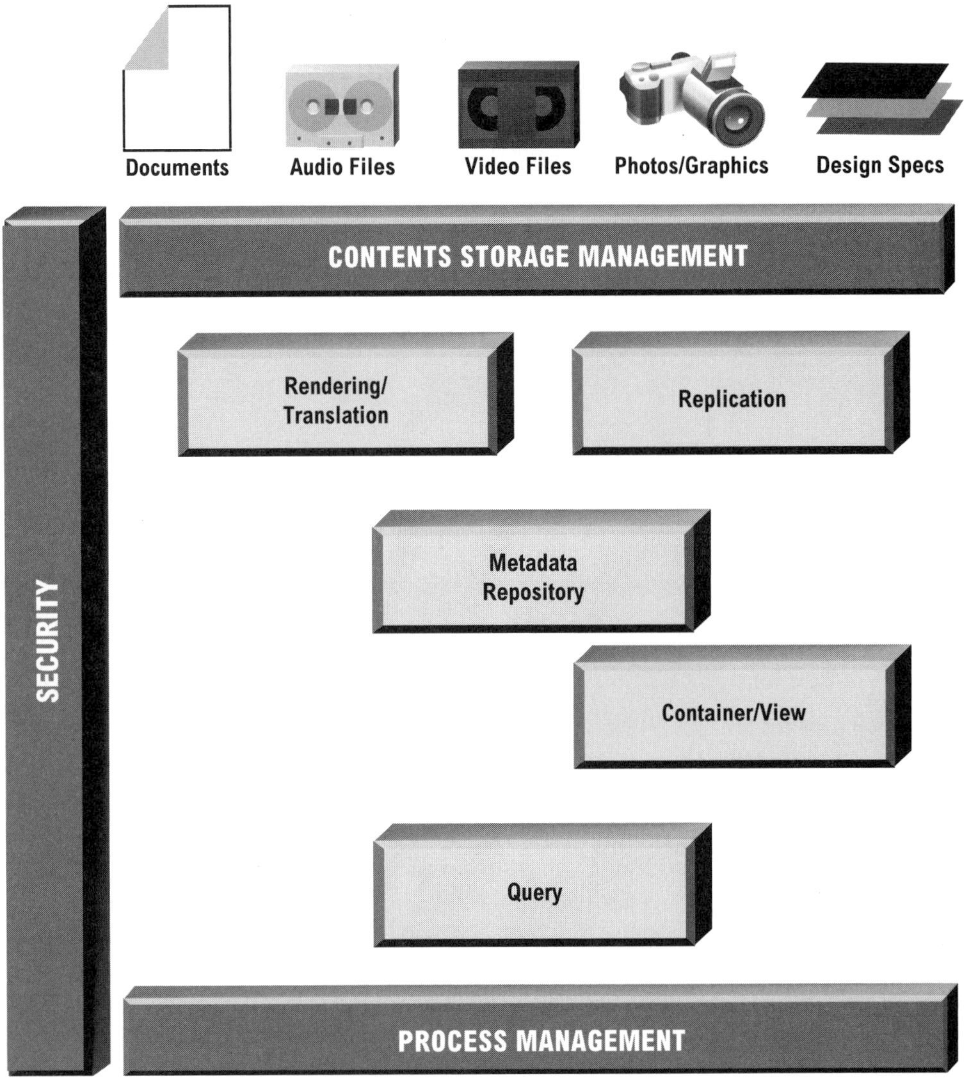

Unstructured Content Integration Reference Architecture

The Unstructured Information Implementation Table specifies all the integration services provided, along with relevant implementation details. Modify the following template to define the specific implementation.>

Integration Service	Vendor/Product	Implementation Notes
ECM	<Vendor name/ product name>	<Modules deployed>
Rendering (translation and transformation)	<Vendor name/ product name if different ECM vendor>	<Formats supported, including HTML, PDF, MS Word, MS Excel, TIFF, JPEG>
Content repository	<Vendor name/ product name if different ECM vendor>	<Types of content supported including documents, images, photos, audio, and video>
Metadata		<Types of metadata descriptions supported including thumbnails, key words; common information management metadata>
Query capabilities		<Ability to query different types of content with a common method; full text query; scanned text query>
Content objects/ containers (views)		<Define content objects that contain other content objects, for example, Web page.>
Content propagation		<Ability to propagate changes across a variety of sources to ensure content is synchronized>
Process management	<Vendor name/ product name if different ECM vendor>	<Modules deployed, including modeling, management dashboard, etc.>
Security	<Vendor name/ product name if 3rd party security vendor used>	<Model and level of security provided>

Unstructured Content Integration Implementation Table

4.3 Metadata Repository Integration

<A metadata repository is essentially a database that contains information about data sources. The enterprise metadata repository contains all of the metadata on information and application sources along with information on how to access this information. An active metadata repository contains the access mechanisms as well. The metadata repository also contains new metadata descriptions, such as canonical format, that can be mapped onto the source metadata either directly or by applying transformation or calculation rules.

Because EII and ECM solutions could each have their own metadata repositories, a company could wind up with multiple repositories to manage, and metadata that needs to be synchronized and integrated. In principle, the metadata repository should provide a level of abstraction that makes it easier to consolidate, integrate, and manage distributed information. In practice, the company may need to create a multi-tiered metadata architecture to provide the levels of abstraction necessary to deliver this agility.

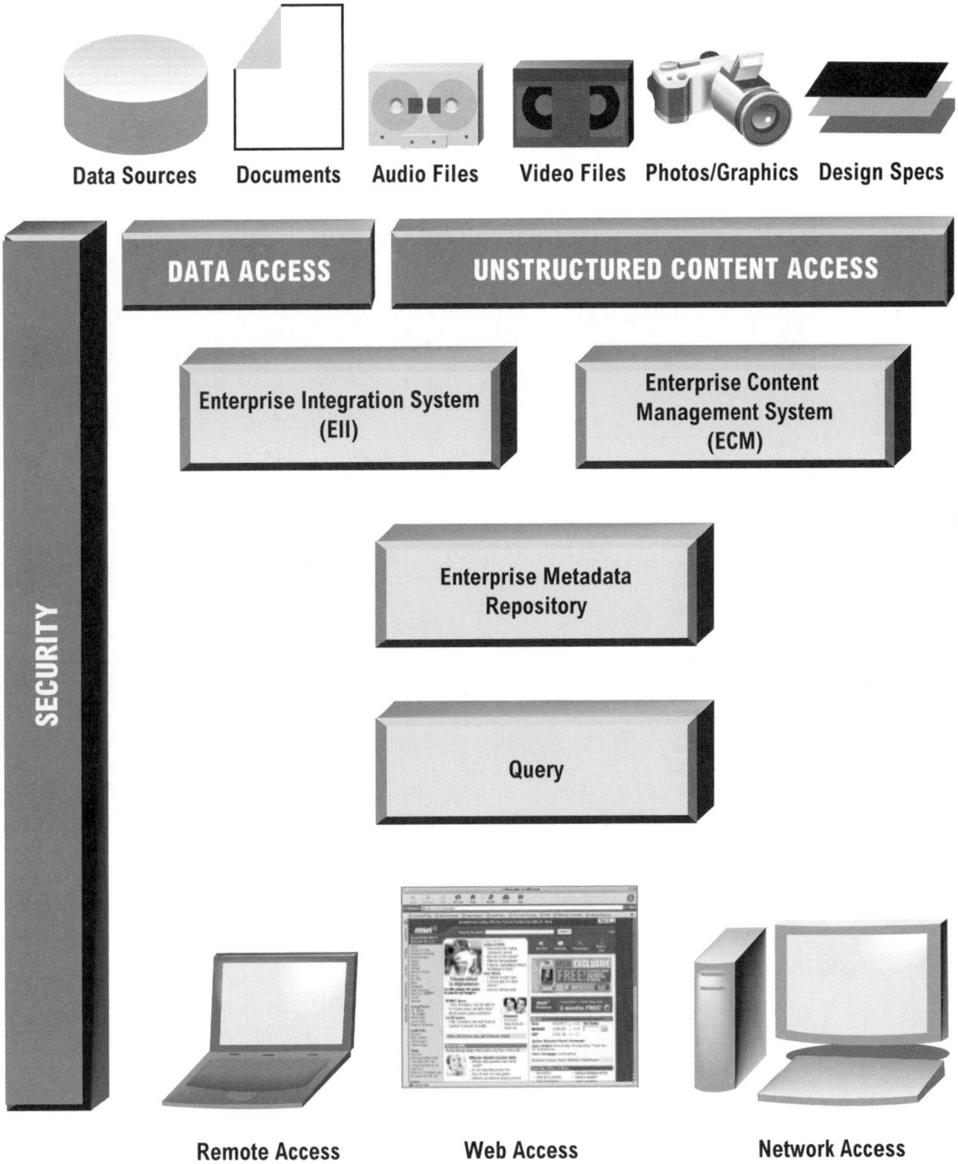

Metadata Repository Integration Reference Architecture

The Metadata Repository Integration Implementation Table details the capabilities of the metadata repository, including which services are supported. Because EII and ECM solutions could each have their own metadata repositories, a company could wind up with multiple repositories to manage and metadata that needs to be synchronized and integrated. In principle, the metadata repository should provide a level of abstraction that makes it easier to consolidate, integrate, and manage distributed information. In practice, the company may need to create a multi-tiered metadata architecture to provide the levels of abstraction necessary to deliver this agility. The architecture diagram and specification table should include all metadata sources. Modify the following template to define the specific implementation.>

Integration Service	**Vendor/Product**	**Implementation Notes**
Metadata repository	<Vendor name/ product name>	<Types of content supported including documents, images, photos, audio, and video>
Canonical format		<XML, proprietary, other>
Translation and transformation/ format rendering	<Vendor name/ product name>	<Formats supported, including XML, other data formats, HTML, PDF, MS Word, MS Excel, TIFF, JPEG.>
Query capabilities	<Language(s) supported>	<SQL; key word search, full text query, other>
Access capabilities	<Vendor name/ product name>	<Database API or gateway, adapter, other>
Replication	<Vendor name/ product name>	<Mechanism for synchronizing changes across sources>
Security	<Vendor name/ product name if 3rd party security vendor used>	<Model and level of security provided>

Metadata Repository Integration Implementation Table

5. Conclusions and Recommended Next Steps

<This section should provide any final comments on implementation.>

Appendix A: References

<The appendix should list any reference documents used in the creation of the document so that its contents can be traced back to their sources if necessary. This should be broken down into internal documents and external documents. Internal documents are those that belong to the organization. External documents are items such as articles, whitepapers, Web sites, or product documentation.>

APPENDIX J

Composite Application Integration Implementation Specification

<ENTERPRISE NAME>

<PLACE LOGO HERE>

<author>
<version>
<revision date>

Template Instructions

This is a template for the Composite Application Integration Implementation Specification. This page should be removed prior to publication of the specification. The template is a guide for the enterprise and should not be blindly followed. The organization should

- *Review the chapter in the book that refers to the template to understand its use.*
- *Examine the template outline and determine what additions might be necessary based on unique organizational needs.*
- *If absolutely necessary, remove any sections that will not apply. (The authors strongly discourage this practice.)*
- *Save the template for future use.*
- *Begin to develop the document.*

Guidance is given for preparation of the document throughout the template.

- *Text shown as normal text should be utilized in the document. It may be modified as necessary.*
- *Text shown in pointed brackets is either instructional guidance in the application of the document or a description of the type of information to be added and should be removed prior to publication.*
- *Text shown in double pointed brackets is a placeholder for the insertion of text by the authors.*

Headers and footers should be customized as necessary as a final step in the completion of the document.

Composite Application Integration Implementation Specification

1. Introduction

<This specification provides implementation guidance for the implementation of a composite application integration based solution. It is most likely that the service oriented design specification from Chapter 7 will form the basis for the implementation.

Composite integration represents a specific style of integration. This style is to solve problems where information from various sources needs to accessed and updated. Types of problems that are well suited to application integration are

- Adding a new functional module to existing applications
- Extending the functionality of packaged applications
- Assembling new business solutions from existing modules

This section describes the specific technical problems that are being addressed in the implementation, and provides a context for the specific implementation.>

2. Scope

<The scope of a Composite Integration Implementation Specification is limited to the specific services, components, and systems that are being integrated. It should cover organizations, information, systems, and the expected end result.>

3. Key Participants

<This section identifies all stakeholders in the implementation; including business managers who control all or part of the systems, the development team who will execute the implementation and any system designers and/or architect(s) who participated. Any other participants or stakeholders should also be identified including their roles.>

4. Composite Application Integration Patterns and Services

<There is really only one composite application integration pattern but there are numerous variations on how it can be implemented. The composite application consists of services and/or components or systems that can be called as services. The services have a standard interface, and are integrated into an application through code logic or an orchestration engine.

The following diagram depicts the Composite Application Integration Reference Architecture with the services essential for composite applications. The services can be implemented through an application platform suite, message broker, ESB, or adapters. Modify this diagram to depict the particular composite application implementation.

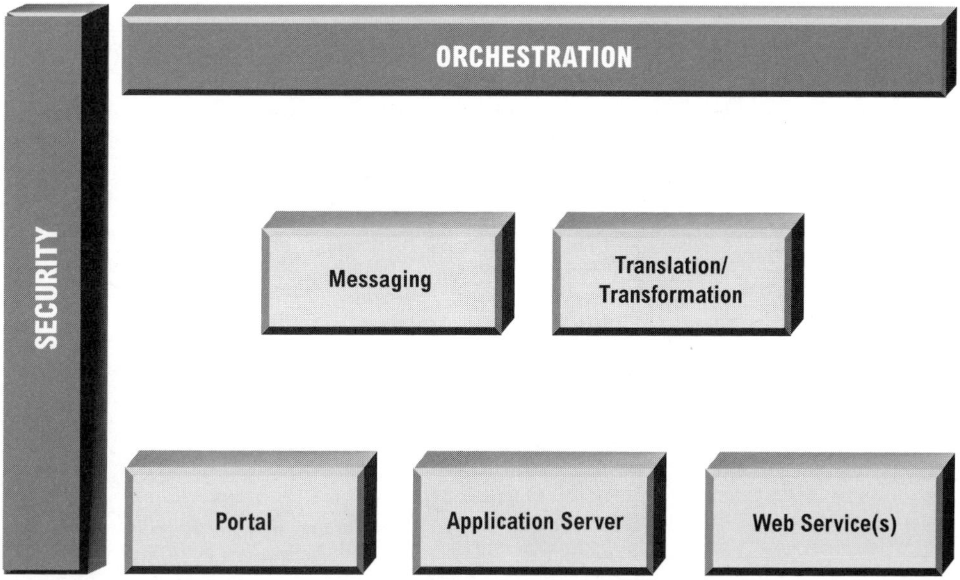

Composite Application Integration Reference Architecture

The Composite Application Integration Implementation Table defines the alternative technologies that can be used to implement the solution. Modify the following template for the specific implementation.>

Integration Service	Vendor/Product	Implementation Notes
Development and deployment	<Vendor name/ product name>	<Application server, Web services development tool>
Service interface	<Vendor name/ product name>	<Web services>
Translation and transformation	<Vendor name/ product name>	<Application platform suite, message broker, other service>
Orchestration	<Vendor name/ product name>	<Web service orchestration, workflow, process engine>
Portal	<Vendor name/ product name>	<Portal services provided such as: transactions, workflow, etc.>
Messaging	<Vendor name/ product name>	<Messaging services provided such as: publish/subscribe, guaranteed delivery, etc.>
Security	<Vendor name/ product name if 3rd party security vendor used>	<Level of security provided>

Composite Application Integration Table

5. Conclusions and Recommended Next Steps

<This section should provide any final comments on implementation.>

Appendix A: References

<The appendix should list any reference documents used in the creation of the document so that its contents can be traced back to their sources if necessary. This should be broken down into internal documents and external documents. Internal documents are those that belong to the organization. External documents are items such as articles, whitepapers, Web sites, or product documentation.>

APPENDIX K

Process Integration Implementation Specification

<ENTERPRISE NAME>

<PLACE LOGO HERE>

<author>
<version>
<revision date>

Template Instructions

This is a template for the Process Integration Implementation Specification. This page should be removed prior to publication of the specification. The template is a guide for the enterprise and should not be blindly followed. The organization should

- *Review the chapter in the book that refers to the template to understand its use.*
- *Examine the template outline and determine what additions might be necessary based on unique organizational needs.*
- *If absolutely necessary, remove any sections that will not apply. (The authors strongly discourage this practice.)*
- *Save the template for future use.*
- *Begin to develop the document.*

Guidance is given for preparation of the document throughout the template.

- *Text shown as normal text should be used in the document. It may be modified as necessary.*
- *Text shown in pointed brackets is either instructional guidance in the application of the document or a description of the type of information to be added and should be removed prior to publication.*

Headers and footers should be customized as necessary as a final step in the completion of the document.

Process Integration Implementation Specification

1. **Introduction**

<This specification provides implementation guidance for the development of a process integration based solution. It is most likely that the process design specification from Chapter 9 will form the basis for the implementation.

Process integration represents a specific style of integration. It manages the integration from an end-to-end business process level. It is appropriate for business process-improvement initiatives, automating iterations between organizational entities, and implementing industry and compliance solutions.

This section describes the context of specific implementation described by this specification.>

2. **Scope**

<The scope of a process integration specification is limited to the business processes that are being automated and integrated. It can include processes within departments or between departments, divisions, territories, companies, and business customers and partners.

In this section, define the scope of the implementation, including all business entities and systems.>

3. **Key Participants**

<This section identifies all stakeholders in the implementation; including business managers who control all or part of the process, system designers and architect(s), and the development team who will execute the implementation. Because there may be multiple managers responsible for parts of the process, continuous process improvement and process optimization will be difficult to achieve without a process owner or manager who is responsible for the end-to-end process. Any other participants or stakeholders should also be identified including their roles.>

4. **Process Integration Patterns and Services**

<Process integration is in the very early stages of adoption, and patterns may emerge over time. Reference architectures are provided for the following patterns:

- Process automation
- Process activity monitoring
- Process collaboration

In this section define the particular pattern that is being used and provide details on the configuration of the specific components of the implementation.>

4.1 Process Automation

<Process automation requires underlying application integration services. The solution may provide integration services such as adapters, or may provide integration with an EAI solution. Many BPM tools do both in order to provide implementation flexibility.

The services included in process automation include process modeling, process simulation, process management including support for long-lived processes and transactions, business rules management, transaction support including compensating transactions, as well as all necessary application integration services. The following figure depicts an example Process Automation Reference Architecture.

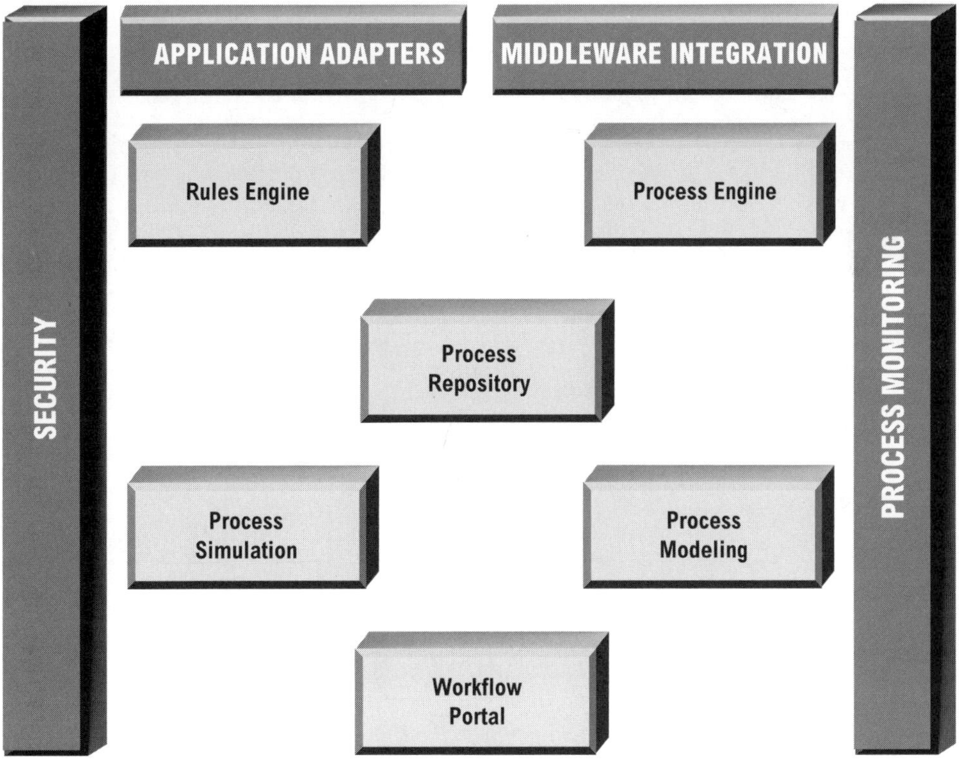

Process Automation Reference Architecture

The Implementation Table specifies all the integration services provided in the Process Automation integration solution, along with relevant implementation details.

Modify the sample following table to specify your implementation.>

Integration Service	Vendor/Product	Implementation Notes
Process modeling	<Vendor name/ product name>	<State of BPEL or other standard models supported>
Process simulation	<Vendor name/ product name>	<Add-on or integrated?>
Process management	<Vendor name/ product name>	<Support for long-lived processes?>
Rules management	<Vendor name/ product name>	<Rules management may replace process management or may augment it.>
Workflow management	<Vendor name/ product name>	<Is there an additional process modeling and management engine?>
Application interface	<Vendor name/ product name or deployment technology>	<Specify: integration broker adapter; Web service; JCA interface; data interface (ODBC, JDBC, OLE DB, ADO).>
Middleware integration	<Vendor name/ product name>	<Integration with other integration technologies>
Process repository	<Vendor name/ product name>	<Part of enterprise repository or content management systems or separate?>
BAM	<Vendor name/ product name>	<Include monitoring capabilities here if it is part of the BPM solution.>

Process Automation Implementation Table

4.2 Process Monitoring

<Process monitoring, also called business activity monitoring (BAM), provides real-time visibility into business processes. BAM can be part of a business process management solution or it can be a stand-alone solution.

The services provided by BAM include a management dashboard with key performance indicators relevant to particular roles in the organization, real-time analytics to populate the dashboard, and the underlying agents or event managers to recognize relevant events. It has some information integration capabilities to pull information from analytical data stores in real time. A BAM solution may also contain modeling or development capabilities to define the BAM solution, as each one is likely to be unique.

Because the BAM market is young and evolving, the current solutions have different focuses and configurations. In this section, define the services included in your BAM solution. The following figure is a sample reference architecture that is likely to evolve significantly as the market matures.

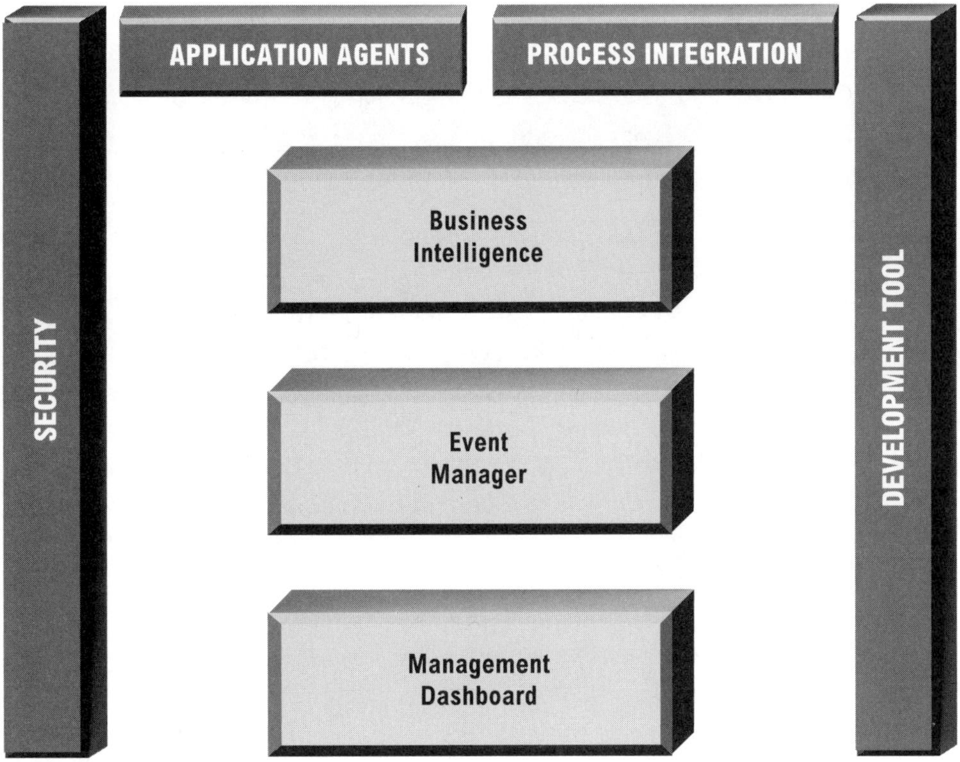

BAM Reference Architecture

The Implementation Table specifies all the integration services provided in the BAM solution, along with relevant implementation details. Modify the following table to specify your implementation.>

Integration Service	Vendor/Product	Implementation Notes
BAM solution	<Vendor name/ product name>	<Users of the solution>
Management dashboard	<Vendor name/ product name>	<Key performance indicators included for each type of user>
Business intelligence	<Vendor name/ product name>	<Define integration technology and analytical data sources>
Event manager	<Vendor name/ product name>	<Event server, process engine event logs>
Application interface	<Vendor name/ product name>	<BAM agents, process or part of BPM solution>
Development/ modeling	<Vendor name/ product name>	<Graphical development to generate BAM solution>

BAM Implementation Table

4.3 Collaborative Process Integration

<Collaborative process integration provides a platform for integrating work from different team members in different locations. Collaborative solutions include a collaboration portal that provides access to all project artifacts including deliverables, meeting notes, discussions, etc. A project repository is important for managing project artifacts. The repository can be part of the collaboration platform, or may integrate with a content management solution. Version control with check-in and check-out facilities can either be part of the platform or provided through integration with a content management system or a version control system (especially important for software development as the code is often managed by an existing version control system). The solution can also be a combination of both.

Project management may also be provided by the platform, or it can integrate with a project management system. Workflow is often included as part of the platform to manage the collaborative process. Project coordination is provided with electronic calendar and meeting scheduling. A facility to support threaded discussions and negotiations, and document decisions is also helpful. Because much project communication is done through e-mail, which is particularly difficult to manage and archive, e-mail integration is becoming more important. The collaboration platform should include role-based security with granular levels of authorization, so access rights can be defined artifact.

As process collaboration integration becomes more firmly entrenched in the organization the architecture is likely to evolve. The following figure is a reference architecture based on the major capabilities currently available.

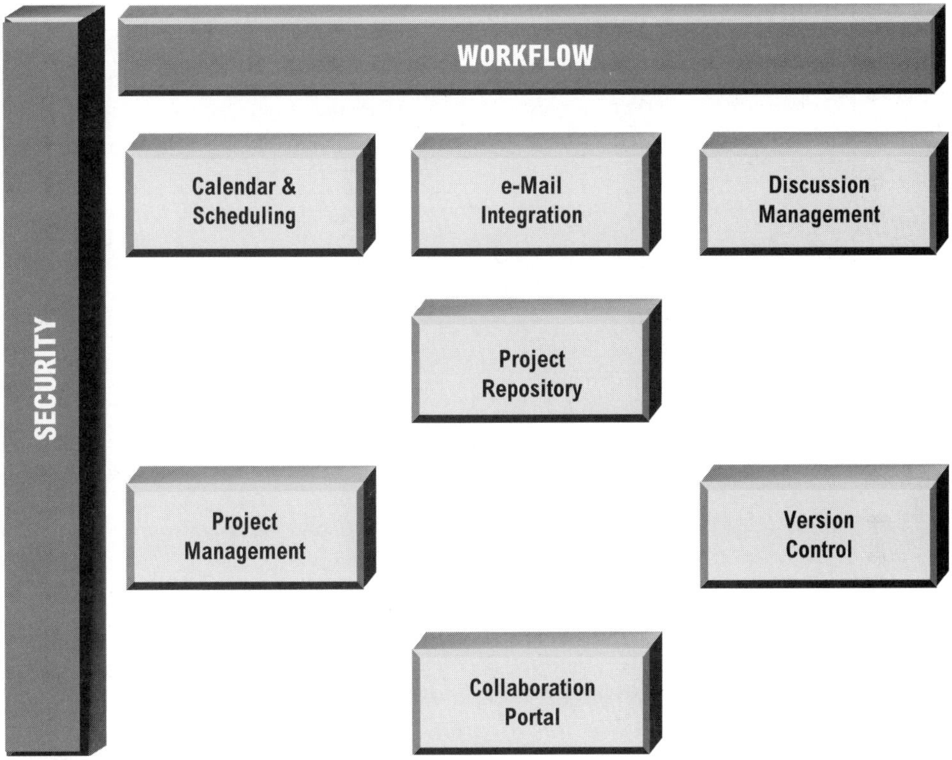

Collaborative Process Reference Architecture

The Implementation Table specifies all the integration services provided in the collaborative integration solution, along with relevant implementation details. Modify the following table to specify your implementation.>

Integration Service	Vendor/Product	Implementation Notes
Collaborative platform	<Vendor name/ product name>	<Hosted within organization or by vendor>
Collaboration portal	<Vendor name/ product name>	<Key features provided>
Project repository	<Vendor name/ product name>	<Part of platform or integration with ECM>
Version control	<Vendor name/ product name>	<Part of platform, part of ECM, third party, combination for different types of information>
Project management	<Vendor name/ product name>	<Part of platform and/or integration with project management tool>
Workflow	<Vendor name/ product name>	<Part of platform or integration with workflow tool>
Calendar and scheduling	<Vendor name/ product name>	<Part of platform or integration with calendaring and scheduling tool>
Discussion management	<Vendor name/ product name>	<Tool for threaded discussions that are part of project history>
E-mail integration	<Vendor name/ product name>	<E-mail integration with project repository>
Security	<Vendor name/ product name>	<Role based security>

Collaborative Process Integration Table

5. Conclusions and Recommended Next Steps

<This section should provide any final comments on implementation.>

Appendix A: References

<The appendix should list any reference documents used in the creation of the document so that its contents can be traced back to their sources if necessary. This should be broken down into internal documents and external documents. Internal documents are those that belong to the organization. External documents are items such as articles, whitepapers, Web sites, or product documentation.>

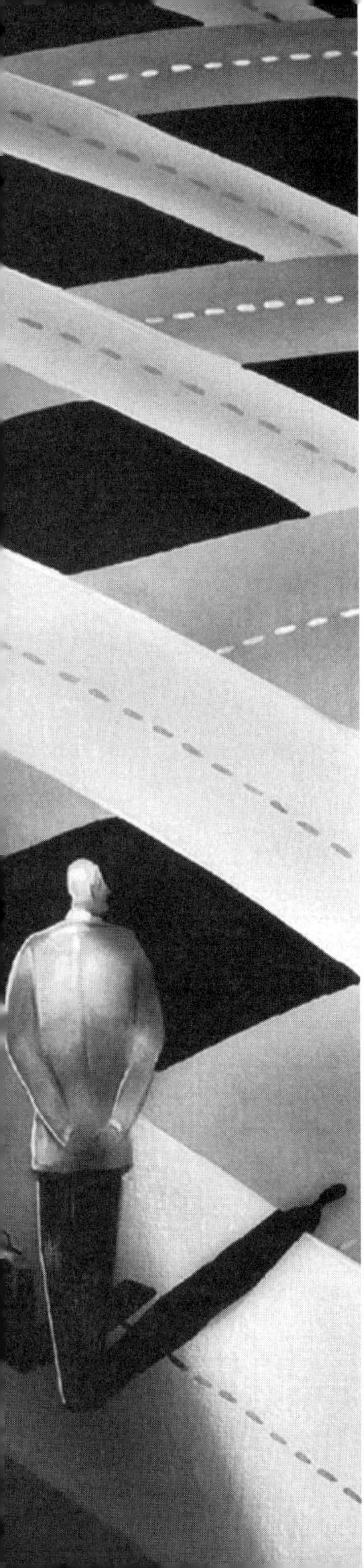

Bibliography

Acharya, Ravi. "EAI: A Business Perspective." *EAI Journal* (April 2003).

Aranow, Eric. "Enterprise Integration: Business' New Frontier." *Distributed Enterprise Architecture Advisory Service, Cutter Consortium* 4, no. 12 (2001).

Arveson, Paul. "Background and History of Measurement-Based Management" (1998). Available from *http://www.balancedscorecard.org/*.

Bacheldor, Beth. "Keep Pace on the Innovation Speedway." *Information Week Magazine* (September 22, 2003).

Berners-Lee, Tim, James Hendler, and Ora Lassila. "The Semantic Web." *ScientificAmerican.com* (May 17, 2001).

"BPM 2002 Market Milestone Report." Boston: Delphi Group, 2001.

Brewin, Bob. "FedEx Readies Rollout of Wireless Handheld." *ComputerWorld* (December 2, 2002). Available from *http://www.computerworld.com/mobiletopics/mobile/handhelds/story/0,10801,76299,00.html*.

"Case Study: CompuCredit's Enterprise Data Architecture Solves Application Integration and Interoperability, Drives Success." *CIO Magazine* (October 2003). Available from *http://www.cio.com/sponsors/100103storage/index.html?page=6*.

"Connecting Minnesota's Criminal Justice Information." *CrimNet* (n.d.). Available from *http://www.crimnet.state.mn.us/About/About.htm*.

Correia, Joanne. Gartner Enterprise Application Integration and Web Services Summit presentation (fall 2002).

Derome, Jon. "2003 Integration Expense Survey." Boston: Yankee Group (n.d.).

Derome, Jon and Kosin Huang. "Business Applications & Commerce." Cambridge, MA: Yankee Group, September 2003.

Dickie, Jim. "The Sales Effectiveness Challenge—Are We Solving the Right Problem?" *Insight Technology Group, CRM Project* 1 (January 15, 1999). Available from *http://www.crmproject.com/documents.asp?d_ID=742).*

Dragoon, Alice. "All for One View." *CIO Magazine* (July 2003).

Dragoon, Alice. "The General Motors Story: Organizing to Achieve." *CIO.com* (April 28, 1998). Available from *http://www.cio.com/conferences/perspectives/042898_1.html.*

"Enabling MyFlorida" in *Enterprise Action Plan 2003,* Appendix A: "Enterprise Integration Architecture Development." State of Florida State Technology Office (n.d.). Available from *http://sto.myflorida.com/cio/action_plan.*

"Ensodex Integration Service and Technology Best Practices Methodology, The." Best Practices White Paper. St. Paul, MN: Ensodex, September 2000.

"EntireX Central Hudson Gas & Electric Corporation: Utility Company Taps Software AG Products to Provide Increased Operational Productivity and Customer Self Service While Minimizing Costs." Software AG Case Report (n.d.). Available from *http://www.softwareagusa.com/media/case_studies/PDFs/centralhudson_cr.pdf.*

Fingar, Peter. "Turning Up Business Velocity: Competing on Time with BPM." ebizQ.net webinar, April 15, 2004. Available *from http://www.ebizq.net/expoq/events/4114.html.*

Girard, Kim. "How Levi's Got Its Jeans into Wal-Mart." *CIO Magazine* (July 15, 2003).

Gold-Bernstein, Beth. "Choosing the Right Integration Solution." *ebizQ.net* (March 22, 2004). Available from *http://www.ebizq.net/topics/int_sbp/features/3998.html.*

Gold-Bernstein, Beth. "Clearing Up BPM Acronym Confusion." *ebizQ.net* (January 27, 2003). Available from *http://www.ebizq.net/topics/eai/features/1627.html.*

Gold-Bernstein, Beth. "Designing Reusable Services to Enable SOAs" *ebizQ.net* (November 17, 2003). Available from *http://www.ebizq.net/topics/soa/features/3301.html.*

Gold-Bernstein, Beth. "Integration from the Top Down." ebizQ webinar, September 25, 2002. Available from *http://www.ebizq.net/expoq/events/2269.html.*

Gold-Bernstein, Beth. "Making SOA a Reality—An Appeal to Software Vendors and Developers." *ebizQ.net* (October 27, 2003). Available from *http://www.ebizq.net/topics/soa/features/3142.html.*

Gold-Bernstein, Beth. "Ten Critical Success Factors for the Real-Time Enterprise." *ebizQ.net* (June 23, 2003). Available from *http://www.ebizq.net/topics/soa/features/2052.html.*

Gold-Bernstein, Beth and Lee White. "Critical Success Factors for the Real-Time Enterprise." ebizQ webinar, June 17, 2003. Available at *http://www.ebizq.net/expoq/events/2237.html.*

Goldenberg, Barton. "KeyCorp Invests in Real Time." *Optimize,* no. 17 (March 2003).

Hammer, Michael. *Reengineering the Corporation: A Manifesto for Business Revolution.* New York: HarperCollins, 1993.

Heflin, Jeff, ed. "OWL Web Ontology Language Use Cases and Requirements." W3C Candidate Recommendation, August 18, 2003. Available from *http://www.w3c.org.*

Herzum, Peter. "Web Services and Service-Oriented Architecture." *Cutter Consortium, Executive Report* 4, no. 10 (2001).

Iansiti, Marco. "Integration the Right Way, the Wrong Way." *CIO Magazine* (May 15, 2003).

Kelly, David A. "Business Process Visibility: Different Approaches." *ebizQ.net* (March 1, 2004). Available from *http://www.ebizq.net/topics/bpm/features/3880.html.*

Kelly, David A. "Connecting the Big (Business) Picture to the Details (IT Infrastructure)." *ebizQ.net* (April 12, 2004). Available from *http://www.ebizq.net/topics/bpm/features/4178.html.*

Kelly, David A. "Tracking Business Transactions Across the Enterprise." *ebizQ.net* (April 26, 2004). Available from *http://www.ebizq.net/topics/bam/features/4256.html.*

Kemp, Ted. "B2B Tech Spending Is Alive and Well." *InternetWeek.com* (April 2, 2001). Available from *http://www.internetweek.com/newslead01/lead040201.htm.*

Kernochan, Wayne. "Enterprise Information Integration: The New Way to Leverage e-Information." Boston, MA: Aberdeen Group, July 2003.

"KeyCorp Invests in Real Time." *Optimize,* no. 17 (March 2003).

"Leading Texas University, A." *Software AG,* (n.d.). Available from *http://www.softwareagusa.com/media/case_studies/pdfs/UofTexas%20cr.pdf.*

Leaver, Sharyn. "Evaluating BPM Products in 2004." Cambridge, MA: Forrester Research, Inc., January 27, 2004.

Lindorff, David. "Case Study: General Electric Time=$." *CIO Insight Magazine* (November 2002).

Linthicum, David. "Will the Real Service Oriented Integration Solution Please Stand Up?" *ebizQ.net* (March 29, 2004). Available at *http://www.ebizq.net/topics/soa/features/4069.html.*

"Logistics EntireX—The Logical Choice for a Leading Transportation Logistics Company." Case Report, EntireX Web Integration, northAmerican. *Software AG* (n.d.). Available from *http://www.softwareagusa.com/media/case_studies/pdfs/nAL%20CR.pdf.*

Lublinsky, Boris and Michael Farrell, Jr. "Top 10 Reasons Why EAI Fails." *EAI Journal* (December 2002).

Lundberg, Abbie. "The IT Inside the World's Biggest Company." *CIO Magazine* (July 1, 2002).

Surmacz, Jon. "Togetherness Pays Off." *CIO Magazine* (April 24, 2002). Available from *http://www2.cio.com/metrics/2002/metric357.html.*

McCoy, David and Benoit Lheureux. "Business Activity Monitoring: Beginning a New Era of Alertness." Gartner Web Services and Application Integration Conference, May 2003.

"MetaObjectFacility (MOF) Specification v. 1.4." Needham, MA: Object Management Group, April 2002.

Mitchell, Pierre. "E-Business Process Management." *AMR Research* (February 2000).

Moozakis, Chuck. "Hard Goods Makers Seek Key ROI Metric." *Internetweek.com* (October, 15, 2001). Available from *http://www.internetweek.com/transformation2001/industries/manufacturing/manu.htm.*

Morris, Rob and Beth Gold-Bernstein. "How the Mainframe Plays a Pivotal Role in a Service-Oriented Architecture." ebizQ webinar, May 20, 2003. Available from *http://www.ebizq.net/expoq/events/2241.html.*

Newport, Billy. "Requirements for Building Industrial Strength Web Services: The Service Broker." July 2001. Available at *http://www.theserverside.com/articles/article.tss?l=Service-Broker.*

O'Donnell, Glenn. "A Disciplined Approach to IT Performance Optimization." Stamford, CT: META Group, June 2003.

Peers, Jennifer. "Costco Electronic Services: A Case Study." *Web Services Journal* (September 2003). Available from *http://www.sys-con.com/webservices/article.cfm?id=645.*

Phillips, Charles and Ryan Rathman. "Morgan Stanley CIO Survey Series: Release 3.6." New York: Morgan Stanley, September 3, 2002.

Powell, Dennis. "e-Finance: Enabling the Enterprise at Cisco Systems." Cisco Systems, August 2003. Available from *http://newsroom.cisco.com/dlls/tln/exec_team/powell/pdf/Basic_e-Finance_Presentation_August_03.pdf.*

Rogers, Sandra. "Exploring Web Services." *IDC* 4, no. 6 (2003).

Ruh, William A., Francis X. Maginnis, and William J. Brown. *Enterprise Application Integration: A Wiley Tech Brief.* John Wiley & Sons, Inc. (2000).

Sacchi, Guido. "Delivering Business Value through a Service Oriented Architecture." Software AG (n.d.). Available from *http://www.softwareagusa.com/advertising/whitepaper/soawhitepaper.pdf.*

"Sacramento County: Modernize Existing Applications to Simplify Government Interactions." Software AG (n.d.). Available from *http://www.softwareagusa.com/media/case_studies/pdfs/Sacremento_CR.pdf.*

Schulte, Roy. "Creating the New Enterprise Agility: Service-Oriented and Event-Driven." ebizQ webinar, April 3, 2003. Available from *http://www.ebizq.net/topics/jms/features/2307.html.*

Schulte, Roy. "Services and Events: The Secret Ingredients in the Agile Enterprise." ebizQ webinar, April 22, 2004. Available from *http://www.ebizq.net/expoq/events/3926.html.*

Schulte, Roy. "Your Enterprise Nervous System: Irresistible Force Meets Immovable Object." ebizQ webinar, September 4, 2003. Available from *http://www.ebizq.net/expoq/events/2404.html.*

"Secure Application Integration Methodology." Mclean, VA: Concept Five Technologies, 2000.

Smith, Howard, and Peter Fingar, "Assimilating BPM: Col. Sanders' Secret Recipe." *ebizQ.net* (April 5, 2004). Available from *http://www.ebizq.net/topics/bpm/features/4133.html.*

Smith, Howard, Douglas Neal, Lynette Ferrara, and Francis Hayden. "The Emergence of Business Process Management." Version 1.0. UK: CSC's Research Services (January 2002).

Software AG, *http://www.softwareagusa.com.*

Soley, Richard Mark. "Model Driven Architecture: An Introduction." Object Management Group (2002). Available from *http://www.omg.org/mda/presentations.htm.*

Stahl, Stephanie, "Editors Note: Adapt or Prepare to Pay the Price." *InformationWeek.com* (June 23, 2003). Available from *http://www.informationweek.com/shared/printableArticle.jhtml?articleID=10700751.*

"State of North Dakota Laptop Legislation and Child Support Status Offered by New 'Webified' Systems." Case Report, EntireX, Software AG, (n.d.). Available from *http://softwareagusa.com/media/case_studies/PDFs/State_of_ND_CR.pdf.*

Tillett, L. Scott and Jeffrey Schwartz. "Delta Syncs Data, Ops." *Internetweek.com* (June 22, 2004). Available from *http://www.internetweek.com/newslead01/lead062201.htm.*

Trimble, Dave. "How To Measure Success: Uncovering the Secrets of Effective Metrics." *BPR OnLine Learning Center* (n.d.). Available from *http://www.prosci.com/metrics.htm.*

"UML Notation Guide, OMG-Unified Modeling Language, v1.5." Needham, MA: Object Management Group, March 2003.

Vijayan, Jaikumar. "NorthAmerican Logistics Cuts XML Translation Costs with Software AG's Tamino." *ComputerWorld* (September 2002).

Wilkes, Lawrence. "Web Services—Right Here, Right Now: Delivering Web Services Today with IBM Solutions." *CBDi Forum* (n.d.). Available from *http://www.cbdiforum.com/index.php3.*

Wu, Jonathan. "Calculating ROI for Business Intelligence Projects." Strategic Technology Consulting Business White Paper Series. Chicago, IL: Base Consulting Group, December 12, 2000.

Young, C. "Enterprise IT Architecture and the Real-Time Enterprise." Stamford, CT: *Gartner Commentary* (March 5, 2003).

Zurek, Bob. "The Future Integration Dream Team." *EAI Journal* (January 2003).

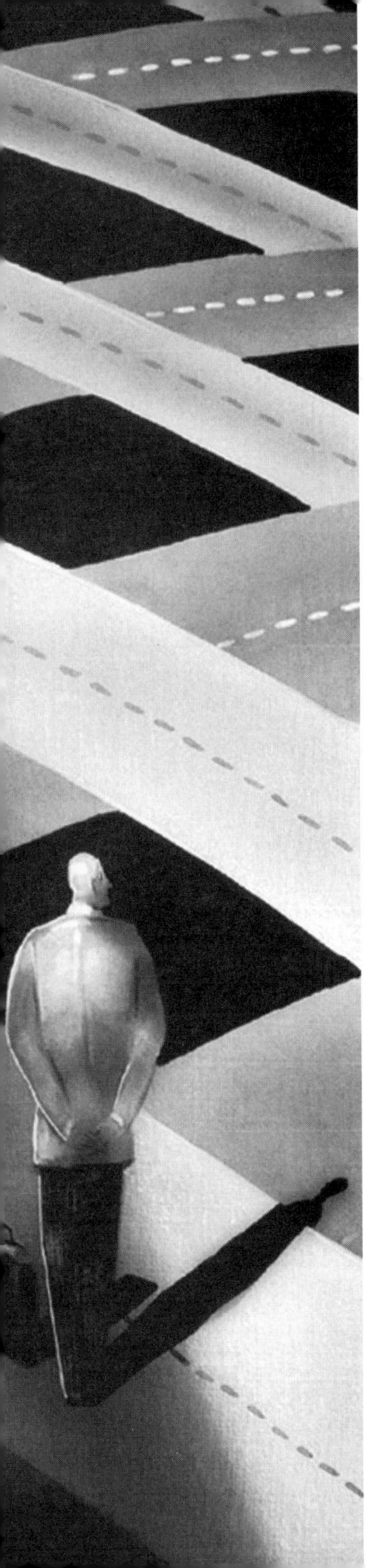

Index

CD-ROM Warranty

Addison-Wesley warrants the enclosed CD-ROM to be free of defects in materials and faulty workmanship under normal use for a period of ninety days after purchase (when purchased new). If a defect is discovered in the CD-ROM during this warranty period, a replacement CD-ROM can be obtained at no charge by sending the defective CD-ROM, postage prepaid, with proof of purchase to:

Disc Exchange
Addison-Wesley Professional
Pearson Technology Group
75 Arlington Street, Suite 300
Boston, MA 02116
Email: AWPro@aw.com

Addison-Wesley makes no warranty or representation, either expressed or implied, with respect to this software, its quality, performance, merchantability, or fitness for a particular purpose. In no event will Addison-Wesley, its distributors, or dealers be liable for direct, indirect, special, incidental, or consequential damages arising out of the use or inability to use the software. The exclusion of implied warranties is not permitted in some states. Therefore, the above exclusion may not apply to you. This warranty provides you with specific legal rights. There may be other rights that you may have that vary from state to state. The contents of this CD-ROM are intended for personal use only.

More information and updates are available at:
http://www.awprofessional.com/